WASHINGTON'S TAIWAN
DILEMMA
✸✸✸✸✸✸✸✸✸ 1949–1950
FROM ABANDONMENT TO SALVATION

DAVID M. FINKELSTEIN

NAVAL INSTITUTE PRESS
ANNAPOLIS, MARYLAND

This book has been brought to publication with the generous assistance of Marguerite and Gerry Lenfest.

Naval Institute Press
291 Wood Road
Annapolis, MD 21402

First Naval Institute Press paperback edition published in 2014.
ISBN: 978-1-59114-252-2 (paperback)
ISBN: 978-1-61251-474-1 (eBook)

The Library of Congress has cataloged the hardcover edition as follows:
Finkelstein, David Michael.
From abandonment to salvation : Washington's Taiwan dilemma, 1949–1950 / David M. Finkelstein
    p. cm.
Includes bibliographical references.
1. United States—Foreign relations—Taiwan. 2. Taiwan—Foreign relations—United States. 3. Taiwan—History—1945– 4. United States—Foreign relations—1945–1953. 5. United States—Foreign relations—China. 6. China—Foreign relations—United States. I. Title.
#183.8.T3F56 1993
327.7305124'9—dc20
                                                                93–3784 CIP
ISBN 0-913969-64-8 (cloth : alk. paper)

♾ Print editions meet the requirements of ANSI/NISO z39.48-1992 (Permanence of Paper).
Printed in the United States of America.

22 21 20 19 18 17 16 15 14   9 8 7 6 5 4 3 2 1
First printing

For my daughters, Allison and Elaina

ACKNOWLEDGMENTS

I am deeply indebted to many persons and institutions over the years that made this study possible.

The faculties and staffs of the department of history and the department of East Asian studies made my time as a Princeton graduate student exciting and challenging. I am forever grateful to Professor Marius Jansen and Professor Frederick "Fritz" Mote for taking me under their wings. When I showed up at "Old Nassau" I was still shaking off the mud from a year-long assignment with an infantry battalion in Panmunjom, Korea. I cannot help but think that their decision to have mercy upon that young, rough-edged regular Army captain was the result of their own service in the Pacific Theater of Operations during the Second World War. I can never adequately thank them.

The department of history at the United States Military Academy at West Point provided funds for an important research trip to the Truman Library. Archivists at Princeton's Seeley G. Mudd Manuscript Library, the Harry S. Truman Presidential Library in Independence, Missouri, and the MacArthur Memorial in Norfolk, Virginia, all provided invaluable assistance in locating and making available hundreds of documents.

Finally, I wish to heartily thank the Naval Institute Press for the decision to republish this study, making it available to readers once again. Susan Todd Brook and the rest of the crew in Annapolis were terrific to work with.

TABLE OF CONTENTS

PREFACE TO THE PAPERBACK EDITION

The renewal of civil war in 1945 between the Chinese communists and the Nationalist government signaled the demise of Washington's wartime hopes that U.S. postwar policy in Asia could be anchored upon a stable China allied to the United States. The establishment of the People's Republic of China under the Chinese Communist Party in October 1949, and the Nationalist government's retreat to Formosa (now known as Taiwan), left American foreign policy officials and military planners with two significant and interrelated dilemmas: how to deal with the new government on the mainland and what to do about Chiang Kai-shek's holdout regime on the island of Taiwan.

Between autumn 1949 and late spring 1950, set against the larger context of the unfolding Cold War with the Soviet Union, the Truman administration's need to make fundamental decisions on these two policy issues became increasingly pressing. In spite of Peking's outward signs of hostility towards the United States, Mao Tse-tung's homegrown brand of Chinese nationalism raised hopes in some quarters of the U.S. government, particularly in the State Department, that the newly founded People's Republic of China might go the way of Yugoslavia under Marshall Tito. What should be done about China? Was it possible that a China under communist rule could be kept out of the Soviet camp? What policies could the United States craft to increase the chances?

Also during this period, it was apparent that the Nationalist government on Taiwan was extremely vulnerable; many feared it would either fall to an invasion or collapse under the weight of its own monumental internal problems. As early as summer 1949 Mao was already instructing his military commanders to prepare plans for the island's capture. Despite the geographic advantages the government on Taiwan enjoyed for its own defense, and despite the enormous operational difficulties an invasion would pose to the mainland armies, many informed U.S. officials believed that in the absence of direct American military intervention, the island would fall quickly. This, they assessed, was the result of a legacy of poor governance since V-J Day, widespread corruption and incompetence within the Nationalist political and military establishments, and popular resentment against the regime. Politically, could the United States afford to "lose" Taiwan after the loss of the mainland? Strategically, what military value to the United States did the island represent? Was the United States willing to commit forces to save Taiwan? Could the island be wrested from Peking without direct U.S. military intervention? If Taiwan could be secured, what price would Washington pay in terms of strategic equities with the new communist regime on the mainland? How U.S. officials grappled with these questions is the grist of the narrative herein.

This book examines the dilemmas of making China policy in 1949 and 1950. The emphasis, however, is on how the Truman administration approached the question of Taiwan in particular. The story is intriguing, for as the reader will see, the historical evidence clearly suggests that right up until the North Korean invasion in June 1950 the Truman administration remained divided on whether Taiwan was worth saving at all.

This is a study that began as a paper for a graduate history seminar at Princeton University in 1982 and 1983, which in turn grew into a doctoral dissertation (1990) and then transformed into a book originally published by George Mason University in 1993. Like many works of history, this book was a child of its time.

The early 1980s, when this research began, was an exciting time for historians of U.S.-Asian relations in general and of U.S. policy toward China in particular. The formal normalization of relations between the United States and China had just taken place in 1979. Nearly concurrently, beginning in the late 1970s and early 1980s, the U.S. government declassification process was methodically placing into the public domain previously classified materials pertinent to U.S. policy toward China at the close of the 1940s and early1950s. Among the many important resources that became widely available to researchers were new volumes of the State Department's Foreign Relations of the United States series for *China* and *The Far East*. In addition, various archival holdings were also opening up.

Also during the early 1980s, a gifted cohort of historians was using these new collections to revisit, explore, and press the boundaries of the narrative of U.S.-China relations during the late 1940s and early 1950s. These historians were demonstrating the art of the possible for the field and for graduate students at the time, I among them. While there are many distinguished individuals among this group that one could name, I will single out two: historians Warren Cohen and the late Nancy Bernkopf Tucker. Their work in particular inspired the seeds of my own research while at Princeton. Although I could not have imagined it while in graduate school, years later I had the great fortune of meeting them and coming to know them both as terrific people as well as terrific scholars.

Beyond the narrative itself, this volume is also a case study of the complex and sometimes messy processes by which foreign policy is made in the United States; a process I vicariously observed and came to appreciate as a U.S. Army China specialist assigned to various positions in Washington, D.C. This volume reveals the tensions, institutional and sometimes personal, that existed within the Truman administration. It highlights the dynamics at the time between a well-established State Department and various newly created entities such as the Department of Defense, the Joint Chiefs of the Staff, and the National Security Council. Indeed, the history of policymaking for China and Taiwan in 1949–50 is also a study in how the U.S. interagency system first developed and dealt with some of its initial foreign policy and security challenges. The story herein also underscores the strains between the executive and legislative branches in the development of foreign policy as well as the domestic dimensions of the process. Finally, this study also brings to light little-discussed and often uncomfortable issues in Taiwan's history, some of which still have resonance on the island even today. These include the legacies of the Japanese colonial experience, the postwar Nationalist occupation, and the first stirrings of the "Formosan independence movement," to name just a couple.

Today, some sixty-four years after the events in this book took place, Taiwan remains a sensitive and sometimes contentious issue in relations between the United States and China. Taiwan's status continues to be a highly charged topic on the mainland, one still subject to domestic politics in Washington and often a partisan issue on Taiwan itself. Especially for today's U.S. officials who still grapple with this issue, I hope that this volume will provide helpful historical context.

INTRODUCTION

By occupying Formosa we would create an irredentist cause about which the Chinese Communists could rally almost universal support within China. At the same time, we would largely nullify one of our major political weapons, namely, exploitation of Soviet encroachment on China from the north....We would create an enduring issue of major proportion between this country and the Chinese Communist regime, an issue in which that regime would enjoy complete support of the Chinese people and from which neither we nor the Chinese Communists could back down without almost impossible loss of prestige.[1]

> Walton Butterworth,
> Assistant Secretary of State
> for Far Eastern Affairs,
> December 16, 1949

Dean Acheson became Harry Truman's Secretary of State in January 1949. Among the myriad of major policy problems he inherited was the issue of Taiwan. By 1949 the Nationalist regime on the mainland had collapsed almost completely. For all practical purposes China was under communist rule. As the last vestiges of *Kuomintang* resistance on the mainland were being snuffed out, Chiang's ever-retreating government established itself on the island of Taiwan, determined to make a desperate last stand.

Acheson and his advisers at the State Department were not anxious to see the island fall. Politically, the Truman administration could not afford another China debacle; it was thoroughly engaged trying to explain why it was Chiang Kai-shek who "lost" the mainland, not the Democratic Party. Diplomatically, the United States did not want another setback in the Cold War by having yet another area in Asia succumb to communism. Moreover, if the strategically located island were in hostile hands during wartime the U.S. defensive perimeter in the Pacific would be threatened. Consequently, in January

1

1949 the State Department and the Department of Defense agreed that Taiwan and the Pescadores should be denied to Peking. The problem, however, was how to accomplish this goal. The United States had already disengaged militarily from the Chinese civil war. But it now appeared that if Washington did not take drastic measures, possibly military intervention, Taiwan would also go under to the Chinese communists. Throughout 1949 the Joint Chiefs of Staff (JCS) were asked time and again by State and the National Security Council to review the implications of the fall of Taiwan to U.S. national security. In every instance, the JCS stated that in time of war Taiwan would have to be denied to hostile forces. However, the island was not deemed so vital to American national security that the Joint Chiefs were willing to recommend armed intervention to rescue Taiwan under conditions short of an actual war in the Far East. With limited forces available to defend even prime interests in Europe, the uniformed services refused to expend resources, or risk a general war with the Soviets, over the fate of Taiwan. This being the case, it became the policy of the Truman administration to attempt to deny Taiwan to the CCP by diplomatic and economic measures.

As far as State was concerned, however, attempting to save Taiwan without U.S. military intervention was as good as writing off the island. The record of KMT rule on Taiwan since V-J Day was abominable. The same nepotism, corruption, and maladministration which helped push the Nationalists out of power on the mainland was also evident on the island province of Taiwan. A string of incapable governors retarded the island's economic rehabilitation since the end of the war. The hundreds of thousands of mainland refugees streaming to Taiwan since 1948 strained the island's infrastructure and economy to the point of collapse. KMT repression of native Taiwanese had resulted in a major uprising in 1947 in which untold hundreds of civilians were massacred. Consequently, it was judged that the internal threat to Taipei remained as great, if not greater, than the threat of external invasion. Moreover, KMT factional politics at the highest levels of national and provincial government, as well as distrust among surviving military commanders, made positive reforms and a good military defense of Taiwan all but impossible.

Nevertheless, Washington sought ways to snatch Taiwan from Mao. Primarily, it attempted to stabilize the internal situation on the island by granting economic assistance. This, however, could only be a stop-gap measure. The key to the survival of Taiwan, believed Foggy Bottom, was political reform. And to this end State attempted to pressure Taipei by issuing threatening *demarches* stating that unless changes were enacted, the U.S. would withdraw its economic aid. Even subversion was considered. In the spring of 1949 Acheson dispatched a special envoy to Taiwan to determine if there was a viable indigenous Formosan independence movement which Washington could manipulate into demanding United Nations intervention at the expense of the KMT. At another point in 1949, the idea of having another Asian nation propose a trusteeship for Taiwan under United Nations auspices was considered.

However, by the winter of 1949 it seemed that none of these measures would produce the desired result. Chiang was firmly in control. There was no organized independence movement which could take over from the KMT. The prospects of imposing a U.N. trusteeship were deemed bleak, and Washington's threats to Taipei did no good. From the State Department's perspective, cosmetic changes in island politics would not suffice. The political and economic situation on Taiwan continued to deteriorate with breakneck speed. Chiang's regime was already so rotten, it was believed, that at the first sign of an invasion Taiwan would collapse. The Joint Chiefs continued to refuse to agree to military intervention, although under pressure from the Secretary of Defense they began to suggest limited military assistance. However, renewed military assistance, the basing of naval assets on the island, or the dispatch of an advisory group was considered pointless by State. Chiang, argued the diplomats, had all the military equipment he needed to defend Taiwan. What was needed was a government worth defending; and only the Generalissimo could provide that. Moreover, moderate military assistance would only delay the inevitable. Acheson and his advisers were unwilling to commit the prestige of the United States to another military failure in the Chinese civil war.

The very real shortcomings of the KMT and the reluctance of the Joint Chiefs to commit troops to the defense of the island were weighty constraints to the policy objective of denying Taiwan to the communists. However, the greatest impediment to attaining that goal was a political constraint imposed by the State Department. Policy toward the island was not made in a vacuum. Throughout this period policy toward Taiwan was subjugated to the larger policy problem of mainland China.

There was no doubt that the communist regime in Peking was there to stay. No one in State believed that Washington's relations with the new China would be cordial. However, Acheson's experts firmly believed that there were deep-seated historical animosities and contemporary arguments between Moscow and Peking which might preclude the mainland from becoming "an adjunct of Soviet power" in the Far East. Although common ideology would initially place China in the Soviet camp, it was judged that the leaders of the CCP were as much nationalistic Chinese as they were communists. Analysts at State argued that Russian imperialism in the Chinese provinces of Sinkiang, Mongolia, and Manchuria would eventually offend the leaders of the Chinese Communist Party. Moreover, it was believed that Mao Tse-tung, as an indigenous leader who came to power on his own, owed nothing to Stalin and may even have harbored deep resentments for the failed policies of the CPSU in China in the 1920's.

The policy, then, which Washington fashioned for the mainland was to wait for the eventual emergence of a "Titoist" regime in Peking. In the meantime, the State Department would do nothing which would distract Peking's attention from the fact that it was the Soviet Union, not the United States, that was the imperialist power to be feared. Consequently, if Taiwan could not be saved by diplomatic and economic methods, if Chiang took no measures to help himself, and the Pentagon refused to declare the island of vital interest to the national security, then State was not prepared to engage in half-measures which would only allow Moscow to point to Washington and scream, "Imperialists!"

State's "hands off" policy toward Taiwan was under attack throughout all the stages of its development. Chiang's powerful lobbyists and his friends in Congress continually attempted to force the administration into positive actions to help Taipei. In Tokyo, General MacArthur pressured the Joint Chiefs of Staff to commit themselves to the island's defense. Secretary of Defense Louis Johnson disagreed with State's policy. He also pressured the JCS to come around. Moreover, he leaked National Security Council decisions to the China Bloc in Congress, attempted to discredit State, and may have provided KMT representatives in Washington with inside information. Even before the ugly specter of McCarthyism appeared in February 1950, Truman's Republican critics had already jumped on China-Taiwan policy as a partisan weapon with which to accuse State of being "soft" on communism. Nevertheless, right up until the invasion of Korea Acheson, supported by Truman, refused to budge on the issue of Taiwan. Chiang Kai-shek would have to help himself this time.

The first two chapters of this study provide background to the policy problem of Taiwan. Chapter 1 recounts the American experience in China during the Second World War and U.S. China policy during the civil war from 1945 to 1949. This bitter experience had a direct impact on State's China hands. After watching Chiang snatch defeat from the jaws of victory so many times, they were reluctant to bet that he could do much better on Taiwan. At the same time, those who demanded active measures to save Taiwan in 1949 were able to play on the emotional theme that the Truman administration was about to sell a valued ally in the war down the river to the communists. Chapter 2 brings Taiwan into focus. It recounts the prewar experience of the islanders under Japanese rule and recounts, from State's perspective, the utter failure of the KMT to capitalize on so great an asset after V-J Day. Chapters 3 and 4 outline how policy toward Taiwan became tied simultaneously to the policy of encouraging a Titoist mainland. Chapter 5 and Chapter 6 examine how State determined that economic and diplomatic measures alone could not secure Taiwan from the CCP. Chapter 7 examines how policy toward Taiwan was incorporated into Washington's larger policies toward the Far East, the various pressures on State to reverse its "hands off" policy, and the ultimate decision to "abandon" Chiang to his own devices to save himself. In Chapter 8, the domestic battles over State's Taiwan policy are reviewed. It is also suggested that, despite the doubts that Dean Rusk came to have over abandoning Chiang, the "hands off" policy remained in effect up until the invasion of Korea.

The United States never did occupy Taiwan. But in June of 1950, as part of the United States' response to the invasion of Korea, President Truman ordered the 7th Fleet to proceed to the Formosa Strait and "neutralize" the island. That decision saved Chiang Kai-shek's Nationalist regime from a communist invasion which, in March 1950, U.S. intelligence predicted would occur as early as that summer. And since 1950, the issue of Taiwan has remained an enduring and major source of friction between Peking and Washington. However, had Pyongyang not launched its invasion of South Korea, the United States, in all likelihood, would not have intervened with military force to preclude the fall of Taiwan to the Chinese communists. In a few short months Taiwan had gone from abandonment to salvation.

Notes

1. Memorandum, Butterworth to Acheson, "Memorandum Respecting Formosa," December 16, 1949, SDF:Reel 3.

CHAPTER 1

The United States and China, 1938–1948: A Frustrating Encounter

Of all the allies of the United States, China excited the highest hopes and ultimately provided the most crushing disappointment.[1]

Gaddis Smith

The debates in Washington in 1949 over policy toward China and Taiwan were conditioned by the American experience in China during the Second World War, Chiang Kai-shek's prosecution of the ensuing civil war, and the Nationalist record of occupation on Formosa after V-J Day. This background is essential to understanding the attitudes of both the detractors of Chiang's regime as well as those of his staunchest friends in court. This first chapter will review the decade of 1938–1948. Chapter 2 will address the legacy of *Kuomintang* rule on Taiwan.

In the grand sweep of U.S.-China relations the Second World War marked a radical departure in the history of American policy toward China. For the first time the United States linked its own security with the fate of China. When the Pacific War commenced in 1941 Washington made the survival of Nationalist China an overarching wartime goal. Planners in Washington, far removed from the realities on the ground, fantasized about a strong and united China whose millions would serve as a great and effective ally in the war against Japan, whose pro-western and democratic government would stabilize postwar Asia, and whose needs would provide an outlet for American goods when the war ended. As the Cold War unfolded after V-J Day the survival of non-communist China was deemed necessary to thwart Soviet influence in Asia as anti-colonial revolutions swept the remnants of former European empires. In short, it was the intention of the United States to see China emerge as a great and friendly power.

To achieve these broad goals the United States wedded itself to Generalissimo Chiang Kai-shek and the Nationalist government. The encounter was not inspiring. The partnership which began with such great promise proved itself, almost from the beginning, to be a chimera. Officials from the State Department and the armed services charged with carrying out these policies quickly discovered that China under *Kuomintang* rule defied the attainment of these goals.

Wartime propaganda not withstanding, "Free China", they found, was neither free nor democratic. Chiang's war aims were not in consonance with the grand strategy of the "Big Three". China was wracked by civil war, revolution, and economic problems of staggering proportions. During and after the Second World War Chiang Kai-shek failed to institute those social, political, and economic reforms suggested by United States representatives which might have slowed the growth of the communist movement. During the civil war he refused as well to heed military advice which could have precluded the ultimate destruction of the Nationalist cause by force of arms.

In the end, China did not play its assigned role in the war against Japan or in the postwar world order which President Roosevelt had envisioned. The wartime experience of the United States in China ensured that the first casualty of the showdown with the communists after V-J Day was the credibility of the Nationalist government; it was dead long before the final battles in 1949. Although material aid continued to be sent to the embattled KMT, no responsible official in the Truman administration was willing to go to war to save a government which seemed so bent on self-destruction.

1.1   THE U.S. AND CHINA ON THE EVE OF THE
   SECOND WORLD WAR

On July 7, 1937 the "Marco Polo Bridge Incident" transformed almost a decade of piecemeal aggression by Japan in northern China into full-scale war. On that day the Sino-Japanese War began in earnest. Although not evident at the time, the war in distant China signaled the beginning of the end of an isolationism to which the American public tenaciously was clinging and hoping to preserve. Slowly and ineluctably, the war in China became linked to events in Europe. The policy of "quarantining" aggressors in 1937 later gave way to economic sanctions against Japan. By 1940 America was allowing the "lend lease" of military supplies to embattled allies. The

United States, while technically not at war on the eve of Pearl Harbor, was hardly uninvolved in the world conflagration.

America's road to war with Japan was not travelled with gay and reckless abandon. Still reeling from the effects of the depression, and with pitifully inadequate armed forces, the United States in 1937 was woefully unprepared for war with any nation. Indeed, the American public was not willing to contemplate a leading role in the troubled events of the times. Also, at the beginning of the war between China and Japan the Roosevelt administration was split in its view of how to react to Tokyo's aggression in China. Some, such as Secretary of State Cordell Hull, felt that the best way for the moment to avoid a conflict with Japan was not to antagonize Tokyo. On the other hand, "hardliners", such as Treasury Secretary Henry Morganthau, Jr. and State Department Far Eastern expert Stanley Hornbeck, were convinced that only strong actions would convince Japan that further aggression would not be in its best interests.[2]

However, as early as 1938 Japan's war in China was coming to be seen as a threat to United States interests. The swift victories which the Imperial Army enjoyed in the first year of the war forced American planners to contemplate the implications of a China dominated by Japan. Prince Konoe's declaration of the "New Order" for East Asia in November 1938 gave notice of Japan's intentions to rid the Orient of the white man. It now appeared that Japanese aggression might not be confined to China proper. While no one in Washington was willing to risk war with Japan at this time, the idea that it was in the interests of the United States for China to survive its war with Japan and continue the struggle began to take hold.

The American public was shocked at the brutality of the Japanese campaign in China. Indeed, the toll of civilian casualties was staggering.[3] The aerial bombing of Shanghai and the "Rape of Nanking" were difficult to countenance. For many Americans the resistance of China against Japan took on heroic proportions. In 1938 *TIME* magazine featured Generalissimo and Madame Chiang Kai-shek as "Man & Wife of the Year", attributing China's continued will to resist exclusively to their leadership and relaying Chiang's message, "Tell America to have complete confidence in us", to millions of readers.[4]

The rationale which eventually made China's cause critical for officials in Washington was less emotional. First, if war with Japan was in the offing the United States would need time to prepare. China could buy America that time by keeping the Japanese bogged down in an indecisive campaign on the continent. Second, China's continued resistance might be able to keep the Japanese from moving into Southeast Asia. This was considered to be of crucial importance to the survival of the United States' European friends. The colonial possessions of Great Britain, France, and the Netherlands in Southeast Asia provided the raw materials which they would need to resist the axis.

In December 1938 President Roosevelt, at the urging of Under Secretary of State Sumner Welles and Treasury Secretary Henry Morganthau, Jr., approved a $25 million commodity loan to the Chinese. While no great sum, the loan represented the beginning of the United States' commitment to China's survival.[5] As war clouds gathered over Europe, and China's plight became critical, this commitment became unshakable.

Between December 1938 and December 1941 American assistance to Chiang's government in exile escalated. Economic assistance took the form of various commodity and currency stabilization loans.[6] Such aid was designed to help battle inflation, bolster confidence in the Nationalist government, maintain China's will to resist, and provide some funds with which to purchase arms.

As with its other future allies, the United States also provided military assistance to China before its official entry into the war. Different, however, was the fact that in China United States citizens participated in the fighting with Washington's approval and military advisors were sent to supervise the use of American equipment.

Americans fought the Japanese as pilots in Claire Chennault's American Volunteer Group (AVG)—the "Flying Tigers". In late 1940, and after intense lobbying, Washington agreed to allow Chennault's agents to travel to American air bases to recruit pilots to fly the hundred-odd Curtis P-40 fighters which were allocated to be sent to China later on through the Lend Lease program. Volunteers were allowed to resign their commissions to fly as private citizens. These men technically were no longer on active duty. However, as soon as the war broke out they, and Chennault, were recalled to active duty and reintegrated into the Army Air Corps.[7] In the interim, the pilots of the AVG fought over the skies of southwest China providing Americans with their first heroes of the war.

Less exciting, but perhaps more significant, was the creation of a military advisory group sent to China. In the spring of 1941 the Lend Lease Act was passed and the United States declared its intent to be "the arsenal of democracy." This pleased the Chinese to no end. They were determined to get their fair share of the military goods.

Chiang Kai-shek had already established a purchasing company in the United States—China Defense Supplies (CDS)—through which military equipment was bought and sent to China. Managed by Chiang's brother-in-law, T.V. Soong, CDS was also a very effective lobbying organization which had the ear of persons in the highest circles of the Roosevelt administration. Through Soong the Chinese issued requests for enormous amounts of the latest military hardware which Chiang's supporters close to the President were inclined to agree to.

The enormous task of supplying finite amounts of equipment to the British, Soviets, and the Chinese required that a certain degree of prioritization be made in order for the program to be effective. Much of the burden for ensuring that equipment shipped to allies supported American strategy fell to Army Chief of Staff George C. Marshall. Marshall was no stranger to Chinese affairs. In the 1920's he served as the commander of the American 15th Infantry Regiment in Tientsin. Marshall was not impressed with the argument that China lacked only adequate arms to defeat Japan. He was worried about the influence the Chinese were accruing within the administration, and he was abashed at the President's own romantic attachment to the Nationalist government; an attachment which in his view was in disproportion to the relative unimportance of China to the future war effort. In short, Marshall was concerned that lend lease to China would not be provided on a rational basis given other commitments.[8] Consequently, in July 1941 he convinced Roosevelt to send a military mission to China which would supervise lend lease to Chungking.

The creation of the American Military Mission to China, AMMISCA, was a significant event in the history of United States foreign military policy and in the history of United States-Chinese relations. First, it was the forerunner of the modern day Joint U.S. Military Assistance and Advisory Group (JUSMAAG)—one vehicle through which the United States today provides military aid to friendly foreign governments. The need to staff these organizations has in large measure justified the training of foreign area experts by each of the armed services. Second, in the context of this period of U.S. assistance to the KMT, AMMISCA provided a skeptical General Marshall with his own eyes and ears in China. Finally, AMMISCA was the first of three military assistance groups which would be sent to China to help the Kuomintang.[9] Before and after the war these missions were an irritant to Chiang. The Generalissimo did not want military advice. All he wanted was American materiel. The fact that China was the only ally to suffer the intrusion of these "experts" was seen as a slap in the face to Chinese sovereignty. Consequently, the suggestions offered by these missions were generally ignored and, as a result, a great deal of ill will toward the KMT developed within the American military establishment.

AMMISCA's formal mission was to assist the Chinese in all phases of procuring lend lease equipment and to help train Chinese personnel in the use and maintenance of such material.[10] Additionally, it was Marshall's intention to use AMMISCA as the nucleus of a joint staff with the Chinese once war with Japan was begun.

The group was commanded by Brigadier General John Magruder, who had previously served as an attache in Peking and was well versed in the China scene. He took with him army officers from all branches of service whom he sent out to KMT units to observe shortcomings and recommend material requirements.[11] The reports that Magruder and his officers sent back to Washington were troubling and were harbingers of the problems which the American effort in China would encounter after Pearl Harbor.[12] Nevertheless, from its arrival in China in October 1941 until the outbreak of the Pacific War AMMISCA did what it could to expedite desperately needed war supplies to Chungking.[13]

The Japanese attack on Hawaii formalized the alliance between the United States and China. In their own hour of darkness, Americans drew courage from the tribulations, perseverance, and tenacity of allies across both oceans. China presented a particularly inspiring image. As the *New York Times* editorialized on December 9th:

> We do not stand alone...We have as our loyal ally China, with its inexhaustible manpower—China, which we did not desert in her own hour of need—China, from whose patient and untiring and infinitely resourceful people there will now return to us tenfold payment upon such aid as we have given.[14]

These hopes, so eloquently expressed, did not materialize.

1.2   THE DIFFICULTIES OF ALLIANCE

For American civil and military officials, the alliance was a nightmare. The realities which they faced in China made the pursuit of United States interests in that theater of war seemingly impossible to attain.

Washington's aims in China were an integral part of the grand strategy pursued by the allies for prosecuting the war against the axis as well as President Roosevelt's vision of the postwar world order.[15] Stated succinctly by wartime Secretary of State Cordell Hull:

> Toward China we had two objectives. The first was an effective joint prosecution of the war. The second was the recognition and building up of China as a major power entitled to equal rank with the three big Western Allies, Russia, Britain, and the United States, during and after the war, both for the preparation of a postwar organization and for the establishment of stability and prosperity in the Orient.[16]

Both objectives required a politically unified China capable of waging total war. Neither condition existed. By 1941 Chiang's crack German-trained troops had long since been destroyed during the Shanghai campaign of 1937 and the retrograde to Chungking.[17] One month after Pearl Harbor the united front with the communists ended as a result of the "New Fourth Army Incident." From January 1941 on forward, what loyal and effective troops Chiang did possess were used to blockade the communists in Yenan instead of prosecuting the war against Japan.[18]

When the United States entered the scene in China it encountered a weary nation on the verge of renewed civil war. The war aim of the KMT was to let the allies win the war against Japan and preserve itself for the inevitable showdown with communist rebels afterwards. The continual prodding of Chiang by General Joseph W. Stilwell to commit American-trained and equipped Chinese troops to battle with the Japanese, and Stilwell's insistence that loyal but incompetent commanders be relieved was, for the Generalissimo, a death wish.[19] In short, America became a player in the Chinese revolution.

Even before Stilwell took command of the China-Burma-India Theater (CBI), Magruder and the officers of AMMISCA were reporting that all was not well militarily in China. Generally, they were aghast at the sorry state of the KMT forces and amazed at what appeared to be a total lack of aggressive spirit among the Chinese troops. Their reports to Washington set the tone for the perpetual frustrations which beset Stilwell and his successor, General Albert C. Wedemeyer.

Comments by AMMISCA artillery advisers Lieutenant Colonels George W. Sliney and Edwin M. Sutherland were common among many of the mission's American personnel. They complained that China's military system was built upon personal loyalties, not competence, and that "The interest of the Chinese towards any aggressive action appears to be quite negligible, regardless of their statements that all they need is airplanes, tanks, and artillery in order to drive the aggressor from their shores."[20] The situation they encountered seemed out of line with the propaganda they had heard in America prior to their arrival. Disheartened, Sliney wrote to Magruder that:

> The general idea in the United States that China has fought Japan to a standstill, and has had many glorious victories, is a delusion...The will to fight an aggressive action does not yet exist in the Chinese Army. If the Government of the United States is counting on such intent it should be cautioned against being too sure of any large-scale offensive action at present...Many small things all pointing in the same direction have caused me to have a feeling, stronger than a suspicion, that the desire of the Chinese for more modern materiel was not, before December 8th, for the purpose of pressing the war against Japan, but was to make the Central Government safe against insurrection...[21]

Magruder's own observations corroborated those of his subordinates. In a biting report to the War Department he warned that, "...China's military successes are being highly exaggerated, by what is given out in American newspapers and over American broadcasting stations." He feared that if such propaganda was continued that it "...could lead to grave defects in American war plans, if our own officials should be influenced by it to even the slightest extent." He opined that Chinese officials were themselves victims of their own propaganda, and that they were living "...in the world of make-believe" as was their habit. Magruder was amazed by the "impossible quantities" and "impractical varieties" of military equipment that was demanded by the Chinese. He complained that officials were "...unwelcome to any helpful suggestions" which might improve their logistics system. Finally, he warned that misconceptions of the potential Chinese contribution to the war effort "...may harm us greatly." He suggested that in the future, the United States will "...have to do away with all sham and pretense" in dealing with the Chinese.[22]

General Stilwell's refusal to bow to "sham and pretense", or confront it gracefully, was the underlying cause of the fatal rift which developed between himself and Chiang and which resulted in very strained relations between Chungking and Washington. During the two years he served as Chief of Staff to the Generalissimo, American Commander for CBI, Deputy Commander for the allied Southeast Asia Command (SEAC), and Washington's agent for Lend Lease to China, "Vinegar Joe" did everything within his power to force Chiang to fight the Japanese. He cared not for the political future of the KMT.

He recognized the shortcomings of the Nationalist armies and set out to correct them. The training bases he established in Ramgarh (India) and Kunming (Yunnan Province, China) proved that if properly fed, equipped, trained, and led the Chinese soldier could become an effective and determined fighter equal to any in the allied cause.

Supported by Chief of Staff General George C. Marshall, Stilwell begged the President to pressure Chiang to fight by threatening to make Lend Lease contingent upon Chinese offensive action and reform of the Nationalist army. Chiang countered by threatening at various points to sit out the war or make a separate peace with Japan.

For Chiang Kai-shek, the survival of the Kuomintang under his leadership as the ruling government of China superseded allied grand strategy. The relief of loyal commanders, the expenditure of resources against the Japanese in occupied China, or the deployment of effective troops to fight a land campaign in Burma would undermine this paramount goal. The tenuous grip which the KMT maintained over China prior to the outbreak of the Sino-Japanese War had loosened considerably since Pearl Harbor. Implementing Stilwell's plans for prosecuting the war, the Generalissimo argued, would destroy it. Consequently, he lobbied General Chennault's case for driving the Japanese from China by air offensives which would not require him to commit his troops to battle.

By 1944 Chiang forced Roosevelt to choose between Stilwell and himself. The President, over the objections of Marshall, chose Chiang.[23] F.D.R.'s decision to support the Generalissimo was predicated upon his long term goal of having a friendly China replace Japan as Asia's premier power after the war. He saw no alternative to Chiang's leadership.

Ironically, the weeks after Stilwell's relief were the darkest for China since 1937. The first major Japanese land offensive since Pearl Harbor—*ICHIGO*—was in full swing, and it appeared that it would achieve its goal of destroying the Nationalist government once and for all. The offensive was launched specifically to eliminate the airbases in China from which the Americans were conducting long range bombings of Japan. Only at the eleventh hour were the Japanese halted. In the meantime, they had destroyed most of the Air Corps' forward bases, coming dangerously close to Chungking itself in the process. The offensive vindicated Stilwell's belief that airpower alone would not win the war in China. His argument that airbases were useless unless adequately defended on the ground was, in the final analysis, correct. The President realized too late that he was wrong to have supported Chiang's and Chennault's plan for air offensives instead of pressing for the reform of the Nationalist army to enable it to recapture occupied China.

At the height of the offensive, when all looked very bleak, the President commissioned a study examining the military and political problems encountered in China.[24] In many ways the study, "The President and U.S. Aid to China-1944," was the predecessor of the more famous *White Paper* which the Truman administration would later issue in the bleaker days of 1949. Both outlined the extent of U.S. aid to China, both decried Chiang's failure to use such aid effectively or implement suggestions to save the day. Fortunately for Roosevelt, the worst never came to pass. F.D.R. would not have to explain the "loss" of China. However, by the end of the crisis the President was himself exasperated by the KMT and no longer suffered delusions that China would make any substantial contribution to the war.

In any event, by 1944 China was no longer a factor in the plans for the defeat of Japan. The successful campaigns in the Pacific waged by General MacArthur and Admiral Nimitz allowed for a straight shot at the Japanese home islands. The east China coast would not be needed as a base from which to launch the final invasion of Japan after all. When Wedemeyer took up his post as Stilwell's replacement he did so only as Chief of Staff to the Generalissimo and guardian of Lend Lease. His mission was primarily to serve as Chiang's adviser and continue the training of the Chinese divisions Stilwell had begun. Hopefully, these forces would help China consolidate its position after the war and enable it to play its designated role of world and regional power. CBI was dismantled into separate theaters, and Roosevelt refused to consider pressing Chiang to appoint another American officer to command Chinese troops. The President did not want the United States to bear the burden of military defeat in China should disaster strike again.[25]

The best that could be hoped for was that unity could be preserved and Chiang's Central Government could be strengthened so that China could truly be one of the "Four Policemen" after the war. But Kuomintang China was as weak politically as it was impotent militarily.

It was quickly discovered that Nationalist rule was predicated upon Chiang maintaining the dubious loyalty of former warlords and playing off against each other the various factions which made up the party.[26] Displaced from the central coastal provinces and urban centers which were the KMT's strongest prewar bases of support, the Central Government resided in a province, Szechwan, over which it had previously exercised only nominal control.[27]

Economically, the government was a basketcase. Staggering inflation kept the country on the verge of bankruptcy—the result of long years of war, fiscal mismanagement, and peculation. Compounding the problem was Chungking's attempt to rectify the problem in the old warlord fashion of printing exorbitant amounts of currency. Additionally, the Japanese occupied the few centers of industry which developed prior to the war, relegating Nationalist China to almost total dependence on the U.S. Army Air Corps for supplies flown from "over the hump" in India to provide for the war effort.[28]

Worse still, the KMT had a talent for misrule. The bureaucracy suffered from levels of corruption unfathomable to outside observers. The burden of taxation and conscription fell mostly on the peasantry, adversely affecting agricultural production and undermining the loyalty of the major segment of the population. General Wedemeyer was so appalled at Chinese conscription methods that he passed on to Chiang the observations of one of his officers that "...Conscription comes to the Chinese peasant like famine or flood, only more regularly—every year twice—and claims more victims.

Famine, flood and drought compare with conscription like chicken pox with plague."[29]

Liberals and intellectuals were equally disillusioned with Nationalist rule. As the war progressed the militaristic, if not fascistic, tendencies of the party destroyed the reformist ideals of the earlier more revolutionary KMT. Chiang brooked no criticism of himself or the government. Censorship of the domestic press was absolute. Foreign correspondents who wrote articles unfavorable to Chinese policies were not permitted to send their dispatches out of the country.[30] Intellectuals were constantly under surveillance—especially those who were thought to have too much contact with foreigners.[31] A brutal secret police, General Tai Li's Central Investigation and Statistics Bureau, terrorized critics. Ambassador Gauss likened it to the German "Gestapo".[32] There did not appear to be much freedom in "Free China."

Just as disturbing was the postwar political outlook. The publication in 1943 of Chiang's manifesto, *China's Destiny*, caused great concern among American officials about the nature of the regime which the United States was trying to prop up and which was expected to serve as a positive example of nationalism in postwar Asia. Intended as a blueprint for the future of China, the book became required reading not just for Party members, but for all Chinese. It was Chiang's attempt to add to his soldier's uniform the trappings of the traditional Chinese sage. The O.S.S. noted with dismay the arguments that "The Chinese must...eliminate adulation of western culture, Liberalism, and internationalism." Equally distressing was the pronouncement that without the KMT China had no future and that "China's destiny is completely entrusted to the Kuomintang." The O.S.S. went on to note that in spite of promises to publish an English language edition of the book none was expected because the anti-western flavor of the text would harm the regime internationally.[33] The State Department also noted that the book would not be translated because of it's "...rejection of the doctrine of liberty and the rights of the individual as known in liberal western nations." The Embassy in Chungking reported that the book was probably written by Tao Shi-sheng, an adherent to "pro-Fascist ideas" and a former Blue Shirt. The pronounced anti-westernism in the book, it was feared, would complicate Sino-western relations in the postwar period. Even more discomforting, the Embassy relayed, was that:

The Generalissimo's insistence on Kuomintang rule to the exclusion of any share in the government by other political parties and his denial of western liberalism should serve to convince all Chinese of liberal tendencies that there is little hope for them from the Kuomintang.[34]

In Washington, a Division of Far Eastern Affairs official lamented that the book was "...an authoritative confirmation of already manifested reactionary Kuomintang views." He went on to add that:

It is only when one realizes the past consistent failure of the Chungking Government to carry out its pledges to the people, the obstinate determination of reactionary Kuomintang elements to preserve their power and opportunities for profit, and the uncompromising attitude toward the Chinese Communists that the unfortunate significance of the book becomes evident.[35]

Finally, to the north, was the specter of an ever-growing communist movement which all observers agreed would pose as a serious challenger for the Mandate of Heaven if the KMT could not recover from the pressures of the war and internal misgovernment.

All of these problems were dutifully reported by Foreign Service Officers posted in Chungking and Washington, as well as by the various wartime intelligence services. Tragically, many of those who continually called attention to the shortcomings of the Nationalist regime or questioned the advisability of wedding America's postwar China policy to Chiang's survival would later be purged during the anti-Red hysteria of the late 1940's and blamed in part for the communist victory in 1949.[36]

As early as 1942 John Carter Vincent, Counselor of Embassy in Chungking, pointed out the discrepancies between the wartime and postwar goals of the United States and the situation in China as he saw it. He described the KMT as a "...congeries of conservative political cliques whose only common denominator and common objective is desire to maintain the Kuomintang in control of the government." Instead of progressive, the Party was becoming increasingly "preservative." The entire political system was kept together solely by the personality of Chiang, who himself was a prisoner of these cliques and therefore unable to address China's ills. He concluded that:

Effective measures for financial, economic and social reform cannot be expected from the present leadership either now or in the post-war period. Whether or not the Kuomintang as presently constituted will be able to maintain its leadership after the war is a question which hinges on unpredictable developments.[37]

John Paton Davies, a Foreign Service Officer attached to Stilwell's staff, an observer in communist-controlled Yenan during the "Dixie Mission", and later George F. Kennan's Asia expert on the State Department's influential Policy Planning Staff was prolific in his analyses of the wartime political situation. Like Vincent, Davies was as concerned about the future as he was about wartime problems. He speculated that the KMT was bent on attempting to destroy the communist movement at the first opportunity. This, he feared, would inevitably "...force the Communists into the willing arms of the Russians," with dire consequences for the United States and the stability of Asia. He prophesied that, in the event of civil war:

> ...we may anticipate that Chiang Kai-shek will exert every effort and resort to every stratagem to involve us in active support of the Central Government. We will probably be told that if fresh American aid is not forthcoming all of China and eventually all of Asia will be swept by communism. It will be very difficult for us to resist such appeals, especially in view of our moral commitments to continued assistance to China during the post-war period.[38]

In spite of the realities which confronted him, Roosevelt never wavered in his crusade to elevate China to the status of a world power with a postwar mission commensurate with that of the United Kingdom, the Soviet Union, and the United States. At the Moscow Conference of Foreign Ministers in October 1943, Roosevelt cajoled the British and Russians into allowing Chiang to be a signatory in absentia to the Moscow Declaration. In effect, China was made a member of the "Big Four", securing for Chiang the role of a world leader.[39] The status of China as a postwar regional power was secured at the Cairo Conference in November 1943, the only major wartime conference that Chiang attended. The Cairo Declaration affirmed the resolve of Great Britain, the United States, and China to pursue as their ultimate war aim in the Pacific the unconditional surrender of Japan and strip it of all territories in Asia and the Pacific which it had taken as a result of the First World War. Additionally, it was declared that "...all territories Japan has stolen from the Chinese, such as Manchuria, Formosa, and the Pescadores, shall be restored to the Republic of China."[40] With the Japanese empire dismantled, China would emerge from the war as the premier power in Asia. Also, as a token of good will, the United States abrogated it extraterritorial rights in China—the last of the "unequal treaties" imposed upon the

THE UNITED STATES AND CHINA, 1938-1948

Ch'ing Dynasty at the turn of the century, and convinced Great Britain to do the same. At Dumbarton Oaks in 1944 the Chinese became a founding member of the United Nations, later to be assigned a permanent seat on the Security Council.

That the President's unshakable faith in China was in stark contradistinction to the situation as reported underscores the fact that Roosevelt rarely put his trust in the State Department. In spite of his own background, F.D.R. was put off by the aristocratic airs of the professional Foreign Service. He considered the diplomatic corps too unimaginative and conservative to meet the challenges of the twentieth century. At best, Roosevelt allowed his Secretaries of State to air their views. More often than not he ignored them. Throughout the Second World War the Department of State sat on the sidelines. Roosevelt took personal control of foreign policy, relying heavily on his military planners and personal envoys for advice.[41]

Nowhere was Roosevelt more personally involved in the conduct of wartime foreign and military policy than in China. He consistently subverted his own military chain of command by encouraging Chennault to write him personally of progress and problems. He acted as a referee in the quarrels between Stilwell and Chiang. Additionally, the President perpetually bypassed the State Department and the Embassy when seeking situation reports and advice on policy matters. Throughout the war Roosevelt sent to China a seemingly unending stream of personal representatives to act as his eyes and ears.[42] Roosevelt's last envoy, Patrick J. Hurley, would have a tragic impact on the conduct of U.S. China policy.

Roosevelt dispatched Hurley to Chungking via Moscow in the summer of 1944 with the primary mission of patching up the differences between Stilwell and Chiang in order to convince the latter to give command of the Chinese armies to Stilwell and to vigorously prosecute the war against Japan.[43] Uninitiated, Hurley was quickly sucked into the intrigues of Chungking politics and coopted by the Generalissimo. After studying the situation he wrote to F.D.R. that Chiang is anxious to fight the Japanese and is willing to allow an American to command his forces. However, Hurley, went on, "...Chiang Kai-shek and Stilwell are fundamentally incompatible. Today you are confronted by a choice between Chiang Kai-shek and Stilwell. There is no other issue between you and Chiang

Kai-shek...”[44] Soon afterwards Stilwell was relieved, Clarence E. Gauss resigned as Ambassador, and Hurley took his place.

Hurley became Ambassador at a major crossroads in the history of American-Chinese relations. By late 1944 the significant concern of the United States toward China was political, not military. China had already proven its inability to contribute to the war effort. However, postwar plans still required a unified China. The KMT-CCP split had to be rectified. Hurley attempted in vain to bring the two sides together. As George Marshall would later find out, reconciliation was impossible. Unlike Marshall, Hurley was singularly incapable of even attempting it. Rarely has a United States Ambassador been so determined to ignore the political realities of the country to which he was accredited.

Hurley, was convinced by Molotov of the Soviet Union that “...the so-called Communists of China are not Communists at all...”, and tried to convince Chiang likewise.[45] He reported to the President that:

> The avowed purpose of Chiang Kai-shek and his government is to make China a united independent democracy. A government of the people, for the people, and by the people, to promote the progress of democratic processes in administration...The Communists also...support the establishment in China of a government “of the people, for the people, and by the people”...There is very little difference, if any, between the avowed principles of the National Government the Kuomintang and the avowed principles of the Chinese Communist Party.[46]

Based on these premises Hurley spent his Ambassadorship negotiating with Chungking and Yenan for unification. His naivete was incredible, but it was also useful to the KMT and the CCP. Neither wanted publicly to seem intransigent; both tried to use Hurley to achieve their aims. Negotiations continued even though both parties considered him a buffoon. As it became clear that unification would not be easily obtained, Hurley’s attitude toward the CCP hardened and he lobbied Chiang’s goals rather than longterm U.S. interests in avoiding civil war.

In the process, Hurley destroyed the morale and effectiveness of his Foreign Service Officers. He allowed no criticism of his views on the nature of the KMT-CCP rift, most of which were completely opposite those of his staff. He rarely kept them informed of the progress of negotiations. Indeed, as a group, he held them in contempt.

Additionally, Hurley allowed no reports unfavorable to Chiang to leave the embassy. The problems between Hurley and his staff reached the point where the Office of Far Eastern Affairs felt a need to write a memorandum criticizing Hurley's treatment of his staff and his conduct of policy in general.[47] Ambassador Hurley was still conducting negotiations between the KMT and CCP when the atomic bomb brought an abrupt end to the war in the Pacific.

1.3 THE AFTERMATH OF V-J DAY

President Roosevelt never lived to see his world order. His successor, Harry S. Truman, was destined to see the nation through the end of the war. Truman, however, was destined as well to witness the virtually instantaneous unraveling of the grand alliance and the beginning of the Cold War. Almost immediately after V-E Day the Soviets were challenging their wartime allies in Eastern Europe. The British and French, even as they licked their wounds, were engaged in plans to reconstitute the former empires which Roosevelt had hoped to see dismantled.

The end of the war brought confusion to the situation in China. A veritable race ensued for control of the mainland. Soviet troops poured into Manchuria. Mao Tse-tung declared the right of the Red Army to accept the surrender of the enemy and issued the appropriate orders. Chinese communist forces in north China and in pockets of resistance behind Japanese lines on the eastern coast scrambled to be the first to disarm Imperial Army garrisons. Washington issued its own orders, General Order No. 1, which directed all Japanese in China (other than those in Manchuria) to surrender only to the armies of Chiang's Central Government.[48]

The Nationalist army, isolated mostly in southwest China, was far from being in a position to accept the Japanese surrender. Consequently, the U.S. Army Air Corps was ordered to airlift three KMT armies to Peking, Nanking, and Shanghai as well as other strategic points in North, East, and Central China. Additionally, approximately 50,000 U.S. Marines were landed in Peking, Tientsin, and other coastal areas in the north. Within a short couple of months between 400,000 and 500,000 KMT troops were moved by air and sea to new positions in order to accept the surrender of the enemy and restore Chungking's control over China.[49] For his part, Chiang was anxious to have his troops redeployed. As Supreme Allied Commander in China he ordered the Japanese to keep their arms and positions until they could surrender to the Nationalists, and fight if necessary to do so. The first moves of renewed civil war were being played out.

American assistance to Chiang in reestablishing the Central Government's control over the mainland in the crucial weeks after V-J Day was in accordance with F.D.R.'s policy of support for Chungking. This policy was validated by President Truman and the influential State-War-Navy Coordinating Committee (SWNCC).[50] However, by October 1945 SWNCC was noting that the political realities in China were too ominous to ignore. While recognition and support for the Central Government of China would continue, the United States did not intend to become involved in a civil war. It became a matter of policy that American military support of the KMT would cease if "...the Chinese armed forces are being used...to engage in fratricidal war..." and that China policy should undergo constant review.[51]

General Albert C. Wedemeyer was in the unenviable position of having to carry out a policy ripe with contradictions. On one hand he was told to assist Chiang's armies reoccupy China. At the same time he was informed that in doing so his actions should "Not prejudice the basic U.S. principle that the United States will not support the Central Government of China in fratricidal war."[52] Throughout the late summer and fall of 1945 Wedemeyer continually pointed out to his superiors in Washington that regardless of intent, the use of American military assets to ferry KMT troops throughout China would be construed by the communists as aid and abetment to their enemy and that wherever KMT troops were landed clashes with the communists were almost certainly to occur. When General Eisenhower replaced Marshall as Army Chief of Staff in November 1945 Wedemeyer lost no time in sending to him a lengthy message outlining the bleak situation in China. He recounted all of the all too familiar political and military weaknesses of the Central Government. It was his frank assessment that the Generalissimo would not be able to consolidate control over North China for months or even years. He feared that Chiang was hoping to use the American Marines in the north to secure his rear as he attempted a campaign of military pacification which Wedemeyer did not believe the Nationalist army was capable of prosecuting successfully. Finally, he warned Eisenhower that it would be impossible for American troops to escape involvement in the civil war if they continued their support mission or remained in north China.[53] Despite Wedemeyer's recommendation that the Marines be withdrawn from China the Soviet forces by then in control of Manchuria dictated that a U.S. military presence in China remain for the time being.

Policy makers in Washington were not insensitive to Wedemeyer's problems in China or unaware of the nature of the KMT. Their concern was keeping the Russians from denying the U.S. influence in China, a real possibility if civil war broke out. Consequently, in the autumn of 1945 the policy of the United States became one of continuing support for Chiang while at the same time doing what it could to preclude the outbreak of full-scale hostilities between the KMT and CCP.[54] General Hurley's role as interlocutor between the two factions was becoming more important to the overall aims of American policy. Soviet posturing in the north made the success of Hurley's negotiations critical.

In spite of Wedemeyer's warning that civil war was almost inevitable, and ignoring the reports of his own military attaches that fighting between the KMT and CCP had already begun, Hurley, in early September, was still officially oozing optimism in his reports to Washington. He dismissed reports of battles opining that they convey "...an impression of civil war more serious than evidence warrants." He confidently relayed to the Secretary of State that:

> ...as I have previously pointed out, events seem to be bringing about a solution to China's internal political difficulties, and even now the Generalissimo and Mao Tse-tung are engaged in conversations, with considerable prospects of success, looking to an agreement between the Government and the Communists.[55]

In his heart of hearts the Ambassador must have surely known that his negotiations were doomed to fail.

Tired, and claiming need of medical attention, Hurley requested leave and returned in September to the United States for what was supposed to be a temporary stay. While back home Hurley continued to read diplomatic cables which totally discounted his estimate of the situation. The opinions he expressed during his consultations back at the State Department put him at loggerheads with the department's China analysts. Having failed to make peace between Stilwell and Chiang he now realized that he had also failed to make peace between the KMT and CCP. In October he offered his resignation to President Truman citing fatigue. The President refused to accept it expressing great confidence in Hurley's abilities to carry on with negotiations.[56] Hurley decided to think over his decision. What he decided was that he was being set up to take the fall for the outbreak of civil war. On November 27th, Hurley stunned the President and the country by publicly resigning.[57]

At 12:30 PM on November 27th, Hurley called a news conference at which he read his blockbuster letter of resignation, as yet unseen by President Truman. Hurley reviewed his wartime service for President Roosevelt. He then went on to declare that the conduct of United States policy during the war was never carried out in accordance with the President's aims. As regards the China debacle Hurley charged that:

> ...it is no secret that the American policy in China did not have the support of all the career men in in the State Department. The professional foreign service men sided with the Chinese Communist armed party and the imperialist bloc of nations whose policy it was to keep China divided against herself. Our professional diplomats continually advised the Communists that my efforts in preventing the collapse of the National Government did not represent the policy of the United States. These same professionals openly advised the Communist armed party to decline unification of the Chinese Communist Army with the National Army unless the Chinese Communists were given control.

He then charged the staff of the Embassy in Chunking and the Chinese and Far Eastern Divisions in the State Department as being singularly determined to destroy the chances of successful negotiations. He charged as well that the United States has not been true to the charter of the United Nations but has been supporting the "imperialistic bloc." Hurley then warned that a third world war was in the making, and that the United States was going to be "sucked into a power bloc on the side of colonial imperialism against Communist imperialism." He ended by accusing the Foreign Service of allowing America's economic strength to defeat American interests.[58]

The contradictions and irrationalities of Hurley's statements aside, his charges of State Department collusion with the Chinese communists were serious enough that conservative Republican Senators such as Kenneth Wherry were able, by early December, to convene a full Congressional inquiry conducted by the Senate Foreign Relations Committee. At the hearings, Hurley would specifically charge FSO's George Atcheson, John S. Service, John Carter Vincent, John Paton Davies, Fulton Freeman, John K. Emmerson, and Arthur Ringwalt as part of a pro-Communist clique in the State Department.[59] As O. Edmund Clubb pointed years later, "It was Hurley—Patrick J. Hurley—really, who planted the seed of McCarthyism."[60]

On the same day that Hurley resigned, President Truman announced that General of the Armies George C. Marshall would proceed to China to attempt to mediate a peace in that troubled land. In his letter of instruction to Marshall, the President wrote that, "Specifically, I desire that you endeavor to persuade the Chinese Government to call a national conference of representatives of the major political elements to bring about the unification of China and, concurrently, to effect a cessation of hostilities, particularly in north China." Marshall's mission was underway.[61]

The General's departure was accompanied by a statement of policy toward China by the President. Truman prefaced those policy statements by declaring that a unified and democratic China was in the best interests of the United States and the United Nations, and that "...a breach of peace anywhere in the world threatens the peace of the entire world." The President stated that the Government of the United States felt that hostilities must end and that a political reconciliation must be realized. Further, Truman proposed that unity and democracy could only be attained if the present one-party government of the KMT was broadened "..to include other political elements in the country" and autonomous armies are disbanded. Accordingly, Marshall was being sent to China not to interfere in its internal affairs, but to assist in achieving a peace for which "...the United States has already been compelled to pay a great price to restore." While placing the ultimate burden of attaining unity on the Chinese themselves, Truman stated that the United States would continue to recognize the National Government of China, continue the mission of the U.S. Marines to assist the National Government "...in effecting the disarmament and evacuation of Japanese troops in the liberated areas", and provide such economic, agricultural, and military assistance necessary to help a united China achieve prosperity and security. Finally, the President stated that "...U.S. support will not extend to military intervention to influence the course of any Chinese internal strife."[62]

The President had no illusions about Marshall's task being an easy one. He was painfully aware of the political and economic deterioration under which the Central Government was suffering. On the eve of Marshall's departure Edwin A. Locke, Jr. presented the President with a lengthy report on the conditions he found as a result of his trip to China on Truman's behalf. After citing China's economic woes he reported on KMT misrule. "The outstanding fact", he wrote, "is that the Central Government has been steadily losing the broad popular support which it had in earlier years...The people in Kuomintang China feel there is little to choose between the Central Government and the Communists as far as their welfare is concerned."[63] Locke suggested that only with massive American economic assistance and political guidance would the Chinese be able to establish a prosperous democracy. He was optimistic that once KMT rule was softened and the economy was resuscitated that civil strife would dissipate.[64]

Marshall did not share Locke's optimism. His initial impressions led him to wonder whether his mission would succeed. Relaying Marshalls' opinions to the President, his attache, James Sheply, reported that the KMT and CCP "...were able to agree to anything in general and almost nothing in specific..." Marshall felt as well that:

> ...both the National Government and the Communist Party were willing to negotiate so long as they could win their own objectives by political means, and that both sides were filled with such a deep-seated distrust of the good faith of the other that no concrete results were likely ever to result from such negotiations if the Chinese factions were left to themselves.[65]

In spite of these reservations, Marshall was able to make headway in his quest for peace. By the end of January 1946 the KMT and CCP agreed to a cease-fire and to convene a Political Consultative Conference (PCC) to work out the terms of a constitutional coalition government. By the end of February a tentative agreement was reached for the integration of the Red Army into the National army. In March, Marshall returned to Washington to secure economic aid for China. However, his temporary departure only proved that his achievements were predicated solely upon his personal presence and that form had triumphed over substance. Armed clashes between the belligerents broke out almost immediately. Upon his return, he spent his time reasoning with, cajoling, and at times threatening the parties to cease hostilities. Marshall pressured the communists. Truman pressured Chiang. In August he wrote to the Generalissimo, through Ambassador Wellington Koo, that:

The Agreements reached by the Political Consultative Conference on January 31st were greeted in the United States as a far-sighted step toward the achievement of national unity and democracy. American disappointment over failure to implement these agreements by concrete measures is becoming an important factor in our outlook with regard to China...Unless convincing proof is shortly forthcoming that genuine progress is being made toward a peaceful settlement of China's internal problems, it must be expected that American opinion will not continue in its generous attitude towards your nation. It will, furthermore, be necessary for me to redefine and explain the position of the United States to the American people.[66]

Peace was not to be had. By the end of the summer of 1946 the KMT and CCP were fighting in Anhwei and Jiangsu provinces. By November the KMT called into session the National Assembly without first having worked out the terms of a coalition government, thereby negating the agreements of January. Chou En-lai, the CCP's chief negotiator, returned to Yenan charging bad faith on the parts of the KMT and the United States.

Marshall, like Hurley before him, had failed. In early January 1947 his recall was announced. On January 7th, Marshall issued a lengthy and bitter statement outlining the reasons for the collapse of his efforts. In it, he berated both the KMT and CCP as acting in selfish bad faith. He blamed reactionaries in each party for deliberately sabotaging progress toward unity. He declared that China's only salvation lay in the leadership of third party liberals who, unfortunately, would not easily be given a chance to exercise political power.[67] That same day, Truman announced his nomination of Marshall for the post of Secretary of State. On January 29th, eight days after Marshall was sworn into office, the United States declared the termination of its efforts in attempting to mediate a peace in China's civil war.

1.4 TRUMAN, MARSHALL AND CHINA, 1947-1949

Under General Marshall the Department of State regained its primacy in the foreign policy making arena. The President held Marshall in great esteem and summoned his counsel regularly. At the same time, Marshall put a great deal of trust in his subordinates, the professional Foreign Service. Accustomed to forcing the chain of command to function, Marshall exercised his "experts" until even the lowliest country desk officer could not help but feel that a new day had dawned at Foggy Bottom. After the gloomy days that State had seen during the war, and afterwards under the secretive, aloof and often absent Secretary of State James Byrnes, Marshall's style was a boon to morale.[68]

Together, Truman and Marshall confronted the Cold War with the Soviet Union. Undoubtedly, the primary security concern of the United States at this time was the challenge which Moscow posed in the west. By the time Marshall assumed his position on the cabinet, Moscow's foreign policies quashed any hopes of cooperation between the former allies. Consequently, it was the object of American foreign policy to halt further Soviet inroads into Europe and the Middle East. The Truman Doctrine and Marshall Plan gave substance to Washington's resolve to contain communism in these areas, considered vital to the security of the United States, through both military and economic assistance.

Unfortunately, as the administration focused its energies on the rescue of Europe the problems in China did not disappear. For the most part, they got worse.

Addressing the situation in China proved problematic for Truman and Marshall. They recognized that it would not be in the interests of the United States to see China overrun by the communists and possibly aligned with the Soviet bloc. However, the administration steadfastly refused to consider committing combat troops to aid the KMT in its war against Mao Tse-tung. Furthermore, the primacy of Europe in the calculus of the U.S. security equation, finite economic and military resources, and no assurance based on past experiences that all-out aid would be successful dictated that the lion's share of foreign aid would not go to China. Consequently, in China the United States followed a policy which Tang Tsou has described as one of "limited assistance."[69]

What was "limited" about this assistance is that the United States would not do for Chiang what he refused to do for himself; successfully wage a war, resuscitate the economy, and reform the political system. What Washington was willing to do, within its means, was to give the Chinese government the wherewithal to address those problems. The United States continued to provide China with various forms of military and economic aid.

Lend Lease military equipment totaling $741,965,650 was continued for six months after V-J Day. Also, American military stockpiles throughout the Pacific, including troop transports, tanks, small arms, artillery, and maintenance facilities, were turned over to the Nationalists after the war. Over one hundred naval landing craft capable of patrolling rivers and coastal areas were sold to the Chinese. Millions of rounds of assorted small arms and artillery ammunition were transferred cost-free by the Marines in North China when they departed in late 1947.[70] Additionally, in early 1946 President Truman approved the creation of a Joint U.S. Military Advisory Group for China (JUSMAGCHINA) to better coordinate the efforts of the few hundred army, navy, and air force advisors who were retained after the war to continue to build the "39 Division Army" which Stilwell had earlier begun. Authorized to attain a strength of 1,000 officers, advisory personnel labored to help Chiang organize, train, and create a modern army as well as instruct the Chinese general staff in operational planning, logistics, and naval and air operations.[71]

Military assistance to the Nationalists entailed very little in the way of new expenditures. Although the value of equipment given under the extended Lend Lease program amounted to hundreds of millions of dollars, the items transferred probably would have been disposed of in the course of the massive demobilization which the American armed forces underwent after the war ended. Many military end items sent to China were purchased outright by the KMT. Only JUSMAGCHINA entailed any substantial outlay of new funds.

Economic aid to the Nationalists was provided more grudgingly by the administration in the form of the China Aid Act of 1948. On January 3, 1948 the 80th Congress was convened. It was the first time in fourteen years that the Republicans had been able to secure both houses of the legislature. A "China Bloc" of intensely pro-KMT conservative Republicans, led at this time primarily by former China missionary Walter H. Judd, Styles Bridges, and House Speaker Joseph W. Martin, was beginning to take form.[72] These representatives and others were demanding that communism in China be contained with the same enthusiasm which the administration was demonstrating toward Europe. Fearful that the legislation for the European Recovery Act would be held up by those who were demanding a "Marshall Plan for China", the administration submitted a separate bill for $570 million in economic assistance to the KMT in February 1948.[73] After much debate between the House and Senate, the bill was tied directly to Marshall Plan. When the omnibus was finally passed in April, it entailed $463 million in economic assistance *plus* $125 million for the purchase of military equipment.[74] As a result, the Economic Cooperation Administration (ECA), the coordinating agency for all foreign economic assistance associated with the Marshall Plan, created a China account and the armed services were instructed to continue to sell military hardware to the Chinese.

Although the rhetoric of containment opened the door for supporters of Chiang to press for greater assistance, neither Truman or Marshall had ever intended for the policy to be universally applied. Both eyed Europe as the specific target of U.S. effort, and, in general, those areas of the world where American aid was perceived as having a good chance of making the difference between the survival of friendly governments or their succumbing to communism. Nothing in the recent history of the United States' dealings with Chiang could convince Truman or Marshall that American aid could make a difference in the situation in China. Marshall monitored the situation in China very closely and ensured that the President was kept informed of events. Throughout 1947 and 1948 reports from the field led the administration to believe that nothing short of armed intervention in the civil war and an overpowering measure of political and economic control over the government of China could save the day. Testifying before the Congress in 1948 Marshall submitted that:

> ...the present Government evidently cannot reduce the Chinese Communists to a completely negligible factor in China. To achieve that objective in the immediate future it would be necessary for the United States to underwrite the Chinese Government's military effort, on a wide and probably constantly increasing scale, as well as the Chinese economy. The U.S. would have to be prepared virtually to take over the Chinese Government and administer its economic, military and governmental affairs...An attempt to underwrite the Chinese economy and the Chinese Government's military effort represents a burden on the U.S. economy and a military responsibility which I cannot recommend as a course of action for this Government...Present developments make it unlikely, as previously indicated, that any amount of U.S. military or economic aid could make the present Chinese Government capable of reestablishing and then maintaining its control throughout all of China.[75]

The controversial fact finding mission of General Albert C. Wedemeyer during the late summer of 1947 only served to convince Marshall that not much had changed since he had left the mainland. Though he advocated increased military and economic aid to the Nationalists, even Wedemeyer, a staunch KMT supporter and virulent anti-communist, was forced to point out to Marshall (and Chiang) that the political, military, and economic disasters of the Central Government were self-inflicted wounds.[76]

Reporting by State Department personnel in China painted an equally gloomy picture. Even as the China Aid Act was being debated in Washington Embassy officials in Nanking, the Nationalist capitol, were reporting a "...heightened tempo of repressive police activities all over the country" and that KMT efforts to liberalize the political system would not be soon in coming. Economic reforms were equally wanting. It was the the view of the Embassy that, "In recent months the Central Government has effected no fundamental reforms nor brought about any appreciable improvement in conditions in the country". Consequently, "...the government has been steadily losing prestige in the eyes of the people and popular support for it has never been at a lower point."[77] In September 1947 Ambassador John Leighton Stuart, in a telegram to Marshall forwarded to the President, reported on the continuing deterioration of the political and economic situation of the KMT. In it, he likened the Nationalist regime to "...an extremely sick man whose will to live begins to show signs of weakening."[78]

Loss of resolve was readily apparent on the battlefield. Throughout 1947 Nationalist forces failed to stem the tide of the Red Army. By the fall of 1948 it appeared that the communists would sooner or later win a political decision by force of arms. All of Manchuria had fallen and, save a few pockets of isolated KMT resistance, most of North China was in communist hands as well. Nanking itself was soon to be threatened. The military situation had deteriorated to such an extent that U.S. military advisers informed the State Department that "..short of actual employment of US troops in China no amount of military assistance can now save the Chiang Kai-shek regime...[79] Chiang realized too late that he had underestimated the abilities of the communist forces and severely overestimated his own military genius. In early November, Chiang, almost hat-in-hand, wrote President Truman asking for American military advisers who he would authorize to direct combat operations.[80] The request was denied. In late November 1948 the Director of Central Intelligence informed the President that the communists were consolidating their grip on North China in preparation for eliminating the last KMT strongholds in North and Central China. In the estimate of the

Central Intelligence Agency (C.I.A.), the communists would have no trouble in doing so. This accomplished, an all-out offensive would ensue with the anticipated result of the collapse of organized military resistance. In most probability, the President was informed, Chiang's government would either "...flee south or surrender to the Communists."[81] A month earlier, the State Department was already anticipating that "...the disappearance of the National Government as we know it is only a matter of time."[82]

Less than one hundred miles off the coast of China lay the island province of Taiwan. In accordance with General Order No. 1, and in anticipation of the fulfillment of the Cairo Declaration, the island was "liberated" by KMT troops after the surrender of Japan. Between 1945 and 1948 American officials looked on in disgust as the very excesses which were soon to doom the mainland to communist rule were tragically repeated.

Notes

1. Gaddis Smith, *American Diplomacy During the Second World War, 1941–1945* (New York: John Wiley and Sons, Inc., 1965), p. 6.

2. For recent scholarship which examines the split in the Roosevelt administration over how best to deal with Japanese aggression see Jonathan G. Utley, *Going to War with Japan, 1937–1941* (Knoxville, Tenn.: The University of Tennessee Press, 1985).

3. Very few military histories of the Sino-Japanese War are to be found in English that do not center around the British or American efforts against Japan in China after the Pacific War began in 1941. One exception is Dick Wilson's *When Tigers Fight: The Story of the Sino-Japanese War, 1937–1945* (New York: The Viking Press, 1982). It was Wilson's goal to write of the war through Chinese and Japanese eyes and to recount the horror of it all. The work, however, is journalistic as opposed to scholarly. Also of interest is Frank Dorn, *The Sino-Japanese War, 1937–1941: From Marco-Polo Bridge to Pearl Harbor* (NY: 1974), and portions of F.F. Liu, *A Military History of Modern China, 1924–1949* (Princeton, N.J.: Princeton University Press, 1956). Dorn was one of Stilwell's aides in China. Liu served as an officer in the Chinese army during the war and subsequently pursued graduate studies at Princeton University.

4. "Man & Wife of the Year," *TIME*, January 3, 1938, pp. 12–16. *TIME-LIFE* publisher Henry Luce was personally committed to the cause of Nationalist China and Chiang Kai-shek. The son of missionaries, Luce grew up in China. He used his influence to rally support for Chiang in the dark days before America's entry into the war. After V-J Day he allowed the "China Lobby" to use his periodicals to condemn the Truman administration's policies in the Far East.

5. Utley, pp. 48–49.

6. For a detailed account of United States financial assistance to China before and after Pearl Harbor see Arthur N. Young, *China and the Helping Hand, 1937–1945* (Cambridge, Mass.: Harvard University Press, 1963). Young, a former Princeton professor and State Department economic consultant, served as China's financial advisor from 1929 to 1947.

7. Chennault, a former Army Air Corps pilot, went to China to serve as Chiang Kai-shek's air force advisor shortly after the war began in 1937. He quickly became a favorite of the Generalissimo's. He was unshakably dedicated to the idea that airpower alone could win the war against Japan by using China as an airbase for long range bombers. Later, as Commanding General of the American 14TH Air Force, Chennault was constantly involved in violent disagreements with General Joseph Stilwell, his superior, over supply priorities and basic strategy. The constant arguments between these two men, and the machinations of Chiang in support of Chennault, were as debilitating to the prosecution of the war in China as any military factor. After the war Chennault became a leading critic of the Truman administration's China policy.

8. For Marshall's attitude see Michael Schaller, *The U.S. Crusade in China, 1938–1945* (New York: Columbia University Press, 1979), p. 57, and Forrest C. Pogue, *George C. Marshall: Ordeal and Hope, 1939–1942* (New York: The Viking Press, 1965), pp. 353–355.

9. The second was JUSMAGCHINA which was created after V-J Day to assist Chiang in his civil war with the Communists. The third and final group, JUSMAAG-C, was established on Taiwan in 1951 to advise the KMT in the defense of the island. (See Chapter 12).

10. Charles F. Romanus and Riley Sunderland, *Stilwell's Mission to China* (Washington, D.C.: Office of the Chief of Military History, United States Army, 1953), p. 30. This work is one of three dedicated to the history of the China-Burma-India theater in the multi-volume collection, *The U.S. Army in World War II*. Along with their other two companion volumes, *Stilwell's Command Problems* (1956), and *Time Runs Out in CBI* (1959), Romanus and Sunderland have produced an operational history of the United States effort in China during the war that remains unsurpassed.

11. American Aid To China, 1942, OSS/SD:reel 1:33–46. As reported by the Office of Strategic Services (O.S.S.), Magruder's group totaled 35 officers. Six of these officers had served previously in China. Three had studied Chinese language for four years or more. The political reporting of this group carried considerable weight in the War Department.

12. The AMMISCA mission ended in 1942 when the China-Burma-India Theater of war was created. Magruder, replaced by Lieutenant General Joseph W. Stilwell, returned to the United States to become an Assistant Director of the Office of Strategic Services (O.S.S.). As deputy to Major General William J. "Wild Bill" Donovan, Magruder lorded over the O.S.S.'s Secret Intelligence and Counter-espionage directorates. Bradley F. Smith, *The*

Shadow Warriors: O.S.S. and the Origins of the C.I.A. (New York: Basic Books, Inc., Publishers, 1983), p. 130 and Anthony Cave Brown, *The Last Hero: Wild Bill Donovan* (New York: Vintage Books, 1984), p. 508.

13. For a summary of the type and amount of materiel sent to China prior to Pearl Harbor see Romanus and Sunderland, *Stilwell's Mission to China,* p. 49.

14. "United We Stand," *The New York Times,* 9 December 1941, p. 30.

15. For F.D.R.'s postwar plans see Robert A. Divine, *Roosevelt and World War II* (Baltimore, Md.: The Johns Hopkins Press, 1969), Robert Dallek, *Franklin D. Roosevelt and American Foreign Policy, 1932–1945* (New York: Oxford University Press, 1979), or Willard Range, *Franklin D. Roosevelt's World Order* (Athens, Ga.: 1959).

16. Cordell Hull, *The Memoirs of Cordell Hull,* 2 vols. (New York: The MacMillan Co., 1948), 2:1583.

17. For the background of the German army training mission to China in the 1930's see F.F. Liu, *A Military History of Modern China, 1924–1949.* For the impact of the Shanghai campaign on the Nationalist army see Ch'i Hsi-sheng, *Nationalist China at War: Military Defeats and Political Collapse, 1937–1945* (Ann Arbor, MI.: The University of Michigan Press, 1982).

18. In this affair troops of the central government attacked and destroyed elements of the communist New Fourth Army, effectively ending the cessation of civil war which had been called in 1936 as a result of the kidnapping of Chiang during the Sian Incident. It has been estimated that Chiang used over 400,000 troops to blockade the communists throughout the war. For official U.S. reporting on the New Fourth Army Incident see FR:41:V:462–472.

19. For the tribulations of General Stilwell see Romanus and Sunderland, *Stilwell's Command Problems.* The recounting of Stilwell's experiences became, in the early 1970's, as controversial as the General himself. In her immensely popular biography, *Stilwell and the American Experience in China, 1911–1945* (New York: The MacMillan Co., 1970), Barbara Tuchman used the General and his bitter experiences with Chiang Kai-shek as an allegorical indictment of United States policies in Southeast Asia. Equally politically charged is Liang Chin-tung's *General Stilwell in China 1942–1944: The Full Story* (New York: St. John's University Press, 1972). A direct rejoinder to Tuchman, Liang, a former Republic of China official, attempts to destroy the hero-sage-martyr image of Stilwell constructed by Tuchman and to place the blame for the communist victory squarely on the shoulders of the irascible general and, ultimately, the United States.

20. "Rpt, Lt Cols George W. Sliney and Edwin M. Sutherland." Item 87, AMMISCA Papers, Folder 4. Cited in Romanus and Sunderland, *Stilwell's Mission to China,* p. 36.

21. "Memo, Sliney for Magruder," 10 Dec 41. Ibid.

22. *The Military Mission in China to the War Department,* February 10, 1942, FR:42:China:13–16.

23. For a distillation of Stilwell's account of his efforts and problems in China see *The Stilwell Papers* (New York: William Sloane Associates, Inc., 1948), edited by Theodore H. White. White, a journalist in China during the war, was representative of those American correspondents whose experiences in Chungking left them disgusted with Chiang and the KMT. For a full treatment of his views see his classic piece, *Thunder Out of China* (New York: William Sloane Associates, Inc., 1946) co-authored by Annalee Jacoby and *In Search of History: A Personal Adventure* (New York: Harper & Row, 1978).

24. The study was reproduced with a commentary by Riley Sunderland under the title, *Roosevelt and China: The White House Story:* "The President and U.S. Aid to China-1944" (Wilmington, Delaware: Michael Glazier, Inc., 1979). The original study was written by a young Naval Reserve Lieutenant assigned to the White House Map Room by the name of George M. Elsey. After his release from service Elsey served on the White House staff as Administrative Assistant to President Truman. As an intimate of the President's, Elsey was witness to the China debacle of 1945–1949 and the debates over policy toward Taiwan.

25. Throughout the crisis of 1944 the tone of Roosevelt's communiques to Chiang lost the quaint cordiality which characterized his earlier missives. His annoyance was apparent and he no longer took into account the matter of "face" when addressing the Genralissimo. Before Wedemeyer took up his new post, the President bluntly told Chiang that "The ground situation in China has so deteriorated since my original proposal (that Stilwell be given direct command of the Chinese army) that I am now inclined to feel that the United States Government should not assume the responsibility involved in placing an American officer in command of your ground forces throughout China." *President Roosevelt to Generalissimo Chiang Kai-shek*, October 5, 1944, FR:44:VI:165. Parentheses added.

26. As early as 1941 the O.S.S. had determined that the K.M.T. was rife with factionalism which might preclude effective prosecution of the war and adversely affect Chiang's ability to institute reforms even if he wanted to. See "Chinese Politico-Military Factions", Coordinator of Information Memorandum No. 14, OSS/SD:China and India, Part III:Reel 1 for the O.S.S's assessment of the various KMT cliques.

27. See Tien Hung-mao, *Government and Politics in Kuomintang China, 1927–1937* (Stanford: Stanford University Press, 1972) for an appreciation of how precarious KMT rule over China was even before the outbreak of the Sino-Japanese War.

28. For the details of Chinese fiscal problems see Arthur N. Young, *China and the Helping Hand*, ibid., and Arthur N. Young, *China's Wartime Finance and Inflation, 1937–1945* (Cambridge, Mass.: Harvard University Press, 1965).

29. Memorandum, Wedemeyer for Generalissimo, 5 Aug 45. Cited in Romanus and Sunderland, *Time Runs Out in CBI*, pp. 368–373.

30. *The Charge in China (Atcheson) to the Secretary of State*, June 23, 1943, FR:43:China:64–65, for the problem of KMT censorship of the foreign press corps.

31. *The Charge in China (Atcheson) to the Secretary of State*, July 20, 1943, Ibid., pp. 76–77.

32. *The Ambassador in China (Gauss) to the Secretary of State*, February 9, 1944, FR:44:VI:China:14–20.

33. *China's Destiny*-by Chiang Kai-shek: A Political Bible for the New China, Office of Strategic Services, R&A No. 951, 15 July 1943, OSS/SD: China and India, Part III: Reel 1.

34. *The Charge in China (Atcheson) to the Secretary of State*, May 31, 1943, FR:43:China:244–248.

35. *Memorandum by Mr. Augustus S. Chase of the Division of Far Eastern Affairs*, August 9, 1943, Ibid., pp. 310–312. An English language edition was not issued until 1947. By then the book had been thoroughly scrubbed for foreign consumption. The authorized translation, forwarded by Lin Yutang and claiming to have notes on all revisions, was released with China already in the grips of civil war and just as the storm around Truman's China policy was building. See Chiang Kai-shek, *China's Destiny*, translated by Wang Chung-hui (New York: The MacMillan Co., 1947). Almost immediately afterward, Philip Jaffe offered a translation noting the original deletions, hoping to bare the true "reactionary" and anti-democratic nature of the Kuomintang. Chiang Kai-shek, *China's Destiny & Chinese Economic Theory: With Notes and Commentary by Philip Jaffe* (New York: Roy Publishers, 1947). This edition was a leftwing riposte to Wang's official translation. Jaffe, of course, was an editor of *AMERASIA*, a leftwing magazine which was investigated in connection with the illegal possession of classified government documents in late 1945. For the details of the case see John S. Service, *The Amerasia Papers: Some Problems in the History of US-China Relations* (Berkely, Ca.: Center for Chinese Studies, University of California, 1971).

36. The most prominent among the Foreign Service Officers who later suffered for their reporting were John Carter Vincent, John S. Service, John Paton Davies, and O. Edmund Clubb. The purge of a whole generation of China experts in the late 1940's and early 1950's was a tragedy not only for the individuals whose lives and careers were ruined, but for the entire nation. It would be decades before the United States government could restaff the State Department and the intelligence agencies with China specialists of such high qualifications. For an overview of the fate of these men and others see E.J. Kahn, Jr., *The China Hands: America's Foreign Service Officers and What Befell Them* (New York: The Viking Press, 1972). See also O. Edmund Clubb, *The Witness and I* (New York: Columbia University Press, 1974), Gary May, *China Scapegoat: The Diplomatic Ordeal of John Carter Vincent* (Washington, D.C.: New Republic Books, 1979), and John Paton Davies, *The Dragon by the Tail* (New York: Norton Books, Inc., 1972).

37. *Memorandum by the Counselor of Embassy in China (Vincent) to the Ambassador in China (Gauss)*, July 22, 1942, FR:42:China:212-226. Vincent returned to Washington in 1944 to become Chief of the Chinese Affairs Division (CA). In 1945 newly appointed Assistant Secretary of State Dean G. Acheson promoted Vincent to the position of Director, Far Eastern Affairs (FE).

38. *Memorandum by the Second Secretary of Embassy in China (Davies), Temporarily in the United States*, "The American Stake in Chinese Unity: Proposals for Preliminary Action," June 24, 1943, FR:43:China:258-256.

39. Herbert Feis, *The China Tangle: The American Effort in China From Pearl Harbor to the Marshall Mission* (Princeton, N.J.: Princeton University Press, 1953), pp. 98-99.

40. "Statement by President Roosevelt, Generalissimo Chiang Kai-shek, and Prime Minister Churchill, December 1, 1943," in *A Decade of American Foreign Policy Basic Documents, 1941-1949* (Washington, D.C.: Department of State, 1985), p. 20.

41. For an overview of Roosevelt's relationship with "Foggy Bottom" see Chapter 2, "The Challenge of Global War: The Roosevelt Era, 1933-1945", in Barry Rubin, *Secrets of State: The State Department & The Struggle Over U.S. Foreign Policy* (New York: Oxford University Press, 1987).

42. Envoys included Lauchlin Currie (twice sent), Wendell Wilkie, Henry Wallace, Harry Hopkins, Admiral William Leahy, Donald Nelson, and Patrick Hurley. Elsey, *Roosevelt and China*, ibid., p. xiii, and William P. Head, *America's China Sojourn: America's Foreign Policy and Its Effect on Sino-American Relations, 1942-1948* (Lanham, Mass.: University Press of America, Inc., 1983), p. 107.

43. For a full treatment of the public life of Hurley and his service in China see Russell D. Buhite, *Patrick J. Hurley and American Foreign Policy* (Ithica, N.Y.: Cornell University Press, 1973).

44. *Major General Patrick J. Hurley to President Roosevelt*, October 10, 1944, FR:44:VI:170.

45. *Major General Patrick J. Hurley to President Roosevelt and the Chief of Staff (Marshall)*, September 7, 1944, ibid., p. 154.

46. *The Appointed Ambassador in China (Hurley) to the Secretary of State*, December 24, 1944, ibid., pp. 745-748.

47. *Memorandum by the Deputy Director of the Office of Far Eastern Affairs (Stanton)*, April 28, 1945. Ibid., pp. 348-350. In this memorandum it was noted that, "...General Hurley's approach to the very complicated political problems in China is characterized by an intransigent and inflexible attitude...a policy which has been described by intelligent observers as 'blank check' support of the Generalissimo...In brief, Ambassador Hurley is conducting this Government's relations with China along lines which we do not approve and which will lead China toward internal chaos and serious external difficulties."

48. *Directive by President Truman to the Supreme Commander for the Allied Powers in Japan (MacArthur), Instruments for the Surrender of Japan, General*

Order No. 1, August 15, 1945, FR:45:VII:530–531. Japanese forces in Manchuria and north of the 38th parallel in Korea were directed to surrender to the Soviets.

49. Tang Tsou, *America's Failure in China, 1941–1950* (Chicago: University of Chicago Press, 1963), p. 308.

50. SWNCC was formed in December 1944. It was a forum held at the assistant secretary level which attempted to insure that government policies of both a political and military nature were coordinated. It was formed as well as a result of Roosevelt's worsening health and his Secretaries' appreciation that F.D.R.'s very personal style of policy making tended to keep decisions compartmented. President Truman relied upon SWNCC very heavily when he assumed the Presidency as a body through which continuity could be maintained and ultimately to perform those policy study and recommendation functions that the National Security Council would later perform. Michael Schaller, *The American Occupation of Japan: The Origins of the Cold War in Asia* (New York: Oxford University Press, 1985), p. 7 and Steven L. Rearden, *History of the Office of the Secretary of Defense: The Formative Years, 1947–1950* (Washington, D.C.: Historical Office of the Secretary of Defense, 1984), pp. 125–126.

51. *Report by the State-War-Navy Coordinating Committee, SWNCC 83/6, Policy of the United States Toward China with Special Reference to U.S. Military Responsibility in the Training and Equipment of Chinese Armed Forces,* October 22, 1945, FR:45:VII:583.

52. *The Commanding General of the United States Forces, China Theater (Wedemeyer), to the Chief of Staff (Marshall),* ibid., p. 532.

53. *The Commanding General, U.S. Forces, China Theater (Wedemeyer), to the Chief of Staff, United States Army (Eisenhower),* November 20, 1945, ibid., pp. 651–660.

54. In September 1945, President Truman extended Lend Lease to China for an additional six months—the only wartime ally to continue to receive military equipment after the cessation of hostilities—and committed the United States to assisting the Central Government train a modern thirty-nine division army.

55. *The Ambassador in China (Hurley) to the Secretary of State,* (September 4, 1945), ibid., p. 550. For the details of the negotiations held between the Nationalists and the Communists see Buhite, *Patrick J. Hurley and American Foreign Policy,* ibid.

56. Buhite, p. 262.

57. Truman is reported to have rushed into a cabinet meeting that day holding the newspaper with Hurley's statement of resignation declaring, "See what a son-of-a-bitch did to me." Robert J. Donovan, *Conflict and Crisis: The Presidency of Harry S. Truman, 1945–1948* (New York: W.W. Norton & Co., 1977), p. 149.

58. *The Ambassador in China (Hurley) to President Truman, Washington,* November 26, 1945, FR:45:VII:723–732.

59. Buhite, ibid., p. 273. For a detailed study of the hearings and the controversies over China policy in the wake of Hurley's resignation see Kenneth S. Chern, *Dilemma in China: America's Policy Debate, 1945* (Hamden, Conn., Archon Books, 1980).

60. Transcript, O. Edmund Clubb Oral History Interview, 1974, p. 34, Truman Library.

61. President Truman to General Marshall, December 1945, HST/PSF/Box 173/China 1945. For a review of the history of the Marshall Mission see Chapters IV-IX in Forrest C. Pogue, *George C. Marshall: Statesman, 1945-1959* (New York: Viking Penguin Inc., 1987).

62. *U.S. Policy Toward China* (Suggested draft of statement by the White House upon the departure of General Marshall for China), December 1945, HST/PSF/Box 173/China 1945.

63. Memorandum to the President From Edwin A. Locke, Jr., 18 December 1945, HST/PSF/Box 173/China 1945.

64. Locke's report was so critical of the KMT and recommended such deep American involvement in China's political and economic affairs that General Marshall and the President decided that it should not be made public for fear of adversely affecting Marshalls' options in conducting his negotiations with the KMT and CCP. Memorandum for E.A. Locke From President Truman, 4 January 1946; Memorandum for the President from Secretary of State James Byrnes, 4 January 1946, HST/PSF/Box 173/China 1946.

65. Memorandum for the President from James Sheply, Attache to General Marshall, 28 February 1946, HST/PSF/Box 173/China 1946.

66. Letter, Harry S. Truman to Ambassador Wellington Koo, 10 August 1946, HST/PSF/Box 173/China 1946.

67. Personal Statement by the Special Representative of the President (Marshall), January 7, 1947, *United States Relations With China With Special Reference to the Period 1944-1949* (New York: Greenwood Press Publishers, 1968), pp. 686-689.

68. For the positive impact that Marshall had on the State Department see Joseph Marion Jones, *The Fifteen Weeks: An Inside Account of the Genesis of the Marshall Plan* (New York: The Viking Press, 1955), pp. 105-109; John Lewis Gaddis, *The United States and the Origins of the Cold War, 1941-1947* (New York: Columbia University Press, 1972), pp. 347-348; and Robert H. Ferrell, and Samuel Flagg Bemis, gen. eds., *The American Secretaries of State and Their Diplomacy* (New York: Cooper Square Publishers), vol. XV: *George C. Marshall* by Robert H. Ferrell (1966), Chapter Three, "The New Department".

69. Tang Tsou, *America's Failure in China, 1941-1950*, ibid. Tsou eventually comes to the conclusion that limited assistance was tantamount to the abandonment of Nationalist China because there was a commitment to an end (saving China from communism) which "could not be achieved with the means employed". While Tsou's work remains a classic for the depth of analysis performed with so little primary material on the subject available at the

time, one must point out that he examines China policy virtually in a vacuum. In his attempt to write the penultimate study on China policy, other Cold War pressures on the United States were virtually ignored. Interestingly, Tsou castigates U.S. policy makers for holding unrealistic illusions about the nature of the KMT during the Second World War while at the same time bemoaning an "unwillingness to use military power" to save it later on (p. ix).

70. NSC 34, United States Policy Toward China, 13 October 1948, DNSC:Reel 1.

71. Directive to Secretaries of State, War, and the Navy, 25 February 1946, HST/PSF/Box 173/ China 1946. The creation of a joint service advisory group was a new concept in the history of the U.S. defense establishment. The internal and bureaucratic problems associated with its creation, as well as delays in the Chinese government agreeing to an appropriate status of forces agreement, resulted in JUSMAGCHINA not becoming fully operational until November 1, 1948. In the interim, however, China was not without active duty U.S. military advisory personnel. From early 1946 until the activation of the JUSMAAG the Army Advisory Group (AAG) and the Naval Advisory Group Survey Board (NAGSB) provided guidance in ground, air, and naval matters to the highest echelons of the Nationalist military establishment. For insight into how the newly established Joint Chiefs of Staff went about creating JUSMAGCHINA see J.C.S. 1330/27, Proposed Directive Governing the Establishment and Operation of the U.S. Military Advisory Group in China, 9 June 1948; Decision on J.C.S. 1330/32, Proposed Directive Governing the Establishment and Operation of the U.S. Military Advisory Group in China, 14 July 1948; J.C.S. 1330/33, Establishment of a Joint U.S. Military Advisory Group to the Republic of China, 28 July 1948; and J.C.S. 1330/34, Designation of Chiefs of the Army, Naval, and Air Force Advisory Divisions of the Joint U.S. Military Advisory Group to the Republic of China, 25 September 1948, RJCS:Reel 1.

72. For a full treatment of the history of the "China Bloc" and the "China Lobby" see Ross Y. Koen, The China Lobby in American Politics (New York: Octagon Books, 1974). While Koen uses the term "China Lobby" to include all persons and organizations who took up support of Chiang and the KMT in the late 1940's, 50's, and 60's, I choose to differentiate between private supporters and supporters serving in the Congress by the terms "China Lobby" and "China Bloc" respectively.

73. William Whitney Steuck, Jr., The Road to Confrontation: American Policy Toward China and Korea, 1947–1950 (Chapel Hill, N.C.: The University of North Carolina Press, 1981), pp. 58–59.

74. Ibid., p. 59. Various versions of the bill can be found in HAS/Box 96.

75. United States Relations with China, ibid., pp. 382–383.

76. William Steuck, The Wedemeyer Mission: American Politics and Foreign Policy During the Cold War (Athens, Ga.: The University of Georgia Press, 1984). Steuck has produced a superb study of the mission and its ramifications for American China policy. Especially interesting is his narrative and analysis

of Wedemeyer's final oral report to Chiang, in which the General publicly berated the Generalissimo for the failures of his regime. Equally interesting is Steuck's analysis of why Wedemeyer's final written report was suppressed by Marshall and the domestic controversy which resulted. For Wedemeyer's version of these events see his memoirs, *Wedemeyer Reports!* (New York: Henry Holt & Company, 1958).

77. Telegram, Nanking to Secretary of State, 12 March 1947; Telegram, Nanking to Secretary of State, 21 March 1947; HST/PSF/Box 173/China 1947. These telegrams were sent by Undersecretary of State Dean G. Acheson to President Truman with a cover memorandum stating that "Secretary Marshall has requested that the attached messages and reports concerning the situation in China be given you."

78. Summary of Telegrams, China, 22 September 1947, HST/NAF/Box 21/Jan–Apr 48.

79. Summary of Telegrams, China, 8 November 1948, Ibid., Sep–Dec 1948.

80. Letter, V.K. Wellington Koo to President Truman, 9 November 1948, HST/PSF/Box 173/China 1948.

81. Memorandum for the President from RADM R.H. Hillenkoetter, Director of Central Intelligence, 24 November 1948, HST/PSF/Box 173/China 1948.

82. NSC 34, United States Policy Toward China, 13 October 1948, DNSC:Reel 1. NSC 34 was prepared by George Kennan of State's Policy Planning Staff (PPS) and was originally submitted to the Secretary of State as PPS/39. See Anna K. Nelson, ed., *The State Department Policy Planning Staff Papers, 1947–1949* 3 vols. (New York: Garland Publishing Company, 1983), vol. 2, p. 412.

CHAPTER 2

The Nationalist Occupation Of Taiwan, 1945-1948: A Less Than Inspiring Record

Our experience in Formosa is most enlightening. The administration of former Governor Chen Yi has alienated the people from the Central Government. The Central Government lost a fine opportunity to indicate to the Chinese people and to the world at large, its capacity to provide honest and efficient administration. They cannot attribute their failure to the activities of the Communists or of dissident elements...The Army conducted themselves as conquerors. Secret police operated freely to intimidate and to facilitate exploitation...There were indications that Formosans would be receptive toward United States guardianship and United Nations trusteeship. They fear that the Central Government contemplates bleeding their island to support the tottering and corrupt Nanking machine and I think their fears well founded.[1]

> GEN Albert C. Wedemeyer
> to Secretary of State
> Marshall, August 17, 1947

On October 25, 1945 General Andô Rickichi, the nineteenth and last Japanese Governor-General of Taiwan, formally surrendered the island to General Ch'en Yi who accepted on behalf of the victorious allied powers. Thus ended fifty years of Japanese rule.

During that half-century the people of Taiwan lived a regimented and often repressive existence as second-class citizens within the Japanese colonial empire. At the same time, however, the same spirit and resolve which Meiji modernizers exhibited in the home islands was applied in their first colonial possession. Japan quickly transformed an underdeveloped and all but neglected frontier area on the fringe of the Ch'ing empire into a relatively modern, economically developed, and self-sufficient island whose inhabitants enjoyed a standard of living in Asia second only to the Japanese themselves.

However, in less than two years of mainland rule Nationalist officials and carpetbaggers handily mismanaged and exploited the island's economy to the point where many wondered if it would ever recover. Unless major reforms were quickly instituted, Taiwan, it seemed, would be destined to sink to the mainland's level of economic chaos.

Furthermore, Chinese cousins from across the Strait came not as liberators but more as occupiers of a population tainted by the stink of a hated enemy. Taiwanese political leaders who looked forward to finally attaining self-rule for the island under a Nationalist democracy on the mainland were hopelessly disappointed. For the common man and woman who cheered the departure of the ubiquitous and all-powerful local Japanese policeman there came instead an equally repressive KMT military regime.

In February 1947 Taiwanese resentment exploded into the streets as rioters reacted to the killing of a woman by occupation police for selling contraband cigarettes. Shortly thereafter, Nationalist troops from the mainland arrived and massacred untold thousands of civilians and arrested hundreds more.

American consular officials in Taipei had been observing and reporting upon the nature of KMT rule on Taiwan since VJ-Day. The picture they painted was not a pretty one. Visiting United States officials such as General Albert Wedemeyer corroborated the desperate state of affairs on the island. Many in Washington feared that unless drastic political and economic reforms were forthcoming Taiwan might fall to the Communists although CCP influence on the island was determined to be negligible! Indeed, at the end of 1948 the Joint Chiefs of Staff, at the request of the Department of State, were tasked to appraise the strategic value of Formosa and the implications for United States security should the island fall to "Kremlin-directed communists."[2] Taiwan henceforth became a variable in Washington's Cold War calculus.

2.1 TAIWAN AND THE CHINESE EMPIRE

Sitting approximately one hundred miles off the eastern coast of Fukien Province, and straddling the sea lanes between Japan and Southeast Asia, Taiwan was a neglected frontier area of the Ming Dynasty (1368–1644). For most of this period the island was inhabited almost exclusively by aboriginal tribes who lived in the eastern mountain ranges and Chinese and Japanese pirates who used the western coast to stage raids on the mainland.

During the age of European exploration Taiwan, named *Ilha Formosa* or Beautiful Island by the Portuguese, was visited by the sea-faring powers as a convenient refitting station. By the early 1620's the Dutch from Java and the Spanish from the Philippines had established settlements on the island's northern tip. From their stronghold, Zeelandia, the Dutch were able to expel the Spanish and from 1628 until 1663 Taiwan was ruled by the Dutch East India Company. During this period a considerable number of Chinese migrated to the island, fleeing the dislocations of the Ming-Ch'ing transition. These adventurous folks would become the ancestors of the Taiwanese ruled in turn by the Ch'ing, the Japanese, and the Nationalists.[3]

In 1663 Cheng Ch'eng-kung (Koxinga), the pirate and self-proclaimed Ming loyalist, displaced the Dutch after a protracted siege of Fort Zeelandia. Until the Ch'ing took the island by force in 1683, the Cheng family ruled Taiwan as an independent principality. After its incorporation into the empire, Taiwan was made a prefecture (*fu*, 府) of Fukien.[4] The Ch'ing initially treated the island as a backwater and imperial magistrates did not invest much time or effort in developing it. At best, assignment to Taiwan was to be endured. Aside from the tropical diseases which made the posting a hardship tour, the independent-minded islanders were an unruly lot over which to preside. In 1714, 1787, and 1833 there were three great rebellions against Ch'ing rule. Consequently, Taiwan became known as an area subject to "an uprising every three years, a rebellion every five."[5]

During the latter half of the nineteenth century, the age of the New Imperialism, Taiwan, like the mainland, was subjected to encroachments by foreign powers. In 1868 the British attacked Fort Zeelandia ostensibly in retaliation for the sacking of Christian missions but more directed at breaking the local government's monopoly in the camphor trade.[6] During the "Taiwan Incident" of 1874 Japan launched a punitive expedition against the island in retaliation for the murder of sailors from Okinawa. While Tokyo's main purpose was to strengthen its claims to the Ryûkyû (Liu-ch'iu) Islands, the affair gave the Japanese an opportunity to test Peking's resolve to maintain control over Taiwan.[7] Finally, throughout 1884 France blockaded and shelled the island during the Sino-French War (1884–1885).[8]

In response, the Ch'ing attempted to strengthen their control over Taiwan and sinicize it. The ban on mainland migration was lifted in 1875 and in 1886 Taiwan was elevated within the empire to a full province (*sheng*, 省).[9] Under the province's first governor, Liu Ming-ch'uan, the celebrated "Self-Strengthener", a program of modest modernization began. Liu improved the island's harbors, established telegraph lines, developed mining, and generally made his realm one of China's most progressive regions.[10] However, the Chinese experiment on Taiwan came to a screeching halt as a result of the Sino-Japanese War.

2.2 THE JAPANESE HALF-CENTURY

On April 27, 1895 Li Hung-chang, representing the defeated court in Peking, affixed his seal to the Treaty of Shimonoseki; the final act of humiliation in China's war with Japan. Among other terms dictated to the Ch'ing, Taiwan was ceded to Japan.[11] Tokyo had gained its first colony.[12]

The Chinese gave up the island with much regret but little protestation. The Taiwanese, on the other hand, did not accept this turn of events so passively. On May 25, 1895 gentry leaders proclaimed the Taiwan Republic.[13] Although the Republic lasted but twelve days armed resistance to Japan's occupation lasted for over half a year.[14] When the insurrection was finally quelled, Tokyo proceeded to write a mixed historical record of rule over the island.

One of the enduring characteristics of Japanese rule was the efficiency with which absolute control over the colonial population was maintained. Only by imposing law and order could any economic benefits be reaped from the island. Also, as a strategically placed outpost of empire, Tokyo could ill-afford to brook internal instability.[15] Although Imperial Army garrison strength in Taiwan was gradually reduced over the years (until, of course, the period of the "China Incident" and the Pacific War) rule over the island had a very martial flair to it. Indeed, except for the years 1919 to 1936 the Governors-General of Taiwan were either Imperial Army Generals or Navy Admirals.

The main instrument of colonial control was the civil police force established in 1898. In the neighborhoods of the cities, the rural lowlands, and even in the remote mountain regions inhabited by the aborigines, the Japanese police officer was present to enforce the policies of the colonial government in Taihoku (Taipei). Whether call-

THE NATIONALIST OCCUPATION OF TAIWAN, 1945–1948   49

ing responsible *pao-chia* (*hokô*) heads to task for local criminal activity, or recruiting laborers for government service, it was the policeman who came to represent the realities of colonial rule for the vast majority of Taiwanese.[16]

Although its colonial possession served both as a status symbol and strategic outpost, it was as an economic asset that Taiwan made its greatest contribution to Tokyo. In the words of Samuel Pao-San Ho, Taiwan, prior to 1930, served as an "agricultural appendage of Japan," providing vast amounts of rice and sugar to the home islands.

The cheap rice sent back to Japan not only fed a work force which was shifting noticeably to the industrial sector, but kept those very industrial wages from rising. Also, colonial sugar production helped to lower Japan's trade deficit around the turn of the century for between 1896 and 1904 fifty percent of Japan's foreign exchange was being applied toward the import of foreign sugar.

After 1930, Taiwan served as a source of industrial products for Japanese heavy industry.[17] Petro-chemicals, aluminum, and ores from Taiwan all served to fuel Japan's war machine.

As with Japan's later possessions, Taiwan existed within the empire solely to serve the needs of the metropole. However, the economic wealth which was extracted from the island was the result of intensive Japanese development. Taiwan, more than any of Tokyo's other possessions, was the beneficiary of a high degree of modernization which ultimately raised the standard of living of the Taiwanese far above that of Chinese across the Strait.[18]

The decision that Taiwan must be economically developed was present from almost the very beginning of Japanese rule. Much of the credit for instituting the programs and policies which allowed the colony to prosper rests with Gotô Shimpei. As Taiwan's fourth civil administrator (serving under General Baron Kodama Gentarô, Governor-General from 1898 to 1906) Gotô initiated far-reaching changes of the social and economic order which, within ten years, "...changed a backward, economically fragmented, and debt-ridden territory into a modern, economically self-sufficient colony."[19] Indeed, by 1904 Japan no longer had to subsidize the maintenance of its new colony.[20]

Taiwan's excellent climate and natural resources made the island ripe for increased development. Also, revenues the colonial government accrued from its various monopolies over camphor, opium, salt, ginseng, and sugar were reinvested in the agricultural sector and in building the island's infrastructure.[21]

However, it was, ironically, the repressive regimentation of the population which accounted for a major transformation of farming techniques and increased agricultural production; the foundation of Taiwan's relative pre-war prosperity. Through village associations (*baraku kai*), the Youth Corps (*Seinendan*), the *hokô* system, farmers associations, and a myriad of other organizations which the people were "encouraged" to join, modern farming methods, enforced by the ever-present police, were introduced. Specifically, as a result of the distribution of superior strains of high-yield rice seeds, the use of chemical fertilizers, and forced labor for riparian and irrigation projects, rice production grew at a steady rate up until the Pacific War. For example, in 1911 Taiwan exported less than 100,000 metric tons of rice to Japan after meeting its own needs. However, by 1937 that amount increased to almost 750,000 metric tons. Sugar production increased from about 80,000 metric tons per annum in the early 1900's to over 900,000 metric tons in the 1930's.[22]

Although the modernization of Taiwan occurred under the whip, so to speak, the people of the island enjoyed a standard of living far above that which the majority of their relatives on the mainland could even imagine.[23] Law and order ended the incessant clan violence and inter-group rivalries which plagued Taiwan under Ch'ing rule. The island's infrastructure was developed. Functioning harbors, railroads, communications, and postal systems became taken for granted. By 1920 Taiwan had 637 KM of railroads and 3,553 KM of roads criss-crossing the island.[24] Public sanitation, waste disposal, and water treatment did much toward eliminating cholera and typhoid. On the eve of the Pacific War Taiwan boasted over 270 hospitals and medical clinics.[25] Indeed, by the end of Japanese rule the life expectancy for native men and women increased by some thirteen and sixteen years respectively.[26] Education for Taiwanese children, though not the upper track of schooling Japanese on the island enjoyed, was the rule rather than the exception. At the end of the war seventy percent of all school-age children were in class.[27] In 1928 Taihoku Imperial University was opened—the empire's seventh Imperial institution of higher learning. In 1936 a medical college was added.[28]

However, for all the benefits of progress, the Taiwanese were politically powerless and their cultural identity was under constant assault. The islanders were never granted all the rights of citizens in the home islands although the Diet declared them Japanese citizens when the Nationality Law of 1899 was passed.[29] They were treated alternately with repressive rule or, under the best of administrations, condescending toleration toward a people who were inherently inferior but capable of being uplifted.

Culturally and socially the idyllic goal of Taiwan's colonial masters was *dôka* (*Tung hua*), or assimilation. In Taiwan (and Korea) it was hoped that through education and social controls colonial subjects could be "Japanized" and molded into "...diligent, loyal, law-abiding 'imperial people's' (*kômin*), imbued with the same values, bearing the same responsibilities, and sharing the same life-styles of Japanese..."[30] The reality was discrimination and subjugation. Responsibilities to the emperor were many, rights under Imperial rule were few. Furthermore, assimilation was anathema to a people who, over the centuries, had developed an indigenous cultural identity.

With the modernization of Taiwan a political consciousness grew among a small but vocal segment of the colonial population. In 1921 the desire for full participation in the island's political and economic life found expression with the founding of the League for the Establishment of a Taiwan Congress (*Taiwan Gikai Kisei Dômei*). The creation of the "Taiwan League," as it was known, was inspired by Wilsonian principles and encouraged by the loosened political atmosphere in Japan itself during the period of "Taishô Democracy." The Taiwan League was most active in Japan proper where thousands of island students were attending institutions of higher learning. On Taiwan long-time political activist Lin Hsien-t'ang (Rin Kendô) came to represent the League and the "Home Rule Movement" itself. The agenda was quite simple. It was desired that Taiwan be recognized as a distinct cultural entity within the empire; that a popularly-elected congress be established to counterbalance the authority of the Governor-General; and that the Imperial Diet include Taiwanese representation. The League petitioned these demands with the Diet every year for fifteen years. At no time did the movement ever call for independence from Japan.[31]

Ignored in Tokyo and often repressed by the colonial administration on Taiwan, the League never accomplished more than attaining some token concessions. The few League activities tolerated by the

Japanese, such as publications, all ceased to be permitted after the invasion of North China in 1937.

However, in the desperate last days of the Pacific War, Tokyo, in a bid to assure the loyalty of the Taiwanese, dramatically altered the status of the island. As the battle for Okinawa began (April 1945), an Imperial Rescript announced the appointment of Lin Hsien-t'ang as a member of the House of Peers. Additionally, Taiwan would no longer be a colony. It was declared that 1945 would be the year that general elections would be held for an island-wide assembly and that representation in the Diet would ensue.[32] It all came too late.

In the end, as Mark Peattie elegantly stated it:

> ...the ethos of Japanese colonialism bequeathed no legacy of cultural deference nor forged any bonds of mutual affection...What did remain behind after the colonial rulers had departed were the standards of success set by Japan in meeting the challenge of modernity.[33]

What also remained behind on Taiwan were aspirations for self-rule. With the surrender of Japan the island's future took unforeseen directions.

2.3 THE NATIONALISTS TAKE CONTROL

The postwar political future of Taiwan was decided at Cairo in 1943. At that time President Roosevelt, Generalissimo Chiang, and Prime Minister Churchill jointly issued their statement declaring that, among other territories, Taiwan would revert back to Chinese rule after the defeat of Japan.[34]

Throughout the war it was assumed that an American invasion of the island would be necessary before the final assault on Japan could occur. However, in the early Autumn of 1944 General MacArthur's "Luzon First" argument carried the day, making the liberation of the Philippines the priority. The invasion of Taiwan was delayed and, ultimately, unnecessary due to the early conclusion of the war.[35] The abrupt ending of the war also negated earlier plans for an initial American occupation of the island. United States troops were rushed instead to Japan and Korea.[36] The occupation of Taiwan became an entirely Chinese affair.[37]

Since Taiwan's eventual reversion to Chinese control was assumed the Nationalists were charged with administering the island on behalf of the allied powers.[38] However, Taiwan did not legally return to Chinese sovereignty immediately after the Japanese surrender. Until a formal treaty with Japan was concluded the island was technically still an integral part of the Japanese empire.

Chiang Kai-shek's selection of General Ch'en Yi as first Governor-General was an unfortunate choice.[39] For the people of Taiwan it was tragic. Under Ch'en's rule from October 1945 to April 1947 the island was brought to its knees economically and the Taiwanese were subjected to repression and, ultimately, atrocities which today still scar relations between native islanders and the former mainlanders who still wield power in Taipei.

Born in the Generalissimo's native Chekiang Province, Ch'en was a 1907 graduate of Japan's *Shikan Gakko*. He aligned his personal army with the Nationalist revolutionary forces in 1926 as the Northern Expedition swept through Chekiang. Chiang and Ch'en were introduced by a mutual acquaintance in 1927 and stayed close associates. Until Ch'en's execution in 1950 Chiang consistently overlooked his excesses and appointed him to prominent positions in the national government.[40]

Ch'en, like many of the Generalissimo's lieutenants, was an opportunist. However, unlike most of Chiang's closest subordinates he was also a rapacious warlord of the first order. Prior to his posting on Taiwan Ch'en was already notorious for his methods as Governor of Fukien (1934-1941). While serving in that position he established extensive provincial monopolies which bled the region economically and lined the pockets of his own aides. He maintained very cordial relations with the Japanese military and conducted a profitable trade with Taiwan. Fukienese who protested his economic policies and collaboration were brutally suppressed. Perhaps fearing that Ch'en would support Wang Ching-wei's puppet regime in Nanking, Chiang transferred him to Chungking in August 1941 where, nonetheless, he was promoted and appointed as Secretary General of the Executive Yuan.[41]

Given his well-known previous record, Ch'en's selection as Governor-General of Taiwan was a shock to those who followed Chungking politics. The Assistant Army Attache in China, LTC David Barrett, reported that many of the Chinese to whom he spoke were incredulous that Chiang would turn over to such a man as Ch'en "...the biggest plum which could possibly fall to an official since the Japanese surrendered..."[42] Ch'en's abysmal record as Governor-General confirmed their worst fears.

In distinct contrast to the Japanese, who almost immediately established order on Taiwan fifty years earlier, Ch'en's administration brought with it a sampling of the chaos and disillusionment which was engulfing the mainland. The first exposure the islanders had to their "liberators" were the KMT troops who were ferried across the Strait. As was usually the case, these troops had little in the way of formal logistical support and foraged for their existence. They commandeered, confiscated, and appropriated private property as they saw fit. In some units wholesale looting of private Taiwanese and former Japanese assets occurred. Those soldiers which did pay for their provisions forced local shopkeepers to sell their wares at ridiculously low prices.[43] The alienation of the Taiwanese by the generally ill-disciplined Nationalist troops was universally observed. It was considered serious enough by the American Embassy in Nanking to cable back to Washington that "...military misbehavior is probably the greatest single liability of the new government (in Taipei), coupled with the general arrogance with which troops and officials treat the native population."[44]

The police function on the island was taken over by mainlanders who were as unruly and unreliable as the regular garrison troops. Many of the police conscripts were illiterate youths "...with no knowledge of local dialects, no comprehension of police duties and reliant only on their arms..." which they used "indiscriminately." The island's criminal element had a field day. The Taiwanese were more fearful of Nationalist police officers than local gangsters and were reluctant to report crimes. The islanders were incensed at the breakdown in law and order and the KMT's inability to provide basic security in what was previously a relatively tranquil territory. "Whereas the Japanese were always known as 'stinking dogs' among the Formosans," commented the American Consul-General in Taipei, "the mainland Chinese are now referred to as 'pigs' who have only voracious appetites and offer nothing of the protection which the 'dogs' afforded."[45]

Moreover, Taiwanese found that they were immediately excluded from any meaningful role in the administration of the island. After years of lobbying Tokyo for "Home Rule" Formosans were crushed to once again find themselves politically disenfranchised in their own land.

The Government-General of Taiwan was a government of military occupation administering over a territory formerly held by a defeated enemy. Ch'en Yi, as Governor-General, ruled on behalf of the Executive Yuan of the Central Government and was responsible solely to the Generalissimo. He was delegated enormous powers by Chiang and was virtually unchecked.[46] The natives were regarded as sympathetic to Japan and, until sinicized, considered unfit for any role in politics. Taipei's official records indicated that Taiwanese were indeed participating as partners in provincial, municipal, and local government. However, most islanders in the government's employ were serving as "...office boys, messengers, charwomen..." and in other such menial positions. The only prominent posts held by Taiwanese were the Vice Commissioner of Education, the Mayors of Taipei and Takao, and the Prefectural Magistrates of Shinchiku and Takao. Even in these cases, each of the men holding the above positions, though born on the island, had been on the mainland for over a decade. At best they were out of touch with local aspirations. For the most part they were active in the promotion of the Nationalist agenda.[47]

The aspirations of the Taiwanese for a major role in the island's political life immediately after the departure of the Japanese were unrealistically high given the facts of life on the mainland and the methods by which the KMT continued to stay in power and govern China. Yet, they had been led to believe that with liberation would come the democracy and self-determination which were the center-pieces of allied wartime propaganda.

Of even greater immediate concern than the political situation was the fact that what private enterprise that did exist under the Japanese was all but eradicated by Ch'en. The Central Government, the Government-General of Taiwan, and private mainland interests closely affiliated with high-level KMT officials monopolized almost every aspect of economic life on Taiwan. As the Embassy in Nanking explained to General Wedemeyer in a briefing during his much publicized mission, the Chinese in Taiwan went further even than the Japanese in Manchuria to attain absolute control over the economy. In Taiwan the KMT "...not only controlled nearly all lucrative enter-prises, but the government also partly owned and endeavored in varying degrees to operate them."[48]

In addition to the previous Japanese monopolies, the Chinese established a Trading Bureau which controlled all of the island's import and export trade. Almost all of the island's trade was directed to Shanghai. It quickly became clear that the mainland could not replace Japan as a source and outlet for goods. Nevertheless, Taiwan's economic well-being was tied to the fortunes of China proper.

The Central Government, through the National Resources Commission (NRC), took over full control of the petroleum, aluminum, gold, and copper industries through fourteen subsidiary organizations. Nanking owned the Salt Monopoly as well. The NRC and the Government-General of Taiwan jointly controlled most former private Japanese industries and companies. Nanking and Taipei shared the revenue accrued from monopolizing electric power, sugar, cement, paper and pulp, alkalis, machine and ship-building, and chemical fertilizers. The Government-General of Taiwan directly controlled iron works, textiles, bricks and tiles, glass, oils and fats, and rubber goods. Additionally, Taipei controlled the monopolies on camphor, wine, cigarettes, and matches.[50]

Taipei exercised control over its monopolies through semi-official corporations in which Ch'en and his Commissioners personally owned major interests. They were able to squeeze out local private businessmen by maintaining licensing authority over iron, steel, ceramics, chemicals, printing, electrical components, textiles, glass, oil and fats, coal mining, marine products, livestock, tea, pineapples, lumber, agricultural produce, automobiles, harbor services, transportation, travel services, medical supplies, engineering firms, and ice. All banks and financial institutions were likewise controlled either by Ch'en or other mainland interests. In some cases influential mainlanders were able to secure protected business rights. For example, T.V. Soong's China Merchants Steam Navigation Company held half interest in the only company authorized to ship goods between the island and the mainland; the Taiwan Water Navigation Company. The Government-General of the island held the other fifty percent.[51]

The few private enterprises allowed to engage in business did so only at the pleasure of Ch'en and his subordinates with the appropriate "squeeze" being exacted in due course. Finally, while foreigners were often hired on as technical advisers in these government ventures, Nanking permitted no foreign companies to participate in the development of Taiwan.[52]

Predictably, the economy, infrastructure, and standard of living on Taiwan fell drastically. By the close of 1947 overall industrial production on the island fell to less than one-third of prewar levels.[53]

The failure of the new administration in Taipei to maintain riparian works and irrigation systems, coupled with a desperate shortage of chemical fertilizer, decimated the rice crops of 1945 and 1946. By the end of 1948 rice production was still over 200,000 metric tons short of 1937 production levels.[54] Rice prices soared and hoarding began. The administration in Taipei had seized all Japanese army grain reserves in 1945 and it was popularly believed that Ch'en was selling the grain on the mainland through the black market. The Governor-General, ostensibly to preclude private hoarding, imposed centralized collection of all crops by the Food Commission, further undermining the population's confidence in the mainlanders' intentions. Consequently, throughout 1945 and 1946 there were fears that rice riots would break out.[55] Sugar production, formerly an indicator of economic well-being on Taiwan, plummeted. In 1947 a crop of only 30,000 metric tons was harvested; a figure far below turn of the century output.[56]

Predictably, the Chinese were incapable of running all of the island's industries and services. Although all Japanese were scheduled to be repatriated by April 30, 1946 it became clear that their departure would result in a near complete shutdown of Taiwan. The Embassy in Nanking enjoined SWNCC, responsible for setting the time tables for repatriation, to consider the negative impact the departure of the Japanese would have. If a minimum number of Japanese technicians were not allowed to stay on there would be chaos. "Lack of competent Chinese personnel and poor showing to date of Chinese official in taking over administration of Formosa," warned the U.S. Embassy in Nanking, "may well mean the island will face serious economic dislocations and possible disorder."[57] Consequently, with the Generalissimo's approval, 5,600 Japanese technicians (and 22,400 of their dependents) were permitted to remain at their posts until January 1, 1947.[58]

The retention of so few trained personnel did not keep the economy and services of the island from deteriorating. After a short few months of KMT administration a noticeably "...sharp increase in numbers of beggars and impoverished peddlers..." could be observed.[59] By the end of 1947 unemployment, almost unknown under Japanese rule, was calculated by American officials as greater than 150,000 persons.[60] Public health services and sanitation instituted by the Japanese ceased to operate. In 1946, for the first time since 1919, bubonic plague reappeared and a cholera epidemic spread across the island.[61] Inflation set in and the price of modern conveniences previously taken for granted quickly slipped out of reach for the common citizen. For example, the cost of electricity increased so drastically that most people in the cities reverted to the use of oil lamps. One year after liberation the cost of public transportation was twenty times as high as under Japanese rule.[62] In summation, by the summer of 1946, the American Consulate in Taipei reported that "Economic paralysis has set in..."[63]

According to the NRC's American technical advisor, Taiwan's economic ills were a function of two major factors. First, China was "...not prepared to replace Japan as a source of materials and equipment necessary to sustain production on the island..." Second, even with the best of intentions, the Chinese did not possess the technical and managerial skills of the Japanese. Although the central and local governments owned and operated all industries, there was a total lack of coordination for the use of scarce resources. Reporting to the NRC, Dr. S.A. Trone complained that "Each factory tries to keep a stock of materials greater than its present needs, for fear of rising prices." Furthermore, there was no plan, rhyme, or reason to the KMT's economic administration. Every factory operated in isolation with one goal; "...the making of inflated paper profits, without regard to sound management, better production, and maintenance of equipment."[64]

Compounding these problems was the fact that Taiwan's resources were being diverted to the mainland. The Consul General in Taipei corroborated reports that over half of the coal produced monthly on the island was being shipped across the Strait.[65] This particular diversion had a "...crippling effect..." on Taiwan's production capacity. Factories were forced to close down and workers either went unpaid or were let go. Experts predicted a total stoppage in the island's production if such exports continued.[66]

Finally, along with the usual gross instances of individual corruption among officials, Taiwan was also subject to rivalry between the various factions of the KMT.[67] Each was determined not to be cut out of what prizes were to be had on the island. Fully one month before the occupation took place a fierce struggle between representatives of Governor-General designate Ch'en, the Ministry of Finance, and the Central Bank of China was joined over future control of Taiwan's financial institutions. At stake were the assets of Japan's Bank of Taiwan and commercial banks established during colonial rule. The Central Bank was able to wrest control of the Bank of Taiwan. Private institutions were divided among Ch'en's administration, the Bank of Communications, the Farmer's Bank, and the Central Trust.[68] The diversification of financial power and the different, often competing agenda of the various parties involved made rational financial planning for the island all but impossible.

Principally, however, the biggest factional struggle over Taiwan was between the Political Science and C-C cliques. Aside from the rush for each to take what they could from Taiwan, the contest between these two groups mirrored the political competition they were engaged in on the mainland for influencing the shape of KMT policies and favor with the Generalissimo. Ch'en Yi, ironically, was supported by the Political Science faction; a relatively liberal group compared to the reactionary C-C Clique.[69] The latter group took great pleasure in denouncing the inadequacies of Ch'en's administration in the press, hoping to bring pressure on Chiang to relieve their rivals' man. On one occasion friction between the two groups reached a point where it was alleged that the C-C faction was responsible for cutting off all scheduled air travel and communication between Taiwan and the mainland for a month in 1946, as well as causing the government communications office in Shanghai to refuse all telegrams from Taipei for two weeks.[70]

Crisis was not far away.

2.4 THE "FEBRUARY INCIDENT" AND THE "MARCH MASSACRE"

The many problems on Taiwan under KMT rule did not surface gradually, nor did they go unnoticed by American officials. Troubles on the island unfolded and compounded with breakneck speed. American officials sent a constant stream of reports back to Washington outlining the Nationalists' failings.

Less than thirty days after Ch'en Yi took control of the island General MacArthur's political advisers in Tokyo sent to the State Department a memorandum describing the widening gap between the Taiwanese and their new masters. "The disillusionment after one month," stated the report, "is apparent and though there is an atmosphere of watchful waiting, a deep ground swell of resentment and reaction is developing. Complaints most frequently voiced include criticism of the government's failure to include Formosan-Chinese in the reorganized administration," and "...the predominance of a closely knit, self-seeking nepotic group from the mainland."[71]

After seven months of occupation the American Embassy in China cabled Secretary of State Marshall alerting him to major problems across the Strait. "Even admitting the National Government's preoccupation with problems of greater magnitude on the mainland," wrote the Charge d'Affairs, "it is difficult to understand why so valuable a colonial asset should have been handed over to a group of officials whose incompetence is increasingly apparent and whole principal concern seems to be their own enrichment."[72]

The Taiwanese were not shy about publicly addressing what they considered to be abuses and shortcomings under Chinese rule. Comparatively highly literate, and experienced in lobbying their interests, local leaders were vocal in their denunciations of the Ch'en administration.

The occasion of the convocation of the officially sanctioned Taiwan People's Political Council (PPC) in December 1946 resulted in a first showdown of sorts between Taiwanese and mainland officials. PPC's were being convened on the mainland at this time in conjunction with a reorganization of the Central Government and the issuing of a new constitution. Such assemblies were called to bring the polity into the process of political reform. A PPC was organized on the island in anticipation of Taiwan's eventual return to China with provincial status. The meetings in Taipei degenerated into a point by point condemnation of Ch'en Yi's rule which ended in the presentation of list of grievances by Taiwanese representatives. However, it was the opinion of the American Consulate that Taiwanese voices were falling upon deaf ears; that the rulers in Taipei acted in word and deed as "...a Government above the people and not answerable to nor dependent upon them."[73] Taipei officials left the meetings shocked by what they considered Taiwanese ingratitude. The Taiwanese left bitterly disappointed.[74]

Tensions between islanders and mainland rulers grew as problems mounted. A series of government initiatives throughout January and February 1947 further stoked the fires of discontent. First, land taxes were increased by thirty percent. Second, Ch'en Yi announced that China's constitution—to go into effect on the mainland on December 25th—would not apply to Taiwan. Third, the administration in Taipei decided to lay off twenty percent of its employees. Cuts would come mostly from the lower echelons of the work force; jobs held almost exclusively by islanders. Fourth, local popular elections were postponed for two years. Fifth, Taiwanese were practically frozen out of the bidding for former Japanese properties through discriminatory credit practices. Finally, on February 15, allegedly on the orders of the Governor-General, the Bank of Taiwan recalled twenty percent of all outstanding loans to private businessmen, causing a good number of commercial enterprises owned by Taiwanese to be bankrupted.[75] It would not have taken much at this point to provoke the population into reaction. The explosion came soon enough.

On the evening of February 27th a woman vendor on a Taipei street was accosted by Monopoly Bureau agents. They accused her of selling illegal cigarettes and attempted to confiscate her wares and cash. She screamed and resisted, causing a crowd to form. In the course of the struggle she was beaten to death. The onlookers surrounded the agents who fired into the crowd to escape. One bystander was killed. The police were summoned and the Monopoly Bureau men were taken away. After they departed the crowd overturned the agents' truck and set it on fire.[76]

The next morning demonstrators estimated at two thousand strong assembled at the Monopoly Bureau demanding that it and the Trading Bureau be abolished. When no one from the Monopoly Bureau met the protesters they marched on the Governor's office. As they reached the plaza in front of the Government Building the crowd, according to the American Consulate, "...without warning was swept with machine gun fire which killed four." At that point they dispersed into the surrounding streets, sacking and burning Monopoly Bureau properties in the city wherever it could be found. Taiwanese anger was then unleashed on mainlanders. "During the afternoon, all (mainlanders) who could be caught were beaten; some were killed." Ch'en, in response, then sent roving patrols of armed soldiers in trucks through the city streets "...which used machine gun and rifle fire against unarmed crowds..." The result was a general slaughter. "The heaviest killing," according to Vice-Consul Kerr, "took place within five hundred yards of the Consulate where 25 were killed and more than 130 reportedly wounded," some with dum-dum bullets. In no instance, reportedly, did Taiwanese use firearms against soldiers.[77] Nevertheless, they remained determined to resist. Within a day the rioting spread across the island.[78] All services ceased to operate. Martial Law was declared. Taiwan was on the brink of open revolt. The "February Incident" would soon lead to even greater tragedy.

Isolated for the moment from reinforcements on the mainland, and faced with the prospect of being overwhelmed by shear force of numbers, Ch'en, on March 1, was forced to accept a delegation of representatives from the Taipei PPC who wished to resolve the incident and discuss wide-ranging reform issues. After a few hours delay, during which he attempted unsuccessfully to bolster Taipei with some 5,000 troops from the south, Ch'en agreed to allow the formation of a "Committee to Settle the Monopoly Bureau Incident." The Committee would be given until March 10th to formulate recommendations for general reforms on Taiwan to be presented to the administration. Additionally, Ch'en agreed to lift martial law as of midnight. In the interim, the Committee would work with the Government-General to restore order on the island.[79]

During the period of 1 through 9 March islanders virtually controlled Taiwan. Only at government-general headquarters in Taipei did Ch'en Yi wield any effective authority. While isolated incidents of violence between government troops and Taiwanese occasionally broke out the island, for the most part, was tense but quiet. Taiwanese employees at public utilities did their best to restore services. Public order was maintained by Taiwanese volunteers recruited for a "Loyal Service Corps" by the Committee.[80] In the meantime, Ch'en allowed the Committee to expand its membership to include a very broad spectrum of the island's leadership; PPC representatives, educators, businessmen, media people, and labor leaders.[81] For the next few days, the expanded Committee met among itself and with representatives of the Government-General to discuss grievances and finalize an agenda to be negotiated for the March 10th deadline.

Also during this period, the American Consulate in Taipei was being looked to by Taiwanese as a means through which to communicate their dilemma to the United States and their desires to the Chinese government. On the fourth of March a petition said to represent some 800 Taiwanese was handed to Consular officials and addressed to Secretary of State Marshall. In it the signitories expressed the view that the only hope for Taiwan was to sever all economic and political ties to the mainland; that the United Nations administer Taiwan with a view toward eventual independence.[82] This approach to the problem seemed, for the moment, to be an "unofficial" view held among a minority of the islanders. On the following day, the Political Reconstruction Promotion Association of Taiwan, a group participating in the Committee, handed the Consulate a memorandum to be sent to the Chinese Central Government through the good offices of Ambassador Stuart. It stated that the civil commotion on the island "...is purely in protest against corrupt officialdom and a demand for political reformation with no other purposes whatsoever." The letter pleaded with Chiang not to dispatch troops but to send instead a high official "...to settle the incident for the sake of the nation."[83] Fearing that the Consulate would become embroiled in the rising storm, Ambassador Stuart in Nanking felt obliged to wire Taipei reminding its staff that it should "...continue to refrain from intercession either official or personal in such internal difficulties while reporting any further approaches...to Embassy.[84]

Prophetically, the Consulate in Taipei predicted further and greater trouble. Although the Taiwanese desired to resolve the "February Incident" by peaceful means, they were distrustful of Ch'en and feared a "...repetition (of the) alleged Fukien massacres occurring under General Ch'en's rule there..." It was reported that in some quarters they were preparing to offer full resistance if threatened.[85] Taipei reported as well that Taiwanese were stressing the United States' responsibility for both the island's current predicament and its future based on Washington's role in the promulgation of the Cairo Declaration, and that they intend to "...appeal for American help in seeking UN intervention pending final transfer of sovereignty to China." Finally, recommending a bold policy which gave credence to Taiwanese fears of impending retribution by the Central Government, the Consulate cabled the Ambassador in Nanking that:

> After gravest consideration Consulate concludes only practicable solution would be immediate American intervention in its own right or on behalf of UN to prevent disastrous slaughter by Government forces if loosed on capital...[86]

By the seventh of March the Committee had drafted and presented to Ch'en their program for reform; the "Thirty-two Demands." The document outlined proposals for political and economic reform, addressed the need for personal safety and the sanctity of private property, and called for individual liberties in line with the United States' own Bill of Rights. Instead of calling for independence from the mainland, the Committee demanded instead that Taiwan become a Province with special autonomous status. The Taiwan Garrison was to be abolished and Formosans would defend the island as members of the Chinese Nationalist Army.[87] It was an ambitious program which was never to be given serious consideration.

On the evening of March 8th Nanking's solution to the Taiwan problem was put into action. An initial force of 2,000 troops, followed within the next few days by between fifty and sixty thousand more, landed on Taiwan.[88] Immediately, and without warning, a reign of terror fell upon the islanders. On the ninth of March martial law was declared once again.[89] Mass arrests and summary executions were the order of the day. The Committee was dissolved. Most of its members were in detention, declared "missing," or known to have been shot. The systematic annihilation of the island's leadership and members of the Loyal Service Corps commenced. The "March Massacre" claimed untold numbers of citizens uninvolved with the Committee as well. It was a clean sweep.[90]

There are still no reliable figures on the final toll of the incident. At the time the Central Government in Nanking reported that there were "...no detailed statistics available on casualties in the Taiwan riots."[91] Kerr has estimated that between five and ten thousand Taiwanese were killed by the end of March.[92] In November 1947 the Central Intelligence Agency reported vaguely to President Truman that "...thousands of Taiwanese lost their lives" in the course of the suppression in March.[93]

2.5 THE REACTION IN NANKING AND WASHINGTON

In the following weeks the Central Government allowed Ch'en to continue a policy which the American Embassy in Nanking, quoting "reputable Formosan sources," described as "...systematic repression...with arrests and executions."[94]

Publicly, Nanking played down the gravity of events on Taiwan. At a news conference on March tenth Chiang Kai-shek explained that order would once again be restored on the island now that regular troops had been dispatched to take up garrison duties. He blamed the Communists for instigating the rebellion. Further, Chiang lamented that a settlement of the "February Incident" would be difficult to achieve since the Committee had made demands which were beyond the authority of Taipei to consider. Moreover, many of the demands were unconstitutional. He added that a government official was on his way to Taiwan to assist in achieving a settlement.[95]

General Pai Ch'ung-hsi, Minister of National Defense, arrived on Taiwan on April 17th and stayed three weeks. As the Generalissimo's personal representative he observed the situation and was charged to make recommendations back to Nanking.[96]

Vice Consul Kerr's assessment of Pai's mission was gloomy. While Pai made sweeping statements promising reforms across the board, there was no reason to believe that they would be more than cosmetic. For example, he recommended disbanding the Trading Bureau and replacing it with a Supply Bureau. According to Kerr, Pai gave the appearance of supporting Ch'en publicly, further alienating the populace. Even as he conducted his mission arrests and executions continued. Kerr felt that Pai's public statement on the situation prior to departing Nanking accurately reflected the Central Government's attitude about the whole affair. Summarized by Kerr, Pai stated that:

> ...the Formosan-Chinese have been misled by long Japanese indoctrination which taught them to vilify the Chinese Government, the people and the troops. Japanese educational influence will be eradicated. Ambitious local politicians and communists have plotted and led the uprisings. They are being eliminated. Students, being impressionable and hasty, followed these local leaders. Under stricter control they will now be led to understand the traditional Chinese virtues.[97]

As Kerr correctly assessed, Pai was also on the island to determine how big a political liability Ch'en had become for the Generalissimo. The C-C Clique was demanding Ch'en's dismissal in debates within the KMT's Central Executive Committee. Up until Pai's return Chiang supported Ch'en within the party as well as publicly.[98] Apparently the situation on Taiwan was worse then Chiang had thought. Ch'en's days as Governor-General were quickly coming to a close.

United States government officials were shocked by the whole affair. Even Ambassador Stuart, who was notable for his consistent ability to find some thin thread of good in the KMT, was sobered by the
outrages on Taiwan. In a message back to State, he wrote that:

> ...the situation in Formosa typifies trends in China with which our associ-
> ation could well become a matter of serious national embarrassment.
> There is little question but that in Formosa there was understandable
> popular reaction against official maladministration and corruption...The
> handling of the problem in Formosa, which is now at an acute stage, may
> offer us an indication of what we may expect elsewhere...In view of the
> foregoing circumstances...it would seem premature for the US to commit
> itself to a course of fulsome support of the Government which has thus far
> given insufficient indication that it will move in directions satisfactory to
> American concepts or that has the capacity to revitalize itself.[99]

Nevertheless, at this point in time Washington was not prepared
to publicly censure Chiang for the mess on Taiwan nor contemplate
intervention in any form on behalf of the islanders.

Before long the American press was reporting on the events of
February and March. In early April Minnesota Senator Joseph H.
Ball wrote to Under Secretary of State Dean Acheson, sending him a
newspaper story citing the "blood bath" on Taiwan. Ball asked if the
State Department could verify the allegations in the article. "If so,"
wrote Ball, "it seems to me we should protest just as vigorously
against such acts by the Chinese government as we do when the Russians perform similar acts in Hungary and Poland."

Acheson's response is worth quoting in its entirety, for it reveals
official thinking, as well as policy, on the Taiwan issue at that point in
time. "For your confidential information...," wrote Acheson,

> ...it can be stated that dispatches and telegrams received through Depart-
> mental sources generally confirm press reports indicating harsh measures
> were employed to suppress the recent uprising there. However, by virtue
> of the Cairo Agreement, a copy of which is attached, this Government is
> committed to the return of Formosa to China. Although the transfer of
> sovereignty has not yet been formalized, China's de facto control over the
> island is generally recognized. Therefore, this Government would not be
> in a position to register with the Chinese authorities a formal protest in
> regard to its activities in suppressing Formosan unrest.[100]

Senator Ball wrote Acheson back unconvinced that the Cairo
statement "...imposes any compulsion on our government to refrain
from protesting to the Chinese about the way they are carrying out

that agreement." He warned that the American people and the Congress would think twice about aid for China if such behavior on the part of Nanking continued. He urged that the U.S. Government, either publicly or privately, protest to the Chinese.[101] Acheson again informed Senator Ball that the United States was not in a position to make a "...formal protest to the Chinese authorities...". However, members of the Embassy staff in Nanking were speaking to various KMT officials about the matter. Indeed, Ambassador Stuart had recently handed Chiang Kai-shek a memorandum concerning problems on Taiwan.[102]

Stuart believed that Chiang was not being told the truth about the situation on Taiwan by his subordinates; a classic case of disloyal advisers surrounding the emperor. During a conversation with Stuart on March 29th, Chiang still "insisted" to the Ambassador that the problems on Taiwan were "...not so serious as reported..." When Stuart asked if the Generalissimo would be interested in reading the Embassy's summary and analysis of events he answered in the affirmative.[103] Later that week Stuart suggested to Chiang that T.V. Soong be appointed Governor-General of Taiwan and that American economic advisers be appointed to assist him. According to Stuart, the Generalissimo "...heartily accepted..." the suggestion.[104] Unfortunately, Chiang's brother-in-law was not interested. Soong told the Ambassador that reform of Taiwan amounted to little more than a drop in a bucket as far as China's ills were concerned. The entire structure of China's government needed to be reformed. "What was needed," Soong said, "was another revolution."[105]

2.6 WEI TAO-MING'S "REFORM" ADMINISTRATION

Whether or not Chiang would have given his brother-in-law the post is moot; the two had often been at odds in the past. In any case, at a press conference in Nanking on April 23, Minister of Information P'eng Hsueh-pei confirmed that Dr. Wei Tao-ming would soon leave for Taiwan to take up duties as the new Governor.[106] Ch'en Yi sailed for Shanghai where he stayed in retirement until July 1948 when Chiang appointed him Governor of Chekiang.

Wei Tao-ming had most recently served as Ambassador to the United States (1942-1946) and as Vice-Chairman of the allied Far Eastern Commission (1946-1947). Additionally, throughout his long career in the Nationalist Government, Wei had acquired a reputation as a reformer. After earning the degree of *Docteur en Droit* from the University of Paris in 1926, he went on to serve as Minister of Justice (1928–30), Mayor of Nanking (1930–31), and Secretary General of the Executive Yuan of the Central Government (1938–41). Before his appointment as Ambassador, Wei served a year in Washington under Hu Shih, whom he succeeded.[107]

Upon receiving the news of Wei's appointment Ambassador Stuart cynically assessed that it was probably "...designed for its affect on the American public."[108] He was probably correct in that assessment. It was the Embassy's opinion that, for Chiang, "...the chief anxiety at this time, is not so much in remedying the conditions that brought the revolt, but rather fear of outside intervention and even the countenance by outside powers of Japanese claims, already voiced, for emigration to and possibly economic influence in Taiwan."[109] Undoubtedly, Wei's appointment would give the impression of a fresh start. To sweeten the outlook for observers Taiwan was granted full Provincial status as well.

It is difficult to assess or pass judgment on Wei's rule. For one thing, he served as Governor only until December 1948. Furthermore, most of his year and a half of service seemed to be spent studying the problems Ch'en Yi left behind and attempting to replace bad officials with his own people. This latter task was a most difficult one. In briefing members of the "Wedemeyer Mission" in August on the situation on Taiwan, Embassy First Secretary Perkins pointed out that "...it would appear plain that a good portion of the old crowd remains in Taiwan and, in fact, the shadow of Chen Yi appears still to haunt the scene."[110]

How much authority was actually invested in Wei as Governor was open to question. In a conversation with the American Consul General Wei once lamented that the Central Government was not responsive to his needs and that only Chiang himself could give him a binding decision on any proposed initiative.[111]

Additionally, the security apparatus and armed forces seemed to ignore him. "Disappearances" continued and secret police activity persisted. The military continued to arrest civilians "...probably largely for private gain..." and, in some cases, military officials blatantly ignored instructions from Taipei. It was the general impression that either "...the new civilian government (was) powerless to control (the) military..." or Wei had given it a "free hand."[112]

Kenneth Krentz, who became Consul General after Wei's appointment, was of the opinion that the Governor was making slow but sure progress in spite of the obstacles in front of him. The few major changes in government personnel that were made were, in his opinion, "markedly for the better." Furthermore, Wei seemed to be "diplomatically steering and pushing officials gradually but surely into corrective measures." Krentz maintained guarded optimism in assessing Wei's prospects for success.[113]

Others did not share Krentz's relatively upbeat assessment. Former Vice Consul Kerr believed that Wei's measures were too gradual. He predicted that unless major movement toward reform was made quickly that "...Formosa will succumb to communism in the near future."[114] In March 1948, based on reports from contacts he maintained on the island, Kerr was likewise convinced as that a second uprising was imminent.[115] Ambassador Stuart, while not yet prepared to predict the worse, was nevertheless worried. After half a year of Wei's rule, observed the Ambassador, "maladministration," and "smoldering discontent" were still evident. More troubling to Stuart were reports that Taiwanese were organizing for revolutionary activities with "virtual autonomy" as its goal.[116]

Probably the harshest critique of Wei's administration was that prepared for the President by the CIA in March 1948. "Although Wei himself has not been accused of corruption," stated the report,

...his rule has failed to correct any of the basic ills of the former regime. The power of the secret police has not diminished and there has been no increase in local autonomy for the Taiwanese; economic conditions have not improved. Definite plans have been made to turn commercial enterprises organized by Chen Yi over to private ownership, but little progress has been made in this direction.

Further, according to the CIA, two new problems had surfaced. First, the increase in Nationalist troops on Taiwan undergoing training was placing a burden on the local economy. Second, Taiwanese were now being conscripted against their will for military service on the mainland.

While there was no evidence to date that discontent had led any substantial numbers of Taiwanese into the Communist camp, analysts judged that "...the opportunity for the spread of Communist influence, here as elsewhere in China, has been created by Nationalist incompetence and greed." The future was not judged bright. CIA saw

no hope for substantial improvements on Taiwan as long as the regime
in Nanking continued to deteriorate. Reports of "...the formation of a
sizable underground..." ensured that Taiwan would continue to be
"...the scene of unrest and occasional uprising." Taiwan's ultimate
fate, in the view of the CIA, would be determined by "...the outcome
of the struggle on the mainland."[117]

2.7 THE STRATEGIC IMPORTANCE OF FORMOSA

If the CIA was correct in its estimate that Taiwan's future
depended on the outcome of the Chinese civil war, then, toward the
end of 1948, there was much to be concerned about. By November
both the CIA and the State Department were on record as predicting
the end of Nationalist control of mainland China in short order.[118]

With this in mind, on November 1, 1948, Acting Secretary of State
Robert A. Lovett wrote Sidney W. Souers, Executive Secretary of the
National Security Council. Lovett requested that the NSC prepare a
study "...as a matter of priority..." which would assess "...the strategic
implications to the security of the United States should Formosa and
its immediately adjacent islands, including the Pescadores, come
under an administration which is susceptible of exploitation by
Kremlin-directed communists."[119]

The study, NSC 37, "The Strategic Importance of Formosa," was
assigned to the Joint Chiefs of Staff. It was the first of many which
would be prepared to assess, analyze, and question the proper United
States policy toward Taiwan. Over the next two years, in the NSC 37
"series" of papers, the Departments of State and Defense would put
forth and argue, sometimes vehemently, their positions. As conditions in East Asia changed, the JCS would time and again be asked to
reassess the strategic importance of Taiwan. These military assessments would form the basis of policy recommendations to the President from the State Department.

In this first study the Joint Chiefs were adamant that the denial of
Taiwan to the U.S. would engender serious strategic liabilities for
national security.

First, it was assumed that Taiwan could only become susceptible
to Communist exploitation if the mainland was already under Communist domination. If that were the case, the ports and airbases on
the China coast would already be denied to U.S. forces. "This would
enhance, from the strategic viewpoint, the potential value to the

United States of Formosa as a wartime base capable of use for staging of troops, strategic air operations and control of adjacent shipping routes." At the same time, "...and of even greater strategic significance...," were Taiwan itself to fall into unfriendly hands, the enemy would have the capability of dominating the sea lanes of communication between Japan and Southeast Asia, improving their power projection potential into the Philippines and the Ryukyu Islands. This, according to the JCS, would be "seriously detrimental" to national security and indeed "...makes it even more essential that strategic control of the Ryukyus, as previously recommended..., remain in United States hands."

The JCS then reminded the NSC readership that the denial of Taiwan to the United States could have dire consequences for Japan. "...Formosa is capable of serving as a major source of food and other materials for Japan, a source that would, of course, be denied under assumed conditions." Whether or not Taiwan's resources were denied Japan "...could quite possibly be a decisive factor as to whether Japan would prove to be more of a liability than a potential asset under war conditions."

Finally, recommending policy, it was stated that:

> Based on the foregoing, the Joint Chiefs of Staff believe that it will be most valuable to our national security interests if, in spite of the current Chinese situation and its obvious trends, Communist domination of Formosa can be denied by the application of such *diplomatic* and *economic* steps as may be appropriate to insure a Formosan administration friendly to the United States.[120]

The JCS were now on record. The loss of Taiwan would seriously impair national security. It would later appear significant to the State Department that the JCS recommended only the use of diplomatic and economic means to secure Taiwan. As events unfolded, State would ask the Joint Chiefs the tougher question. Did Taiwan's strategic importance warrant the use of American forces to deny it to the Communists?

2.8 RETREAT

The KMT leadership and Chinese people were not blind to their own situation. Those who had no means to leave would be left on the mainland to come to terms with the new Communist government. For those fortunate others, the exodus began as early as the spring of 1948. Taiwan was the refuge of choice. Consul General Krentz was worried by the numbers of mainlanders who were already arriving in May. "There are many indications that many rats are leaving what they perceive to be a sinking ship," he cabled to Stuart, "and they do not mind being shipwrecked on this rich and beautiful island."[121]

By winter Manchuria had fallen and the KMT was preparing for a defense south of the Yangtze River. The end was in sight and elements of the armed forces and government were preparing to leave.

By mid-December, as the disastrous Hwai-Hai Campaign was being played out, the Chinese Air Force and Navy were already in the process of removing equipment and personnel to Taiwan, leaving the ground forces with precious little strategic and tactical air support or coastal and river transportation.

The Air Force requested United States assistance in moving its heavy equipment and maintenance facilities from Shanghai to Taiwan. While Ambassador Stuart did not want to see the equipment fall into Communist hands, he was not certain that he could recommend that the U.S. Government go too far in helping the KMT remove to the island. His fear was that the great influx of mainlanders—especially military personnel—would reignite the tensions of the past year and ultimately end in a rebellion which would end in Communist domination. Stuart, probably registering the level of crisis in which the mainland was now gripped, was convinced that the proper course for the United States was to hold Taiwan "...in trust for people of China under UN with US as administering trustee until ratification Japanese peace treaty." He stated in no uncertain terms that the United States "...should avoid, through action of any of its agencies in China, giving the appearance of assisting transfer of authority of Nationalist Government to Taiwan."[122]

By the close of 1948 there could be no doubt that Chiang Kai-shek did not intend to lead a serious last stand on the mainland. As of December 16th Nanking requested that sixty percent of the American military equipment destined for China under the China Aid Act of 1948 be diverted to Taiwan.[123] By December 24th the Chinese Ambassador in Washington informed the State Department that it was now the desire of the Chinese Government that *all* future shipments of military goods be sent directly to Keelung.[124]

In the next few days it became clear the Chiang was about to disassociate himself from the final act of a tragedy he helped to write. On December 29th, it was announced that Dr. Wei would be replaced by

General Ch'en Ch'eng who would serve as Chairman of the Provincial Government of Taiwan as well as Commander-in-Chief of the Taiwan Garrison Command.[125] General Ch'en, who in effect was second in command of the Nationalist armies, served notably as Chiang's Chief of Staff during the Second World War. He was one of the Generalissimo's oldest, most loyal, and trusted lieutenant's.[126]

The implications of the events of December 1948 were obvious. As Ambassador Stuart cabled to Washington, "This appointment, plus knowledge coming to us of shipment automobiles, certain Generalissimo's files and house effects to Taiwan may be straws in wind indicating Generalissimo's intentions."[127]

Chiang was soon to resign, leaving Vice President Li Tsung-jen to preside over the Nationalist defeat by the Communists. The Generalissimo would repose to his ancestral home in Chekiang and later reemerge as the leader of "Free China" on Taiwan.

As President Harry S. Truman began his second term of office he would be faced with developing a policy for two China's; a mainland dominated by the Communists and the KMT's last bastion on Taiwan.

Notes

1. *General Wedemeyer to the Secretary of State*, August 17, 1947, FR:47:VII:725.

2. NSC 37: The Strategic Importance of Formosa, December 1, 1948, HST/PSF/MNSC/Box 205/NSC Meeting #31, cover sheet.

3. On the sometimes confusing question of who is a Taiwanese, E. Patricia Tsurumi's definition is most appropriate: "Native islanders of Chinese ancestry who had crossed the Taiwan Strait and settled on the island largely between the seventeenth and nineteenth centuries, but in some cases even earlier." E. Patricia Tsurumi, "Colonial Education in Korea and Taiwan," in *The Japanese Colonial Empire, 1895-1945*, eds. Ramon H. Myers and Mark R. Peattie (Princeton, New Jersey: Princeton University Press, 1984), p. 279. Myers' and Peattie's volume is significant in that it is the first English language work to bring together scholarship on the internal dynamics of the Japanese colonial experience.

4. Leonard H.D. Gordon, "Taiwan and Its Place in Chinese History," in *Taiwan: Studies in Chinese Local History*, ed. Leonard H.D. Gordon (New York: Columbia University Press, 1970), p. 1.

5. George H. Kerr, *Formosa: Licensed Revolution and the Home Rule Movement, 1895-1945* (Honolulu, Hawaii: The University Press of Hawaii, 1974), p. 15; Harry J. Lamley, "The 1895 Taiwan War of Resistance: Local Chinese Efforts against a Foreign Power," in Gordon, p. 30.

74   FROM ABANDONMENT TO SALVATION

6. Leonard H.D. Gordon, "Taiwan and the Powers, 1840-1895," in Gordon, p. 102-103.

7. Marius B. Jansen, *Japan and China: From War to Peace, 1894-1972* (Chicago: Rand McNally College Publishing Company, 1975), p. 18; Gordon, "Taiwan and the Powers, 1840-1895," pp. 103-106. The incident brought Japan and China to the brink of war.

8. Gordon, ibid., pp. 106-107.

9. Kerr, *Formosa: Licensed Revolution*, pp. 11; Gordon, "Taiwan and the Powers, 1840-1895," p. 93.

10. For the details of Liu's administration see Samual Chu, "Liu Ming-ch'uan and the Modernization of Taiwan," *The Journal of Asian Studies* Vol. XXIII, No. 1 (November 1963): 39-53.

11. For the other terms of the treaty see Jansen, *Japan and China: From War to Peace, 1894-1972*, p. 25.

12. The deliberations in Tokyo leading to the decision to take Taiwan as a term of the treaty can be followed in Edward I-te Chen, "Japan's Decision to Annex Taiwan: A Study of Itô-Mutso Diplomacy," *Journal of Asian Studies* Vol. XXXVII, No. 1 (November 1977): 61-72.

13. For an overview of the short-lived independence of Taiwan see Harry J. Lamley, "The 1895 Taiwan Republic: A Significant Episode in Modern Chinese History," *Journal of Asian Studies* Vol. XXVII, No. 4 (August 1968): 739-762.

14. For a brief account of the struggle against Japan see Harry J. Lamley, "The 1895 War of Resistance: Local Chinese Efforts against a Foreign Power," in Gordon, pp. 23-77. In this "war" which the Japanese commander merely termed an action to mop-up "local brigands and insurgents" (*doki sôzoku*) the occupiers lost 164 troops killed in action, 515 wounded in action, and over 4,000 dead from disease! Kerr, *Formosa: Licensed Revolution*, p. 21.

15. While Douglas MacArthur was fond of referring dramatically to Taiwan as "an unsinkable aircraft carrier," the Japanese military was keen in alternately speaking of the island as the key to a "southern advance" (*nanshin*) or "a stone aiming at the southeast" (*Tônan no seki*). Mark R. Peattie, "Japanese Attitudes Toward Colonialism, 1895-1945," in Myers and Peattie, p. 90.

16. To appreciate the very wide range of duties entrusted to the police in enforcing laws and assisting in colonial administration see Ching-chih Chen, "Police and Community Control Systems in the Empire," in Myers and Peattie, pp. 213-239. According to Chen (p. 215), by 1945 there were at least 1,000 police substations throughout the island.

17. Samuel Pao-San Ho, "Colonialism and Development: Korea, Taiwan, and Kwangtung," in Myers and Peattie, pp. 348, 350-351.

18. For works on the agricultural and industrial development of Taiwan see George W. Barclay, *Colonial Development and Population in Taiwan* (Princeton, New Jersey: Princeton University Press, 1954; Ramon H. Myers, "Taiwan as an Imperial Colony of Japan," *Journal of the Institute of Chinese*

Studies (Chinese University of Hong Kong) Vol. VI (December 1973): 425-451; Ramon H. Myers and Adrienne Ching, "Agricultural Development in Taiwan Under Japanese Colonial Rule," *Journal of Asian Studies* Vol. XXIII, No. 4 (August 1964): 555-570; Samuel P.S. Ho, "Agricultural Transformation Under Colonialism: The Case of Taiwan," *Journal of Economic History* Vol. XXVIII (September 1968): 314-360; and Samuel P.S. Ho, "The Developing Policy of the Japanese Colonial Government in Taiwan, 1895-1945," in *Government and Economic Development*, Gustav Ranis, ed., (New Haven, Conn.: Yale University Press, 1971).

19. Mark R. Peattie, Introduction, in Myers and Peattie, p. 19. For more on Gotô see, Chang Han-yu and Ramon Myers, "Japanese Colonial Development Policy in Taiwan, 1895-1906: A Case of Bureaucratic Entrepreneurship," *Journal of Asian Studies* Vol. XXII, No. 2 (August 1963): 433-449 and Yukiko Hayase, "The Career of Gotô Shimpei: Japan's Statesman of Research, 1857-1929," Ph.D. dissertation, The Florida State University, 1974.

20. Ho, "Colonialism and Development: Korea, Taiwan, and Kwangtung," p. 358.

21. According to Ramon Myers and Yamada Saburô, between 1900 and 1938 "...between one-fifth to one-third of the government-created capital formation went for agriculture..." Myers and Saburô, "Agricultural Development in the Empire," in Myers and Peattie, p. 434.

22. Ho, "Colonialism and Development: Korea, Taiwan, and Kwangtung," pp. 379, 364.

23. The term "modernization" is subject to a myriad of definitions. However, its use here is in the context of Rozman et. al. in *The Modernization of China*, Gilbert Rozman, ed. (New York: The Free Press, 1981), p. 3. In the view of the authors, modernization is "...the process by which societies have been and are being transformed under the impact of the scientific and technological revolution." Certainly, Taiwanese society was transformed as a result of the science and technology imported from Japan. Taiwan was a very different place in 1945 from the island taken from China in 1895.

24. Ho, "Colonialism and Development: Korea, Taiwan, and Kwangtung," p. 351.

25. Kerr, *Formosa: Licensed Revolution*, p. 84.

26. Ho, "Colonialism and Development: Korea, Taiwan, and Kwangtung," p. 380.

27. Tsurumi, "Colonial Education in Korea and Taiwan," p. 291. Certainly, the administration in Taihoku used schooling to indoctrinate and control the younger generation of colonial subjects as well as to enhance the productive abilities of its people. For a more detailed study of education under Japanese rule see E. Patricia Tsurumi, *Japanese Colonial Education In Taiwan* (Cambridge, Mass.: Harvard University Press, 1977).

28. Tsurumi, "Colonial Education in Korea and Taiwan," p. 290.

29. Edward I-te Chen, "The Attempt to Integrate the Empire: Legal Perspectives," in Myers and Peattie, pp. 245-246.

76   FROM ABANDONMENT TO SALVATION

30. Peattie, Introduction, in Myers and Peattie, p. 40.

31. Chen, "The Attempt to Integrate the Empire: Legal Perspectives," p. 253. For the evolution of the Home Rule Movement see Kerr, *Formosa: Licensed Revolution*, pp. 113–130. For a comprehensive survey of Taiwanese political activities see Edward I-te Chen, "Formosa Political Movements Under Japanese Colonial Rule, 1914–1937," *Journal of Asian Studies* Vol. XXXI, No. 3 (May 1972): 477–497.

32. Kerr, *Formosa: Licensed Revolution*, pp. 229–230.

33. Peattie, "Japanese Attitudes Toward Colonialism," p. 127.

34. While the ultimate return of Taiwan to China was not questioned by U.S. officials during the course of the war, there was disagreement within the State Department, and among the various postwar planning committees, as to the timing of the transfer of sovereignty after surrender and the process by which control of the island would be turned over to the Chinese. See Leonard Gordon, "American Planning for Taiwan, 1942–1945," *Pacific Historical Review* Vol. XXXVII (1968): 201–228.

35. For an excellent review of the the fierce debate between MacArthur, Nimitz, and the Joint Chiefs over whether Taiwan or the Philippines was to be the critical objective for late 1944 see Robert Ross Smith, "Luzon Versus Formosa," in *Command Decisions*, ed. Kent R. Greenfield (Washington, D.C.: Department of the Army, Office of the Chief of Military History, 1960), pp. 461–477.

36. Not long after Pearl Harbor, Schools for Military Government were established at leading universities such as Harvard, Princeton, and the University of Chicago. At these institutions foreign area and administrative experts began training military officers for occupation duties across the globe. In 1943 the "Formosa Unit" was established at Columbia University. Dr. Phillip Jessup was a co-director of the curriculum. Lieutenant Francis Cleaves (USNR) was responsible for supervising translation work. Lieutenant George H. Kerr (USNR) was Officer-in-Charge of producing area handbooks for Taiwan. In the 1930's Kerr, a student of Japanese history, had studied and taught in Taiwan. When the unit disbanded in late 1944 he served as Assistant Naval Attache in Chungking. After VJ-Day he reverted to duty with the Foreign Service and was Vice-Consul of the first Consulate on Taiwan. Almost all of the reporting on conditions in Taiwan during Governor Ch'en Yi's rule in the State Department files and in the *Foreign Relations* series is his. Many of the initial reports Ambassador Stuart forwarded to Washington about conditions on the island under his name were in fact written by Kerr. A witness to the "February Incident" and the "March Massacre," Kerr became a vocal advocate for Taiwanese independence. He left government service in late 1947 to become a guest lecturer at the University of Washington. For a vigorous condemnation of KMT occupation policies on Taiwan see Kerr's *Formosa Betrayed* (Boston: Houghton Mifflin Co., 1965).

37. The American military presence on Taiwan after VJ-Day was about 120 officers and men. They served as members of the Formosa Repatriation

Group (established to assist in repatriating to Japan members of the Imperial Armed Forces and their dependents), a graves registration team, and a "Search Detachment" which searched the island for the remains of aircraft and crew members reported as downed during the war. *The Consul at Taipei (Blake) to the Ambassador in China (Stuart)*, January 10, 1947, FR:47:VII:424.

38. The demise of Nationalist control over the mainland by 1949, and the subsequent re-establishment of the Central Government in Taipei in the absence of a treaty with Japan (1951), made tenuous the KMT's claim to the island. The question of the legality of Chiang's hold over Taiwan would be debated in the United Nations, exploited by the Communists, and manipulated by various policy-making bodies in Washington and the China lobby to support or change U.S. policy toward the island.

39. The two Generals Ch'en Yi, Nationalist (陳 儀) and Communist (陳 毅) are not to be confused.

40. For a brief biography see Howard L. Boorman and Richard C. Howard, eds., *Biographical Dictionary of Republican China* Vol. I (New York: Columbia University Press, 1967), pp. 250-254.

41. Ibid., p. 223. Also see Kerr, *Formosa Betrayed*, pp. 53-56 for Ch'en's governorship of Fukien.

42. *Report by the Assistant Attache in China (Barrett)*, FR:47:VII:125. According to the American Consulate in Taipei, the Taiwanese were convinced that "...the Generalissimo and the Party handed Taiwan over to Ch'en Yi for a period of exploitation as repayment for a political debt, said to have been created when Ch'en Yi, then Governor of Fukien, disbanded and destroyed the Ninth Route Army after its defense of Shanghai in 1931." Message, American Consulate Taipei, August 12, 1946, SDF: Reel 1. The incident described above refers to the "Fukien Rebellion" of 1932-1934. The revolt was staged by the Nineteenth Route Army, not the Ninth, and Ch'en was made Governor of Fukien after the revolt had been put down.

43. Message, American Embassy Nanking to Secretary of State, "Conditions on Formosa," May 21, 1946, SDF:Reel 1; Message, American Consulate Taipei to American Embassy Nanking, "Political and Social Conditions on Formosa," August 12, 1946, SDF:Reel 1. For the details of KMT troop behavior in the initial phase of the occupation see Kerr, *Formosa Betrayed*, pp. 97-105. The initial occupation force numbered about 12,000 troops. By 1946 the Taiwan Garrison Command comprised about 30,000. Kerr, ibid., pp. 73, 103.

44. Message, Robert L. Smyth, Counselor of Embassy Nanking to Secretary of State, "Conditions in Formosa," March 18, 1946, SDF:Reel 1. Parenthesis added.

45. Message, American Consulate Taipei, "Political and Social Conditions on Taiwan," August 12, 1946, ibid.

46. *The Consul in Taipei (Blake) to the Ambassador in China (Stuart)*, January 10, 1947, FR:47:VII:425.

47. Message, American Consulate Taipei, "Political and Social Conditions in Taiwan," August 12, 1946, SDF:Reel 1.

48. Message, American Embassy Nanking to Secretary of State, "The Situation in Taiwan," August 22, 1947, SDF:Reel 1. SDF:Reel 1. The enclosure to this message is a transcript of the briefing given on the above subject to General Albert C. Wedemeyer and members of his mission on August 9, 1947.

49. Ibid.

50. Letter, S.A. Trone to Secretary of State George C. Marshall, February 24, 1948, SDF:Reel 1. Trone served for three years as Adviser to the National Resources Commission and the Central Bank of China. He forwarded to the State Department a copy of a very detailed memorandum which he prepared for the NRC that underscored the economic problems KMT policies on Taiwan had created.

51. Message, American Embassy Nanking to Secretary of State, "The Situation in Taiwan," August 22, 1947, ibid.

52. *The Counselor of Embassy in China (Smyth) to the Secretary of State*, July 14, 1946, FR:46:X:1379. When pressed by the State Department to allow American companies to do business in Taiwan the Central Government explained that their denial of commercial opportunities was a political matter; that "...the people (of Taiwan) would not stand for it." Parentheses added.

53. "Memorandum of a Report on Taiwan to Ambassador By Dr. S.A. Trone," March 4, 1948, SDF:Reel 1.

54. "Special Report on Taiwan (Formosa) Submitted by COL. N.H. Vissering, Office of the Food Administrator for Occupied Areas, Department of the Army," June 3, 1948, SDF:Reel 3. In 1947, for example, only ten percent of the prewar levels of chemical fertilizers used in rice production was available. This was a result of the general breakdown in industrial output attendant with the Chinese government's control over production on the island.

55. Kerr, *Formosa Betrayed*, pp. 106–109; Message, American Consulate Taipei to American Embassy Nanking, "Political and Social Conditions on Formosa," August 12, 1946, SDF:Reel 1.

56. Kerr, *Formosa Betrayed*, p. 109. Throughout the 1900's sugar production hovered around 80,000 metric tons. Ho, "Colonialism and Development: Korea, Taiwan, and Kwangtung," in Peattie and Myers, p. 364. Kerr's figure for 1947 is not far off the mark. A report by the Department of the Army's Food Administration for Occupied Areas put sugar production for 1946–1947 at 34,000 metric tons. "Special Report on Taiwan (Formosa) Submitted by Col. N.H. Vissering, Office of the Food Administrator for Occupied Areas, Department of the Army," June 3, 1948, SDF:Reel 3.

57. *The Counselor of Embassy in China (Smyth) to the Secretary of State*, March 20, 1946, FR:46:X:891.

58. *The Counselor of Embassy in China (Smyth) to the Secretary of State*, April 6, 1946, ibid., p. 892. SWNCC concurred pointing out that, "The Formosan economy would...be severely crippled for some years if all or most

of the highly trained Japanese in industry and agriculture were repatriated now." *Memorandum by the State Department Member of the State-War-Navy Coordinating Committee (Hilldring) to the Secretary of State*, June 27, 1946, ibid., p. 899.

59. Message, American Embassy Nanking, "Political and Social Conditions and Personalities and Group Interests on Taiwan," September 14, 1946, SDF:Reel 1.

60. Message, American Consulate General Taipei to American Embassy Nanking, "Tentative Assessment of the Situation in Taiwan," January 26, 1948, SDF:Reel 2. Kerr, in *Formosa Betrayed*, p. 234, states that UNRRA observers placed unemployment at more than 300,000 at the end of 1946, a figure "...which did not include *under-employed* Formosans..." (Italics are Kerr's).

61. Message, American Embassy Nanking, "Political and Social Conditions and Personalities and Group Interests on Taiwan," September 14, 1946, SDF: Reel 1.

62. Ibid.

63. Ibid.

64. "General Report on Taiwan," Dr. S.A. Trone, Advisor to the National Resources Commission and the Central Bank of China to Dr. Wong Wen Hao, Chairman, National Resources Commission, January 21, 1948, SDF:Reel 2.

65. Message, American Consulate General Taipei to American Embassy Nanking, "Tentative Assessment of the Situation in Taiwan." Ibid.

66. "General Report on Taiwan," Dr. S.A. Trone, ibid.

67. Corruption on Taiwan was described by Ambassador Stuart as, "...more, perhaps, than the usual amount of graft..." to be found on the mainland. *The Ambassador in China (Stuart) to the Secretary of State*, March 19, 1947, FR:47:VII:71. The Vice Consul-General in Taipei alleged that the sordid story of corruption on Taiwan starts with Ch'en himself, reporting that "It is a popular belief that the Governor General has amassed more than US $3,000,000 during the first six months in office." Message, American Embassy, Nanking, "Political and Social Conditions and Personalities and Group Interests on Taiwan," September 14, 1946, SDF:Reel 1.

68. *The Ambassador in China (Hurley) to the Secretary of State*, September 8, 1945, FR:45:VII:1144–1145.

69. *The Ambassador in China (Stuart) to the Secretary of State*, March 19, 1947, FR:47:VII:71–72.

70. Message, American Consulate Taipei to American Embassy Nanking, "Political and Social Conditions in Taiwan," August 12, 1946, SDF:Reel 1.

71. Message, Office of the Political Adviser, Tokyo to the Department of State, "Report on Current Public Opinion on Formosa," January 28, 1946. Forwards report dated November 23, 1945. SDF:Reel 1.

72. Message, American Embassy Nanking to Secretary of State, "Conditions on Formosa," May 21, 1946, SDF:Reel 1.

73. *The Ambassador In China (Stuart) to the Secretary of State*, December 4, 1946, FR:46:X:590. In this report it was stated that: "...the Government's

representatives were met in the People's Political Council with 'outspoken and forceful criticism from an articulate and intelligent body of local representatives, spokesmen for a public whose general level of education and information is considerably higher than the average for the mainland from which the government officials come. Attempts to limit debate, questioning and criticism and to slur over important but embarrassing problems met with spirited opposition.'"

74. For details of the results of the PPC see Kerr, *Formosa Betrayed*, pp. 196–203.

75. Kerr, *Formosa Betrayed*, pp. 239–248.

76. Message, American Consulate Taipei to Embassy Nanking, "Review of the Crisis in Taiwan," March 3, 1947, SDF:Reel 1; Kerr, *Formosa Betrayed*, p. 255. Kerr, an eyewitness to the events of the following days and the "March Massacre" was the author of almost all reporting on these incidents. Reports in the *Foreign Relations* series almost invariably cite information he sent in messages from the Consulate.

77. "Review of the Crisis in Taiwan," ibid.

78. Kerr, *Formosa Betrayed*, p. 257.

79. "Review of the Crisis in Taiwan," ibid.; Kerr, *Formosa Betrayed*, pp. 258–259; *Memorandum on the Situation in Taiwan, United States Relations with China*, pp. 926–927.

80. Kerr, *Formosa Betrayed*, p. 269. Message, American Consulate in Taiwan to Embassy Nanking, "Review of the Crisis in Taiwan," March 3, 1947, SDF:Reel 1. The Loyal Service Corps consisted mainly of high school students and recent graduates of Japanese-run Middle Schools. These young men were said to be well-trained for their mission. The American Consulate in Taipei reported that between "...20,000 and 30,000 Formosan youths received some elementary military training from the Japanese...Many of these youths have boasted of their superiority over Chinese troops from the mainland and it is believed not impossible that if the situation breaks into wide civil warfare, these youths may form the nucleus of Formosan-Chinese resistance to Chinese Army forces."

81. Kerr, *Formosa Betrayed*, p. 265.

82. *The Ambassador in China (Stuart) to the Secretary of State*, March 5, 1947, FR:47:VII:430.

83. *The Ambassador in China (Stuart) to the Secretary of State*, March 7, 1947, FR:47:VII:435.

84. *The Ambassador in China (Stuart) to the Secretary of State*, March 5, 1947, ibid., p. 430.

85. *The Ambassador in China (Stuart) to the Secretary of State*, March 5, 1947, ibid., p. 431. Parenthesis added.

86. *The Ambassador in China (Stuart) to the Secretary of State*, March 6, 1947, ibid., p. 433.

87. *The Ambassador in China (Stuart) to the Secretary of State*, March 11, 1947, ibid., p. 439. A full translation of the "Thirty-two Demands" can be found in Appendix I, in Kerr, *Formosa Betrayed*, pp. 475-479.

88. *The Ambassador in China (Stuart) to the Secretary of State*, March 9, 1947, ibid., p. 438; *Memorandum by the Vice-Consul at Taipei (Kerr) to the Ambassador in China (Stuart)*, ibid., p. 456. This last document is undated but a footnote indicates that it was prepared prior to Kerr's departure from Nanking for Washington on April 28, 1947. The figures Kerr cites are based upon a report of observations made by Assistant Military Attache to China Colonel F.J. Dau during a trip to Taiwan shortly after the initial landings.

89. Message, Embassy, Nanking to Secretary of State, No. 499, March 9, 1947, SDF:Reel 1. Martial law on Taiwan remained in effect until 1987.

90. Kerr's eyewitness account is still one of the few ever published. For his observations see Chapter XIV, in *Formosa Betrayed*.

91. *The Ambassador in China (Stuart) to the Secretary of State*, March 20, 1947, FR:47:VII:442. In this message Ambassador Stuart quoted from a Ministry of Information press conference.

92. Kerr, *Formosa Betrayed*, p. 310.

93. CIA Report SR-8, "China," November 1947, HST/PSF/Box 259, p. I-12.

94. Message, Embassy Nanking to Secretary of State, No. 539, March 13, 1947, SDF:Reel 1.

95. Message, Embassy Nanking to Secretary of State, No. 527, March 11, 1947, SDF:Reel 1.

96. Pai's delegation included fourteen military and political leaders which included Chiang Ching-kuo, the Generalissimo's son and later his successor on Taiwan. *The Ambassador in China (Stuart) to the Secretary of State*, March 18, 1947, FR:47:VII:442.

97. Message, American Embassy Nanking to Secretary of State, "The Mission of General Pai Chung-hsi to Taiwan," April 15, 1947, SDF:Reel 1. This memorandum was prepared by Kerr who, at this time, was recalled to the Embassy to brief the Ambassador and his staff on the situation on Taiwan. The message was forwarded to Washington by W. Walton Butterworth, Minister-Counselor of Embassy, and soon to become the much-embattled Director of the Division of Far Eastern Affairs in the State Department. Butterworth's cover letter to Kerr's report stated that "Mr. Kerr's personal observation of the bloody events in Taipei and the subsequent brutal suppression of representative Taiwan elements perhaps makes his comments appear highly keyed in tone and in certain instances catagoric in content. However, with the continuation of Chen Yi's regime in power in Taiwan, there is coming to be less and less middle ground which can be occupied by cooly impartial opinion."

98. Ibid.

99. *The Ambassador in China (Stuart) to the Acting Secretary of State*, March 21, 1947, FR:47:VII:76. This lengthy message dealt with the reorganization of the KMT which was underway at the time. Stuart recommended that

the US Government take a close look at the new players and policies in Nanking before reassessing China policy. He added that all should realize that the KMT reorganization was taking place while fighting a "powerful and determined enemy." As Stuart messages went, however, this particular one was as close to a general condemnation of Chiang's rule as any would come.

100. Letter, Senator Joseph H. Ball to Under Secretary of State Dean Acheson, April 4, 1947, (Newspaper article, "Editor Describes Atrocities in Rebellion, Chinese Kill 5,000," *Minneapolis Morning Tribune*, March 31, 1947 attached), Letter, Dean Acheson to Senator Ball, April 11, 1947, SDF:Reel 1.

101. Letter, Senator Joseph H. Ball to Under Secretary of State Dean Acheson, April 19, 1947, SDF:Reel 1.

102. Letter, Under Secretary of State Acheson to Senator Joseph H. Ball, April 26, 1947, SDF: Reel 1. The very lengthy memorandum Ambassador Stuart handed Chiang on April 18th was prepared by Taipei Vice Consul Kerr; one of Kerr's last official acts before returning to the United States and separating from government service. In the memo Kerr outlined all of the economic and political problems the Chinese had created on Taiwan since VJ-Day. The urgent necessity for reform was underscored. Chiang had a choice. He could either continue the repression of the Taiwanese and face a protracted struggle or reform and allow Taiwan to become an economic asset for China. *The Ambassador in China (Stuart) to the Secretary of State*, ("Memorandum for the Ambassador on the Situation in Taiwan" enclosed), FR:47:VII:450-455. The memorandum handed Chiang by Stuart was an abbreviated version. The full text can be found in *United States Relations with China*, pp. 923-938.

103. *The Ambassador in China (Stuart) to the Secretary of State*, March 29, 1947, FR:47:VII:90.

104. *The Ambassador in China (Stuart) to the Secretary of State*, April 4, 1947, ibid., p. 96.

105. *The Ambassador in China (Stuart) to the Secretary of State*, April 12, 1947, ibid., pp. 96-97.

106. *The Ambassador in China (Stuart) to the Secretary of State*, April 23, 1947, FR:47:VII:455. Wei did not actually arrive on the island until May 13th. *The Ambassador in China (Stuart) to the Secretary of State*, May 17, 1947, ibid., p. 464.

107. Boorman and Howard, *Biographical Dictionary of Republican China*, Vol. III, pp. 406-408.

108. Message, American Embassy Nanking to Secretary of State, No. 893, April 25, 1947, SDF:Reel 1.

109. Message, American Embassy Nanking to Secretary of State, "The Situation in Taiwan," August 22, 1947, SDF:Reel 1.

110. Message, Embassy Nanking to Secretary of State, "The Situation in Taiwan," August 22, 1947 (script of briefing to Wedemeyer Mission enclosed), SDF:Reel 1.

111. Message, American Consulate General, Taipei to Embassy, Nanking, "Wei Tao-Ming as Governor of Taiwan," May 4, 1948, SDF:Reel 3.

112. *The Ambassador in China (Stuart) to the Secretary of State*, July 8, 1947, FR:47:VII:467–8. Parentheses added.

113. "Wei Tao-Ming as Governor of Taiwan," SDF:Reel 3.

114. *Memorandum by Mr. George H. Kerr to the Director of the Office of Far Eastern Affairs (Vincent)*, May 26, 1947, FR:47:VII:466.

115. Letter, George H. Kerr (Visiting Lecturer, University of Washington) to Walton Butterworth (Office of Far Eastern Affairs, Department of State), March 29, 1948, SDF:Reel 2.

116. *The Ambassador in China (Stuart) to the Secretary of State*, November 17, 1947, FR:47:VII:470.

117. Appendix I "Taiwan (Formosa)," March 1948, to CIA Report SR-8, "China," November 1947, HST/PSF/Box 259.

118. See Chapter 1.

119. Letter, Robert A Lovett to Sidney W. Souers, November 1, 1948, SDF:Reel 1.

120. NSC 37: The Strategic Importance of Formosa, December 1, 1948, HST/PSF/MNSC/Box 205/NSC Meeting #31. Italics added.

121. Message, American Consulate Taipei to American Embassy Nanking, "Implications of Impending Political Battle for the control of Taiwan," May 13, 1948, SDF:Reel 2.

122. Telegram, American Embassy Nanking to Secretary of State, No. 2545, December 17, 1948, SDF:Reel 2.

123. *Memorandum by the Director of the Office of Far Eastern Affairs (Butterworth) to the Acting Secretary of State*, December 16, 1948, FR:48:VIII:233.

124. *Memorandum of Telephone Conversation, by Chief of the Division of Chinese Affairs (Sprouse)*, December 24, 1948, ibid., p. 237.

125. Memorandum from Mr. Butterworth (FE) to the Secretary of State, December 29, 1948, SDF:Reel 2.

126. See Boorman and Howard, Vol. I, pp. 152–160.

127. Telegram, American Embassy Nanking to Secretary of State, No. 2668, December 30, 1948, SDF:Reel 3.

CHAPTER 3

Acheson's China Policy: Banking on Mao Tse-Tito

...the interests of China and the Soviet Union were really conflicting and not complementary, and that properly handled that situation could be developed, and that should be the main line of policy.[1]

Dean Acheson
Princeton, 1953

By the end of Truman's first administration it was acknowledged by the President's foreign policy experts that mainland China would soon be ruled by the communists. This could not be reversed. The KMT was deemed incapable of saving itself. American attempts at mediating a political solution failed. Military intervention on Chiang's behalf was out of the question. The best that could be done was to find a way for the United States to cut its losses.

The defection of Marshall Tito from the Soviet camp in 1948 suggested that the communist bloc was not as solid as was previously thought. For some at Foggy Bottom—especially George Kennan's Policy Planning Staff—Tito's break with Moscow had direct implications for the situation in China. It raised the possibility that a communist-dominated China did not necessarily mean a Moscow-dominated China.

As a result of this line of reasoning the President, by March 1949, approved a series of policy papers which fixed as the primary objective of the U.S. in China the goal of keeping a communist-ruled mainland from becoming "an adjunct to Soviet power."

While no one at the State Department ever argued that a communist-dominated China would be friendly to the United States, analysts did believe that there were enough strains, past and potential, in CCP-CPSU and Sino-Soviet relations to make Chinese communist subservience to the Kremlin a moot question. It would only be a matter of time before real frictions between the two arose.

It was recognized that there was very little that the U.S. could do to accelerate the inevitable break between the Chinese and Soviet communist parties. However, Washington had to be wary of inadvertently driving the CCP into the waiting arms of the Soviets by misguided initiatives on its part. Unhappily, waiting for the emergence of Chinese "Titoism," and being prepared to encourage it when it developed, was believed to be the best policy the United States could pursue to attain its stated objective of keeping the inevitable CCP victory in China from benefiting Moscow.

Throughout 1949 this policy was woven throughout the fabric of decision papers, public statements, and confidential discussions dealing with China and Taiwan. It was a policy which had its roots in the last days of General Marshall's tenure as Secretary of State, but which flourished during Acheson's watch. It was a policy which was largely a result of the analysis of George Kennan and John Davies, but one which other top advisers in State endorsed. Indeed, Secretary Acheson himself was to become its greatest exponent.

In the final analysis, however, it was a policy devised and subscribed to by a group of men who brought to their positions very definite ideas about the situation in China and the limits of what the U.S. could do to influence events there. The policy of pursuing "Mao Tse-Tito" was most definitely the State Department's brainchild.

3.1 FOREIGN POLICY MAKERS, 1949: THE DEPARTMENT OF STATE

The very special trust and confidence which President Truman reposed in Dean Acheson made the Secretary of State almost without equal in the ability to influence the President in foreign affairs and national security matters. Not until General Marshall was recalled from retirement for the second time in September 1950 to become Secretary of Defense did Acheson have a colleague on the cabinet of equal stature in the President's eyes.

Acheson was well aware of the power he wielded and was not shy about exercising it.[2] Confident to the point of arrogance, the Secretary was notorious for the tutorials he felt obliged to give those who did not quite understand the correctness of department policies. Far East policy offered ample opportunities for such lectures, for State was under perpetual attack for its handling of the China debacle.

Acheson's introduction to the China tangle came during his tenure as Undersecretary of State (1945–1947). Of particular significance, he was intimately involved in General Marshall's ill-fated mission to China. Assigned to act as the General's liaison back in Washington, Acheson kept the President abreast of progress and problems, ensured Marshall's messages were delivered to the appropriate agencies, and provided support for the mission members as required. During that time Acheson developed a deep and abiding respect for Marshall. He shared with the General the frustrations of dealing both with the KMT and the communists, and developed, as a result, a marked contempt for both parties. Acheson also shared Marshall's opinion that intervention in China's civil war was not in the United States' best interests.

Acheson took office as the fifty-second Secretary of State on January 21, 1949—the same day Chiang Kai-shek resigned. In his memoirs he lamented that "I arrived just in time to have him collapse on me."[3] It is an ironic twist of fate that unending crises in Asia burdened the eurocentric Acheson throughout his tour of duty.

Precisely because his interests and instincts lay elsewhere, Acheson, in developing policies for the Far East, relied heavily upon the advice of a handful of key advisors.[4] In 1949 these included George F. Kennan, W. Walton Butterworth, Philip D. Sprouse, Dr. Philip C. Jessup, and Dean Rusk. All had also served Secretary Marshall.

When Acheson took office George Kennan was serving as the Director of the Policy Planning Staff (PPS). The staff, established in May 1947, was the brainchild of Secretary Marshall. It was created to bring together the best minds in the Department. Detached from the daily crises they dealt with in their former functional or regional offices, PPS analysts were formed into a "think tank" charged to project future problem areas for United States foreign policy and recommend appropriate courses of action. Marshall asked Kennan to be the staff's first director.[5]

At the time Acheson took over State, PPS was *the* most influential organization within the department. It became, as well, an important source of the administration's foreign policies. It was PPS analysts who drafted Department of State position papers for submission to the National Security Council. When Secretary Acheson argued Department positions he was often arguing PPS recommendations. There was no issue which was not within the purview of the PPS. As Kennan later wrote, "...the world was our oyster; there was no problem of American foreign policy to which we could not address ourselves..."[6]

Although a Soviet affairs expert, Kennan had very definite opinions about the situation in China. In general, he felt that China "...was not the great power of the Orient" and that the United States "...need neither covet favor, nor fear the enmity, of any Chinese regime." Further, he declared to have "...no use for either of the two regimes..."[7] In notes to himself written in 1948 Kennan submitted that there was nothing "...very practical or effective which America might do..." to turn the tide for the KMT. "You can help any government but the one which does not know how to govern."[8] Concerning Chiang Kai-shek, he felt that:

> The Generalissimo's demands upon us for aid...have been motivated basically not by a determination on his part to employ that aid effectively...but by the hope that he might in this way involve our responsibility to a point where we would be obliged to take upon ourselves the main burden of his struggles...enabling him to conserve his own strength for the protection of his personal political position vis-a-vis other groups in China...[9]

Ultimately, Kennan felt that United States security was *not* tied to the fate of China and those wringing their hands over Chiang's prospects were a tiresome lot.

Kennan's chief analyst for Asian affairs on the PPS was John Paton Davies, Jr. A career China FSO, Davies spent the war assigned to Stilwell's staff as a political adviser. Having served in both Chungking and Yenan he had first-hand knowledge of the KMT and CCP leadership. As a result of the accusations surrounding the resignation of Ambassador Hurley Davies was transferred from China to the Embassy in Moscow. It was there that he and Kennan met. The latter was duly impressed. Davies, wrote Kennan, had a "brilliant" and "imaginative mind...He was a man of broad, sophisticated, and skeptical political understanding..." Kennan credits Davies with educating him about Soviet policies and intentions in the Far East during their service in Moscow.[10]

As previously mentioned, Davies predicted postwar problems for the United States in China with uncanny accuracy.[11] He was convinced that the KMT would fight a civil war with the communists which it would lose. His greatest fear was that unqualified American support of Chiang would force the Chinese communists directly into the Soviet camp. As early as 1943 he was cautioning Washington that in order for the United States to maintain influence in China after the war;

> ...we should avoid committing ourselves unalteringly to Chiang. We should be ready during or after the war to adjust ourselves to possible realignments in China. We should wish, for example, to avoid finding ourselves at the close of the war backing a coalition of Chiang's Kuomintang and the degenerate puppets against a democratic coalition commanding Russian sympathy.[12]

During the war Davies, along with Stilwell, led the fight for the establishment of the Dixie Mission in communist-held Yenan. Stilwell's interest was military in nature; he favored a mission in order to gauge the CCP's potential for fighting Japan. Davies's interest was more political. Washington had no first-hand intelligence about the CCP leadership. He had heard rumors that the communist Chinese leadership was split in its loyalty to Moscow; a state of affairs which needed to be verified. "This probable schism within the Party," wrote Davies in 1943, "may prove at some later date to be of major importance."[13] Without realizing it at the time, Davies underscored the basis of the United States policy toward China in 1949; a policy which he would assist in articulating.

Kennan has bemoaned, and some scholars have written, that PPS declined in power ("importance," to quote Warren Cohen) under Acheson.[14] Certainly this was true as a *relative* statement about PPS's status in the bureaucracy. Under Acheson the staff did not enjoy the direct access to the Secretary that it had under Marshall. However, it would not be correct to say that PPS no longer had *influence*. The staff continued to play a major role in shaping U.S. policy throughout 1949 and beyond.[15]

Acheson, however, "...was a man who dealt, in his inner world, not with institutions but with personalities."[16] One of his closest advisers on China matters was Kennan's Princeton classmate (1926), W. Walton Butterworth. A close personal friend of Acheson's, Butterworth's views heavily influenced the Secretary's thinking about the Far East in general and China in particular.[17]

Butterworth served as Director of the Office of Far Eastern Affairs (FE) from 1947 through the late spring of 1950. In 1949, when the position was upgraded, he was confirmed as Assistant Secretary of State for Far Eastern Affairs.

A career Foreign Service Officer, Butterworth served in the American Embassy in Spain during the Second World War. Prior to his assignment to the Embassy in Nanking in 1946 he had never served in China. His reputation for handling tough assignments, coupled with the fact that he had no prior connection to China policy, made him State's choice to run the Embassy in Nanking for Ambassador Stuart. Hurley's resignation, his outrageous charges, and the Senate hearings resulting from them took their toll on Embassy morale. Butterworth was sent in to keep the ship afloat.[18] While serving as Minister of Embassy in China Butterworth met and worked with General Marshall, then on his mediation mission. When Marshall became Secretary of State in 1947 he recalled Butterworth from his post and made him Director of FE.

Butterworth once remarked that during his career as an FSO he was "...a firehorse ready to respond to the fire."[19] To be sure, his China sojourn was a five-alarm affair. Throughout his tenure at FE Butterworth was subjected to unceasing attacks by all who disagreed with United States policy in the Far East. As Warren Cohen put it, he was viewed as "...the evil genius behind the policies of Marshall and Acheson."[20]

A realist, Butterworth did not nurture any optimism whatsoever about the prospects for the success of Marshall's mission. He did not believe that the "lambs and lions" were about to live in harmony. He felt that the communists were deadly serious about usurping total power. Moreover, he believed that they were not merely "agrarian reformers"—a term which Butterworth later stated was Patrick Hurley's "contribution to misunderstanding."[21]

Although he believed a communist-dominated China would be inimical to the United States, Butterworth was not prepared to recommend that Washington underwrite the KMT indefinitely. What Chiang needed, he felt, was not more money and military assistance but bold solutions to the country's myriad of political, economic, and social problems. The KMT, he was convinced, had all the money and arms it needed. What it lacked was the ability to reform itself. Consequently, Butterworth opposed the passage of the China Aid Act of 1948 and all policies which attempted to solve the China problem by merely throwing money at it.[22] He earned the enmity of the KMT and its American friends for his role in classifying General Wedemeyer's mission report, the publication of the China "White Paper," and the tough, no-nonsense way in which he dealt with Chinese diplomats.[23]

Serving directly under Butterworth as Director of the Office of Chinese Affairs (CA) was Philip D. Sprouse. Also a career FSO, Sprouse (who did a year of graduate work at Princeton in 1929) was a China specialist; one of the Department's "China Hands." From 1935 until his assignment back to Washington in 1947 he served almost continually in China, assigned to postings in Peking, Hankow, Chungking, Kunming, and Nanking.[24]

Like Butterworth, Sprouse met Marshall during the General's mission to China, serving as Marshall's political adviser at Executive Headquarters in Peking. When the mission ended Sprouse was entrusted with the weighty task of writing, for the General's signature, the official after-action report sent to the President. Sprouse admired Marshall very much and once commented that, "I sensed that here was *real greatness,* greatness in a way that I never had seen before."[25]

Sprouse was assigned back to State as Assistant Director of CA about the same time Marshall returned to become Secretary. Within a year, he took over as Director.[26] While Sprouse was serving as the number two man in CA, Marshall, in 1947, appointed him Political Adviser to the Wedemeyer Mission. This assignment allowed the future CA Director to travel through parts of China, Taiwan, and Korea which he had not been able to reach during the war. Sprouse served as a principle drafter of Wedemeyer's controversial after-action report.[27]

Sprouse went on to become Director of CA shortly after the Wedemeyer Mission ended. He served in that capacity through Acheson's first year and a half as Secretary, leaving CA in June 1950. Sprouse held Acheson, like Marshall before him, in high esteem. Acheson, in his estimation, was a man of "...honesty and integrity and courage."[28] For their part, Butterworth and Acheson both put great stock in Sprouse's opinions. Butterworth considered him one of the "...two most outstanding..." China FSO's that State had at that time.[29]

Sprouse, like Marshall, Acheson, and Butterworth, was convinced that military aid was not the answer to the KMT's problems. He endorsed the assessment of JUSMAG Chief General David Barr that Chiang possessed sufficient military equipment to defeat the CCP.[30] The answer, he felt, was a program of wide-ranging political, economic, social and military reforms.

Sprouse was convinced that Chiang, if left to himself, would not enact the changes needed.[31] Consequently, the United States would have to force Chiang into a program of reform. The only leverage Washington had was economic and military aid. Therefore, Sprouse reasoned, United States aid to the KMT on the mainland had to be conditional. The Central Government, while there was still time, had to be forced to reform by being given specific measures to accomplish. Should the Nationalists fail to comply then the United States would be free to walk out on Chiang completely.[32]

To Sprouse's frustration, Marshall's policy of "limited aid" for the mainland was never really conditional. With no reason to have to reform Chiang went along as before. Later, when Taiwan policy was being formulated, the idea of conditional aid would be resurrected as a way to force the KMT to save itself on its final island battleground.

Also wielding considerable influence as advisers to Secretary Acheson were Dean Rusk and Dr. Philip C. Jessup. Both played important roles in the formulation of Far Eastern policy.

Jessup, Professor of International Law at Columbia University, was a member of the United States' delegation to the U.N. during Truman's first administration.[33] A friend of Acheson's, he served in the Department as Ambassador-at-Large during Truman's second term. Acheson used Jessup as a sounding board for all manner of policies and questions. He was a trusted "outsider" and was a regular participant at the Secretary's daily briefing each morning at 9:30.[34] Acheson also relied upon him to take up special tasks. It was Jessup whom Acheson designated as the general editor of the China "White Paper." Furthermore, he was sent on missions to Asia to speak with American officials on the scene, hear their views, and report back to State on conditions in the Far East. In the autumn of 1949, Jessup was tasked to put together and direct the efforts of a small group of consultants from outside the government. Known as the "The Wise Men," their mandate was to offer fresh recommendations for U.S. Asia policy after the declaration of the People's Republic of China.

A Rhodes Scholar and college professor before WW II, Dean Rusk served on General Stilwell's staff in CBI as a reserve Colonel.[35] Though no Asian specialist, Rusk's wartime experience generated within him a great interest in that part of the world. Toward the end of the war he was assigned to the War Department.[36] Discharged in 1946, Rusk crossed the Potomac, making the long swim from the Pentagon to the State Department where he worked on United Nations affairs with John Foster Dulles and Dr. Jessup.

As one of Acheson's Deputy Under Secretaries, Rusk kept an eye on Far Eastern affairs precisely because the Secretary did not care to on a daily basis.[37] That alone was great service rendered the beleaguered Acheson. Above and beyond, however, Rusk had a great gift to offer; he had the ability to get along with Republican Congressmen. Consequently, Rusk was charged with building bipartisan support for State's initiatives across the globe. China policy offered a certain challenge in that regard. Later, in the spring of 1950 Rusk would have a key role in developing China policy, for he would replace Butterworth as Assistant Secretary for Far Eastern Affairs.

3.2 "TITOISM" and CHINA: ROOTS OF A POLICY

The defection of Marshall Tito from Moscow on June 28, 1948 was a welcomed sign in Washington. It offered hope that the power of the Soviets over their satellites was not immutable; that the bonds created by common ideology were not necessarily strong enough to overcome the forces of nationalism presumed to be latent in any country. Kennan wasted no time in commenting on Tito's defection from the COMINFORM. Within two days, the PPS director was circulating a paper, PPS 35, entitled "The Attitude of this Government Toward Events in Yugoslavia."[38]

Kennan warned that it would be "...a frivolous and undignified error on our part to assume that because Tito had fallen out with Stalin he could now be considered our 'friend.'" Yugoslavia would remain a communist country dedicated to "...an ideology of hostility and contempt" toward the capitalist West.

On the other hand, Belgrade's defection, it was argued, introduced "A new factor of fundamental and profound significance...into the world communist movement." It demonstrated that "...the Kremlin can be successfully defied by one of its own minions," and that:

> ...the aura of mystical omnipotence and infallibility which has surrounded the Kremlin power has been broken. The possibility of defection from Moscow, which has hitherto been unthinkable for foreign communist

leaders will from now on be present in one form or another in the mind of every one of them.

Whether or not Tito's defection would hold or, more importantly, whether others in the Soviet bloc would likewise attempt to leave the fold would depend very much, suggested Kennan, on how the United States handled Belgrade in the present circumstances. To "fawn" upon Tito now that he had made his break would do no good. Obsequious behavior on the part of the West might very well cause such revulsion on the part of Yugoslavia's communist leadership that Tito's independent stance might be undermined. Also, reasoned Kennan, condescending behavior toward the communist leader would be degrading to the United States and without much popular support at home. At the same time, if the West was too quick to spurn Tito, his international isolation might not only send him back to Moscow, but demonstrate to others that choosing communism meant choosing the Kremlin by default. Consequently, Kennan lectured that the U.S. would have to walk a fine line in its dealings with Tito.

United States officials, Kennan recommended, should make it be known that Washington "...would welcome a genuine re-emergence of Yugoslavia as a political personality in its own right." At the same time, U.S. officials should make the point that Belgrade's internal political system and its ideology is "deeply distasteful" to this country. Nevertheless, while relations would never be cordial or intimate, American relations with Yugoslavia would be predicated upon how Tito behaved toward the United States. Yugoslavia's communist ideology need not necessarily stand in the way of political or economic relations "...provided Yugoslavia is willing to adopt a loyal and cooperative attitude in its international relationships." Further, the United States would not stand in the way of Yugoslavia establishing "better relations" with countries currently benefiting from ERP aid.

Tito's defection occurred at a time when the State Department was being pressured to review China policy. It was evident that limited military aid would not turn the tide for the KMT. The impetus within the government to review U.S. initiatives was, according to Kennan, "...largely a result of the wide-spread feeling, which Secretary Forrestal appears to hold, that we 'have no policy' with relation to what is now happening in China and that something should be done about it."[39]

Kennan found the call for action most frustrating. In the first place, he did not feel that in the conduct of its diplomatic relations, the United States was required to have "...'a policy' with respect to internal events in another country." This concept contradicted the "deeply sanctioned" principle of the U.S. Government of refraining from involvement in the internal affairs of other nations. Further, if such intervention were to be undertaken then it must be shown where such actions were vital to the national security, and that the means were available to make intervention successful. In the case of China, Kennan doubted that the prospect of communist domination presented a direct threat to United States security. Even if it did, it was doubtful that the United States had the military and economic wherewithal to affect the outcome of the civil war.[40] Nevertheless, Kennan and the PPS Staff, in coordination with Sprouse and the Office of Chinese Affairs, set down on paper for the National Security Council the views of the Department of State concerning a "policy" for China.

The paper, PPS 39: "United States Policy Toward China," was commissioned in January 1948 at the request of the NSC pursuant to Secretary Forrestal's concerns. Its completion and submission was deferred on several occasions due to the quickening pace of events in China as well as disagreements within the policy community over what type of paper it should be. It was not until the summer of 1948—after Tito's break with Moscow—that analysts at State began to craft their paper.[41] It was completed in early September.[42]

PPS 39 was a watershed paper because it contained within it the core ideas which characterized the approach to China the Truman administration would promote until Chinese intervention in Korea. It recognized that U.S. policy toward China should not be predicated upon the survival of the Nationalist regime. The best that could be hoped for would be to aim for keeping a communist-dominated China from abetting Soviet power. Finally, it assessed that, just as in Yugoslavia, if the U.S. played its hand correctly, it might be able to keep the CCP from embracing the Soviets. It implied that Mao could yet turn out to be another Tito.

If a policy for China was needed, began the analysis, it was not a policy which proposed how to better assist Chiang Kai-shek. The KMT was on the verge of losing its civil war and there was nothing the U.S. could do to change that fact of life.[43] Indeed, the civil war itself was symptomatic of "...tremendous, deepflowing indigenous forces which are beyond our power to control."[44] What was needed was to recognize this, and develop a policy "... defined in the most flexible and elementary terms" which would allow Washington to cope with an ever-changing situation in China as the inevitable came to pass. Specifically, PPS 39 recommended that, for the moment, the U.S. should continue to recognize the National Government. Second, after the National Government "as we now know it" falls, "...make our decision regarding recognition in light of the circumstances at the time." Third, and finally, the U.S. should "...prevent so far as possible China's becoming an adjunct of Soviet politico-military power."[45]

Highly significant was the analysis of Soviet goals in China and the problems they faced in dealing with their clients, the CCP. Within this analysis is to be found the roots of the reasoning which resulted in policies which were designed to encourage "Titoism" on the mainland. Kennan and Davies must be credited for initiating the search for Mao Tse-Tito.

It was PPS's view that Moscow's ultimate goal in China was to "...expand its influence there and eventually to control all of the territory comprising China." However, the "unromantic men in the Kremlin" did not desire to control China because they harbored any illusions about its military potential. On the contrary, the Soviet interest in China was political.

> In the struggle for world domination—a struggle which the Kremlin pursues essentially through political action (even in civil war)—the allegiance of China's millions is worth striving for. That allegiance is worth striving for if only to deny it to the free world. In positive terms, China is worth having because capture of it would represent an impressive political victory and, more practically, acquisition of a broad human glacis from which to mount a political offensive against the rest of East Asia.[46]

In pursuit of this goal, reasoned Kennan and company, the task in front of the Soviets was not how to help the CCP win the civil war (a job which they were doing well enough by themselves), "...but how to ensure complete and lasting control..." over the Chinese communist movement after victory was secured.[47] This, it was reckoned, presented potential problems for Stalin on two counts. First, Mao himself had to be coopted or replaced. "It is quite true," went the analysis, "that a common body of ideology is a strong bond; but to the old conspirators of the Kremlin the questions to ask about any foreign communist party are: who controls the party apparatus; who controls the secret police; who controls (if they exist) the armed forces; and does the foreign leader love power more than he fears the Kremlin."[48]

If the answers to these questions as applied to China are as unsatisfactory to the Kremlin as they turned out to be in the case of Yugoslavia, Moscow faces a considerable task in seeking to bring the Chinese Communists under its complete control, if for no other reason than that Mao Tse-tung has been entrenched in power for nearly ten times the length of time that Tito has.[49]

Second, it was reasoned, even if Mao could be controlled, the Soviets, in their quest to dominate China, would have to deal with the very strong forces of Chinese nationalism which resided within the CCP. The drafters of PPS 39 pointed out that after the Chinese communist victory over Chiang was complete, the ties between the CCP and CPSU would be exposed. "And if the Chinese Politburo is revealed as subservient in any way to the Kremlin, the Chinese Communist leadership is in for difficulties from the powerful sentiments of nationalism and xenophobia, on the part of both the Chinese public and the nationalist elements in the party."[50] In a highly significant passage, it was pointed out that:

It is a nice piece of irony that at precisely the time the Chinese Communist leadership is most likely to wish to conceal its ties from Moscow, the Kremlin is most likely to be exerting utmost pressure to bring the Chinese Communists under complete control. The possibilities which such a situation would present us, provided we have regained freedom of action, need scarcely be spelled out.[51]

Butterworth concurred with the paper's analysis and recommendations; ensuring Secretary Marshall's approval as well. In October 1948, PPS 39 was circulated as a working paper within the National Security Council as NSC 34.[52]

3.3 U.S. AIMS IN CHINA ARE ARTICULATED

With the analysis in PPS 39/NSC 34 before it, the policy-making community was able, by early January 1949, to produce a paper, NSC 34/1, in which United States goals in China were clearly articulated. Prepared jointly by the NSC staff, representatives from State, the uniformed services, and the Central Intelligence Agency, NSC 34/1 drew heavily from the analysis in PPS 39.[53] Unlike PPS 39, it was remarkably brief and to the point.

1. The objective of the U.S. with respect to China is the eventual development by the Chinese themselves of a unified, stable, and independent China friendly to the U.S., in order to forestall threats to our national security which would arise from the domination of China by any hostile power.

2. The U.S. should recognize that the development of a unified, stable and independent China acceptable to the U.S. is not likely to be accomplished by any apparent Chinese group or groups within the foreseeable future.

3. *The immediate aim of the U.S. should, therefore, be to prevent China from becoming an adjunct of Soviet power.* In pursuing this aim the U.S. should:

    a. Make appropriate plans and timely preparations in order to exploit opportunities in China while maintaining flexibility and avoiding irrevocable commitments to any one course of action or to any one faction.

    b. Regard efforts with respect to China as of lower priority than efforts in other areas where the benefits to U.S. security are more immediately commensurate with the expenditure of U.S resources.[54]

Dean Acheson had been in office less than two weeks when NSC 34/1 was presented at the 33rd meeting of the NSC for consideration on February 4, 1949. While he felt that the report was "...general and somewhat obscure in phraseology..." he nevertheless agreed that "...from a strategic point of view, China was an area of lower priority, especially since the house appeared to be falling down and there was not much to be done until it had come down." He recognized that the policy outlined in NSC 34/1 was "not positive" and "open to attack", but felt that "...hasty positive action might commit us to an unpredictable course of action." Not much would be able to be done "...until it was clear what would be left in China."[55] After a minimum of discussion, the NSC adopted the paper without change and the President approved it the same day.[56] As a result, it was henceforth a matter of official policy that the immediate aim of the United States in China was to prevent the soon-to-be-victorious communist regime "...from becoming an adjunct of Soviet power."

While not in disagreement with the policy he inherited Acheson was uncomfortable with the vagueness of NSC 34/1. Furthermore, almost half a year had lapsed since the Policy Planning Staff offered its original analysis in PPS 39. Consequently, the staff took another look at the situation in China in late February 1949.

The reassessment, PPS 39/2, did not *not* change the aims of U.S. policy in China as defined in NSC 34/1.[57] For the most part, the paper analyzed the problems the CCP, the Soviets, and the United States would *all* have to deal with in China in the not too distant future. Mao and his followers, having moved "...from caves to chancelleries for the first time...," would face great problems in administering the country and rehabilitating the Chinese economy. The Soviets, projected the paper, would have problems in their attempts to influence the Chinese communists.

For the United States, three major difficulties were identified. First, for the present and foreseeable future, Washington was going to have to live with a China "...deeply suspicious and hostile..." to it. Second, it was pointed out that the "...natural points of conflict between the Chinese Communists and the U.S.S.R...." had not yet "developed." Finally, there did not yet exist in China a political force capable of resisting the communists.

However, the PPS allowed that in China time was on the side of the United States. In the not too distant future, "... conflict between communist theory and Chinese environmental realities..." was destined to send the CCP seeking economic ties with the West. Further, it was thought inevitable that a political force capable of resisting the CCP would emerge, "...simply because a China under the Communists will breed it just as surely as Chiang's Kuomintang was the forcing ground of the Communists." The United States would have to wait for the counter-revolution, then "nourish" it and bring it to power.

> This is obviously a long-term proposition. There is, however, no short cut. Consequently, we have no sound alternative but to accommodate our native impatience to this fact. The Kremlin waited twenty-five years for the fulfillment of its revolution in China. We may have to persevere as long or longer. But in one respect at least we can wait with greater confidence: we are under no Byzantine Tartar compulsion to shackle as our own captive the revolution which we seek to release.

It was subsequently recommended that the United States "avoid" military and political support of any non-communist regime in China unless such regimes "...are willing actively to resist communism with or without U.S. aid and, unless further, it is evident that such support would mean the overthrow of, or at least successful resistance to, the communists." Continued military support of ineffective groups of dubious resolve, it was made clear, would only drive the CCP closer to the Soviets. The immediate aim of the United States continued to be preventing the victory of the CCP from adding to the power of the Soviets. Consequently, it was recommended as well that:

> While scrupulously avoiding the appearance of intervention, we should be alert to exploit through political and economic means any rifts between the Chinese Communists and the U.S.S.R. and between the Stalinist and other elements in China both within and outside of the communist structure.

Furthermore, it was suggested that "...principal reliance on combating Kremlin influence in China..." should be on Chinese dissident elements supported by the United States "...through appropriate clandestine channels." PPS 39/2 was circulated within the National Security Council as NSC 34/2.[58]

3.4 NSC 41: PURSUING CHINESE TITOISM

NSC 34/2 did not lend itself to translating the aims of NSC 34/1 into a policy which could be implemented. It failed to offer any concrete examples of just what the United States could do to further its stated aims in China. The analysis of the situation, while intriguing, was too general to serve as a practical guide for decision-makers hard-pressed to deal with the crisis in Asia. The paper which *did* address many of these shortcomings was NSC 41: "United States Policy Regarding Trade with China." Prepared by the State Department, it was circulated to the NSC on February 28th; the same day as NSC 34/2.[59]

From a policy-maker's point of view NSC 41 was an outstanding study. It clearly stated U.S. aims in China, acknowledged constraints to achieving those aims, and offered solid recommendations for what could be done. Most significantly, the document provided a definitive expression of U.S. policy toward China—a policy aimed at encouraging an independent, "Titoist" CCP.

The study began by reiterating that the primary objective of United States policy in China as defined in NSC 34/1—"to prevent China from becoming an adjunct of Soviet power"—remained in effect. It was then suggested that at the moment any leverage the U.S. might have over the communist Chinese regime was "in the field of economic relations."

China, it was recognized, could remain self-sufficient at its present level of development due to the fact that its economy was largely agrarian-based. Also, it was pointed out, based on the historical experience of the Soviets, "...that a determined and ruthless leadership can survive and even consolidate itself in the face of extreme economic hardships..." Nevertheless, if the Chinese communists desire to "...rehabilitate and expand..." its industrial base and raise the level · of its economy, then they will be "dependent" upon a resumption of regular trade relations with the West and Japan.

Given the aims of the U.S., and the economic leverage which it could exercise, there were two courses which could be followed.

The first approach would seek to keep the CCP regime from augmenting Soviet power by mobilizing against it "...the political and economic power of the western world..." Such a policy would be employed "...(a) to force the Chinese Communists, by threat or application of severe economic restrictions, to resist Kremlin pressure..." and adopt policies acceptable to United States interests, or "...(b) to isolate China completely from Japan and the Western world in an attempt to bring about the overthrow or collapse..." of the CCP. This particular course of action was quickly dismissed. In the first place, it was reasoned, it was doubtful that "...the necessary degree of concerted action could be obtained from all western nations so as to make effective the imposition of severe embargoes on trade with China." Second, an economic blockade by the West could work to the benefit of the communists by making the CCP, once again, a rallying-point for Chinese nationalism. Also, an effective boycott of China would preclude the resumption of trade with Japan. This would work against Japanese economic rehabilitation—already a stated policy objective of the United States in Asia.[60] Indeed, the failure to resume the patterns of pre-war trade between North China, Manchuria, and Japan, it was pointed out, would only prolong the burden the United States had assumed in underwriting Japan's economic recovery. Further, such a policy would certainly mean the expulsion of whatever American business interests were still operating on the mainland. But finally, "and most important";

> ...the course of action described above probably would compel the Chinese Communists to eliminate any divergences of opinion within the party and tend to drive the regime into a position of complete subservience to the USSR, thus making impossible of attainment the primary objective towards which it was directed.

Consequently, it was recommended that "...a restoration of ordinary economic relations with China..." be permitted in order to

"...augment...such forces as might operate to bring about serious rifts between Moscow and a Chinese Communist regime."

> Although the leaders of the Chinese Communist party are doctrinaire Marxists, politically hostile to the United States and other western nations, and predisposed to cooperate with the USSR, the germs of friction between a Chinese Communist regime and the Kremlin undoubtedly exist in the Chinese situation.

The Soviets, it was predicted, would attempt to harness China's economic assets for its own. Moscow could be counted upon as well to "...exploit its special position in Manchuria..." to its economic benefit. Such policies on the part of the Soviets would offend all Chinese—communist and non-communist—and could very well generate a great deal of friction between the CCP and CPSU. It was noted as well that at the moment the CCP was not yet "...dependent upon the USSR for maintenance and expansion of its military and political position in China." Consequently, it was implied, it was still not too late to offer the CCP an alternative source of trade.

Were trade between a communist-dominated China and Japan and the West allowed to resume, then, it was reasoned, the growing importance of that trade to the CCP, when juxtaposed next to attempts by the Kremlin at "...political and economic exploitation...," might in itself "...bring about serious conflicts between the Kremlin and the Chinese Communist regime." It was realized, however, that any rifts which occur between the CCP and the CPSU will more likely "...be occasioned by Kremlin policy and actions, and that there is very little the United States can do initially, beyond the policy here proposed, to contribute to creation of a conflict."

In its concluding section, NSC 41 offered the following policy recommendation summation:

> The United States Government should maintain its freedom of action by following initially a policy designed to augment such forces as might operate to create serious rifts between Moscow and a Chinese Communist regime. This policy would permit, so far as the United States is concerned, restoration, under essential security safeguards, of ordinary economic relations between China on the one hand and Japan and the western world on the other. It might enable, at least over the short run, the acquisition from China of commodities important to Japanese self-support, and some continued operation in China of private American interests. If the Communists should not by their actions make this policy untenable, the importance to the Chinese Communists of

trade relations with Japan and the west might foster serious conflicts between Kremlin and Chinese Communist policy and thereby tend to produce an independent Chinese Communist regime. This policy would make it possible for the United States to exploit frictions between a Chinese Communist regime and the USSR should they arise, or to adopt a restrictive trade policy if the Chinese Communists were to demonstrate their determination to follow a course inimical to United States strategic interests.

Just as Yugoslavia's access to western economic trade depended upon Belgrade's behavior in conducting its foreign relations, so too would trade with the CCP be conditioned by its policies toward the West. The policy recommended in NSC 41, it was emphasized, "...should be reviewed constantly, in light of Chinese Communist policies and actions..."

On March 3, 1949, at the 35th meeting of the National Security Council, both NSC 34/2 and NSC 41 were adopted without change. The President approved both papers later that same day.[61]

Before Truman's second administration was even two months along the situation in China was reassessed. It was determined that there was little or nothing that could be done to affect the events unfolding on the mainland. The best Washington could do was to bank on the emergence of "Mao Tse-Tito" at some undefined time in the not too distant future. Mainland China was doomed to communist rule. It remained to be determined if the United States was equally powerless to snatch the strategically important island of Taiwan from the claws of the CCP.

Notes

1. Princeton Seminars, July 23, 1953, reading copy 22–23 July 1953, folder 2, p. 676, DGA/Box 75.

2. For full treatments of Acheson see David S. McLellan, *Dean Acheson: The State Department Years* (New York: Dodd, Mead, & Company, 1976) and Gaddis Smith, *Dean Acheson* (New York: Cooper Square Publishers, Inc., 1972). Also of note for those interested in the lives and times of Acheson and his contemporaries (Lovett, McCloy, Harriman, Bohlen, and Kennan) is *The Wise Men: Six Friends and the World They Made* (New York: Simon and Schuster, 1986) by Walter Isaacson and Evan Thomas.

3. Dean Acheson, *Present At The Creation: My Years in the State Department* (New York: W.W. Norton & Co., 1969), p. 257.

4. For an outstanding piece on the Secretary and his advisors for Far Eastern policy see Warren I. Cohen, "Acheson, His Advisers, and China, 1949–1950," in *Uncertain Years: Chinese-American Relations, 1947–1950,* ed.

Dorothy Borg and Waldo Heinrichs (New York: Columbia University Press, 1980), pp. 13–52. The Borg/Heinrichs volume was a pathbreaking study. When it was published its papers (commissioned in the late 1970's) were among the first to use declassified government documents from the Truman period.

5. George F. Kennan, *Memoirs, 1925–1950* (Boston: Little, Brown, and Co., 1967), pp. 325–327; Forrest C. Pogue, *George C. Marshall: Statesman, 1949–1959* (New York: Viking Penguin, Inc., 1987), pp. 150–151. For a recent biography of Kennan see David Mayers, *George Kennan and the Dilemmas of US Foreign Policy* (New York: Oxford University Press, 1988).

6. Forward, p. VII, in Volume One of *The State Department Policy Planning Staff Papers, 1947–1949*, 3 vols., ed. Anna Kasten Nelson, (New York: Garland Publishers, Inc., 1983). Nelson has brought together some of the best of the declassified PPS papers written through 1949. Many of the NSC papers dealing with China approved by President Truman originated in the PPS; a testament to the influence of this body. Future references will be cited as *PPS Papers*.

7. "Unfinished Paper: Summary by George F. Kennan on points of difference between his views and those of the Department of State," September, 1951, GFK/Box 24.

8. GFK/Box 23/1948–Notes on China. This file contains handwritten notes made by Kennan on China issues.

9. Letter, George F. Kennan to Karl Lott Rankin, August 9, 1950, KLR/Box 17.

10. Kennan, *Memoirs, 1925–1950*, p. 239. For Davies' autobiography see *Dragon by the Tail* (New York: Norton Books, Inc., 1972).

11. See Chapter 1.

12. *The Second Secretary of Embassy in China (Davies) to Mr. Harry Hopkins, Special Assistant to President Roosevelt*, December 31, 1943, FR:43:China:399.

13. *Memorandum by the Second Secretary of Embassy in China (Davies), Temporarily in the United States*, "The American Stake in Chinese Unity: Proposals for Preliminary American Action," June 24, 1943, FR:43:China:260.

14. Kennan, *Memoirs, 1925–1950*, pp. 426–427, 465–470; Cohen, "Acheson, His Advisers, and China, 1949–1950," p. 20.

15. Indeed, Kennan's replacement as PPS Director in 1950 was none other than Paul H. Nitze; up until recently still on active duty as one of this country's top strategic arms negotiators with the former Soviet Union. It is also worth pointing out that in 1949 PPS led the effort in producing one of the most powerful and influential policy papers in the postwar history of the United States; NSC 68. For the history of NSC 68 and Nitze's role while director of PPS see Steven L. Rearden, *The Evolution of American Strategic Doctrine: Paul H. Nitze and the Soviet Challenge* (Boulder, CO.: Westview Press, 1984). According to Rearden (p. 19), NSC 68 was "...written mainly by members of State's Policy Planning Staff."

16. Kennan, *Memoirs, 1925–1950*, p. 426.

17. John Foster Dulles Oral History Collection, Interview with Ambassador W. Walton Butterworth, September 8, 1965, Seeley Mudd Library, Princeton University, p. 7. On his friendship with Acheson Butterworth remarked that "We go back to before he was in the government and when I was in Washington prior to taking my Foreign Service exams. We have country places near each other, and we had a personal relationship quite apart from any official one."

18. Transcript, W. Walton Butterworth Oral History Interview, July 6, 1971, p. 19, Truman Library. Future references will be cited as "Butterworth Oral History." As Butterworth put it, "...a new broom was needed to run the Embassy in China..."

19. Butterworth Oral History, p. 24.

20. Cohen, "Acheson, His Advisers, and China, 1949–1950," p. 19. Butterworth was well aware of the difficult situation which he faced. He realized that his unpopular views on China and his lack of experience in Far Eastern affairs made him a political liability. He urged General Marshall not to appoint him Director of FE in 1947 and advised Dean Acheson not to nominate him for the Assistant Secretary of State position in 1949. However, his realism and candor appealed to both Secretaries of State. When he was confirmed in the post of Assistant Secretary, Butterworth jokingly remarked to his staff that he was "...the first in a long line of expendable Secretaries of State for Far Eastern Affairs." Butterworth Oral History, pp. 53–54.

21. Butterworth Oral History, pp. 28, 31.

22. Butterworth Oral History, pp. 36, 38, 40.

23. For Butterworth and the Wedemeyer report see Stueck, *The Wedemeyer Mission*, pp. 87–92. For Butterworth's no-nonsense approach to Chinese officials he perceived to be out to bilk the United States see William Whitney Stueck, Jr., *The Road to Confrontation: American policy Toward China and Korea, 1947–1950* (Chapel Hill, N.C.: The University of North Carolina Press, 1981), pp. 48–49. Stueck quotes Nanking FSO John Melby recording that "...Butterworth's toughness is most disturbing to the Chinese..." Nancy Bernkopf Tucker, "Nationalist China's Decline and Its Impact on Sino-American Relations, 1949–1950," in *Uncertain Years*, eds. Borg and Heinrichs, p. 164, relates Chinese Ambassador to the United States V.K. Wellington Koo's uneasiness around Butterworth. "I felt Butterworth looked upon me as if I were the Soviet Ambassador, judging from the caution and reserve he assumed, so unusual for an American diplomat in his attitude and action toward an accredited Chinese representative."

24. Transcript, Philip D. Sprouse Oral History Interview, February 11, 1974, pp. 1–8, Truman Library. Future references will be cited as "Sprouse Oral History."

25. Ibid., pp. 8–9, 10. The emphasis is Sprouse's.

26. Ibid., p. 11.

27. For Sprouse's role during the mission, see William Stueck, *The Wedemeyer Mission: American Politics and Foreign Policy during the Cold War*

(Athens, GA.: The University of Georgia Press, 1984). Unlike the situation when he drafted Marshall's report, Sprouse did not entirely agree with Wedemeyer's analysis or recommendations.

28. Sprouse Oral History, p. 65.

29. Butterworth Oral History, p. 34. The other FSO mentioned was Sprouse's Assistant Director at CA, Fulton (Tony) Freeman. Given the situation in China at the time of his appointment as CA Director, one may assume that Sprouse's superiors had a great deal of respect for his abilities and opinions. Indeed, according to Sprouse, CA's role in the formulation of China policy at State was pervasive. It received and analyzed reports from the Embassy in China and the various consular stations, prepared State Department officials for Congressional hearings, and, along with PPS, wrote departmental position papers for the NSC. Sprouse Oral History, p. 95.

30. Sprouse Oral History, pp. 30–31. Butterworth Oral History, p. 41. Acheson, Butterworth, and Sprouse were all fond of referring to Barr's testimony regarding the futility of military aid to the KMT whenever the subject came up. The passage most paraphrased (see "White Paper" p. 358) was usually Barr's bottom line that "No battle has been lost since my arrival due to a lack of ammunition or equipment. Their military debacles in my opinion can all be attributed to the world's worst leadership..."

31. Sprouse Oral History, p. 84. On Chiang and the revolution Sprouse has commented that "I think if you singled out responsibility for what happened in China—much of it of course is historical beyond anybody's control—but if one man had to be singled out, I'd single out the Generalissimo, because he alone had the authority and the possibility of doing the very things that had to be done. But he was not a product of the mid-20th Century and I think he really didn't understand the political and social forces at work within his own country..."

32. On Sprouse and "conditional aid" see Stueck, *The Road To Confrontation*, pp. 49–50; Stueck, *The Wedemeyer Mission*, pp. 77–78; Sprouse Oral History, pp. 69–71, 82–84; and *Memorandum by Mr. Philip D. Sprouse to General Wedemeyer, "Present Situation in China,"* September 19, 1947, FR:47:VII:741–759. For an idea of what specific reforms he would have Chiang put into effect see *Memorandum by Mr. Philip D. Sprouse to General Wedemeyer,* 17 August 1947, FR:47:VII:726–730.

33. For Jessup's memoirs see *The Birth of Nations* (New York: Columbia University Press, 1974).

34. Robert M. Blum, *Drawing the Line: The Origins of the American Containment Policy in East Asia* (New York: W.W. Norton & Company, 1982), p. 16.

35. Though Rusk has no personal papers for the historian to look through, there is enough of his thinking contained in recently declassified government documents to be able to gauge the man. Biographies are few. Of note is Warren I. Cohen, *Dean Rusk* (Totowa, N.J.: Cooper Square Publishers, 1980), and more recently, Thomas J. Schoenbaum, *Waging Peace & War: Dean Rusk in the Truman, Kennedy & Johnson Years* (New York: Simon & Schuster,

1988). Rusk's autobiography, *As I Saw It*, (N.Y.: W.W. Norton Co., 1990) is very disappointing in that Rusk gives almost no insights into this period of his government service.

36. One of the great footnotes of postwar history is that Rusk, while serving as a War Department staff officer assigned to SWNCC, was the person who recommended the 38th parallel as the line of demarcation between the American and Russian zones of occupation in Korea after VJ-Day.

37. Cohen, "Acheson, His Advisers, and China, 1949–1950," p. 18.

38. Nelson, *PPS Papers*, Vol. 2, pp. 317–322; DNSC:Reel 1. This paper was circulated within State as PPS 35. It was circulated within the NSC verbatim, and with the same title, on July 6, 1948 as NSC 18. Quotations in the next four paragraphs are drawn from the body of PPS 35/NSC 18.

39. *Memorandum by the Director of the Policy Planning Staff (Kennan)*, November 24, 1948, FR:48:VIII:211. This memo was sent to Secretary Marshall and Under Secretary of State Lovett.

40. *Memorandum by the Policy Planning Staff*, PPS 39/1, "U.S. Policy Toward China," November 23, 1948, FR:48:VIII:208–211.

41. *Memorandum by the Deputy Director of the Policy Planning Staff (Butler)*, July 27, 1948, FR:48:VIII:122–124.

42. PPS 39 can be found in FR:48:VIII:146–165. While this version contains all key sections of analysis, it does not include the first section which provided demographic, economic, military, political, and historical background information. A complete version can be found in Nelson, ed., *PPS Papers*, Vol. 2, pp., 412–446.

43. FR:48:VIII:150. The document was quite clear about the folly of a U.S. policy in China founded upon support of the KMT. "This continuing exclusive commitment to Chiang is understandable, but it is not good diplomacy. It binds this Government to a single course, leaving no alternative, no latitude for maneuver...In the present situation...we need the freedom to tack, or perhaps even to lie at anchor until we are quite sure of our bearings." In discussing PPS 39 the FRUS version will be referenced.

44. Ibid., p. 154.

45. Ibid.

46. PPS 39, FR:48:VIII:147.

47. Ibid., p. 148.

48. Ibid.

49. Ibid.

50. Ibid. p. 153.

51. Ibid. pp. 153–154.

52. NSC 34 and PPS 39 are identical throughout. NSC 34: "United States Policy Toward China," October 13, 1948, DNSC:Reel 1. In as much as FR:48:VIII carries PPS 39, NSC 34 is not included as a separate item.

53. NSC 34/1: "United States Policy Toward China," January 11, 1949, DNSC:Reel 1; HST/PSF/MNSC/Box 205/NSC Meeting #33. This paper may also be found in FR:49:IX:474–475.

54. Emphasis in paragraph 3 added.

55. Memorandum for the President, February 4, 1949, HST/PSF/Box 220/NSC Memos to the President, 1949. This memorandum is a transcript of discussion at the 33rd meeting of the NSC, February 4, 1949.

56. Memorandum for the National Security Council, February 4, 1949, HST/PSF/MNSC/Box 205/NSC Meeting #33.

57. PPS 39/2: "United States Policy Toward China," February 25, 1949, Nelson, ed., *PPS Papers*, Vol 3, pp. 25–28.

58. NSC 34/2: "U.S. Policy Toward China," February 28, 1949, HST/PSF/MNSC/Box 205/NSC Meeting # 35; DNSC: Reel 1; and FR:49:IX:491–495. The copies of NSC 34/2 in the Truman Papers (HST), the DNSC collection, and the *Foreign Relations of the United States* series have been sanitized to delete paragraph 18 which called for clandestine activity to exacerbate CCP-CPSU frictions. Indeed, in the Truman Papers the minutes of the 35th meeting of the NSC were likewise sanitized due to a discussion of this item. Paragraph 18 is printed in PPS 39/2 in Nelson, ed. *PPS Papers*, Vol. 3 cited above.

59. NSC 41: "United States Policy Regarding Trade with China," HST/PSF/MNSC/Box 205/NSC Meeting #35; DNSC:Reel 1; FR:49:IX:826–834. I have not been able to fix NSC 41 as strictly a PPS product. As with most of the NSC papers prepared within State dealing with China, a great amount of coordination between PPS and FE (Office of Chinese Affairs) undoubtedly occurred on this piece. Nevertheless, the analysis contained within NSC 41, as well as the style of writing, bear the PPS signature. The parallels between the thinking in NSC 41 and previous papers on Yugoslavia lead one to surmise that Kennan worked on this paper.

60. For an outstanding study of U.S. post-war policy toward Japan see Michael Schaller, *The American Occupation of Japan: The Origins of the Cold War in Asia* (New York: Oxford University Press, 1985). See especially Chapter 10, "Japanese Recovery Prospects in the Wake of China's Revolution," pp. 178–195. Schaller's contribution to the historiography of the occupation is his ability to put it into the broader context of the challenges faced by the United States in the Far East during the early years of the Cold War.

61. Memorandum for the President, (Summary of the discussion at the 35th meeting of the NSC), March 4, 1949, HST/PSF/Box 220/NSC Memos to the President, 1949; Minutes of the 35th Meeting of the National Security Council, March 3, 1949, HST/PSF/Box 205/NSC Meeting #35.

CHAPTER 4

In Search Of A Taiwan Policy:
January–March 1949

The situation in Taiwan is steadily growing more critical for the US because of Taiwanese discontent, Chinese Nationalist preparation of the island as a last bastion, and increasing Chinese Communist interest in and capabilities toward the island. Assuming US inactivity, Taiwan will eventually pass to the control of the Chinese Communists. The strategic implications to US security of such a development would be seriously unfavorable. In any US program to prevent Communist control of Taiwan, the advantages to be gained thereby from the strategic military viewpoint would have to be weighed against unfavorable political consequences, the extent of which would vary depending upon the selection and timing of measures for implementing the program.[1]

Central Intelligence Agency
March 1949

At the same time that the Truman Administration was devising a policy toward mainland China (January through March 1949) it was grappling, as well, with the problem of Taiwan. As the new year began the situation on the island deteriorated. Unless the U.S. acted, it was judged that Taiwan would more than likely fall to the communists. Both the Department of State and the Department of Defense agreed that this would be unacceptable.

The need to prevent the fall of Taiwan was in no way the result of any feelings of affection for the ruling Kuomintang. To the contrary, it was Taiwan's strategic importance to United States regional security as a geographic entity which made it the object of a rescue attempt. The dilemma which faced policy-makers, however, was finding a way to detach Taiwan from the mainland without subverting U.S. policy aimed at fostering "Titoism" in a China soon to be dominated by the communists.

4.1 JANUARY 1949: THE SITUATION ON TAIWAN WORSENS

The last weeks of 1948 and the first few of 1949 were disastrous ones for the Nationalists on the mainland. In early December 1948 a KMT army of 500,000 was defeated in the north-western reaches of Kiangsu Province. That same month the communists launched their Peking-Tientsin offensive. On January tenth the Hwai-Hai campaign ended in ignominious defeat for the Central Government with the capture of General Tu Yu-ming. South China was now vulnerable to the advance of the People's Liberation Army (PLA). By January 15, 1949, Tientsin was in communist hands. On 22 January General Fu Tso-yi, reacting to the announcement of Chiang Kai-shek's retirement, and conceding the impossibility of his own situation, negotiated the surrender of his forces in the north. As a consequence, the PLA, on January 31, marched unopposed into Peking.

The general panic which characterized the last days of Nationalist rule in China began in earnest. Madame Chiang was sent to the United States where, during a protracted stay, she attempted to lobby the Truman Administration for increased aid to prolong the KMT's eleventh hour.[2]

The disintegration of the situation on the continent had a direct impact upon Taiwan. Consular reporting from Taipei in the early weeks of 1949 left no doubt that Taiwan was intended to serve the KMT as the "...last bulwark of its struggle against the communists."[3]

The appointment of General Ch'en Ch'eng as Provincial Governor in late December 1948 came as a bolt from the blue. According to Consul General Krentz in Taipei, even Wei Tao-ming had no idea he was to be replaced.[4] Krentz considered Ch'en "...one of the few generals who could be depended upon to stick with the Generalissimo to the last ditch..." Consequently, it had to be assumed that his mission was to prepare Taiwan for Chiang's eventual arrival.[5] Krentz's suspicions were heightened during the first week of January 1949. Chiang Ching-kuo, the Gimo's eldest son, was rumored to have been appointed Chairman of the Taiwan Provincial KMT Headquarters. He was also believed to be slated to be the next mayor of Taipei.[6] Additionally, intelligence sources indicated the Generalissimo's automobiles, files, and household effects had already been shipped to the island.[7] Later that same month K.C. Wu, mayor of Shanghai, confided to JUSMAG and ECA officials that "...2,000,000 million ounces of gold had already been shipped to Taiwan and that he was asking transfer of 500,000 more ounces of the 800,000 remaining in Shanghai."[8]

Throughout January 1949 a general exodus of monumental proportions was under way from the mainland to the island. By mid-month one report estimated that at least 300,000 civilian refugees had arrived at the port of Keelung alone. There was no idea of how many had arrived at the southern port of Kaohsiung or by air.[9] Included in these numbers were believed to be the majority of the KMT's "...die-hard reactionaries..."[10]

The influx of civilian refugees strained housing and sanitation facilities to the breaking point. The island was quite incapable of providing shelter for so many. Of the quarter-million or so refugees 100,000 were estimated to be crammed into Taipei.[11] With immigration regulations all but discarded a general epidemic was feared. By the end of January a rise in the incidence of smallpox was being watched with trepidation.[12]

It was the arrival of scores of Nationalist military units, however, which compounded the chaos exponentially. The turmoil they created was far out of proportion to the mere fifty-odd thousand troops which were estimated to have landed in January. This was due to the fact that major headquarters and their powerful officers, not just troop units, had arrived.

In mid-January the Ministry of Defense had given orders to all major commands which could evacuate to Taiwan to do so. A myriad of organizations such as the Military Medical College, the Air Defense Academy, and the Ordnance Department all relocated *en masse*. So too did the Chinese Navy and the haughty, down-right abusive Chinese Air Force (CAF).[13] The island, in the words of one American official, was being turned into "...an armed camp."[14] Consul General Krentz reported that, "Chinese soldiers and military officers, especially those of the CAF, can be seen in the streets all times of the day. Military jeeps driving at high speed have become a common sight in Taipei."[15] In typical fashion, the military commandeered what it wanted, paid for nothing, and abused Taiwanese and Chinese civilians alike.[16]

Furthermore, the armed forces had taken over the transportation and communication hubs of the island. Airports, railheads, and especially the key ports of Keelung and Kaohsiung were "...for all practical purposes..." under the control of the Army.[17] Harbor management broke down. All available warehousing was filled with evacuated military equipment. Pilfering became rampant and the amount of "squeeze" required to use Taiwanese ports skyrocketed. It became impossible for ships to dock or depart the island. In Keelung an ECA official observed that:

> The harbor is crowded with ships which refuse to return to the mainland for fear of military seizure. Other ships cannot leave because they cannot get to a dock to dispose of their cargo. It is reported that some foreign ships have refused to enter the harbor owing to congestion.[18]

Under these circumstances, Taiwan was in danger of being cut off from external trade and aid at the very moment it was most needed.

The massive influx of military, government, and civilian refugees to Taiwan put a terrific strain on the economy. Needless to say, there were not enough goods and services for such a swollen population.[19] The black market did a lively business. Inflation, exported from the mainland, hit the island very hard. As always, the price of grain was the first to rise. On 21 January the cost of one catty of rice reached a "new height" of 1,800 Yen.[20] By February 15th the same catty had risen to "the appalling height" of 3,300 Yen.[21] As ever, the Central Government's response was to issue more currency. By the end of January, 300,000,000,000 Taiwan Yen were in circulation. Provincial Finance Commissioner Yen Chia-kan was non-plussed, declaring at a press conference that "inflation in coordination with industrial development is not detrimental to local economy."[22] Rice-hording, rationing, and panic buying quickly engulfed the island.

Through the chaos of January U.S. officials were being warned that another Formosan uprising was imminent. From Hong Kong came rumors that the fall of Nanking would be the signal for a general uprising of Taiwanese.[23] George Kerr, then teaching at the University of Washington, wrote Philip Sprouse at State warning that letters from his Formosan acquaintances "indicate a growing tension which is bound to break into violence when it appears that Chiang's present government is finished."[24] Krentz in Taipei advised his superiors in Washington that many Taiwanese believe a revolt must take place before the KMT is dug in too deeply. "I attempt to counsel patience and am urging Chinese moderation," he reported, "but feel situation deteriorating rapidly..."[25]

Communist agitators were believed poised to fan the flames of discontent. Taiwan was now embroiled in China's civil war.

4.2 STATE CALLS FOR A TAIWAN POLICY

The crisis on Taiwan could no longer be brushed off by the State Department as an internal problem for the Nationalist Government as was the case after the riots of 1947.[26] In the last weeks of 1948 the possibility that Taiwan would fall became all too real. The prospect of such a turn of events was recognized as engendering immediate implications for the regional security interests of the United States. By mid-January 1949, although he had not yet formally assumed his new duties, Dean Acheson was receiving briefings on the situation in Taiwan from Acting Secretary of State Lovett and Walton Butterworth.[27]

The Taiwan problem was first raised to the NSC in November 1948 when State asked that the Joint Chiefs of Staff be tasked to assess the implications of the fall of the island for U.S. security. In December 1948 the JCS rendered their judgment. The Joint Chiefs were of the opinion that Taiwan's strategic location demanded that it be denied to unfriendly governments.[28]

The fledgling CIA concurred with the JCS. In their own study (January 3, 1949) the military significance of the island was underscored. It was considered "...of major importance to the US strategic position in the Far East to deny Taiwan to effective Soviet exploitation."[29] The CIA, however, was much more sanguine than the JCS about the need to station American forces on Taiwan. Whereas the uniformed services did not feel a need to occupy the island—denial to the enemy was considered a sufficient objective—CIA was convinced that it was imperative that military bases be established there. In assessing the island's future prospects, the CIA predicted that it was bound to fall to the CCP. "Assuming US inactivity, Taiwan will eventually, but probably not immediately, come under the control of the Communist government in China."[30]

The State Department concurred with the JCS judgment that Taiwan had to be denied to the communists.[31] It agreed as well with CIA that only positive action on the part of the United States would preclude its loss to the communists. Unlike the situation on the mainland, where time was viewed as working in favor of U.S. objectives, time was working against U.S. interests on Taiwan. Consequently, the NSC, on January 6th, directed that a study be prepared "as a matter of urgency" which would consider just what the United States policy should be.[32] Acting Secretary of State Lovett requested that State, not the NSC staff, prepare the study, and that it not be acted upon until Acheson was on board. Both requests were approved. The study, NSC 37/1: "The Position Of The United States With Respect To Formosa," was completed and submitted by January 19th.[33]

NSC 37/1 was not a paper which inspired optimism. It affirmed that the "basic aim" of the United States should be "to deny Taiwan and the Pescadores to the Communists." Doing so, however, might prove difficult. No course of action which might be followed was without risk or cost. The NSC readership was told that "... much the same as in many other areas of Asia—the choice is not between satisfactory and unsatisfactory courses of action but rather of the least of several evils or an amalgam of the lesser of them."

On the island itself, the impact of any U.S. action had to take into account the reactions of three groups: the native Taiwanese, the ruling mainlanders, and the Communists. The Taiwanese were recognized as having "...a strong sense of regional autonomy..." and hatred for the mainlanders but were without "...political experience, organization, or strong leadership." Formosan independence groups on the island, the mainland, and in Hong Kong were few in number and deemed incapable, by themselves, of executing a successful revolt. As for the ruling mainlanders, they had "...displayed a genius for misgovernment..." since VJ-Day. Nevertheless, Ch'en Ch'eng seemed capable of developing a stable non-communist regime. Unfortunately, his efforts were daily being undermined by the thousands of KMT refugees repairing weekly to the island. Too many of those arriving were the very politicians and "militarists...whose gross incompetence has played into the hands of the Communists in China." Finally, the communists on Taiwan were still a negligible group. However, they posed the threat of subverting the armed forces or brokering a deal between the CCP and the government in Taipei. In sum, there were not many groups or individuals which might be able to assist the United States achieve its objective.

Four possible courses of action were offered. First, the United States could occupy Taiwan under the terms of the Japanese surrender either with KMT consent or "by direct action" after the collapse of the Central Government. It was not believed that the Nationalists would agree to such a transfer of power. In regard to direct action, not only might the U.S. encounter armed resistance by the KMT, but *"...there is no doubt that it would galvanize all mainland Chinese opinion in support of the Communists, the very thing we must avoid if our political warfare is to have any degree of success in China.*"[34]

Second, the U.S. could negotiate with the ruling KMT for "extra-territorial and base rights" on Taiwan. However, it was judged doubtful that bases would be granted for any other reason than to drag the United States into the civil war. In any case, U.S. military bases would not solve the problem. They would be no more than "...an illusory defense against Communist capture of power through either penetration or a deal." Experience had proven that military bases "...are not a sovereign remedy against Communist infection in a foreign country. As often as not they are an aggravating factor." A U.S. military presence on Taiwan, it was argued, would be a propaganda coup for the CCP who would attempt to "...rally public support of mainland Chinese to themselves with the result that the U.S. position on the mainland would be jeopardized."

The third option was to "...support on Formosa the National Government or a rump thereof as the recognized Government of China."[35] This possible course of action was given the shortest treatment. It seemed clear that to recognize Taiwan as the seat of Nationalist China would lead immediately to an uprising and provide "the most fertile environment" for the growth of communism on Taiwan. Additionally, to take this path "would greatly complicate" the U.S. in its dealings with the mainland and "...hamstring our tactical flexibility toward China Proper."

The fourth and final course of action outlined was to support "continued local non-Communist Chinese control" of Taiwan "using our influence wherever possible to discourage the use of Formosa as a refuge for National Government remnants."[36] Unfortunately, went the analysis, the fact that Chiang had recently appointed a governor loyal to him mitigated against the success of this approach. Indeed, one of the main problems the United States had labored under so far in molding the policies on the island was the utter lack of "an alternative to National Government leaders which we could use to pressure..." the ruling clique. Without alternative Chinese leaders in hand which the U.S. could flash before the Gimo's face, the KMT "...would continue to ignore our recommendations and endeavor to blackmail us with their indispensability in preventing Communist control of the island."

The policy recommendation offered in the paper was the fourth course of action above.

> When the situation in China has developed to the point where we know what governing groups we will have to deal with in Formosa, the U.S. should seek to develop and support a local non-Communist Chinese regime which will provide at least a modicum of decent government for the islands.

It was recommended as well that the U.S. use what influence it had to discourage a further influx of refugees. Also, when the governing authorities were identified, a *demarche* should be issued which made it clear that:

(a) The U.S. has no desire to see chaos on the mainland spread to Formosa and the Pescadores;

(b) The U.S. has not been impressed by Chinese administration on the islands and believes that if there is continued misrule the Chinese authorities would inevitably forfeit the support of world opinion which might be expected to swing in favor of Formosan autonomy;

(c) U.S. support for the governing authorities of Formosa will inevitably depend in a large measure upon the efficiency of their regime and the extent to which they are able to contribute to the welfare and economic needs of the Formosan people and permit and encourage active Formosan participation in positions of responsibility in Government.

(d) The U.S. cannot remain unconcerned over possible developments arising from the influx of large numbers of refugees from the mainland and the consequent effects, including the increasing burden on the island's economy, and is disturbed at the indication of the Chinese belief that the building up of military strength on Formosa will in itself provide an effective barrier to Communist penetration;

(e) The U.S. expects that the lessons to be drawn from developments on the mainland and from previous Formosan reactions to Chinese rule will not be overlooked by the Chinese authorities in dealing with the problems of the island and with the Formosan people.

The recommendation preceding this proposed *demarche* exposed the lack of confidence the drafters of this document placed in the prospects for success of this course of action. It was suggested that the United States "...also seek discreetly to maintain contact with potential native Formosan leaders with a view at some future date to being able to make use of a Formosan autonomous movement should it appear to be in the U.S. national interest to do so."

On February 3, 1949 the NSC held its 33rd meeting; a meeting devoted exclusively to China-related issues. The first item on the agenda, NSC 34/1, was adopted without all that much discussion. It

was concluded that keeping a communist-dominated China from con-
tributing to Soviet power should be the immediate aim of the U.S.
The policy of encouraging the development of Chinese Titoism was
evolving.[37] NSC 37/1 was the next item on the agenda. It is clear from
the official minutes of the meeting that the Taiwan issue dominated
the discussion that day.[38]

The comments of Dean Acheson revealed that he and his advisors never believed that anything short of armed intervention of one
sort or another, or a Formosan revolution which would justify United
Nations action, would result in Taiwan's salvation. Taiwan needed a
clean slate.

Acheson began by reading selected cables on the situation on the
island; cables which highlighted deteriorating conditions and the
possibility of another general uprising. He then came right to the
point: "...we may not succeed, through diplomatic and economic measures, in preventing the communist infiltration and domination of
Formosa." Referring to the JCS assessment of Taiwan's strategic
importance, an assessment in which he concurred, Acheson felt
pained to point out that the policy proposed in NSC 37/1 had, "at
best", a sixty percent chance of success. The possibility that the
Nationalist armed forces might go over to the communists, coupled
with the fact that a Taiwanese revolution would be unlikely to succeed
on its own, led Acheson to believe that it would be best "... to face now
the exact significance to our security of such an eventuality." He then
suggested that the JCS prepare a new study on the strategic importance of Formosa—a study "...which would indicate whether we
should, if necessary, use military forces to deny Formosa to the communists in the event that other measures are not successful."[39]

Acting Secretary of the Army Draper asked if the granting of
bases on Taiwan by the KMT might not enhance the U.S.'s position.
Acheson responded that basing troops on the island was not a solution
to creating a friendly, non-communist, and stable Taiwanese government. Likewise, unilateral armed intervention by the U.S. was viewed
by Acheson as a last resort to be used to save the island if it were
deemed of such strategic importance that such action was warranted
regardless of the political liabilities associated with it.

What the Secretary of State announced that he "preferred" as a
contingency (should the recommended course of action in NSC 37/1
fail) was to "...try to develop a spontaneous independent movement in

Formosa which could then lead to an agreement in the UN for a new deal for Formosa. This way...we could get international sanction for U.S. intervention." Admiral Hillenkoetter, Director of Central Intelligence, did not see Acheson's contingency scenario as out of the question. He was confident that "...we could have a revolution there in a week if we wanted it." Walton Butterworth pointed out that the legalities of authorizing "the appropriate agency to get in touch with Formosans..." required that NSC 37/1 be approved.[40]

Paul Hoffman of the ECA proposed that the NSC "confirm the present policy of continuing a vigorous program of aid to Formosa..." Economic assistance would help the ruling authorities address fiscal problems which were undermining confidence in Taipei's abilities.[41] At the end of the meeting it was agreed that a new paragraph would be added to NSC 37/1 which strongly endorsed continued economic aid to Taipei.[42]

The recommendations in NSC 37/1, along with Hoffman's additional paragraph, were adopted by the NSC and forwarded to the President for his approval as NSC 37/2. It was agreed that State would prepare a study recommending immediate diplomatic and economic measures which could be taken to save Taiwan. Likewise, the Joint Chiefs would prepare a study for the NSC estimating "...the extent of the threat to U.S. security..." the fall of Taiwan would pose should "...diplomatic and economic steps to deny communist domination of Formosa prove insufficient..." and recommend "...what, if any, military measures should be taken in that event."[43]

President Truman approved the recommendations in NSC 37/2 the next day, February 4th.[44]

4.3 TAIWAN AS A DIVISIVE ISSUE BETWEEN STATE AND DEFENSE

The Department of Defense (DoD) played a poor second to State in the formulation of foreign affairs and national security policy. The new department, created as a result of the National Security Act of 1947, was hampered by ongoing and extensive organizational changes and adjustments to its authority as late as the summer of 1949 when amendments to the act were put before the Congress.[45]

The early history of the DoD is the story of the struggle of the Office of the Secretary of Defense to gain control over a vast military establishment formerly made up of separate cabinet-level departments and independent-minded—sometimes outright rebellious—

uniformed services. It is the story of the search for a proper role for the newly created position of Chairman of the Joint Chiefs of Staff, the problems of defining the mission of the Joint Staff, and the creation of a new service—the Air Force.

Adding to DoD's organizational problems in 1949 was the very real problem of providing for the nation's security. The Department was operating under the most adverse constraints. The Soviet challenge had been growing since the end of the Second World War. The United States, as the undisputed leader of the "free world," was committed to a policy of containing Soviet influence around the globe. Nevertheless, since the end of the war the American military establishment had undergone a massive demobilization. On VJ-Day the armed forces of the United States numbered more than 12 million men in uniform.[46] By 1949 only 1.5 million were on active duty.[47] Selective Service had ended in March 1947 and the services were dependent upon volunteers.[48] The defense budget had likewise atrophied dramatically. In 1945 (FY 1946) the Pentagon was allocated $42 billion. In 1949 (FY 1950) that figure shrunk to $13.9 billion.[49] Given these constraints, the neophyte Joint Staff was reluctant to commit U.S. forces to any peripheral engagement which might escalate and result in the siphoning off of forces from defending vital interests.

Taiwan presented a dilemma for the Joint Chiefs. The island was deemed essential to the defense of the U.S. strategic position in the Far East. However, the JCS were not of the opinion that Taiwan was so directly vital to U.S. national security that they were willing to risk a major or protracted engagement of forces to keep Taiwan from the communists. Consequently, they constantly qualified their judgments about Taiwan's strategic importance and refused to commit themselves to a policy which would employ military force as an option short of a situation in which general war was already under way. Indeed, it was the JCS, in NSC 37, which first suggested that diplomatic and economic means be employed to detach the island from China.

Dean Acheson was constantly exasperated by DoD. It was very difficult to get Defense to speak with one voice. The Joint Chiefs, divided by parochial interests, rarely agreed with each other on any particular issue. Further, they did not always agree with or support the views of the Secretary of Defense. Also, when policy recommendations were required the lumbering Joint Staff took an inordinate amount of time to generate position papers.

From Acheson's perspective, the JCS refused to commit them-selves to an estimate of Taiwan's strategic value. This was unaccept-able. State was going to incur real political risks in attempting to detach the island from China. This being the case, the Secretary of State wanted to be sure that the risks were worth taking. At stake was the possibility that this policy would force the CCP into the willing arms of the Soviets.

The diplomats at Foggy Bottom were never convinced that diplo-matic and economic steps alone would succeed in saving Taiwan. In a memorandum on the subject to President Truman on January 14th, Acting Secretary of State Lovett pointed out that political means of denying the island to the communists were not yet exhausted and the possibility existed that a "Chinese non-communist local government" might yet be fostered which was capable of defending Taiwan. How-ever, Lovett pointed out that the United States had to "prepare for the failure" of political devices "and put itself in a position to inter-vene with force if necessary."[50] State needed to know whether Taiwan's value was such that the Joint Chiefs would be willing to intervene with military force. None of these questions, initially, were answered to the satisfaction of Acheson and company. State's constant harping on the JCS for a resolute statement on Taiwan caused a good deal of friction between the two departments.

Above all, when Louis Johnson was appointed Secretary of Defense on March 28, 1949 relations between State and Defense deteriorated quickly and almost completely. To say that Acheson and Johnson disliked each other would be an outrageous understatement. In his memoirs, Acheson felt obliged to point out that Johnson's behavior in office led him to believe that the Defense Secretary was "mentally ill."[51] These two men engaged in a clash of personality and ego which spilled over to most policy issues that required coordina-tion between their two departments. In fact, Johnson, early on in his tenure, declared that no one in the Department of Defense could coordinate with State on his own. Only one person in all of DoD was authorized contact with State.[52]

Johnson used the very partisan issue of policy toward Taiwan to undermine Acheson. By appearing as a hard-line supporter of the KMT on Taiwan he earned the support of conservative Republicans, the China Lobby, General MacArthur, and the Nationalist Chinese themselves. Some evidence suggests that Johnson, prior to the out-

IN SEARCH OF A TAIWAN POLICY121

break of the Korean War, may have engaged in policy leaks and collusion with MacArthur and KMT officials to trip up State's Taiwan policy and generally make trouble for Acheson and his principal deputies. Without a doubt, Johnson, in late 1949, browbeat the JCS into reversing their long-standing view that committing U.S. forces to save Taiwan would be a mistake.

All of these problems would transpire soon enough. In the meantime, Acheson's immediate concern was tying down the Joint Chiefs to an evaluation of Taiwan's military importance so that political decisions could be made.

4.4 DEFENSE AND STATE RESPOND TO THE NSC

The Joint Chiefs were formally tasked to prepare their study by Secretary Forrestal on February 7th, and were required to present it to him within three days.[53] They met their suspense and, on the eleventh, their paper was circulating within the NSC.[54]

The JCS reiterated that the loss of Taiwan to the communists would still be considered a serious threat to United States security and the analysis offered in their original study (NSC 37) still held true. The denial of mainland facilities to U.S. forces enhanced the strategic value of Taiwan in case of war. Hostile control of Taiwan would compromise the sea lanes between Japan and the straits in Southeast Asia. Taiwan's fall to the CCP would make it impossible for the island to be an asset in the economic recovery of Japan. Finally, in the hands of the enemy, Taiwan could serve as a base for hostile power projection deep into the U.S.'s interior lines and sea lanes in the Western Pacific.

It was then pointed out that the JCS previously recommended that economic and diplomatic means be used to deny Taiwan to the communists, and that "...resort to military measures was tacitly excluded." That judgement, they reported, continued to be valid.

> The Joint Chiefs of Staff are still of the opinion that any overt military commitment in Formosa would be unwise at this time. In spite of Formosa's strategic importance, the current disparity between our military strength and our many global obligations makes it inadvisable to undertake the employment of armed force in Formosa, for this might...lead to the necessity for relatively major effort there, thus making it impossible then to meet more important emergencies elsewhere.

In short, Taiwan was not considered so "directly vital to our national security" that finite forces should be committed to battle at the risk of being unable to cope with crises in areas of greater importance. Nevertheless, given Taiwan's great strategic importance, the Joint Chiefs were prepared to offer a military option, short of a commitment to use force, in support of the "...vigorous prosecution of the approved diplomatic and economic steps..." adopted in NSC 37/2.

Although Secretary Acheson was already on record as not being in favor of the establishment of military bases on Taiwan, that is exactly what the Joint Chiefs suggested. They recommended the "...stationing of minor fleet units at a suitable Formosan port or ports, with such shore activity associated therewith as may be necessary for maintenance and air communication and for the recreation of personnel."

It was admitted that there existed the possibility of "unfavorable diplomatic repercussion" due to "what might be termed a show of force." However, the stationing of naval elements on the island, given its importance, was a reasonable recommendation worth the "diplomatic risks" involved.[55]

On February 18th the State Department submitted to the NSC the recommendations it was tasked to provide for "specific and immediate" diplomatic and economic measures in support of the policy adopted in NSC 37/2.[56]

It was recommended that State "strengthen" its representation on Taiwan by immediately sending "a high-ranking officer" to Taipei. Upon his arrival, this officer was to "approach" Governor General Ch'en Ch'eng and deliver the *demarche* proposed in NSC 37/2. It was further recommended that, after receiving assurances from Ch'en that the governing authorities in Taipei were prepared to rectify the shortcomings outlined in the *demarche*, the official from State should be authorized to tell the Governor General that the U.S. is prepared "...to give economic support for the economy of Formosa, designed to assist in developing and maintaining a viable, self-supporting economy on the island." At that point the ECA could forge ahead with surveys of industrial projects which would contribute to Taiwan's economic self-sufficiency. Also, ECA would then be tasked to prepare and submit a recommended program for "overall economic assistance to Formosa." Finally, it was urged that "...every effort should be exercised to minimize the appearance of United States official activities on Formosa..."[57]

4.5   THE 35TH MEETING OF THE NSC: TITOISM AND TAIWAN LINKED

The 35th meeting of the NSC, held March 3rd, was a significant affair.[58] As a first order of business it was established that the United States would follow a policy toward the communist-dominated mainland aimed at working toward the encouragement of the inevitable split between the CPSU and CCP. The adoption of NSC 41 and NSC 34/2 signaled the beginning of the search for Chinese Titoism. At the same time a strategy was sought which would support the goal of separating Taiwan from the mainland without undermining the Titoist policy toward the Chinese communists. It was the issue of Taiwan which dominated the afternoon.

Prior to the meeting, the NSC staff prepared and circulated a working paper (NSC 37/5) which outlined the recommendations previously submitted by the Departments of State (NSC 37/4) and Defense (NSC 37/3) and which offered the staff's own policy recommendations.[59] The NSC staff was in complete agreement with Secretary of State Acheson's opinion that the establishment of bases on Taiwan—that which the Joint Chiefs recommended in their latest study—would be counterproductive to the policy objectives of the United States toward both the island itself and mainland China. It was reasoned that:

> ...the establishment of U.S. bases on Formosa in the present situation would be not only diplomatically disadvantageous but also, and far more importantly, a heavy political liability for us. A show of military strength would be of dubious efficacy in preventing communist agitation and infiltration or conspiratorial negotiations between communist emissaries and Nationalist commanders on Formosa.

Furthermore, the NSC staff offered that, "A show of military strength would have serious political repercussions throughout China; it might create an irridentist issue just at the time we may wish to exploit Soviet action in Manchuria and Sinkiang."

Consequently, it was the recommendation of the NSC staff that fleet units not now be stationed on or off Taiwan.[60] It was suggested that the diplomatic and economic measures put forth by State in NSC 37/4 be adopted.

Acheson kicked more dirt on the JCS proposal when the meeting turned its attention to the Taiwan issue. The Secretary of State read to the gathering a prepared statement on Taiwan, copies of which he passed around the table.[61]

As a first point Acheson stated that the JCS paper did not provide "with sufficient clarity" answers to the questions they were asked. In his view, NSC 37/3 failed to provide a clear estimate of the threat the fall of Taiwan to the communists would present to U.S. security in the event that economic and diplomatic means failed. Also, he did not think that the question of possible military measures was adequately addressed by the JCS. "I feel," he said, "that it would be helpful if they would do so."

He then went on to reject the JCS recommendation of stationing naval forces on Taiwan. Such a move, felt Acheson, "...would impair the efficacy of what we are trying to do through diplomatic and economic means." Expanding on this point, Acheson articulated the dilemma for U.S. policy posed by the situation on Taiwan.

> In attempting to develop separatism on Formosa, we are up against the potential threat of irredentism spreading throughout the great expanse of continental China. We are most anxious to avoid raising the spectre of an American-created irridentist issue just at the time we shall be seeking to exploit the genuinely Soviet-created irridentist issue in Manchuria and Sinkiang. We cannot afford to compromise an emerging new US position in China by overtly showing a pronounced interest in Formosa. It is a cardinal point in our thinking that if our present policy is to have any hope of success in Formosa, we must carefully conceal our wish to separate the island from mainland control.

Acheson admitted that State was "under no illusions" that Taiwan could be denied to the communists merely through diplomatic and economic means. Indeed, at some later date, he said, "we may conclude that it is impossible" to do so. At that point, a reexamination of the Taiwan problem would be in order. However, the Secretary had no doubts whatsoever that any military option "short of complete blockade and occupation" would be ineffective in combating the fall of Taiwan by internal communist subversion or a deal struck between Taipei and the CCP. Consequently, the establishment of bases on the island would gain nothing and jeopardize the already slim chances of success for Taiwan's rescue by political reform and economic assistance. Acheson concluded his statement by enjoining his colleagues not to make public the U.S. Government's desire to detach Taiwan from China, and by asking that the JCS "...not exclude from its thinking and planning the possibility that it might later be called upon to employ modest military strength in Formosa in collaboration with other friendly forces."[62]

After reading the statement Acheson again reiterated to the group that he did not feel that the JCS had clearly answered the question as to whether Taiwan's importance warranted "overt military action." He interpreted NSC 37/3 as implying that the service chiefs were not prepared to recommend the employment of force "...at this time or under any foreseeable circumstances." However, not being sure how to interpret the Joint Chiefs on this point Acheson felt that they should be asked to prepare in writing another statement on the issue. Additionally, the Secretary of State took exception to the JCS judgment that "the United States faces the prospect of strategic impotence on the continent of Asia."[63]

Defense Secretary Forrestal jumped into the discussion by pointing out that the JCS had already given their opinion on Taiwan's value. The key to understanding the JCS position, he said, was in their assessment that the island was indeed crucial to regional security but not "directly vital to our national security." Army Secretary Royall reminded the group of the United States' many commitments across the globe. He offered that he had recently asked for a complete survey of commitments in the Pacific, and that his feeling was that there was going to be, among the service chiefs, "serious differences of opinion as to whether Formosa was not more important than Japan, particularly in the light of the importance of Formosa to the defense of the Philippines and Okinawa."[64]

Acheson thought that was all well and good. However, he pointed out that the NSC (at the 33rd Meeting) had already rejected the proposal of stationing naval units on Taiwan and that "the Department of State did not like the proposal..." He reminded the group that "Since we have little chance of success in our Formosan aims under any circumstances, the stationing of fleet units would reduce what little chance we did have to practically nothing." Forestall then asked Acheson how State would react if the JCS recommended "direct military action in Formosa." Acheson replied that he would reject overt, direct, and unilateral action.

> If the Joint Chiefs were to recommend the occupation of Formosa, then the Department of State would recommend attempting taking over the island under the front of international action, first by underground

encouragement of a revolution and then UN action to establish a trustee-ship for the island. Thus...we might avoid Chinese resentment over direct U.S. intervention as well as having things go to pieces underneath if we took direct control.[65]

Acheson went on to recommend for approval the policy set forth in NSC 37/5 and call once more for all concerned agencies to keep official American interest in Taiwan low key.

At the close of the meeting NSC 37/5 was adopted without any changes by the NSC membership. The JCS were tasked to clarify their thoughts on Taiwan's strategic importance and confirm or refute the Council's interpretation of their view that "overt military action by the U.S. in Formosa is not recommended either at this time or under any foreseeable circumstances in the future."[66] President Truman approved NSC 37/5 later that same day.[67]

The President's signature on NSC 37/5 put Taiwan policy into motion. Washington's preferred course of action was to promote a stable and efficient Chinese regime on the island—one which would not be susceptible to communist subversion due to misrule. Diplomatic and economic means would be used to pursue this strategy. Specifically, pressure on Taiwan's governing authorities by the U.S. to reform its ways would be balanced by holding out the prospect of economic assistance if they followed Washington's advice.[68] Should this fail, Taiwan would have to be snatched from the grips of the CCP by more devious means. The United States would clandestinely instigate a Formosan uprising. A call for United Nations intervention—possibly in the form of a multi-national military occupation—would be made. A UN Trusteeship for Taiwan would be secured. In this way the U.S. would be blameless for detaching Taiwan from China.

To implement the decisions reached in NSC 37/5, a high-level State Department representative had to be dispatched to Taipei. That official was Livingston T. Merchant.

Notes

1. "Probable Developments In Taiwan," ORE 39–49, Central Intelligence Agency, 14 March 1949, HST/PSF/Box 256/ORE 1949, #28–#45.

2. Madame Chiang stayed in the U.S. from December 1948 until January 1950 acting as the Generalissimo's personal representative. Her portfolio included lobbying the Truman Administration for aid, lending her prestige to the efforts of the China Lobby and China Bloc in Congress, and generally keeping tabs on the machinations of those Chinese eager for US aid but not necessarily in favor of her husband's return to power. After the situation on

the mainland became hopeless, she turned her efforts to attempting to save Taiwan from the communists for the Gimo and the Soong-Kung faction. Blum, *Drawing the Line*, p. 21. For the various KMT faction vying for U.S. support see Tucker, "Nationalist China's Decline and its Impact on Sino-American Relations, 1949–1950," in Borg/Heinrichs, eds. *Uncertain Years*.

3. Message, American Consulate General, Taipei to American Embassy Nanking, "Local Political developments and rumors," January 11, 1949, SDF:Reel 2.

4. Ibid. Ch'en officially assumed his duties on January 5, 1949.

5. *The Consul General at Taipei (Krentz) to the Secretary of State*, January 15, 1949, FR:49:IX:268. Ch'en Ch'eng had been a loyal subordinate of Chiang Kai-shek's since 1924 when he served as an instructor at the Whampoa Military Academy. In the years that followed he served the Gimo faithfully as a staff officer and commander. Chiang's enemies were Ch'en's enemies. Whether fighting recalcitrant warlords such as Feng Yu-hsiang and his *Kuominjun*, communist "bandits," or Japanese invaders, Chiang could always count upon Ch'en's political reliability and talent. In 1944 Ch'en succeeded General Ho Ying-ch'in as Minister of War. Boorman and Howard, *Biographical Dictionary of Republican China*, Vol. I, pp. 152–160. Ch'en was married to T'an Hsiang, daughter of T'an Yen-kai, in 1932. It was widely believed that the Generalissimo and Madame Chiang acted as the go-betweens for this politically prestigious match. Memorandum, Sprouse to Butterworth, February 4, 1949, SDF:Reel 3. This State Department biography incorrectly identified Ch'en's wife as T'an Chang. See Boorman and Howard, Vol. III, p. 233.

6. Message, "Local Political developments and rumors," ibid; Message, Taipei to Secretary of State, January 8, 1949, SDF:Reel 1.

7. Message, Nanking to Secretary of State, December 30, 1948, SDF:Reel 3.

8. Message, Shanghai to Secretary of State, January 28, 1949, CMC/Box 2/China Folder #2. Present at the meeting with Wu was General Barr (Commander, JUSMAG), Admiral Badger (Commander, U.S. Naval Forces, Western Pacific), Admiral Crawford (Commander, U.S. Naval Forces, Shanghai), Raymond Moyer (U.S. Representative, Joint Commission on Rural Reconstruction), and Roger Lapham (Chief, ECA Mission, China).

9. Letter, L.F. Craig (Chief, Taiwan Regional Office, Economic Cooperation Administration) to Harlan Cleveland (Director, China Program, Economic Cooperation Administration) January 13, 1949, SDF:Reel 2.

10. Message, Taipei to Secretary of State, January 2, 1949, SDF:Reel 3.

11. Message, "Local Political Developments and Rumors," January 25, 1949, SDF:Reel 2.

12. Message, American Consulate General, Taipei to Secretary of State, January 28, 1949, SDF:Reel 2.

13. Message, "Local Political Developments and Rumors," January 25, 1949, SDF:Reel 2.

14. Letter, Roger D. Lapham (Chief, China Mission, ECA) to Paul G. Hoffman (Administrator, ECA), 15 February 1949, SDF:Reel 3.

15. Message, "Local Political Developments and Rumors," January 25, 1949, SDF:Reel 2.

16. Consul General Krentz, in one report, gave the following example of gross misconduct:

> ...an army truck driving at terrific speed mowed down a horse cart and instantly killed the driver leaving the horse and a boy of 16 unhurt. The truck stopped and the men climbed down, not to examine the damage or give compensation but only to flog the young survivor of the cart to death.

Message, American Consulate General, Taipei to Embassy, Nanking, "Local Political Developments and Rumors," February 21, 1949, SDF:Reel 2.

17. Letter, Craig to Cleveland, January 13, 1949, ibid.

18. Ibid. The same official, Craig, reported that conditions in Kaohsiung were no better and that in both ports the main problem was "military commandeering of facilities."

19. It was reported that Governor Ch'en expected at least one million refugees to arrive before the exodus came to an end. Message, "Local Political Developments and Rumors," January 25, 1949, SDF:Reel 2.

20. Ibid.

21. Message, American Consulate General, Taipei to American Embassy, Nanking, "Local Political Developments and Rumors," February 21, 1949, SDF:Reel 2.

22. Ibid.

23. Message, Consulate General, Hong Kong to Secretary of State, January 27, 1949, SDF: Reel 2.

24. Letter, George H. Kerr to Philip Sprouse, January 15, 1949, SDF: Reel 1.

25. Message, Taipei to Secretary of State, February 8, 1949, SDF:Reel 3.

26. See Chapter 2.

27. Memorandum, Butterworth to Lovett, January 12, 1949, SDF:Reel 2. Based on his discussions with Acheson on the subject, Butterworth reported to Lovett that Formosa would be a "hot" topic "from here on out."

28. See Chapter 2.

29. Intelligence Memorandum No. 111, Strategic Importance of Taiwan, 3 January 1949, HST/NSC-CIA/Box 2/Dec 48–Dec 49.

30. Ibid.

31. *Memorandum by the Acting Secretary of State to President Truman,* Subject: U.S. Armed Forces at Tsingtao; Problem of Formosa, January 14, 1949, FR:49:IX:265–267. "The Department of State concurs in the Joint Chiefs of Staff conclusion that it is in our strategic interest that Formosa be denied to communists."

32. Footnote 27, FR:49:IX:270.

33. For copies of NSC 37/1 see HST/PSF/MNSC/Box 205/NSC Meeting #33; DNSC:Reel 1; or FR:49:IX:270–275.

34. Emphasis added.

35. Underlining as presented in original.

36. Emphasis as in original. The use of the term "Chinese" by the drafters of this paper implied mainlanders recently arrived since VJ-Day, as opposed to native Taiwanese.

37. See Chapter 3.

38. Minutes of the 33rd Meeting of the National Security Council, February 3, 1949, HST/PSF/MNSC/Box 205/NSC Meeting #33. NSC Members present included: Secretary of State Acheson (presiding), Secretary of the Treasury John W. Snyder, Secretary of Defense Forrestal, Acting Secretary of the Army W.H. Draper, Under Secretary of the Navy W. John Kenny, Secretary of the Air Force W. Stuart Symington, Acting Chairman, National Security Resources Board John R. Steelman, and Economic Cooperation Administrator Paul G. Hoffman. Also attending were Rear Admiral R.H. Hillenkoetter (Director of Central Intelligence), W. Walton Butterworth (State Department, FE), and Robert Blum (Office of the Secretary of Defense).

39. Ibid.

40. Ibid. Acting Army Secretary Draper asked Acheson if there was not an apparent inconsistency in pursuing as a national objective a stable government on Taiwan while at the same time stirring up a revolution. Interestingly, Acheson did not see an inconsistency in this approach.

41. Ibid. Always wary of giving the KMT a free ride with no return on the U.S. investment, Butterworth "...cautioned, with respect to the aid program, of the importance of timing in showing out hand."

42. The new paragraph was as follows:

> The U.S. Government, through the most flexible mechanisms possible, should conduct a vigorous program of economic support for the economy of Formosa, designed to assist the Formosans in developing and maintaining a viable, self-supporting economy.

NSC 37/2: "The Current Position Of The United States With Respect To Formosa," February 3, 1949, HST/PSF/MNSC/Box 205/NSC Meeting #33. NSC 37/1 was renumbered NSC 37/2 when Hoffman's paragraph was added. NSC 37/2 may also be found in FR:49:IX:281–282.

43. Minutes of the 33rd Meeting of the National Security Council, ibid.

44. *Memorandum by the Executive Secretary of the National Security Council (Souers) to the Council,* February 4, 1949, FR:49:IX:282; Memorandum for the National Security Council, The Current Position With Respect To Formosa, February 4, 1949, HST/PSF/MNSC/Box 205/NSC Meeting #33.

45. For a fascinating organizational history of DoD see Steven L. Rearden, *History of the Office of the Secretary of Defense: The Formative Years, 1947–1950* (Washington, D.C.: Historical Office, Office of the Secretary of Defense, 1984). Future references will be cited as *History of the OSD.*

46. Rearden, *History of the OSD,* p. 12.

47. Kennith W. Condit, *The History of the Joint Chiefs of Staff: The Joint Chiefs of Staff and National Policy*, Vol. II, 1947–1949 (Wilmington, DE.: Michael Glazier, Inc., 1979), p. 561. This multi-volume series on the history of the Joint Chiefs was prepared by the Historical Division, Joint Secretariat, JCS. Future references will be cited as *History of the JCS*.

48. Rearden, *History of the OSD*, p. 12–13. As a result of manpower cuts the Army—91 divisions strong in 1945—shrunk, by 1947, to 10 divisions, only two of which were fully equipped.

49. Ibid.; Condit, *History of the JCS*, p. 563.

50. *Memorandum by the Acting Secretary of State to President Truman*, January 14, 1949, FR:49:IX:265–267.

51. Acheson, *Present at the Creation*, p. 374.

52. Princeton Seminars, October 10, 1953, reading copy 10–11 October 1953, folder 2, pp. 778 and 782, DGA/Box 75. For more on the Acheson-Johnson feud see, Rearden, *History of the OSD*, pp. 128, 238, 306, and 526–527; Blum, *Drawing the Line*, pp. 16–18, and 168; and Stueck, *The Road to Confrontation*, pp. 141 and 162.

53. JCS 1966/5, 7 February 1949, The Strategic Importance of Formosa, RJCS:Reel 2.

54. The study was circulated within the NSC as NSC 37/3: "The Strategic Importance of Formosa." FR:49:IX:284–286; HST/PSF/MNSC/Box 205/NSC Meeting #35. It was numbered JCS 1966/6 within the Joint Staff. JCS 1966/6 (Strategic Importance of Formosa), 10 February 1949, MJCS:Reel 1.

55. NSC 37/3, ibid.

56. NSC 37/4: "The Current Position Of The United States With Respect To Formosa," February 18, 1949, HST/PSF/MNSC/Box 205/NSC Meeting #35; DNSC:Reel 1; FR:49:IX:288–289.

57. Ibid.

58. For a transcript of the discussion at the meeting see Memorandum For The President, March 4, 1949, HST/PSF/Box 220/NSC Memos To President, 1949. Attendees at the meeting were: Dean Acheson, Treasury Secretary Snyder, James Forrestal, Secretary of Commerce Charles Sawyer, Secretary of the Army Kenneth C. Royall, Under Secretary of the Navy W. John Kenny, Air Force Secretary Symington, John Steelman of the National Security Resources Board, Paul Hoffman from ECA, Admiral Hillenkoetter (DCI), and Walton Butterworth (State, FE), Minutes Of The 35TH Meeting of the National Security Council, HST/PSF/MNSC/Box 205/NSC Meeting #35.

59. NSC 37/5: "Supplementary Measures With Respect To Formosa," March 1, 1949, HST/PSF/MNSC/Box 205/NSC Meeting #35; DNSC:Reel 1; FR:49:IX:290–292.

60. The rejection of naval bases on the island was not categorical. NSC analysts pointed out that their recommending against it was "...without prejudice to a reexamination of this possible course of action should developments on Formosa so justify."

61. Statement By The Secretary of State at the 35th Meeting of the National Security Council on *The Formosan Problem*, HST/PSF/MNSC/Box 205/NSC Meeting #35; FR:49:IX:294–296.

62. Ibid.

63. The specific point to which Acheson referred was on page 2 of NSC 37/3:

> In general terms, it having become more apparent than ever that the United States faces the prospect of strategic impotence on the continent of Asia, our military capabilities in the Western Pacific must rest primarily on control of sea lanes and maintenance of strategic air potential from strategically tenable island positions. Enemy control of Formosa would seriously jeopardize our capabilities in these respects while constituting, on the other hand, a major contribution to enemy capabilities.

64. Memorandum For The President, ibid.

65. Ibid.

66. Ibid.

67. Memorandum For The President, March 3, 1949, HST/PSF/MNSC/Box 205/NSC Meeting #35; *Memorandum by the Executive Secretary of the National Security Council (Souers) to the Council,* March 3, 1949, FR:49:IX:296–297.

68. Philip Sprouse undoubtedly endorsed what amounted to a conditional aid policy.

CHAPTER 5

The Mission Of Livingston T. Merchant: March–May 1949

> In acting with respect to Formosan situation Dept is relying on your recommendations at every stage in game.[1]
>
> Acheson to
> Merchant
> April 1949

Between March and May 1949, the Truman administration attempted to put into motion the Formosa policy promulgated by NSC 37/2 and 37/5. Onto the shoulders of Livingston T. Merchant fell the weighty responsibility of assessing the political situation on the island and delivering to the ruling authorities on Taiwan the *demarche* incorporated into NSC 37/2.[2] If all went well, Taiwan's KMT rulers would offer, through word and deed, appropriate assurances of good government. The United States would begin to provide the economic aid deemed necessary to stabilize the island, and, hopefully, Taiwan could be saved without Washington incurring the wrath of the CCP. As it turned out, the ambitions of this plan did not square with the realities in the field.

5.1 MERCHANT AND HIS MISSION

Livingston T. Merchant ("Livie" to his friends) was not one of the State Department's China hands. After graduation from Princeton in 1926, he went directly into private business. Only after the Second World War had begun did he enter government service. During the war, Merchant served in Washington with State's War Areas Division and the Division of Defense Materials. From 1945 to 1948 he was assigned to the United States Embassy in Paris as an economic counselor. Merchant's subsequent assignment in 1948 to the American Embassy in Nanking was his first brush with China.[3] Like Walton Butterworth, Merchant was untainted, so to speak, by prior China service. Ultimately, while serving in Nanking, Merchant was detailed

as the "high ranking officer" to be sent to Taiwan in accordance with
NSC 37/2 and 37/5.

Very little has been written about Merchant's Taiwan sojourn.[4]
Although some works of the past few years have referenced his
mission, none has devoted any substantial space to it.[5]

Merchant's tasks were two-fold. First and foremost, he was to
study the political situation on Taiwan. He was to determine which
Chinese leader was running the island. Having done that, Merchant
was then to assess if that leader would be able, as NSC 37/2 put it, to
"...provide at least a modicum of decent government for the islands."[6]
If he felt that the individual concerned could provide stable and efficient government, then, and only then, would Merchant deliver the
demarche as written in NSC 37/2 and inform Washington that
economic assistance to bolster the island could begin. This was
Merchant's primary mission.

Merchant's second task was to provide another vantage point
from which to assess the the Taiwanese independence movement
which was reported to be active on the island. State and the CIA
would conduct investigations as well. Dean Acheson had already
decided, and the NSC concurred, that if Taiwan's Chinese (ie., KMT)
government was incapable of governing the island in such a manner as
to deny it to the communists, then the U.S. would have to be prepared
to use clandestine means to instigate a Formosan uprising in order to
justify a United Nations action. This mission, however, was ancillary
to the first.[7]

Acheson and other members of the NSC were very concerned
that Merchant's activities would expose the desire of the United
States to detach Taiwan from the mainland. Such a turn of events
would arouse the ire of the Chinese communists and undermine the
broader goal of allowing Titoism within the CCP to mature. Consequently, Merchant was specifically instructed to retain his title as a
Counselor of Embassy in Nanking. He was instructed to say, when
asked, that his trip to Taiwan was merely to "...oversee expanded US
representation on that island..." In other words, he was to claim to be
on an inspection tour of the Consulate in Taipei. Furthermore,
Merchant was ordered to avoid at all costs any implication that he was
now transferred to Taiwan. To assist him in his deception of purpose,
Merchant was authorized to travel between Taiwan, Shanghai, and
Nanking as he saw fit. However, his orders emphatically stated that he

was not to allow himself to be captured by the communists while back in China.[8] By the first week of March 1949, Livingston Merchant was in Taipei.

5.2   WHOM TO APPROACH? WHEN TO APPROACH HIM?

It was originally believed by State that Merchant would deliver the NSC's *demarche* to Governor Ch'en Ch'eng.[9] However, by the first week in March, whether Ch'en would survive in his current position was in question, for rumors were circulating that he soon might be replaced.[10] Therefore, one issue with which Merchant had to deal immediately was whether an approach to Ch'en made any sense before the question of the governorship was resolved. If Ch'en was in fact replaced after being given promises of American aid in return assurances of decent government, then those assurances would be useless and Merchant would run the risk of tipping Washington's hand in regard to Taiwan. On the other hand, if the NSC program was delayed until Nanking politics ran its course, then the fast-breaking events on the mainland might render economic aid to Taiwan useless. Time was of the essence if Taiwan was to be saved from communist domination.

Dean Acheson was very aware of these problems and outlined them very succinctly for Merchant on the second of March in one of their first communications during the latter's mission. Acheson conceded that approaching Ch'en was fraught with danger if the governor was to be ditched by Li Tsung-jen. On the other hand, Acheson noted that continuing reports of deteriorating conditions on the island argued for an early approach in order to "stabilize" the situation on Taiwan and "...enable ECA (to) carry out its plans." Acheson believed that an early approach was the safest bet for other reasons as well. First, there was apprehension in Washington that Chinese officials on Taiwan would participate in the coalition government with the CCP that Li Tsung-jen was attempting to negotiate. Second, the more time that passed, the more opportunity the communists would have to infiltrate the Chinese armed forces on the island. Also, local Chinese military commanders might lose their resolve in the face of continued Red Army victories and go over to the CCP even if the Governor did not. Likewise, the passage of time would only permit communist forces to build up a capability for mounting an assault on the island; a target deemed worthy of the cost given the fact that the KMT's national treasury was now located there. Having laid out these and other thoughts, Acheson requested Merchant's views; especially on the issue of the timing of the approach.[11]

Merchant's views were not long in coming. On the sixth of March he wired back to Acheson that an approach to Ch'en Ch'eng at this point would be a mistake. While the time factor was a real one, Merchant opined that the real key to successfully implementing the NSC program revolved around the Governorship of Taiwan. Ch'en Ch'eng, he offered,

> ...lacks the qualities provide liberal efficient administration needed. Moreover, as GIMO man he cannot be relied on to prevent or discourage continued influx least desirable main-landers although mass migration now checked.[12]

Moreover, Merchant agreed with Taipei's Consul General, Kenneth Krentz, who argued that "larger policy decisions" and "firm commitments" be placed on hold because of "nebulous and changing political conditions." Krentz recommended that "...we should now mark time hoping for changes which may enable us to obtain self-help conditions on more certain terms than hitherto."[13]

Merchant went one step further than Krentz. Not merely arguing against an early approach to Ch'en, Merchant recommended to Acheson that the U.S. Government attempt to have the governor replaced! It was Merchant's recommendation that State instruct Ambassador Stuart to "encourage" Acting President Li Tsung-jen to sack Ch'en and replace him with General Sun Li-jen. Sun's ascension to the Governorship, Merchant felt, "...seems on balance solution best suited to our interests."[14]

At the time of Merchant's mission General Sun Li-jen was serving on Taiwan as the Commander-in-Chief of Chinese Army Training Headquarters.[15] Sun, a graduate of George Marshall's alma mater, the Virginia Military Institute, distinguished himself during the Second World War as one of Chiang Kai-shek's most honest and capable field commanders. His operational achievements during the Burma campaigns earned him the respect of General Stilwell. After the war he toured the battlefields of Europe at the invitation of Dwight Eisenhower.[16] The fact that Sun was not one of the Whampoa Clique, Stilwell's wartime praise, and Sun's capabilities as a field soldier all insured that he would remain distrusted by the Gimo. It was reasoned that he might therefore be eager to assist the

U.S. in return for a position which Chiang would never accede to give him otherwise.

Two days after Merchant suggested to Acheson that Sun be made Governor, the Secretary of State sent out his initial reaction. On the whole, Acheson was not convinced that it would be wise to pressure Li on the issue of replacing Ch'en with Sun. He conceded to Merchant that Sun's reputation was good and that he would be "well disposed" toward the United States. Nevertheless, Acheson did not feel that Sun Li-jen had enough administrative experience to make a go of reforming the politics and economy of the island. Furthermore, Acheson was fearful that if the U.S. pressured Li Tsung-jen into a change of governorship there would be no guarantee that a person less capable than either Ch'en Ch'eng or Sun would not be appointed. The Secretary also offered that if the U.S. were to cause Ch'en's relief, then he "...would become disgruntled over efforts remove him and he and his and Gimo followers would sabotage Sun or any other successor."[17]

Merchant was not convinced that Acheson's arguments were valid. Between the ninth and fourteenth of March, while shuttling between Taipei, Shanghai, and Nanking, he continued to lobby his views with the Secretary of State. Merchant responded to Acheson's concerns before departing for a visit to Shanghai by arguing that:

> To me prime need is for governor who is honest, liberal, effective and not so bound to Generalissimo as to permit move by latter to Formosa for last ditch fight if Li negotiates mainland peace nor so blind to China's interests as to deliver island to coalition government under any mainland peace terms.
>
> I agree your doubts Sun but he meets foregoing requirements on all points save administration experience which he is understood willing to supplement by qualified advisers. Moreover, Sun personally controls troops and probably risks less sabotage than any Chen successor by reason his established position on island.

Merchant also mentioned to Acheson that it was his understanding that Li Tsung-jen had already informed Ambassador Stuart that he intended to appoint Sun the next governor. Merchant argued that if Stuart failed to show enthusiasm for this initiative then Li might read U.S. disapproval into it. Merchant then reiterated his position that Stuart offer "discreet encouragement" to Li for appointing Sun, and "...no approach to Chen unless it develops we must deal with him..."[18]

From Shanghai, on the eleventh, Merchant followed up this cable with another. On April third Congressional authorization funding ECA projects in South China would expire. If the NSC plan for Taiwan could be put into effect before that date, then previously appropriated monies could be used to bolster Taiwan without identifying the island as the object of U.S. interest. Funds requested after that date would drag Taiwan into public view in the course of the Congressional hearings required to appropriate new monies. This was a situation which the administration desired to avoid. However, so convinced was Merchant that the key to the Taiwan problem rested with the governorship, that he was willing to wait right up until the last minute (April 3rd) before committing to Ch'en. Merchant recognized the gains to be made if the U.S. could "camouflage" economic aid to Taiwan by "lumping" it with South China projects. However, Merchant still insisted to Acheson that Ch'en was "unreliable" and that he was "reluctant" to recommend that talks commence with Ch'en, for it would only "...encourage him and strengthen his position..." on Taiwan.[19]

Acheson responded to Merchant's Shanghai communique the same day, March eleventh. With what appears to have been a bit of reluctance, Acheson decided to accept Merchant's recommendation. He informed Merchant that State believed that he deserved to have "...a certain latitude dealing with problem." If Merchant could convince Ambassador Stuart that having Sun Li-jen appointed governor was the best bet, then, Acheson told Merchant, it would be fine with him as well. Acheson then added that if Ambassador Stuart agreed with Merchant, then Stuart should be the one to broach the subject of Sun with Li Tsung-jen, not Merchant. Acheson was concerned that if Merchant personally lobbied Li for Ch'en's removal then Merchant would be a useless envoy if Ch'en remained.[20]

By the fourteenth of March Merchant, who flew out to Nanking two days earlier, had secured Ambassador Stuart's concurrence. Stuart agreed to indicate to Li Tsung-jen that he and the United States Government had the highest confidence in Sun's qualifications for promotion to the governorship of Taiwan. Merchant informed Acheson of Stuart's concurrence and added that he believed the prospects for Sun's appointment to be "promising." "Pending clarification governorship," Merchant told Acheson, "I do not contemplate opening negotiations unless you instruct me otherwise."[21] With that, Merchant planned to leave Nanking and, after a short stop in Canton, return to Taipei by March 17th. It was now time to wait and see what transpired.

5.3   THE SEARCH FOR AN INDIGENOUS POLITICAL FORCE

While Merchant and Acheson waited for the issue of the governorship to be resolved, State, Defense, and the CIA attempted to assess whether there was a viable indigenous political force on Taiwan which could be successfully exploited in the event that Chinese officials were not deemed capable of providing those reforms which would save the island.

Identifying and assessing local opposition groups was, no doubt, a very difficult task, for it required a human intelligence collection capability focused on Taiwan which probably did not exist at the time. The OSS had long been disbanded, there were no military attaches assigned to the island, and the CIA was a very young organization. In a letter to Philip Sprouse, George Kerr, State's former Taiwan expert, underscored this shortfall. "Certain Washington intelligence offices," he wrote, "have sent people around to ask me all manner of questions since my return. If I am to judge by the list of points they grasp in their hot little hands, they are shockingly unprepared. I must admit that while I was in Washington in the several Government offices, I received the impression that not much comprehensive reporting has been done."[22]

It was almost natural, therefore, that the Japanese were sought out on this issue. Having dealt with all manner of Formosan independence groups before and during the war they probably had plenty of information to offer. Only the KMT would have had more intelligence and they obviously could not be queried.

Professor Suzuki Gengo, an economic adviser to the Secretariat of the Japanese Finance Ministry, was interviewed by members of the U.S. Embassy in Tokyo on at least two occasions in March. Suzuki was formerly a professor of economics at Taipei's Taihoku Imperial University. After the war, he continued to teach at the school, subsequently renamed Taiwan University. He assisted the U.S. military in their role in transferring rule of the island from Japan to China. Prior to returning to Japan he served as an adviser to the new Chinese government on Taiwan. He maintained contacts with Formosan independence advocates active in Japan and was considered to have studied opinions on the independence movement.

It was Suzuki's opinion that the independence movement was not "particularly strong" or that it could become "an effective force." He pointed out that the February uprising of 1947 was a spontaneous affair. Only since then had any underground independence groups been organized on the island. However, the groups were, in his opinion, "small scale." Suzuki then offered the judgment that it was the independence groups outside of Taiwan which had the most potential for mischief. He believed that these outside groups were determined "to precipitate" a violent uprising on the island "with the full realization that it will fail but with the hope that it will attract attention and arouse interest in the problem of Formosan independence."[23]

The group which apparently became the focus of U.S. interest was the Formosan League for Re-emancipation (FLR). The FLR was formed in 1948 by Joshua Liao (Liao Wen-kuei) and his younger brother Thomas (Liao Wen-yi); the scions of a wealthy Formosan family. The Liao brothers left Taiwan for the United States in the 1920's to pursue their education. Joshua Liao, a political scientist, received an M.A. from the University of Wisconsin and a Ph.D. from the University of Chicago. Thomas, a chemical engineer, was awarded his masters certification from Michigan and his doctorate from Ohio State University. Both ultimately married American women. After VJ-Day they became outspoken critics of Nationalist rule on Taiwan. Joshua Liao was arrested in Shanghai by that city's Garrison Command in 1947 and charged as an instigator of the February uprising. Upon Joshua's arrest Thomas, who in 1946 had campaigned unsuccessfully for a seat in Taiwan's Provincial Assembly, fled to Hong Kong. He was later joined there by his older brother after the latter's release from prison in Shanghai.[24]

It was the intention of the Liao's that the FLR bring together various non-communist advocates of Taiwan independence in order channel the movement's energy effectively. From Hong Kong, Thomas allegedly directed FLR activities in the British colony, FLR activists still on Taiwan, and the actions of those Taiwanese activists who chose to reside in Japan in order to escape KMT oppression. Joshua, on the other hand, worked with activists still on the mainland; mostly in Shanghai and in Nanking. It is still unknown how large an organization they commanded, if there was an organized FLR at all,

or to what extent they were infiltrated by communists. What is clear is
that the two brothers were very visible. They maintained contact with
American and other foreign diplomats in the Far East and regularly
published manifestos declaring that the allied powers had no basis for
ceding Taiwan to China after the war. They demanded that the
United Nations grant the Taiwanese people self-determination. At
times the Liao's confused U.S. officials by working at cross purposes
with each other. Moreover, they sometimes antagonized U.S. officials by publicizing their contacts with Americans.

Although the FLR was of major interest to the U.S. in its assessment of the Taiwan independence movement, very little was known
about who these men were or what the FLR was all about. State
Department officials constantly made discreet inquiries about the
FLR with some foreign diplomats, yet with others tried not to show so
much interest that speculation about United States intentions would
result. For example, when Jean Daridan, Counselor of the French
Embassy in Washington, asked State's John Allison (Northeast Asian
Affairs) if the U.S. is aware of the existence of the FLR, Allison coyly
replied that "...we did know of the existence of this so-called
Formosan Emancipation League in Japan, but that we did not have
any great detail regarding it."[25] On the other hand, in a conversation
with J.F. Ford, First Secretary of the British Embassy, Philip Sprouse
confided that "...the Department was interested in the activities of
the Formosan League for Re-emancipation and had instructed the
appropriate consular offices to keep in touch with League representatives and report to the Department on their activities." Sprouse then
pointed out to Ford that the League was operating from Hong Kong
and asked if the British government could provide information about
the FLR and its aims.[26]

U.S. consular officials did in fact talk with the Liao brothers.
Joshua Liao communicated with the American Consulate in
Shanghai and Thomas with State Department officers in Hong Kong.
Both offered messages of impending revolt, communist subversion,
and the need for the United States to act.

In Shanghai Joshua informed Consul General Cabot that the
Taiwanese were "...well armed and trained and sure of success..." the
next time they rise against the KMT. He offered that the fall Nanking
would be the event which would trigger the next Formosan revolt and
that sabotage and assassination would be the first actions the natives

would take. He told Cabot that he was counselling restraint, but that his more restive followers could not be held in check indefinitely. The elder Liao also took the occasion to protest to Cabot the fact that American military equipment continued to be sent to Taiwan, an act he viewed as giving tacit support to KMT oppression by bolstering the "SS troops" which occupied the island. The Consul General had doubts about Liao's prediction of a victorious uprising. In commenting on his conversation, Cabot reported to State that Liao's comments led him to believe that "...he may envisage 'success' in terms less of military victory than of world dramatization of his people's predicament which will gain attention and sympathy of UN."[27]

In Hong Kong, Thomas Liao informed Consul General Hopper, just as his brother had done in Shanghai, that a Taiwanese uprising was imminent. Liao offered that he had to send a special representative to the island (one Philip Huang) to cool down those who were anxious to begin the revolt. He further stated that the FLR would not initiate its revolt until the United States gave some indication of its intentions in the event of an uprising. Specifically, Liao wanted to know if MacArthur's troops would be sent to intervene to maintain order and wrest control of Taiwan from the Chinese. After all, Liao said, the communists were now very active on the island and in the event of a revolt they would attempt to seize the hour for the CCP.[28]

In conducting their campaign for U.S. or U.N. intervention, the Liao brothers also communicated with MacArthur in Japan, leaked inside information about U.S. intentions of economic aid for Taiwan to the press (presumably to force the U.S. position), and held talks with other foreign officials in the region. Thomas Liao sent MacArthur a petition demanding an end to Chinese rule on Taiwan and listing, in descending order, four alternatives: full independence, a U.N. trusteeship, a trusteeship under U.S. auspices, and finally, a return to Japanese rule.[29] Joshua Liao admitted to the Consul General in Shanghai that he was the "anonymous" Formosan leader quoted in an Associated Press dispatch in which it was demanded that ECA aid going to Taiwan be closely supervised so that it would do good for the Taiwanese and not benefit the "...island's new 'conquerors'." Liao told Cabot that his intent was to communicate this concern to ECA head Paul Hoffman in Washington. He also admitted that he was going to attempt to meet with ECA Chief for China Roger D. Lapham in the near future.[30] Finally, Thomas Liao very openly apprised U.S. officials in Hong Kong of his liaison with the Government of the Philippines. The younger Liao confided that he had met with Philippine Consul General Mariano Ezpeleta. According to Liao, Ezpeleta stated that his mission from Manila was to investigate the problem of Taiwan. Ezpeleta offered to send Liao and an aide (Huang) to Manila to brief Philippine government officials on their program and discuss the future of Taiwan. Ezpeleta further suggested that Liao and Huang make visits as well to Indonesia, and Australia.[31]

In these and other ways, the Liao's, realizing that the United States government was interested in the FLR, attempted to give the impression of a large and well-organized group representing the Taiwan independence movement that would orchestrate a successful revolt. By raising the specter of KMT collapse, Chinese communist activism on Taiwan, and, on one occasion, even Soviet activity on the island, the Liao brothers hoped to move the United States into action. However, the claims of the Liao brothers were met with skepticism as well as outright disbelief.

CIA analysts gave a very low probability to the success of the revolt which both Joshua and Thomas claimed would topple KMT rule. By mid-March it was Langley's view that:

> A successful Taiwanese rebellion against the Chinese Government in the near future is quite improbable, owing to lack of effective organization and leadership and the presence of Nationalist military forces on the island. It is quite probable, however, that the Taiwanese may resort to acts of violence and sabotage at any time in protest against the current influx of mainland Chinese. These outbreaks may be prompted, not so much by hope of success as by a desire to draw the attention of world opinion to the Taiwanese problem.

CIA further believed that the native independence movement was highly susceptible to communist infiltration.[32]

SCAP's military intelligence organization (G-2) noted the FLR in one its intelligence summaries. According to the Military Attache in Nanking, the FLR was claiming to have the support of "several Chinese and Taiwanese military leaders." The FLR's plan, as told by one representative, was to "...take advantage of the weakness of the Nationalist Government and to persuade the Chinese Nationalist forces in Taiwan to lay down their weapons in order to prevent bloodshed." The same FLR representative confided that the plan "won't work." In commenting on this report, SCAP G-2 recognized

the genuine desire of Taiwanese for independence from China but at
the same time indicated that "...the instigators of the present independence movement may have some personal gain in mind..."[33]

More pointedly, Taipei Consul General Kenneth Krentz
believed that little hope should be placed in the FLR (or any group)
being able to provide the type of action required to support the NSC's
contingency plan. Most independence groups, he felt, were "disuni-
fied." The FLR in particular was of "small influence." He suggested
that the FLR and others were attempting "...to force outside action by
exaggeration." The leadership of these groups, he judged, "...is so
compounded of patriotism, irresponsibility and greed as give doubt
effectiveness beyond flash in pan."[34]

Before any final assessment of the FLR could be made, the
Chinese communists made clear that they were aware of
Washington's interests. All good propaganda must have an element
of truth to be stretched if it is to be effective. The following piece had
more stretch than truth; but if nothing else, this broadcast from North
Shensi (forwarded to Washington) must have been unnerving to those
working the FLR problem.

> The "movement for Taiwan Independence" which again has
> appeared in the market recently is made in America with MacArthur
> trade mark. On February 28 and March 1 a small number of American
> running dogs in the names of "Japanese-returned Students Federation in
> Taiwan" and "Federation for the Independence of Taiwan" clamored for
> independence of Taiwan in Tokyo and Hong Kong.
>
> There are not more than a dozen members in these so-called
> Taiwanese groups, and their leaders are the Liao Wen-yi and Liao
> Wen-kuei brothers. This pair of American slaves were originally big land-
> lords in South Taiwan. When Taiwan was under Japanese control, they
> picked on the Taiwanese and robbed them of their lands in collaboration
> with the Japanese Government. After the takeover of Taiwan by the
> KMT reactionary Government, they became officials of the KMT
> Government and helped oppress the people of Taiwan. Because they
> were hated by the Taiwanese, the KMT Government finally dismissed
> them.
>
> Liao Wen-yi and Liao Wen-kuei were American-educated and mar-
> ried American wives. Therefore with American help they acquired the
> monopoly of selling American goods in Taiwan after the Japanese sur-
> render, and became compradores for this American economic aggression
> against Taiwan. Shortly afterwards they were employed by an American

espionage organ as its agents and travelled between Tokyo, Hong Kong and Shanghai. For a long time they have set about goading the Taiwanese to demand independence for Taiwan.

The so-called Taiwan independence movement is just another name for American engulfing of that island. On February 10 a Hongkong newspaper said that America was promoting independence for Taiwan and would raise the issue before the United Nations. She would ask the UN to permit Taiwan to send a representative to the Far Eastern Commission, and MacArthur had already appointed Liao Wen-yi as this this so-called representative. Recently national traitor Liao Wen-yi and his friends again clamored for independence for Taiwan because MacArthur instructed them to do so.[35]

The fact that the FLR and the Liao brothers were linked to the United States by the CCP probably did more to undermine their utility to Acheson and the NSC than any negative assessment of their worth from the field.

Which independence groups or representatives Livingston Merchant may have met with personally during his stay on Taiwan remains unclear. Undoubtedly, he was being briefed by officials in the field who were in contact with these men. By the end of March, Merchant had reached his conclusions about the independence movement. In the assessment he sent back to Acheson, Merchant quashed any hope that a local movement could rise up, depose the KMT, and provide political leadership unassisted. "Though my knowledge is limited," he told Acheson,

> my impression is that Formosan independence groups currently are disunited, politically illiterate, imperfectly organized and in general worthy little reliance. There is no doubt that general and growing discontent exists but effective leadership and organization are still absent.[36]

There was no doubt that an uprising could be instigated. However, with no outside military aid the rebellion would be decisively crushed by the KMT forces on the island. The United States would not provide such assistance unilaterally because it was feared that by doing so Washington would antagonize the CCP and push it into the Soviet camp. Even if some members of the NSC had wanted to intervene at this point (and none did) the Joint Chiefs were still unwilling to commit forces to Taiwan.

5.4 THE PENTAGON RESPONDS TO THE NSC

At the 35th meeting of the NSC (March 3rd) Dean Acheson asked that the Joint Chiefs clarify their position on the strategic importance of Taiwan. Specifically, the Secretary of State's reading of the JCS position was that under no circumstances would the military recommend the use of overt military force to save the island; even if all other means failed. The rest of the council membership agreed with Acheson that the JCS needed to comment on this interpretation.[37]

On March 7th, the Secretary of Defense passed the requirement for a clarification to his joint chiefs.[38] On March 22nd the Joint Strategic Survey Committee completed its response.[39] Finally, on April 2nd, Secretary of Defense Louis Johnson forwarded the JCS clarification to the NSC. The Joint Chiefs responded that the NSC's "...interpretation that this estimate means that overt military action by the United States in Formosa is not recommended by the Joint Chiefs of Staff, either at this time or under any foreseeable future circumstances, is generally correct..." They went on to pen words which, by now, were familiar to the NSC readership:

> The Joint Chiefs of Staff do not believe that the strategic importance of Formosa justifies overt military action at this time or in the event that diplomatic and economic steps prove insufficient to prevent communist domination so long as the present disparity exists between our military strength and our global obligations.

Added to this old song was the new clarification which, hopefully, would satisfy the council.

> However, it should be pointed out that there can be no categorical assurance that other future circumstances extending to war itself might not make overt military action eventually advisable from the overall standpoint of our national security.[40]

There is no record of Acheson's or the NSC's reaction to the JCS response. One can imagine, however, that the Secretary of State was still frustrated by what he would have certainly perceived as more muddled talk and equivocation. But, a bottom line he asked for, and a bottom line he got! Only in event that the United States became involved in a general war in the Far East would the strategic importance of Taiwan be elevated to the point where overt military force might be required to secure it. In April 1949, this scenario probably seemed remote. Unfortunately, it would turn out to be prophetic.

5.5   STUCK WITH CH'EN

Ch'en Ch'eng and Sun Li-jen were not oblivious to the fact that the United States was taking stock of their worth. Neither were they abstaining from playing on the very confused field of KMT politics; and in the early months of 1949 a confused political situation it was! Chiang Kai-shek's retirement was only nominal. With his base of operations in Ch'i-k'ou, his home town, the Generalissimo was still directing loyal troops against a Red Army that was plowing ever southward. Moreover, he still controlled the bulk of the KMT treasury, much of which he had already sequestered on Taiwan with Ch'en Ch'eng as watchdog. At the same time, Li Tsung-jen was attempting, with little success, to give real meaning to his title of Acting President. Recognizing imminent military defeat, he decided that the only way the KMT would survive on the mainland was to engage in negotiations with the communists and attempt to secure favorable terms for a coalition government. Li's willingness to let Mao Tse-tung dictate terms and his overtures to the Soviet Union to assist in negotiations only served to alienate his KMT allies. Sun Fo, son of Sun Yat-sen and President of the Executive Yuan, took such violent exception to Li's approach to negotiations that in February he moved the cabinet out of the capital city of Nanking to Canton. Only in March, with Sun's resignation and the appointment of Ho Ying-ch'in in his stead, did Li recover control of the government.[41]

Throughout March and April, Ch'en Ch'eng and Sun Li-jen jockeyed for position on Taiwan by making trips back and forth to the mainland to enlist support. State Department officials took note of these and other trips, but were hard-pressed for inside information as to just what was transpiring.

During the third week of March, Ch'en Ch'eng flew to Nanking. The Consul General in Taipei was certain that Ch'en would not have left Taiwan if he thought his position was insecure. Rumors were even floating about that Sun Fo, before resigning, further increased Ch'en's powers as Governor by placing all civil and military organizations directly under his control. If this was the case, argued the Consulate in Taipei, then Ch'en was now just as powerful, or even more so, than Acting President Li.[42] Ambassador Stuart also attempted to shed some light on Ch'en's activities. He reported that Ch'en was in Nanking to observe the political situation under Li Tsung-jen. Primarily, however, Stuart opined that Ch'en's purpose "...was political fence-mending under the new regime and that he departed moderately satisfied." Ch'en, offered Stuart, was not about to relinquish the Governorship of his own volition.[43]

Sun Li-jen's circuit included Tokyo, Ch'i-k'ou, and Nanking. Sun flew to SCAP headquarters in early March, a fact which was picked up by a *Newsweek* correspondent. It is not known if he saw MacArthur. However, a dispatch from the Embassy in Tokyo back to State apprised Butterworth that Sun's presence was noted by the local reporter. According to the dispatch, the Embassy, when queried, merely stated to the correspondent that Sun was in Japan to see General David Barr on business concerning the end of JUSMAG activities in China.[44] In early April, Sun had an audience with Chiang Kai-shek and debriefed the U.S. Embassy in Nanking on his meeting with the Gimo. According to Sun, Chiang received him quite cordially, and "...told him to go back to Taiwan and keep up his good work training (the) Chinese Army."[45] If the subject of Sun replacing Ch'en as Governor was discussed, then Sun was unwilling to tell Stuart about it. If Sun's account of the meeting was to be taken at face value, then the implication was that Chiang had no intention of endorsing him as Governor.

Moreover, it soon became apparent that Li Tsung-jen did not have the power to appoint or dismiss the Governor of Taiwan. On April 10th Ambassador Stuart reported to State that in a conversation with Li, the Acting President let it be known that if the United States Government wished Ch'en dismissed and Sun Li-jen appointed, then Chiang Kai-shek was the man to lobby. Furthermore, if the Ambassador wished to have a Chinese interlocutor pass on this suggestion, then he had best find one who has the Gimo's confidence, because Li did not.[46]

Li Tsung-jen's inability to have Sun promoted to Governor, the possibility of a coalition government, as well as his pessimistic assessment of the independence movement caused Merchant to begin to doubt the prospects for the success of the NSC policy toward Taiwan. He suggested to Acheson that even if a decent governor for the island could be installed, the U.S. might soon have to contend with a CCP-KMT coalition on the mainland with claims to Taiwan. If Washington encouraged Taiwan to declare its autonomy from such a coalition, then some American support would be required to help it survive. Military intervention, Merchant believed, would not be a

wise option because it would only result in "...inflaming (the) vast
majority (of) mainland Chinese as well as some Formosans and griev-
ously injuring US moral position (in) all Asia." He pointed out that
local independence groups could not by themselves save the island
from ultimate communist domination. More and more, Merchant
was coming to believe that the best chance for keeping Taiwan out of
CCP hands was to initiate a multilateral military intervention under
United Nations auspices or, failing that, an extra-U.N. military intervention with the British, French, Australians, and possibly India.[47]

Acheson thanked Merchant for the above "well reasoned presentation." However, the Secretary reminded his special representative
that the policy directed by NSC 37/5 was still operative and that further delays in putting it into effect (by not approaching the Governor)
only increased the risk of Taiwan being included in a CCP-KMT coalition. Acheson assured Merchant that there were no thoughts in
Washington of unilateral military intervention in Taiwan in the event
of a mainland coalition government. However, if diplomatic and economic means to keep the island out of CCP hands proved inadequate,
then the U.N. option would be pursued. Acheson told Merchant that
he recognized the weakness of the independence movement. However, the movement could still be of use in the event that appeals for
U.N. intervention from islanders were needed for justification. The
Secretary informed Merchant that State was already attempting to
discreetly assess the attitudes of the French, British, and Philippine
governments toward possible U.N. intervention. That contingency
aside, Acheson asked Merchant if he still believed that he should
delay his approach to Ch'en Ch'eng even though Ch'en's recent trip
to Nanking indicated that he had been given increased powers on the
island?[48]

By the first week of April Merchant's position was an uncomfortable one. From the beginning, he doubted that Ch'en Ch'eng would
institute the types of political reforms necessary to stabilize the
island. He asked Acheson to delay the NSC plan in the hope that Li
Tsung-jen could be pressured into replacing Ch'en with Sun Li-jen.
Acheson, against his own inclinations, agreed to let Merchant have a
go at it. The plan failed. The Secretary was asking him once again to
justify why the approach to Ch'en should not be made. There was
nothing left for Merchant to do other than to agree with Acheson that
it was time to put NSC 37/2 and 37/5 into motion.

In answering Acheson's message, Merchant, on April 6th, pointed out to the Secretary that rumors that Ch'en had acquired new "sweeping powers" remained unconfirmed. He also offered that Li Tsung-jen may have only deferred taking action on replacing Ch'en with Sun; implying that it could still happen. However, Merchant had no choice but to "reluctantly conclude" that Ch'en was not going to be replaced any time very soon and that Ch'en "meets description paragraph 1" of NSC 37/2. Furthermore, sensing the "urgency" that State obviously felt about getting the program underway, Merchant told Acheson that "I believe we must deal with him." But Merchant refused to guild the lily for the Secretary. He judged that Ch'en will be delighted by the prospect of economic aid from the United States. However, Ch'en's ability to institute positive changes would continue to be constrained by "...his loyalty to Gimo and friends." Merchant warned Acheson not to expect Ch'en to supplement ECA funds by dipping into the KMT's gold stocks on the islands; a reserve now reliably reported at some two million ounces. Furthermore, Merchant told the Secretary that Ch'en could be expected to protect the political and financial interests of the C-C Clique and rule "in traditional Chinese style." Yes, he admitted, Ch'en will refuse to participate in a coalition with the CCP, but, Merchant adjudged to Acheson, "My doubts remain nevertheless regarding his ability to provide sufficiently enlightened government to satisfy Formosan aspirations and provide popular native base necessary for effective resistance." Having unburdened himself of these thoughts, Merchant told Acheson that he was prepared to deliver the *demarche* to Ch'en as written in NSC 37/2 and work with local ECA representatives to develop a program of aid.[49]

5.6 MERCHANT'S VIEWS RECEIVE A REPRIEVE

Acheson did not disagree with Merchant's view that Ch'en was unsuitable for the purposes of the NSC plan. Neither did the Secretary believe that economic aid without political reform would suffice to save Taiwan from the communists. The urgency which Acheson continually communicated to Merchant was due to two factors. First, Acheson worried that an early communist victory on the mainland or a deal for a coalition government would *de facto* result in a CCP-controlled Taiwan. Second, Acheson feared that even if Taiwan remained out of CCP hands for the near-term, the administration would be unable to provide economic aid to the island without exposing to the communists the intentions of the United States Government. Because the ECA funds intended for Taiwan were authorized by the China Aid Act of 1948, and that the original legislation provided that all aid to China would end abruptly on April 3, 1949, funds required to support Taiwan after that date would require new Congressional hearings. That being the case, the NSC plan to keep Taiwan out of communist hands would undoubtedly become public.

However, in the winter and spring of 1949, both State and the Congress attempted to find some means of extending the life of unobligated China Aid Act funds past the April 3rd deadline. They did so for different reasons. The China bloc in Congress wanted to extend the life of the legislation in order to bolster the Nationalists on the mainland with China Aid Act monies earmarked for military assistance. State's motives were different. Foggy Bottom had already written off the mainland and was now concentrating on saving Taiwan by using ECA funds authorized by the Act. Happily, on April 14th, the Congress passed legislation which permitted the President to continue to support the Nationalists with unobligated funds left over from the original China Aid Act appropriations. His authority to do was extended through February 1950.[50] As of April 3rd, approximately 54 million dollars in ECA funds remained.[51] These funds could be put to use in Taiwan.

By April 7th, the day after Merchant reluctantly recommended approaching Ch'en, Acheson was confident that legislation extending the China Aid Act would pass. He cabled Merchant and asked for his views on the Taiwan problem in light of the fact that the April 3rd deadline was all but done away with.[52]

Merchant, who was engaged in consultations in Nanking and Shanghai, did not have a chance to read Acheson's cable until April 12th. But he lost no time in responding to the Secretary's request for his views. Unencumbered by the April 3rd deadline, Merchant spoke his mind. Precisely because Ch'en Ch'eng and the Gimo were firmly in control of Taiwan, Washington could rest assured that their self-interest would dictate that Taipei would refuse to participate in any coalition government Li Tsung-jen might achieve. Washington's interests would be served by Chiang's own intransigence on this point. Consequently, the dangled carrot of U.S. economic aid would not be needed to push them in that direction. "On the other hand," he reasoned, "knowledge (which would unavoidably soon become public) of substantial US aid forthcoming would give Communists new handle to propaganda jug, disappoint Formosans who resent present Chinese authorities and confirm widespread mainland Chinese fears we have imperialistic designs on Island." In the final analysis, Merchant believed that for the moment there was "...nothing to be gained and much to be lost by approaching Governor Ch'en with view committing US economic aid beyond routine continuation present modest ECA commodity imports and current slow moving JCRR program." With that, Merchant formerly withdrew his previous telegram recommending that Ch'en be approached and urged Acheson to defer any commitment to him.[53] Later that day he further recommended that he be recalled to Washington for consultations so that he could offer policy makers a full report.[54]

5.7 SPROUSE SUGGESTS A MODIFIED *DEMARCHE*

Acheson and his advisers at State concurred with Merchant's recommendations.[55] However, they had one last task for their special representative. Sometime during the first week of April, while Merchant was in Nanking, T.V. Soong, Chiang's brother-in-law, arrived on Taiwan.[56] On April 9th, Soong requested a meeting with Taiwan Consul General Edgar. He told Edgar that he was on Taiwan at the request of Chiang who sent him to propose a "...political, economic, and military formula..." to preclude a communist takeover of the island. Soong claimed to be well-versed in Taiwan's political problems and the plight of the Formosans; that he had a survey group with him, and that he was to report back to Chiang. Soong admitted to Edgar that the KMT military was still "50 years behind times" and agreed that the military was a real problem in solving Taiwan's political ills. At the same time, Soong denigrated "synthetic democracy" as a solution. Soong, perhaps sent to see Merchant all along, then requested an interview with an American official conversant in economics, but rejected Edgar's suggestion that he meet with the Consulate's economic officer. Consul General Edgar requested guidance from Washington.[57]

State accepted Merchant's recommendation not to convey to Ch'en the full *demarche* included in NSC 37/2. However, Philip Sprouse saw Soong's approach to Edgar as an opportunity to inform the KMT of the views of the United States concerning Taiwan.

Sprouse recommended to Acheson that Merchant be authorized to see Soong in order to "dispel any illusions the Chinese Government may have with regard to possible action by the U.S. Government" on Taiwan. It disturbed Sprouse that reports from the field indicated that Chiang's group believed that Washington considered Taiwan "an essential link in its Western Pacific defense chain" and that the U.S. would never let the island go under. Sprouse was determined to correct Chiang on this point, and make him understand that any aid the U.S. offered to Taiwan would be dependant upon "self-help" measures the Chinese themselves instituted on the island. Sprouse agreed that after Merchant delivered this abbreviated *demarche,* he should be recalled to Washington.[58]

Acheson concurred with Sprouse and on 15 April directed Merchant to talk with Soong. "Since Soong probably has some directive from Gimo and no doubt wished to obtain firm indication US attitude re Formosa," the Secretary told Merchant, "it seems desirable give him some indication US Govt views on subject and disabuse him of some illusions." Acheson told Merchant that the point must be made to the Gimo that only if the KMT demonstrates a firm commitment to political and economic reform on Taiwan will the United States consider any type or amount of economic aid. The Secretary underscored his belief that in the absence of genuine Chinese reform, any U.S. program aimed at saving Taiwan will fail. Merchant was to tell Soong, quite pointedly, that the although United States Government did not want to see Taiwan fall to the CCP: (1) the U.S. did not consider Taiwan all that important strategically, (2) the U.S. has no intention of intervening with military force to save the island, and (3) the U.S. will not establish bases on Taiwan. The onus was to be placed firmly on the KMT to make a go of the island and Chiang and his supporters must be made to understand that.[59]

Merchant did not believe that he should rush off to speak with Soong and said as much to Acheson. He had grave doubts about Soong's "motivations and intentions." Additionally, there was no real proof that Soong was in fact on a mission for Chiang. Consequently, Merchant requested from Acheson the authority to use his own discretion in determining the best moment to deliver Sprouse's modified *demarche.* Acheson gave Merchant the authority he requested.[60]

5.8   MERCHANT QUESTIONS THE NSC PLAN
FOR TAIWAN

Merchant never delivered Sprouse's modified *demarche* to T.V. Soong. In Merchant's mind, more fundamental issues needed to be addressed. Catastrophe on the mainland, continued KMT in-fighting between the Li Tsung-jen and Chiang Kai-shek cliques, and a reprieve from the 3 April deadline for the use of ECA funds emboldened Merchant to suggest to Acheson that the entire NSC plan for Taiwan required rethinking.

The week of 17 April was a busy one for Merchant. On that day he commenced a series of meetings in Shanghai, Hong Kong, and Nanking. Primarily, he met with U.S. Consular and Embassy officials to assess the KMT political situation. He also consulted with ECA representatives to discuss the pros and cons of economic aid for Taiwan. As fate would have it, Merchant was in Nanking as the People's Liberation Army crossed the Yangtze River and stormed the city. On April 24th, he made good his escape to Canton on a B-17 bomber assigned to the Embassy's military attaches in a hair raising last minute drive through the Nationalist's panic stricken capital. From Canton he returned to Taipei.[61]

On May 4th Merchant cabled Acheson. He felt that events on the mainland and Taiwan justified a fundamental change in the NSC's plans toward the island. "I now believe," he told Acheson, "revision of US policy as laid down in NSC 37 series is indicated rather than mere delay in its execution." Merchant judged that there would be no organized or coordinated Nationalist resistance to the communists on the mainland. The PLA was marching southward unopposed. Nanking was gone. Shanghai was next. Li Tsung-jen and Chiang Kai-shek were still battling for control of the KMT. On Taiwan, he told Acheson, things were looking bleaker. Regardless of who governed the island, Taiwan, he felt, would be built up into a military bastion. The loss of mainland markets were sure to lead to increased inflation. The transfer of troops from Shanghai to Taiwan would not result in bolstering the island's defenses. To the contrary, argued Merchant, the economic burden they would now create would only worsen conditions and possibly lead to chaos and sell-outs to the CCP by military commanders. Finally, Merchant judged that previous reports that the fall of Nanking would be the occasion for a general insurrection by Taiwanese had little basis in fact. He told Acheson that, "...there is no new evidence that local independence groups are sufficiently organized, well armed and well led to knock out garrison and successfully establish anti-Communist pro-US native Formosan government..." Merchant further judged that there was no chance that either Li or Chiang would govern Taiwan in an enlightened fashion or take into account the aspirations of the Formosan people. Under either of the two, the island was destined to become an armed camp. Furthermore, Merchant did not believe that modest American economic aid could save Taiwan.

> Formosa cannot now be turned into a welfare laboratory without far larger subsidy than US has so far considered. New and powerful forces of economic deterioration are at work. Even with massive aid there is little chance governing group with its attitudes and available technical brains could effectively and wisely use such aid. American advisers or a large ECA mission could not compensate for these deficiencies. The US would have to exercise direct authority commensurate with any responsibility it assumed for Formosa's economic well being. That would be a large order and have to be skillfully presented in order to avoid effective attack on US by Communist propaganda throughout Asia.

But all was not lost. Merchant told Acheson that he believed Taiwan could be "run on a seige basis for a considerable period." Indeed, Merchant felt that given the number of troops and the amount of gold stocks on the island, the KMT could hold out against the communists for at least one to two years ("or possibly longer"). Thus, he argued, U.S. strategic interests could be served without the expenditure of U.S. aid. He did not believe that American economic aid would enhance the will of the KMT to resist. To the contrary, Merchant argued to Acheson that Washington's aid would only benefit the ruling group and underwrite their military occupation. Merchant believed that the liabilities of ECA aid outweighed any potential benefits.

> First, we would give Communists resounding irredentist tub to thump on mainland and throughout southeast Asia. This would not only be effective as attack on US but would embarrass any effort our part to hammer Soviet steals from China. Second, if having given aid we fail and island is lost to Communists, we have strengthened it for latter's benefit. Finally, we use US resources with slight hope of strategic return.

Merchant stated to the Secretary that his arguments rested on the assumption that it was still U.S. policy not to provide military forces for the defense of Taiwan and not to assume responsibility for governing the island through unilateral occupation.

Merchant then recommended that "US should abandon contemplated ECA reconstruction program on Formosa." He realized that it would be difficult for Washington to "accept this negative conclusion." In offering what could be done, Merchant suggested a strong Consular presence to pressure the governing group for liberal reforms, maintaining "discreet contact with independence leaders as a long shot," and consulting with other nations on the possibility of Taiwan as a U.N. issue.[62]

Two hours after this hard-hitting message was transmitted, Merchant offered Acheson one other alternative. If the U.S. was willing to reverse its basic policies and blatantly go to the defense of Taiwan, then all-out military and economic aid should be offered. Military supplies could be provided the Taiwan Garrison Command and massive economic assistance programs could be put into motion. The *quid pro quo* from the KMT would be the lease of naval and air facilities to the United States, placing Sun Li-jen in overall command of military forces on the island, and the hiring of certain American economic advisers by the Governor in Taipei to oversee economic reconstruction. An "aggressive, frank presentation" by the U.S. would be required to convince other nations that these actions were "no more invasion of sovereignty than grant by US, for example, of B-29 bases."[63]

Merchant realized that he was recommending that the entire basis of U.S. policy toward Taiwan as stipulated by the NSC 37 series of decisions be trashed. He realized as well that he was making his recommendations in "isolation" from the bigger picture of policy goals and constraints. Consequently, he recommended to Secretary Acheson, once again, that he be recalled to Washington for consultations.[64]

On May 9th, Acheson responded to Merchant's long telegrams. He instructed Merchant to return to Washington for consultations as soon as possible. Before doing so, however, Acheson desired Merchant to approach Ch'en Ch'eng (or K.C. Wu if Merchant preferred an indirect channel to the Governor) and let it be known that given the rapidly deteriorating situation on the mainland, the United States Government wished to express its concern that the chaos across the Straits not spread to Taiwan. Merchant was to also tell the Governor that he should not allow a new wave of refugees to further undermine the island's situation. Finally, Merchant was to let it be known that he was being recalled to Washington to report on the situation on Taiwan, and to assess whether the KMT's efforts to prevent CCP capture of the island—either through infiltration or direct attack—were going to be successful.[65]

Merchant chose to approach Ch'en Ch'eng directly. On May 12th, Merchant and Consul General Edgar met with the Governor and Finance Commissioner C.K. Yen. Merchant expressed his concern about the large influx of refugees flooding the island. Ch'en dismissed these reports and assured Merchant the refugee problem was under control. Ch'en refused to answer Merchant's question about the present KMT troop strength on Taiwan or how many mainland troops were expected. Ch'en would only say that the number of troops allowed onto Taiwan "would be held to number he considered necessary for defense." The Governor assured Merchant that he and his soldiers would fight on to the end. Ch'en also "took pains" to tell Merchant that because of his long years of service under Chiang, he would not stop the Generalissimo from residing on Taiwan should he decide to do so. Overall, Merchant told Acheson, his talk with Ch'en was "unrewarding."[66]

That same day (May 12th), Merchant departed Taiwan for the United States via Hong Kong. His mission on the island was over. Acheson's decision not to approach Ch'en with the NSC 37/2 *demarche*, Merchant's talk with Ch'en, as well as Merchant's recall, were reported to the NSC in a progress report on 18 May.[67] Upon his return to Washington, Merchant became Walton Butterworth's assistant at FE and was promoted to the position of Deputy Assistant Secretary of State for Far Eastern Affairs. His insights into the situation in China and on Taiwan would be sorely needed. For as the summer of 1949 rolled on, problems in Asia would take up a good deal of the attention of the Truman administration. The mainland was now all but lost to the CCP and the NSC's original plans to save Taiwan were now being called into serious question.

Notes

1. *The Secretary of State to the Consul General at Shanghai (Cabot)*, April 20, 1949, FR:49:IX:316.
2. See Chapter 4 for the full text of the demarche.

3. Transcript, Livingston T. Merchant Oral History Interview, May 27, 1975, Truman Library, pp. 1–5.

4. Merchant's own papers at Princeton's Mudd Library contain no references to his mission. However, the intent of the policy which sent him on his way and the prosecution of his mission can be gleaned from the *FRUS* series, State Department files, and the NSC papers maintained at the Truman Library.

5. The one exception is June M. Grasso, *Truman's Two-China Policy* (Armonk, N.Y.: M.E. Sharpe, Inc., 1987). For a review of this book see Arthur Waldron in *The China Quarterly* (114, June 1988), p. 299. Even here, however, the coverage of this important mission was not put forth in great detail.

6. NSC 37/2: "The Current Position of the United States with Respect to Formosa," February 3, 1949, HST/PSF/MNSC/Box 205/NSC Meeting #33.

7. In his oral history for the Truman Library in 1975 (p. 31), Merchant stated that the reason he was to contact the resistance was because Washington was afraid that, "...the Nationalists would not be able to get over there (Taiwan) in sufficient force and power to dominate the island" and keep it out of communist hands. His recollection is inaccurate. The administration was absolutely frantic that the opposite was in fact true; that the KMT *was* coming over to Taiwan in force. This, it was believed, was the cause of much of the political unrest and economic problems which would eventually cause the locals to go over to the communists. The very *demarche* Merchant was to deliver specifically mentioned that further KMT migration to Taiwan would lead to its economic collapse. Unhappily, Professor Grasso takes Merchant's oral history statement at face value (p. 48). A close reading of the primary documents refutes this assertion most conclusively.

8. *The Secretary of State to the Ambassador in China (Stuart)*, February 14, 1949, FR:49:IX:287–288.

9. *Note by the Executive Secretary of the National Security Council (Souers) to the Council*, February 18, 1949, FR:49:IX:288; NSC:37/4, "The Current Position of the United States with Respect to Formosa," February 18, 1949, HST/PSF/MNSC/Box 205/NSC Meeting #35.

10. Message, Acheson to Merchant, March 2, 1949, SDF:Reel 2. Ch'en, of course, was Chiang Kai-shek's man. With Li Tsung-jen now presiding as acting President, there was probably good reason to believe that he would replace Ch'en with one of his own stalwarts.

11. Ibid. At the end of this message Acheson specifically instructed Merchant to send his reply directly to him with no other distribution. Throughout the course of their subsequent three-month communication, messages between Acheson and Merchant were almost invariably classified "Eyes Only" cables.

12. Message, Merchant to Secretary of State, March 6, 1949, SDF:Reel 2.

13. *The Consul General In Taipei (Krentz) to the Secretary of State*, February 25, 1949, FR:49:IX:289–290.

14. Message, Merchant to Secretary of State, March 6, 1949, SDF:Reel 2.

15. Stueck, *The Road to Confrontation: American Policy toward China and Korea, 1947–1950*, p. 119.

16. Boorman and Howard, *Biographical Dictionary of Republican China*, Vol. III, pp. 167.

17. Message, Acheson to Merchant, March 8, 1949, SDF:Reel 2; FR:49:IX: 297.

18. *The Consul General at Taipei (Edgar) to the Secretary of State*, March 9, 1949, FR:49:IX:298–299.

19. *The Consul General at Shanghai (Cabot) to the Secretary of State*, March 11, 1949, FR:49:IX:299.

20. *The Secretary of State to the Ambassador in China (Stuart)*, March 11, 1949, FR:49:IX:299.

21. *The Ambassador in China (Stuart) to the Secretary of State*, March 14, 1949, FR:49:IX:299–300.

22. Letter, George H. Kerr to Philip Sprouse, January 15, 1949, SDF: Reel 1.

23. Memorandum of Conversation, "Conditions in Formosa," FSO Charles Nelson Spinks with Professor Suzuki Gengo, Tokyo, March 3, 1949, SDF:Reel 2; Message, United States Political Adviser for Japan to Department of State, "Conditions in Formosa," March 10, 1949, SDF:Reel 2.

24. Kerr, *Formosa Betrayed*, pp. 201–203, 454, 457.

25. *Memorandum of Conversation, by the Deputy Director of the Office of Far Eastern Affairs (Allison)*, January 18, 1949, FR:49:IX:269–270.

26. Memorandum of Conversation, Subject: Formosa and Formosan League for Re-emancipation, Ford and Sprouse, March 23, 1949, SDF:Reel 3; see also *Memorandum of Conversation, by the Chief of the Division of Chinese Affairs (Sprouse)*, March 23, 1949, FR:49:IX:301. Ford admitted no personal knowledge of the FLR but promised to query his government for information.

27. *Consul General at Shanghai (Cabot) to the Secretary of State*, January 26, 1949, FR:49:IX:276.

28. *The Consul General at Hong Kong (Hopper) to the Secretary of State*, January 27, 1949, FR:49:IX:277.

29. *The Consul General at Shanghai (Cabot) to the Secretary of State*, February 13, 1949, FR:49:IX:287. Joshua Liao admitted knowledge of the petition to SCAP to Consul General Cabot but added that his brother had not consulted him prior to sending it.

30. Ibid.

31. Message, Consul General Hong Kong to W. Walton Butterworth, March 15, 1949, SDF:Reel 3.

32. CIA ORE 39-49, 14 March 1949, "Probable Developments in Taiwan," HST/PSF/Box 256/ORE 1949, #28–45.

33. Message, United States Political Advisor in Japan to John M. Allison, March 11, 1949, SDF:Reel 3. Attached to this message was a copy of *Intelligence Summary* No. 2370, 6 March 1949, from SCAP Headquarters.

34. *The Consul General at Taipei (Krentz) to the Secretary of State*, February 3, 1949, FR:49:IX:280.

35. Message, American Embassy Nanking to the Department of State, "Transmission of Complete Texts of Two North Shensi Broadcasts Criticizing American Policy in Taiwan," March 23, 1949, SDF:Reel 2. It is not surprising that the CCP was able to uncover the fact that the Liao brothers were in touch with U.S. officials. The FLR would have been a prime target for CCP intelligence operations. If George Kerr is to be taken at face value, the weakest link in FLR security was right at the top. The Liao brothers, he says, talked with Formosan communists on a rather regular basis if for no other reason than to try to convince them not to turn to the CCP for the liberation of Taiwan. Kerr states in *Formosa Betrayed* (p. 459) that Thomas was at loggerheads on this issue with Miss Hsieh Hsueh-hung, Taiwan's most notorious communist.

36. *The Ambassador in China (Stuart) to the Secretary of State*, March 23, 1949, FR:49:IX:303.

37. See Chapter 4.

38. JCS 1966/10, Memorandum from the Office of the Secretary of Defense to the Joint Chiefs of Staff, March 8, 1949, RJCS:Reel 2.

39. JCS 1966/11, Report by the Joint Strategic Survey Committee to the Joint Chiefs of Staff, March 22, 1949, RJCS Reel 2.

40. Memorandum for the Executive Secretary of the National Security Council from the Secretary of Defense, April 2, 1949, HST/PSF/MNSC/Box 205/NSC Meeting #35.

41. For brief, but excellent overviews of KMT politics at the time see Nancy Bernkopf Tucker, *Patterns in the Dust: Chinese-American Relations and the Recognition Controversy, 1949–1950* (New York: Columbia University Press, 1983), pp. 59–80, or Tucker's "Nationalist China in Decline and Its Impact on Sino-American Relations, 1949–1950," in Borg and Heinrichs, eds., *The Uncertain Years: Chinese-American Relations, 1947–1950* (New York: Columbia University Press, 1980), pp. 131–171.

42. *The Consul at Taipei (Edgar) to the Secretary of State*, March 19, 1949, FR:49:IX:300.

43. *The Ambassador in China (Stuart) to the Secretary of State*, March 31, 1949, FR:49:IX:306.

44. Message, Tokyo to Butterworth, March 11, 1949, SDF:Reel 2.

45. *The Ambassador in China (Stuart) to the Secretary of State*, April 10, 1949, FR:49:IX:312. Parenthesis added.

46. Ibid.

47. *The Ambassador in China (Stuart) to the Secretary of State*, March 23, 1949, FR:49:IX:302–303. Parenthesis added.

48. Message, Acheson to Merchant, March 30, 1949, SDF:Reel 3.

49. *The Consul at Taipei (Edgar) to the Secretary of State*, April 6, 1949, FR:49:IX:308–309.

50. *United States Relations with China With Special Reference to the Period 1944–1949* (New York: Greenwood Press, 1968), p. 408. (Also known as the

China White Paper, abbreviated here as *USRC*). For background on the China Aid Act of 1948 see Stueck, *The Road to Confrontation*, pp. 58–59, 61–67, 70, 136, 146, 280; Blum, *Drawing the Line*, pp. 25–30, 72–73, 102, 141, 193; and Tucker, *Patterns in the Dust*, 184, 197, and 311.

51. *USRC*, p. 408.

52. *The Secretary of State to the Consul General at Shanghai*, April 7, 1949, FR:49:IX:309–310.

53. *The Consul at Taipei (Edgar) to the Secretary of State*, April 12, 1949, FR:49:IX:313–314.

54. *The Consul at Taipei (Edgar) to the Secretary of State*, April 12, 1949, FR:49:IX:314–315.

55.. HST/NAF/Box 21/January–April 1949. On 13 April State reported to the President that "Our special representative in Formosa states that he does not believe that the decisions of the governing group there as to accepting the authority of a Communist dominated Chinese government or their chances of resisting such a government will be affected by a promise of US economic aid at this time. At the same time he thinks that public knowledge of substantial US aid to the present regime in Formosa would disappoint the Formosans and confirm Chinese fears of American imperialistic designs on the island. Our representative therefore thinks that there is nothing to be gained by making any commitment at this time to the present governor concerning increased aid."

56.. *The Consul at Taipei (Edgar) to the Secretary of State*, April 11, 1949, FR:49:IX:311.

57. Message, Edgar to Acheson, April 11, 1949, SDF:Reel 2.

58. Memorandum, Sprouse (through Butterworth) to Acheson, April 13, 1949, SDF: Reel 2.

59. *The Secretary of State to the Consul at Taipei (Edgar)*, April 15, 1949, FR:49:IX:315–316; HST/NAF/Box 21/January–April 1949.

60. *The Consul General at Shanghai (Cabot) to the Secretary of State*, April 21, 1949, FR:49:IX:316; *The Secretary of State to the Consul General at Shanghai (Cabot)*, April 21, 1949, FR:49:IX:317.

61. Excerpt From "Nanking Letter," April 24, 1949, LTM/Box 1. Merchant's "Nanking Letter" to his wife is a wonderful slice of history. In it he paints moving images of the last moments of the city before capture by the Red Army. One can hear the artillery and machine gun fire, see panicked masses fleeing the city, and watch looters with nothing left to lose steal what they can from abandoned shops.

62. *The Consul at Taipei (Edgar) to the Secretary of State*, May 4, 1949, FR:49;IX:324–326. Merchant's recommendations were circulated within State and probably seen by the President, for they were included in State's daily *Summary of Telegrams*. HST/NAF/Box 21/May–August 1949.

63. *The Consul at Taipei (Edgar) to the Secretary of State*, May 4, 1949, FR:49:IX:326–327.

64. *The Consul at Taipei (Edgar) to the Secretary of State,* May 5, 1949, FR:49:IX:327–328.

65. *The Secretary of State to the Consul at Taipei (Edgar),* May 9, 1949, FR:49:IX:329–330. K.C. Wu (Wu Kuo-chen), Mayor of Shanghai, arrived on Taiwan after the fall of Nanking. He approached Consul General Edgar on 29 April to offer his services as a "channel" to Ch'en Ch'eng, confiding that Ch'en usually heeded his advice. Wu went out of his way to let Edgar know that he believed that the key to Taiwan's salvation was in economic, not military, programs. He saw a need for "liberal civilian advisors" to help Ch'en make the right decisions. He decried the excesses of "mainland carpet baggers" and said they had to be eliminated. He assured Edgar that while Ch'en was a "narrow reactionary," he was also "sincere, honest, clean." By KMT standards a genuine progressive, Wu was soon to become a major figure in U.S. and KMT plans for Taiwan. *The Consul At Taipei (Edgar) to the Secretary of State,* April 29, 1949, FR:49:IX:320–321 and Message, Edgar to Acheson, April 29, 1949, SDF:Reel 2; Message, Edgar to Acheson, April 30, 1949, SDF:Reel 2.

66. Message, Merchant to Acheson, May 13, 1949, SDF:Reel 2.

67. Progress Report to the National Security Council by the Secretary of State on the implementation of NSC 37/2 and NSC 37/5, May 18, 1949, HST/PSF/MNSC/Box 205/NSC Meeting #35.

CHAPTER 6

Taiwan Policy Reviewed:
May–November 1949

No one could have had very high hopes that economic and diplomatic steps alone could guarantee the denial of Formosa to a government unfriendly to us.[1]

> Merchant to Butterworth
> May 24, 1949

Livingston Merchant's return to Washington on May 18th initiated a review of Taiwan policy that lasted almost six months. It was Merchant's and State's opinion that economic and diplomatic efforts alone would not suffice to save the island. CCP advances on the mainland and seriously deteriorating conditions on Taiwan made communist control almost certain. Consequently, Acheson called upon the NSC to reopen discussions on the issue. The Joint Chiefs of Staff were afforded what many believed would be one last opportunity to reassess the island's strategic significance before the inevitable occurred. The Pentagon, however, would not support armed intervention. As the military reviewed the issue, various elements in State set to work devising schemes to keep the island out of Mao's grip. However, with the military unwilling to use force, all that the NSC could come up with was a modification to its previous policy. Chiang would be put on notice that no U.S. forces would come to his assistance. He would have to use the island's own ample resources to save it. If he could show legitimate progress, then increased American economic aid might later be afforded him. But no one in Washington really believed that this policy would save Taiwan. Abandoned to Chiang, Taiwan was as good as abandoned to the CCP.

6.1 CHINA TROUBLES PLAGUE THE STATE DEPARTMENT

Merchant's return coincided with what turned out to be a period of mounting troubles for the State Department over China issues.

Foggy Bottom faced China problems on various fronts; from the Congress, from the Department of Defense, from the Chinese Communists, and from the Nationalists on Taiwan.

The Congress

The China Bloc in Congress hounded Acheson as it did Marshall before him. Some members of this group seriously sought to reverse Truman's policy of non-intervention in the Chinese civil war. Others merely used the China debacle to attack this latest Democratic administration. As the Nationalist's fortunes plummeted in the spring, summer, and fall of 1949, China Bloc initiatives intensified.

The McCarren Bill, which called for $1.5 billion in aid for China, was all but killed by the middle of March. However, on the tail end of that controversy came the issue of the extension of the China Aid Act of 1948. Ultimately, on April 4th, the administration received the extension it required. Nevertheless, the issue provided the China Bloc a platform from which to lambaste Truman's China policy and individual members of the State Department. Because Walton Butterworth represented the administration's views in this matter, he became the prime target of China policy critics.[2] Butterworth soon suffered more pointed attacks. In June, confirmation hearings were held to act upon his nomination for the position of Assistant Secretary of State for Far Eastern Affairs.[3] Once again, Butterworth became a scapegoat for China Bloc displeasure with Truman's policies in Asia. The hearings dragged on until late September, and although Butterworth won confirmation, his reputation was done serious damage. For the China Bloc in Congress he became, as Styles Bridges publicly accused him, "...the symbol of failure and of a tragic era in our relations with China."[4]

Also in the summer of 1949, legislative action on the Mutual Defense Assistance Act commenced. This executive branch initiative was originally intended to bolster the members of the newly created North Atlantic alliance by allocating funds for military aid through a Military Assistance Program (MAP).[5] However, the bill was eventually broadened to provide monies worldwide to nations engaged in fighting communism. Consequently, the China Bloc, led by Senator William Knowland (R, California), launched an offensive to include MAP funds for Nationalist China. Although MAP funds for China was a relatively inconsequential part of the overall bill, the ensuing debate on this issue was bitter and partisan. At one point, stalemate over China MAP funds threatened to preclude passage of the legislation. Based on the KMT's poor showing to date, administration supporters argued that allocating funds for China would be a criminal waste. China Bloc members countered that the Nationalists were fighting communism as much as any nation and deserved support—even at the eleventh hour. As ever, this group took advantage of the opportunity to decry China policy and policymakers. It was not until September 28th that the bill passed both houses. When the smoke cleared, the Act provided military assistance funds for the North Atlantic Treaty countries (Title I), Greece and Turkey (Title II), and Iran, Korea, and the Philippines (Title III). The battle for China MAP funds ended in a draw. While no funds were allocated specifically for the KMT, $75 million was appropriated for the "general area" of China. Section 303 of Title III stated that:

> In consideration of the concern of the United States in the present situation in China, there is hereby authorized to be appropriated to the President, out of any moneys in the Treasury not otherwise appropriated, the sum of $75,000,000 in addition to funds otherwise provided as an emergency fund for the President, which may be expended to accomplish *in that general area* the policies and purposes declared in this Act. Certification by the President of the amounts expended out of funds authorized hereunder, and that it is inadvisable to specify the nature of such expenditures, shall be deemed a sufficient voucher for the amounts expended.[6]

All parties were satisfied. The wording of Section 303 did not obligate the administration to provide MAP monies to the Chinese. Indeed, as Robert Blum has effectively argued, 303 funds allowed Truman and Acheson to plan support for countering communism in Indochina instead.[7] China Bloc members were satisfied because they believed, mistakenly, that by authorizing the President discretionary funds Truman might actually conduct covert operations in support of isolated Nationalist forces still holding out against the CCP.[8]

Unfortunately, another result of the MAP debates was the collapse of bipartisanship on Far Eastern policy. But that was certainly helped along by the publication of the controversial China *White Paper* on August 4th. Acheson had hoped that the *White Paper* would put to rest, once and for all, the argument that CCP victory on the mainland could have been averted by greater American efforts. It was a bold attempt to explain a century of revolution, the failures of the Nationalists, and the impotence of substantial American assistance without concomitant internal reforms by Chiang Kai-shek. Unfortunately, the document was unreadable to the average citizen, and in the end only served to rally the China Bloc to charge the administration with abandoning a steadfast ally from World War II. In short, the document backfired. But the *White Paper* was only one salient of a two-pronged offensive by State. The *White Paper*, it was hoped, would clear up misconceptions about past policies; but it was future policies toward Asia which concerned the Secretary of State. Consequently, when the *White Paper* was released, Acheson announced the formation of a group of advisers not in government who would help State develop a Far Eastern policy which would face up to the challenge of new regional realities. Fully integrated into the State Department, these consultants would have access to officials, documents, and be free to consult with Asia experts in academia and the business community. Two men were selected to work under Ambassador-at-Large Philip Jessup in this new group; Everett Case, President of Colgate University, and Raymond Fosdick, a former President of the Rockefeller Foundation. Together, the three became known alternately as the "wise men," the "Jessup Committee," and the "Far Eastern Consultants." Acheson hoped that they would be able to assist State in forging a new consensus in Far Eastern affairs which could not be attacked by partisan interests.[9] Their challenge was great. They were to suggest policies which could accommodate growing Asian nationalism while at the same time counter the spread of communism.[10]

The Department of Defense

But Congress was not the only source of domestic trouble for Acheson. The *White Paper* provided another occasion for disagreement between Secretary of Defense Louis A. Johnson and Dean Acheson. The personal animosity between these two men was spilling over into policy issues; and China policy was an area which was more and more becoming an area of glaring disagreement between the two.[11]

The *White Paper* had been in preparation in the Department of State since April 1949 under Butterworth's overall direction, and with Jessup as editor. The final draft, a tome of 1,054 pages, was completed in mid-July. Considering the fact that much of the document dealt with U.S.-China military relations during the Second World War and post-war military assistance to the KMT, it is truly amazing that the Department of Defense was never intimately involved in its preparation. One must wonder if Acheson purposely kept DoD in the dark. It was Truman who suggested to Acheson on July 14th that the Pentagon be given a chance to review it.[12] Originally scheduled for publication on July 22nd, DoD was only given one week to comment.[13] This short suspense must have annoyed Johnson to no end. However, he was able to trip-up Acheson, if only ever so slightly. On July 21st, on the eve of the original publication date, the Secretary of Defense forwarded the views of the JCS. The Joint Chiefs objected to publishing the document until the U.S. Communications Intelligence Board could be certain that release of the myriad of formerly classified messages in the *White Paper* did not compromise signals intelligence.[14] The document was submitted for review and received clearance from the Intelligence Board on July 28th.[15] Ultimately, Johnson was only able to delay its publication by two weeks. Nevertheless, his objections to publishing the *White Paper* went beyond intelligence security concerns. Johnson was fundamentally opposed to a document which threatened to pull the rug out from under the KMT in what appeared to be their final hours. To Acheson, he posed the fundamental question: "Does its publication serve the national interests?" He also asked Acheson for assurances that "...nothing will be said or written by the Department of State which indicates that the National Military Establishment, or its officials, have participated in preparation or publication of the Paper." Acheson gave Johnson the assurances he requested. The Secretary of State also assured Johnson that it was his belief, as well as that of the President's, that the national interest was served by publishing the document. He told Johnson that there is a "...pressing necessity for informing the Congress and the American people concerning the facts bearing upon our relations with China..." so that past problems are not now compounded.[16] And so, over Johnson's reservations, the *White Paper* was published.

United States-CCP Relations

The Chinese communists also proved troublesome throughout the spring, summer, and fall of 1949. Their actions sent mixed signals to Washington, making it difficult for State to determine whether the CCP was already in the Soviet camp, or whether they could be weaned from Moscow.

On the one hand, the communists were exhibiting very blatant anti-Americanism. The most publicized act of CCP hostility was the arrest and trial of Mukden Consul General Angus Ward and the confinement of the Consulate staff; an affair which lasted from November 1948 to December 1949.[17] Equally outrageous was the break-in of Ambassador Stuart's personal quarters by PLA soldiers on the morning of April 25th; the day the communists took Nanking. The ambassador was still in bed when a dozen red soldiers rousted him out of his sleep and scuffled with his assistants. The soldiers soon departed and Stuart was safe; but the incident shook both the ambassador and Washington.[18] Also, throughout the spring of 1949, CCP propaganda took on an ominous cast. The North Atlantic Treaty, signed in April, was denounced in CCP radio editorials. It was declared that in the event of a general war, China would stand by its "ally, the Soviet Union."[19] By then, even Ambassador Stuart was having doubts about the communists. He reported to Washington that communist pronouncements were more and more being colored with "vitriolic abuse" of the United States.[20] Most disturbing, at least in retrospect, was the publication between June and August of a series of speeches and articles by Mao Tse-tung. *On the People's Democratic Dictatorship,* (June 30th) declared that China would have to "lean to one side." *Cast Away Illusions, Prepare for Struggle* (August 14th), and *Farewell, Leighton Stuart* (August 18th) attacked Acheson, his Letter of Transmittal in the *White Paper,* and U.S. policy toward China.[21]

On the other hand, there was still good reason to believe that the Chinese communists were not opposed to accommodation with Washington. Significantly, it was in April and May that the first Stuart-Huang talks occurred and the "Chou *Demarche"* was delivered."[22] Both Huang Hua and Chou En-lai expressed the interest of the CCP in recognition and economic aid from the United States. Chou En-lai even intimated that the party leadership was split between moderates who believed that only the West could provide the economic assistance needed by China to modernize and radicals who were determined to look to the Soviets for such help. Foreign Service Officers debated the true motives behind these events and their implications.[23] Acheson, however, saw in them the correctness of the policy of pursuing Chinese Titoism.[24] Indeed, in August, he reported to the NSC that State was continuing to implement actions in support that goal. Although the communists did not recognize U.S. diplomatic personnel, State FSO's were attempting to maintain contact with local CCP officials. In CCP-controlled areas, United States Information Service (USIS) programs were being carried out "within the limits imposed by those authorities." Voice of America (VOA) radio programs in Mandarin had been doubled and an English and Cantonese service was established and transmitting. Acheson went on to explain that:

> One of the objectives of the Voice of America and other informational programs within China is to foster possible rifts between Chinese Communists and the USSR by emphasizing the imperialistic aims of the USSR in China as evidenced in Manchuria, Sinkiang, and Mongolia and by destroying the fiction that the USSR is the champion and protector of nationalism. Means are being sought...regarding trade policy with China, for exploiting possible rifts between the Chinese Communists and the USSR. As the Communist organizational structure in China emerges more clearly, opportunities will be sought to create and exploit any rifts between the Stalinists and other elements in China.[25]

But the issue of Taiwan had begun to loom as a major impediment to Washington's pursuit of Chinese Titoism. Taiwan was a ready-made issue which the Soviets could use, and did use, to counter U.S. propaganda. For example, in June, Moscow's foreign affairs weekly, *New Times,* ran an article which alleged that the FLR was actually the creation of the U.S. clandestine service. It was further stated that the U.S. was planning to incite this group of "Formosan quislings and reactionaries" to stage a rebellion, declare independence, and appeal to the United Nations for American occupation troops.[26] In July, the CCP's news service, *Hsinhua,* picked up the article and published it under the title, "American Imperialism in Taiwan."[27] In Tientsin, the U.S. Consul General reported rumors that communist soldiers were being told that the CCP would soon have to invade Taiwan because it was believed that it was virtually a U.S. territory ruled by MacArthur.[28] Also, during June talks between Ambassador Stuart's personal secretary, Philip Fugh, and Huang Hua, the issue of Taiwan was reported to have come up. Fugh related to Stuart that Huang wished the ambassador to press State to make a "...public statement...about the legal aspects of the island..." (presumably a reiteration of the Cairo Declaration) and for the U.S. Government to discourage Chiang Kai-shek from establishing a base there.[29]

Problems on Taiwan

Finally, in the summer of 1949, the situation on Taiwan itself presented Washington with a good number of problems. The fall of Shanghai on May 25th sent another massive wave of refugees to

Taiwan; many of them retreating Nationalist troops. By the first of July it was estimated that 300,000 KMT soldiers were now on the island.[30] By June the strain was showing. Every conceivable area in which troops could be billeted was taken over. Harbor activities in Keelung were once again at a standstill. Rice was nowhere to be bought. Soldiers continued to commandeer what they wanted. It was reported that Formosans were beginning to listen to CCP broadcasts, and defeatism washed over soldiers and civilians alike. Provincial officials who could escape to the United States did so. The American ECA representative reported that the economy was "completely out of hand" and requested to be recalled.[31] As the weeks rolled on public order began to break down. Looting was on the rise. Hostile acts against foreigners began to occur. By the end of the summer the Provincial Government was holding daily executions of those disturbing public order.[32] Additionally, all Hong Kong English language newspapers were banned.[33]

The situation on Taiwan, and in Washington, became even more complicated by the reemergence of Chiang Kai-shek. In late June, the U.S. Consulate in Taipei reported rumors that the Gimo was back on the island.[34] The guesswork on this issue was soon eliminated. On July 4th, Chiang, in Taipei, granted an interview to Clyde Farnsworth of Scripps-Howard. The Generalissimo declared his continued "revolutionary leadership" of the Chinese people, called for aid from the United States, denounced the Soviets as treaty breakers "bent upon world domination," and predicted that the Chinese people would soon rise up to overthrow the communists. Chiang also pointed out, in a lengthy discourse, that Mao Tse-tung was no Tito, and that a policy based on this hope was doomed to fail. It was also announced by Chiang that Taiwan would be the site of KMT Provisional Headquarters.[35] With this, Taiwan officially became the last political and military bastion of Republican China.

Chiang's interview pulled the rug out from under Acting President Li Tsung-jen who was now left stranded on the mainland, virtually cut-off from KMT assets on Taiwan. At the same time, Chiang's reemergence also precipitated a power struggle between the leading military men on Taiwan. Two issues were at hand. The first issue encompassed control of the Southeast China Headquarters; a new organization established by Chiang for the immediate defense of Taiwan. In this competition, Ch'en Ch'eng and P'eng Meng-chi were pitted against Sun Li-jen; all of whom were attempting to win command from Chiang. At the same time, the newly arrived commanders of the KMT Air Force (General Chou Chih-jou), Navy (Admiral Kwei Yung-ching), and Armored Command (General Chiang Wei-kuo) were refusing to subordinate the remnants of their units to anyone but Chiang himself. Newly-appointed Consul General John J. MacDonald watched the factions jockey with horror. As happened on the mainland, he reported, the military, once again under Chiang, was playing politics "while Rome burns."[36]

But Chiang did not confine himself to stirring up KMT politics. In the summer of 1949 he stepped out into the realm of international diplomacy. In mid-July he travelled to Baguio in the Philippines to meet with President Elpidio Quirino. There he attempted to enlist Quirino in an effort to form a "Far East Union" ostensibly to combat communism in East Asia and the Pacific. K.C. Wu, a member of the Gimo's delegation, gave Edgar in Taipei a full debriefing of the trip so that Washington could have "the whole story." According to Wu, Chiang viewed China, Korea, and the Philippines as "Far East orphans" as a result of the State Department's unwillingness to to take decisive action to counter communism in Asia. The pact (Quirino preferred "Pacific Union" to Far East Union) would mirror the North Atlantic Treaty in its aims. Allegedly, Chiang would invite Thailand and Quirino would invite Indonesia to join in the pact. Those countries in the British camp (Australia, New Zealand, Burma, and India) would not be approached. Whether Indochina would be invited to join depended on the fate of Bao Dai. Japan would not be contacted until it could be determined if an approach to Japan meant an approach to MacArthur. The Gimo's initiative was viewed by State as an attempt gain some publicity and stir up trouble for the administration with a Congress Chiang was sure would rise once again to support his cause. K.C. Wu, however, vehemently denied that this was the Generalissimo's intent. U.S. intelligence was also able to learn that during his meeting with Quirino, Chiang raised the possibility of transferring a portion of the KMT's gold reserves on Taiwan to the Philippines—just in case.[37]

Escalating troubles in Taiwan; deteriorating economic conditions, in-fighting between generals, and the KMT's annoying international initiatives, were viewed by Dean Acheson as a direct result of Chiang Kai-shek's meddling. And when in September, in a conversation with Governor Dewey, the latter suggested that Henry Luce be sent "quietly" to Taiwan to persuade the Gimo to retire in exile from the scene (but not in the U.S. or France), the Secretary of State did not object.[38] The Gimo's reemergence on the island was another major obstacle to be faced by State in its attempt to save Taiwan from collapse.

Thus, as Taiwan policy underwent review it took place in most complicated foreign and domestic context.

6.2 MERCHANT REPORTS BACK TO STATE

On May 24th, Merchant submitted to Walton Butterworth his formal assessment of the situation on Taiwan and the prospects for the success of Taiwan policy as laid down in NSC 37/2 and NSC 37/5. In doing so, he reiterated the themes contained in his last messages from Taipei (see Chapter 5), and reopened the issue of U.S. policy toward the island.

"No one," Merchant offered, "could have had very high hopes that economic and diplomatic steps alone could guarantee the denial of Formosa to a government unfriendly to us." Furthermore, he stated that since the time that current Taiwan policy was first formulated, there had been significant developments on the island that needed to be factored into policy. First, positive developments. The current government on Taiwan, he reported, was determined to defend the island against the CCP, both internally and externally. This was in the interests of the U.S. Government, and Washington need not do anything to encourage this, "...for it is based on the strongest of all instincts, personal self-preservation." Moreover, there was no reason to believe that a communist invasion of Taiwan was imminent. Such an operation, Merchant believed, would take at least six months to prepare for. Consequently, the U.S. now had more time than it thought to assess its policy. On the negative side, Merchant submitted that there was no indigenous revolutionary organization on Taiwan that is capable of overthrowing the KMT. The Nationalists now had enough troops on the island to bloodily suppress a revolt. Also mitigating against the original plan for Taiwan was the fact that the island's economy was in such shambles that only a major U.S. economic effort could prop it up. Finally, and most damning, Merchant saw no prospect of U.S. diplomatic overtures having any significant impact on the political style of the ruling authorities on Taiwan.

> To summarize and over-simplify, we find ourselves faced on Formosa with a situation very similar to that which confronted us on the Mainland a year ago. The Government in power is corrupt and incompetent. Self preservation dictates that it advance our national interest in the process of attempting to preserve its collective neck. The people which it rules hate not only the Government but will hate any foreign country which morally and materially gives its support to that Government. Yet, there is no possibility, short of the dangerous and risky effort to finance and promote a coup d'etat, that the present Government will be replaced or alter its character in the direction of liberal political rule and wise economic action.

More than likely, the communists would be able to take the island by infiltration and political work. Consequently, Merchant believed that armed intervention was the only action which could guarantee the security of Taiwan. But in as much as the JCS continued to refuse to support such a move, and the conditions he outlined were operative, it was clear that the current policy was doomed to failure. Therefore, Merchant recommended that the matter of Taiwan be raised by State in the NSC to attempt to find a way to adjust policy.

In recommending that the issue be reopened, Merchant offered three possible lines of action. The first alternative was to proceed with the program engendered in NSC 37/2 and 37/5. Merchant, however, saw no positive results which could come from it. While economic aid might provide encouragement to Taipei, ECA assistance could only slow down, not cure, the island's economic ills. Furthermore, Merchant assessed that this program would undermine "the reservoir of Formosan goodwill to America," give the communists a "ready-made irredentist weapon for their propaganda," and "increase, rather than reduce the vulnerability of many Chinese on this island as well as the Formosans themselves to Communist agitation." The second alternative was to make a bold economic and security commitment to Taiwan. This Merchant rejected because it would create a much more serious challenge to the CCP, undermine the ultimate goal of pursuing Titoism, and commit U.S. forces to defend the island; an option which the Pentagon continued to reject. Ultimately, the course of action which Merchant recommended was one which he described as one of "calculated inaction colored with opportunism." The island was not in any real danger at the moment, and the authorities were already determined to make a stand. Consequently, the U.S. now had a window of opportunity to consult with other friendly nations interested in keeping the island out of CCP hands and raise the issue of Taiwan in the United Nations. Implied, though not stated, was the desire to place Taiwan under a U.N. Trusteeship.[39]

Merchant's assessment made an impact within State. Throughout the last week in June he consulted with George Kennan and John Davies (Policy Planning Staff), and Philip Sprouse and Kenneth Krentz (former Consul General in Taipei) from FE's Division of Chinese Affairs. These men concurred with Merchant's basic arguments. Together, they redrafted and modified Merchant's 24 May report into a much tighter memorandum intended for the Executive Secretary of the NSC. It was stated up front that State believed that "...United States policy with respect to Formosa should be re-examined" and that the current NSC policy holds "little prospect" of attaining United States objectives. Merchant's original paragraph on overall conditions was recast and made more powerful:

> The fact is that we face on Formosa today a situation analogous to that which confronted us on the mainland of China a year ago. The government in power is corrupt and incompetent. It lacks the wisdom and will to take the necessary political and economic steps to modify the deep and growing resentment of the Formosans. The burden of supporting the mass of nationalist troops and other governmental establishments is so great as to accelerate the economic disintegration of the island. Moreover, economic aid from outside cannot in the absence of a basic change in the government alter or cure this situation, and so long as it endures the passage of Formosa under Communist control, by external or internal action is only a matter of time.

The same three possible courses of action were again put forward. However, the negative implications of both bolder economic and military support (the first alternative), and continuing the current policies in NSC 37/2 and 37/5 (the second alternative; now termed "a policy of calculated inaction") were more strongly worded. The hands of Kennan and Davies were evident in the pointed statements made about the need to "...seek and exploit fissures between China and the U.S.S.R." This argument, central to State's overall China policy, mitigated against greater economic and military support. Sprouse, Merchant, and Krentz left their mark on the reason why continuing along with current policies was unacceptable. It was pointed out that it was daily becoming uncertain how long the authorities on Taiwan would be able to maintain "...the will and ability to resist any external or internal attack..." against the communists.

The course of action this group recommended, in almost frantic fashion, was "...immediate commital of the problem of Formosa to the United Nations." It was suggested that a "...friendly and interested power, such as India or the Philippines..." be persuaded to place the question of Taiwan on the agenda of the U.N. Trusteeship Council and request "...that a temporary trusteeship be established by the United Nations over Formosa until such time as its people are given the opportunity in a free and secret election to decide their own destiny." The group further recommended that at the time that Taiwan is raised in the U.N. there be issued a "...forthright public statement by the Secretary of State disclaiming for the United States any designs, territorial or otherwise, on Formosa." (A draft statement was attached to this paper). It was the belief of this group of drafters that such a course of action, while not without disadvantages, would relieve the United States "...of any accusation that it was acting unilaterally and imperialistically." They believed that the "...right of self-determination is difficult to quarrel with and is certainly appealing throughout Asia." They further argued that the placing of Taiwan on the U.N. agenda might even serve "...as a deterrent to overt or covert action by the Chinese Communists to take over the island."

The new memorandum was sent to Walton Butterworth, who concurred with the group that theirs was a reasonable paper. Butterworth then forwarded the memo to Assistant Secretary of State Dean Rusk for his thoughts and for permission to forward the paper to the NSC. Butterworth added in his cover letter to Rusk that some discussion on the tactics of raising the issue in the U.N. were still warranted. He believed that the British should be consulted immediately. After that, an approach to the Indians, the Philippines, and Australia should be made to determine which of the three should raise the issue in the General Assembly. Ultimately, Butterworth thought that those three nations should be given joint administrative power over Taiwan in any trusteeship arrangement and that the U.S. should have no affiliation with it whatsoever.[40]

In the course of the next two weeks, (3 through 15 June) Dean Rusk mulled over the paper forwarded by Butterworth. At the same time, both Rusk and Butterworth consulted with State's Division of United Nations Affairs to determine both the feasibility and mechanics of securing a United Nations Trusteeship for Taiwan. While these issues were being researched, all parties in State were daily more and more convinced of the wisdom of revising policy toward Taiwan. All were becoming more proactive in devising possible schemes to preclude the island's passage to the communists. The urgency with which they labored was a function of the bleak reports they were receiving about possible defections from the KMT camp. For example, unconfirmed intelligence reports alleged that General P'eng Meng-chi was currently in Hong Kong conferring with communist agents. This report was the nightmare all had dreaded. It was believed that if P'eng went over to the CCP he could very well precipitate a complete takeover of the island from within. His troop strength was far greater than that of Sun Li-jen's. Sun's forces, each day, were being pared down by a jealous Gimo. There was also little doubt that P'eng was capable of major treachery, for he was considered "...one of the most thoroughgoing scoundrels in the Chinese Army." This report, in Kenneth Krentz's opinion, made action on Taiwan absolutely urgent, because the U.S. Government could now be faced with a "...*fait accompli* within a matter of weeks which would make the situation irretrievable..."[41]

Unfortunately, after looking into the matter, it was determined that a U.N. trusteeship for Taiwan was not currently within the realm of possibility. First, it was pointed out by Dean Rusk's staff that the U.N.'s limited resources would make it virtually incumbent upon the United States "...to accept a major share of responsibility..." for supporting and supervising a trusteeship. This, of course, would place the U.S. in too high profile a role on the island and undermine other major policy goals. Second, there would have to be a public justification for reversing the Cairo Declaration. Third, it was pointed out that many member nations of the U.N. were reluctant to have that organization embroiled in issues related to the settlement of the Second World War. Fourth, the Nationalist Chinese delegation might fight such a move. Fifth, unless Taiwan were invaded by the CCP, or the island was plunged into widespread civil war, an appeal for U.N. intervention by Formosan natives would not be considered justified under current regulations. Sixth, even if the Trusteeship Council raised the issue of Taiwan in its upcoming meeting (end of June), it was believed that the most it would do would be to pass on to the General Assembly (GA) responsibility for major decisions. In as much as the GA was not to convene until the following autumn, it could be five or six months before any real action to save the island could be accomplished. In that amount of time Taiwan could very well fall. Finally, even if a plebiscite were held on Taiwan, the possibility that the Formosans would vote for a return to the mainland could not be discounted.[42]

Dean Rusk strongly agreed with Butterworth that the situation in Taiwan did in fact require an immediate reassessment of policy. Consequently, Rusk had Merchant take the kernal of latter's arguments about the need for a policy relook, his appraisal of deteriorating conditions on Taiwan, and Merchant's prophesy that NSC 37/2 and 37/5 would fail, and radically redraft the memorandum for the NSC. Added to it, Rusk had Merchant review for the NSC why United Nations action would not suffice. The new conclusions of State's memorandum for the NSC were even more ominous than the original. It deemed a full economic and military commitment by the United States to Taiwan as the only way in which the island could be saved. The new memorandum also called upon the Pentagon to very seriously consider the consequences of a Taiwan in communist hands.

> The almost certain prospect of ultimate failure for our present policy suggests the necessity of a reassessment by the Joint Chiefs of Staff of the strategic implications to the United States of the passage of control of Formosa to a chinese national communist government, with a view to a reaffirmation or modification of their statement, as expressed in NSC 37/3, that United States military forces are not available for the occupation or defense of the island. In this connection, it is believed that nothing short of the assumption of administrative responsibility for the civilian rule and economy of the island by the United States, in addition to military responsibility for its defense, would provide the assurance of internal tranquility neccesary to our purpose.[43]

This newest draft was not sent out to the NSC. Its conclusions were debated within State. Given the poor prospects for United Nations action, deteriorating conditions on Taiwan, and the fact that this newest memorandum in actuality sent Taiwan policy back to the drawing board, Kennan and the PPS had another suggestion. As Merchant confided to Butterworth, "It is now my understanding that Mr. Kennan proposes a different course of action and that Mr. Davies is drafting a paper on the subject for the Under Secretary."[44]

6.3 KENNAN'S RADICAL SOLUTION

Merchant's statement that Kennan was proposing "a different course of action" was an understatement of the highest order. Kennan's suggestion for the salvation of Taiwan, set forth in PPS 53, "United States Policy Toward Formosa and the Pescadores," was bold beyond words. What he recommended was an American military action to depose the Nationalist Government on Taiwan and the establishment of either a unilateral occupation of the island, or one jointly administered by a select group of nations that defeated Japan in the Second World War.[45]

Kennan began his paper by pointing out, as others in State had already, that the current NSC policy toward Taiwan was doomed to fail. He then got right to the point.

> It would now seem clear that the only reasonably sure chance of denying Formosa and the Pescadores to the Communists and insulating the islands from mainland authority would lie in the removal of the present Nationalist administrators from the islands and in the establishment of a provisional international or U.S. regime which would invoke the principle of self-determination for the islanders and would eventually, prior to a Japanese peace settlement, conduct a plebiscite to determine the ultimate disposition of Formosa and the Pescadores. Formosan separatism is the only concept which has sufficient grass-roots appeal to resist communism.

Kennan then offered that there were only two ways in which a change in administration of the island could take place. One way would be to "induce" other Asian powers to "take the lead" in mounting an international political offensive to wrest control of Taiwan from the KMT. The other way would be for the United States to declare that the assumptions upon which the Cairo Declaration was promulgated were no longer valid, and unilaterally intervene and take over the administration of the islands. Either of these courses of action, Kennan pointed out, would have to be accomplished by military intervention by the United States and require the Pentagon to reverse its current position. Either course, he went on, would provide the Kremlin and the CCP with a major propaganda vehicle. Finally, he submitted, both courses of action would make it incumbent upon the United States to forcibly remove from Taiwan the many KMT forces on the island, and force the repatriation of thousands of mainland refugees. Kennan admitted that this would involve "...a considerable amount of pushing people around, which would be unpleasant and might lead to serious moral conflicts within our own people and government." But Kennan did not feel that the U.S. should be constrained by these negative factors if it was serious about saving Taiwan.

Ultimately, Kennan felt that the "international outcry" approach to deposing the KMT would require the cooperation of so many individuals and nations as to make it almost impossible to accomplish. Consequently, the PPS Director offered that only unilateral U.S. action would be timely and successful. He then reported that he had been raising this possibility with others in State, and that no one he spoke with concurred with his solution. He pointed out that all in State believed that the U.S. Government should "reconcile" itself "...to the prospect of Formosa's falling into the hands of the Chinese Communists." Kennan rejected this notion. "I personally feel," he went on, that if the U.S. intervened unilaterally, and it was "...carried through with sufficient resolution, speed, ruthlessness, and self-assurance, the way Theodore Roosevelt might have done it, it would be not only successful but would have an electrifying effect in this country and throughout the Far East." He admitted that he had no basis to believe this except his own instincts, and that the success of his plan would depend upon the President "having the same instinctive concept and a readiness to assume gladly and with conviction" the risks involved. Intervention would depend as well on the willingness of the military to take on an invasion. Consequently, Kennan offered this solution to Acheson with great reservations. He suggested that the Secretary discuss this idea with the President and the other members of the NSC. He told Acheson that he should point out to all that this was only way in which Taiwan could be spared from the communists. "If they feel as strongly as I do," he wrote, "that our situation in the Far East will not permit further inaction in areas where our military and economic capabilities would be adequate to meet the possible commitments flowing from intervention; if they agree, as the NME has hitherto been reluctant to do, that Formosa and the Pescadores is such an area; and if they are prepared to assume their full share of the responsibility for initiating and pursuing such a course—then my personal view is that we should take the plunge."

If on the other hand, said Kennan, the NSC is unwilling to take this action, then State should have it formally recorded that in its view later attempts to save Taiwan will be ineffectual. He implied that U.S.

planners should write off the island as of the moment intervention was rejected. Finally, if intervention was rejected, Kennan, in a rare burst of emotion, stated that the administration should "...set about to prepare U.S. and world opinion as best we can for a possible further significant extension of Chinese Communist control—this time to an area close to our military position in the Ryukyus, close to the Philippines, and relatively inaccessible to military attack by land forces from the mainland in the face of even the most rudimentary air and naval opposition, and above all to an area populated by a dependent people for whom we have a certain specific responsibility and for whom such control would constitute an oppressive alien domination."

Attached to Kennan's basic memorandum was a detailed plan dealing with the political aspects of U.S. intervention (he left military planning to the Pentagon). In it he wove an intricate web of international intrigues involving the U.K., Australia, the Philippines and India which would justify a U.S. invasion. He also outlined some very interesting propaganda and psychological warfare initiatives to gain domestic support as well as assist in some aspects of the military operation. For example, he recommended that the administration begin to leak to the press reports about Nationalist misrule and the plight of the Formosan people. He suggested that the Philippines be urged to grant the FLR a full range of media opportunities to publicly call for autonomy. Kennan also felt that a full chapter in the *White Paper* should be devoted to KMT atrocities and incompetence on Taiwan (in the end, the *White Paper* did address the problems on the island). He also suggested that, prior to invading Taiwan, General Sun Li-jen be afforded the opportunity to throw his lot in with a new independent Formosan government; thereby dividing KMT forces on the island, providing additional forces for fighting KMT holdouts, and having some Chinese representation in the new administration. As for Chiang Kai-shek, Kennan suggested that he be allowed to remain on the island, but in the sole status of a "political refugee."

PPS 53 was never offered to Acheson as a formal, and fully coordinated paper from the Policy Planning Staff. Kennan felt that it was too controversial a paper, and implied that even within the PPS there was little enthusiasm for his suggestions. However, Kennan did forward the paper to Acheson, and may have followed up with conversations with the Secretary. What reactions Acheson had to Kennan's ideas remain unknown.[46]

Nevertheless, the boldness of Kennan's paper was remarkable. His willingness to take the very action which would destroy his own brainchild—the pursuit of Chinese Titoism—was very telling. It bespoke both of his core belief that, ultimately, China did not matter, and represented the frustration many in State were probably feeling in their quest to save Taiwan. And it is telling, as well, that many in State were moving inexorably to the conclusion that Taiwan was becoming a military problem, not a political one. This shift in perspective was probably reinforced by the Central Intelligence Agency. On 16 June, CIA's latest assessment, *Probable Developments In China*, judged that within the "next few months" the CCP would acquire the amphibious capability to invade the island, and that "...US economic and military aid, short of armed intervention, would probably not significantly assist the Nationalists in holding Taiwan..."[47]

6.4 NSC 37/6: FEELING OUT THE DEPARTMENT OF DEFENSE

It was not until August 5th that State was able to produce a paper which all parties concerned—Acheson, Rusk, FE (Butterworth and Merchant), CA (Sprouse and Krentz) and Kennan—considered appropriate for forwarding to the National Security Council. The paper, NSC 37/6, was apparently intended to see if the issue of the strategic importance of Taiwan could evoke an unqualified response from the Pentagon.[48] In it, previous actions pursuant to NSC 37/2 and 37/5 were reviewed, Merchant's assessment of deteriorating conditions were spelled out (his very quotable paragraph "....We face on Formosa today a situation analogous to that which confronted us on the mainland..." was included), and it was pointed out that the island could go under "at any time" due to mutiny and treason, confronting the U.S. with a *"fait accompli."*

Given the situation as it now existed, State called for the NSC to put under review the entire question of policy toward Taiwan. But before doing so, Acheson recommended that the JCS be asked once again to give their views on the importance of the island.

> In view of the foregoing developments, and since there now appears no certain assurance that these islands can be denied to Communist control by political and economic measures alone, the Joint Chiefs of Staff should be asked to review their memorandum dated February 10, 1949, on the strategic importance of Formosa to the United States. Upon receipt of the current views of the Joint Chiefs of Staff, the NSC would be

in a position to review the present policy in Formosa after considering the strategic factor and all political implications arising from our present global foreign policy.

But State had gone through this drill once before. They had continually asked Defense to give an unqualified response to what had always seemed a simple question: how important was Taiwan? This time, Acheson gave the drafters of NSC 37/6 specific guidance to couch their question to the JCS in the most direct manner possible.[49] Consequently, NSC 37/6 continued with a direct query to the JCS. "It would be helpful," it was written, "if the reexamination of the strategic factor by the Joint Chiefs of Staff would include a reply to the following question:"

> Under conditions short of war and on the assumption that in the absence of military measures Formosa and the Pescadores will sooner or later come under Communist control, do the Joint Chiefs of Staff regard these islands as of sufficient military importance to the United States to commit U.S. forces to their occupation?

Then, State went on to offer the JCS even more scenario-specific guidance to mull over when considering the basic question. First, they asked the Pentagon to consider an occupation scenario in which there was "initial opposition from Nationalist forces on the island." Interestingly, this first scenario seemed to take account of Kennan's latest scheme. Second, the Joint Chiefs were asked to consider the consequences of a post-occupation attack from the CCP on the mainland. Finally, the JCS were asked to comment on the implications of a relatively peaceful U.S. occupation "by agreement with existing authorities on the island with implicit responsibility for the maintenance of internal security and external defense." The Pentagon's response to the NSC was requested "as a matter of priority."

6.5 THE PENTAGON IS NOT WILLING TO ACT

On August 22nd, the Department of State received its response from the National Military Establishment.[50] The Joint Chiefs continued to maintain that Taiwan was indeed strategically important to the United States for the reasons originally set forth in NSC 37/3 (February 1949). They also offered that "...the continuing sweep of Communist conquest in China has strengthened that view." However, despite this and other more ominous developments, the Joint Chiefs continued to argue that:

...the strategic importance of Formosa does not justify overt military action, in the event that diplomatic and economic steps prove unsuccessful to prevent Communist domination, so long as the present disparity between our military strength and our global obligations exist, a disparity that may well increase as a result of budgetary limitations and the commitments implicit in the North Atlantic Treaty.

Additionally, the Joint Chiefs, in answering State's basic question, declared that they *"...do not regard Formosa and the Pescadores as of sufficient military importance to the United States, under circumstances set forth above, to commit United States forces to their occupation under conditions short of war and on the assumption that in the absence of military measures these islands will sooner or later come under Communist control."*[51]

Furthermore, the JCS rejected an occupation under conditions in which Nationalist resistance was encountered or which precipitated a CCP invasion on the grounds that either scenario "...could easily lead to the necessity for a relatively major effort, thus making it impossible to meet more important emergencies that might develop elsewhere." Moreover, even if an occupation could be arranged with the consent of the ruling authorities, taking on the responsibility for the island's defense would be a policy almost impossible to reverse, and could in itself lead to greater commitments should the situation demand it. While rejecting any occupation or use of force at the moment, even if it meant the fall of Taiwan, the Joint Chiefs cautioned State and the NSC, once again, that in the event of a general war, national security could very well demand overt military action to defend (or, it was implied, retake) Taiwan. However, they believed that it was preferable "...to face this future contingency as one of the many military problems that must be considered in the event of incipient or actual overt war than to risk undue military commitment in the Formosan area under present circumstances."

Finally, the Joint Chiefs offered that "the probabilities of the Formosa situation" (nice words for Taiwan's inevitable fall to the CCP) made it more important than ever to strengthen and "forestall any weakening" of the position of the U.S. in Asia. Specifically, the importance of the Philippines, the Ryukyus, and Japan, was now "greatly magnified."

It now appeared that the JCS were reconciled to the eventual fall of Taiwan. And while this would be a serious blow to the U.S. position in East Asia, the nation's military planners were not willing to expend precious resources, now stretched ever thinner due to new European commitments, to defend or occupy the island. Even those generals in Washington who had a personal and professional concern with Asia, men such as Albert Wedemeyer, were hard-pressed to endorse the use of force to save Taiwan. Indeed, Wedemeyer, now Army Deputy Chief of Staff for Plans and Combat Operations, was more and more concerned with a strategic perimeter in the Far East which ran from Japan, through the Ryukyus, and to the Philippines. In fact, on August 26th, Wedemeyer wrote to the Assistant Secretary of State for Public Affairs, suggesting that if Taiwan falls, State should consider "information measures" designed to lessen the "ill effects on the governments and peoples" of those nations so as not to weaken their resolve.[52]

6.6   TAIWAN POLICY IS ADJUSTED

The unwillingness of the Joint Chiefs to intervene in Taiwan sent State Department officials scrambling to find a way to ensure that the island could be kept out of CCP control. But the demise of a military option tied their hands considerably. Consequently, diplomatic action was once again considered. Ambassador Jessup tried unsuccessfully to find legal loopholes in the various agreements stemming from the Second World War which could be used to justify an end to Nationalist Chinese possession.[53] At the same time, the British were consulted on their assessment of the situation on the island and possible ways to keep out the communists.

On September 9th, Butterworth, Merchant, and Fulton Freeman (CA) met with members of the British Embassy in Washington. Also present was Mr. Maberly E. Dening, visiting Under Secretary for Far Eastern Affairs from the British Foreign Office. State Department officials gave their British colleagues a frank overview of the situation in Taiwan as they saw it, as well the current views of the United States Government. They also conveyed the views of the Department of Defense as stated in NSC 37/7. Because DoD had ruled out a military option, Merchant told the British, the U.S. Government was now forced back onto diplomatic and economic efforts to save Taiwan. However, Merchant stated that "...the Department was of the opinion that it could not be held indefinitely by the present government; and that the probabilities were that the island would eventually be taken over by the Communists." Merchant pointed out the "illogic" of Taiwan's predicament:

(1) Formosa is completely self-supporting; (2) the Nationalists on Formosa have a well-equipped army, air force and navy; (3) the Communist forces have no air force or navy; (4) the Nationalists on Formosa have an abundance of foreign exchange; (5) it would appear on the surface that the Nationalists under good leadership could establish themselves in an impregnable position for an indefinite period; and yet (6) there is every evidence that the Communists will be able to gain control of the island.

Dening took all of this in with great interest. He then commented on the FLR. He acknowledged that the FLR was opposed to communism; but that was the best that could be said about organization. Their leaders, he submitted, were "unsavory characters." Dening further offered that the possibility of this or any other group in Taiwan successfully appealing to the U.N. for a plebiscite was remote. As long as Chiang Kai-shek remained in control of the island this would not happen. On this point Butterworth was in agreement with his British guest. As the meeting came to a close, Mr. Dening read from a paper prepared for him by the Foreign Office in London on the subject of Taiwan. In it were five salient points. It was the view of the British Government that: (1) both the KMT and the CCP would continue to claim sovereignty over Taiwan; (2) the legal status of Taiwan could not be changed without "Four Power agreement," meaning the inclusion of the Soviets and the Chinese; (3) it was unlikely that the U.N. would be able to resolve the Taiwan question, and that even raising it in that forum would result in more harm than good; (4) the ultimate outcome of control of Taiwan was destined to be determined by "the present struggle between the Communists and the Nationalists;" and (5) Taiwan would probably fall to the CCP and "all that can be done is to hope that occupation of the island by the Communists will not prove disastrous."[54]

These views destroyed any hopes State might have had that the British would assist the U.S. in a United Nations offensive for a Formosan plebiscite and in reversing the Cairo Declaration. It made clear as well, that the British could not be counted upon for support should the U.S. decide to exercise a military option in the future. Consequently, on October 6th, State submitted to the National Security Council a new document, NSC 37/8.[55]

The document began by citing State's previous judgment that conditions on Taiwan made the passage of the island to Communist hands quite probable. Added to this was a recent CIA assessment that without U.S. military intervention the island "probably will be under Chinese Communist control by the end of 1950." It was further stated up front that recent conversations with the British indicated that London was reconciled to the ultimate fall of Taiwan and that the British government could not suggest any realistic measures which could keep this from happening. It was further pointed out that the Joint Chiefs did not consider Taiwan so important strategically as to justify overt military action. Then, the very crucial point was made that, given the Pentagon's assessment, State judged that, *"The political importance of Formosa does not give rise to considerations of such importance as to justify overriding, on political grounds, the views of the Joint Chiefs of Staff...respecting the military importance of the islands."*[56] Indeed, State believed that the use of military force would be destructive to its overall aim of fostering a split between the CCP and CPSU.

The paper then rhetorically offered a program of "greatly expanded" economic aid as a possible course of action, coupled, perhaps, with a program of military assistance—even the reestablishment of a military advisory group. However, this alternative was rejected out of hand. It was argued that the present crisis on Taiwan was not the result of lack of arms or lack of funds; there was plenty of both to be found on the island. To the contrary, the problem on Taiwan was singularly the result of "...the transfer to the Island of the ills and malpractices that have characterized the Kuomintang in China." Were the U.S. to now engage in an expanded program of military and economic assistance, then, it was argued, the rulers on the island would be lulled into a false sense of security that Washington felt Taiwan so important strategically that it would never let it go under. At the same time, increased aid would destroy any incentives for the present rulers on Taiwan to take for themselves those measures of self-help, politically and economically, that would ensure their survival. Furthermore, increased aid at this time would commit the prestige (and resources) of the U.S. Government to a regime that is determined to destroy itself. It would invite charges of U.S. imperialism in China and throughout Asia, and possibly consolidate Formosan support behind a Communist government. It would "...nullify our efforts to exploit Chinese irredentism arising from Soviet action in the North."

What State did offer as a course of action was a modification to the present policy toward Taiwan as delineated in NSC 37/2 and 37/5. It was recommended that the current "modest" level of ECA assistance be continued; just enough of a carrot to keep spirits on the island bolstered, and point out the possibility of greater aid in the future.[57] But the crux of the new policy would be a diplomatic initiative. The Chinese on Taiwan had to be made to understand that the United States was not going to commit troops to defend the island; that they held their fate in their own hands, and that the degree of U.S. economic support for Taiwan would be directly tied to efforts they made on their own behalf to cure economic and political ills of their own making. And since "...the real source of authority on Formosa..." was now the Generalissimo himself, State strongly recommended that the following *demarche* be directed to him personally:

> The U.S. has no designs on Formosa and seeks no military bases or special privileges of any kind on the island. The U.S. Government will not commit any of its armed forces to the defense of the island. It is concerned, however, lest the chaos of the mainland spread to Formosa and believes that a higher level of political and economic well-being must be provided if serious unrest is to be avoided and the legitimate aspirations of the population of Formosa met. The previous misgovernment of Formosa has been a cause for serious concern on the part of the U.S. and there have been disturbing indications of unrest among the population of Formosa as civilian refugees and military forces have arrived in large numbers on the island. The U.S. attitude toward Formosa will depend largely on the action of the present Chinese administration in establishing an efficient administration which would seek to bring to the people a higher level of political and economic well-being. The resources on the Island, together with the material assets available to the Chinese administration are believed to be sufficient to enable that administration substantially to improve conditions through its own efforts. Unless effective steps are taken initially by the Chinese administration itself, external aid would be of little benefit and would be largely dissipated. The U.S. Government will, therefore, continue to watch with interest the efforts of the Chinese administration to initiate those measures which are necessary to provide the basis of effective administration and effective utilization of the resources of Formosa. While the U.S. Government will continue to furnish economic assistance to Formosa under existing legislation, the provision of any additional aid will depend upon the future performance of the Chinese administration on Formosa.

State further believed that "maximum effectiveness" would be derived from this *demarche* if it was accompanied by a public statement to both the Chinese and American peoples. The proposed press release which was drafted read as follows:

> Since V-J Day, this Government has watched with deep concern periods of serious misgovernment of Formosa. In recent months the civil conflict in China has spread over a wider area and there have been disturbing indications of unrest among the population of Formosa, as civilian refugees and Chinese military forces have arrived in large numbers on the island, with serious resultant disruption of the economy.
>
> The United States has no armed forces on Formosa and no intention of placing such forces there; it seeks no military bases or special privileges of any character whatsoever on the island. It is, however, rightfully concerned for the peace, prosperity and future of those whose home is on Formosa, to the liberation to which it contributed. The United States Government would view with concern the spread of chaos from the mainland to Formosa and this Government believes that a higher level of political and economic well-being must be provided if serious unrest is to be avoided and the legitimate aspirations of the population of Formosa met.
>
> The United States is continuing the implementation of the ECA economic assistance program under existing legislation on Formosa with a view to assisting in bringing economic and political stability to the population of the island. The Chinese administration on Formosa has sufficient resources at its command to develop and defend the island for months if not years to come, if these resources are used effectively. This Government will continue to follow closely the manner in which existing resources are developed and used, for this will be a major factor in determining the extent to which further United States aid might be helpful.[58]

This course of action—sending a bolt of reality through the Gimo—now seemed to State to be the only real hope for Taiwan's salvation. The paper concluded by recommending that this course of action be brought before the NSC, approved, and sent to the President for his signature.

Before the paper was forwarded on to the NSC, it was sent to Philip Jessup (still working U.N. affairs in New York), and Far Eastern consultant Raymond Fosdick for final coordination.[59] Fosdick was not bothered by State's new paper. "I think it is the best we can do," he commented, "and it doesn't discourage me."[60] Charles Yost, an advisor to Jessup at the U.N., told the latter that he was "not happy about the proposed policy..." but was "...inclined to believe that we have no alternative but to accept it..." because of "...the attitude of the JCS..., the unwisdom of our supporting Chiang without being able to control him; and the improbability of being able to obtain UN control of the island." And although he believed this policy would not be successful in preventing the fall of Taiwan, Yost, too, came to the conclusion that it was the best State could do. However, Yost did take exception to the draft public statement. He believed that the first paragraph could very well incite Formosan unrest, and that the very last sentence might unduly raise Chiang's hopes "...of aid beyond which we are unlikely to furnish."[61] For his part, Jessup agreed with Yost's comments about the press release. However, Jessup also felt that ECA aid should be increased to Taiwan. Finally, Jessup was concerned about whom would deliver the demarche to Chiang. He wanted to be sure that the person delivering it could do so with force and effectiveness.[62] In the end, however, neither Jessup nor Yost desired to stop NSC 37/8 from going forward. Merchant assured both that Butterworth would give them an opportunity to edit or redraft the press release should the NSC adopt State's paper. Furthermore, they would be consulted on procedural details such as how the *demarche* would actually be delivered.[63] With that, NSC 37/8 was sent to NSC Executive Secretary Sidney Souers.

NSC 37/8 was taken up by the NSC at its 47th meeting, held either on the 19th or 20th of October. The group which convened was relatively small. In the absence of the President, the meeting was chaired by Secretary of State Acheson and attended by Defense Secretary Louis Johnson, JCS Chairman Omar Bradley, Treasury Secretary Snyder and Mr. William C. Foster, Deputy Administrator of the ECA. Taiwan was not the only issue on the agenda. Discussions were also held on the status of negotiations for a treaty with Austria, as well as British policies toward Hong Kong.[64]

NSC discussion notes for the President taken on the issue of Taiwan were to the point. Secretary of Defense Johnson did not see how State's paper constituted a change of policy. Also, he did not see why the major recommendation in the paper—the *demarche*—required immediate implementation. It was Johnson's opinion that action on the paper should be deferred and included in NSC 48, "United States Policy Toward Asia"; a paper in progress, the aim of which was to determine an overall, coordinated Far Eastern policy for the U.S.[65] Furthermore, Johnson objected to a press release timed to the *demarche*. A public statement, as proposed by State, "would prejudice our best interests and limit our possible future courses of action." However, the Defense Secretary did agree with Acheson that a *demarche* should be given privately to Chiang, and suggested two changes in language. Whereas State categorically declared that Washington sought no military bases or special privileges on Taiwan, Johnson had that sentence struck out completely. Also, where State declared, without qualification, that the U.S. "will not" commit its armed forces to the defense of Taiwan, Johnson changed the "will not" to "does not intend."[66] For his part, General Bradley was also opposed to the press release. Significantly, Bradley stated that "...we ought not to publicize such a communication since we might change our mind in light of the overall Asia policy..." (a reference to NSC 48). Bradley added that whereas the JCS did not feel that the military should go into Formosa now, "...the situation might change."

The notes of the 47th meeting of the NSC do not reflect the discussions between Acheson, Bradley, and Johnson that undoubtedly occurred as a result of remarks by the latter two men. It is simply stated that Acheson acquiesced to the language changes suggested by Johnson as well the recommendation to kill the press release. It was agreed, however, that the *demarche* would·be delivered to Chiang, and that State's paper (NSC 37/8) would be forwarded to the NSC staff for inclusion into NSC 48.

Read in isolation from later events, as Acheson must have read them at the time, wordsmithing on the *demarche* by Defense seemed to mean little, and was an easy compromise to make in exchange for consensus on shaking up the Gimo. Also, General Bradley's remarks were consistent with the continual qualifications the military added to their previous statements about the strategic importance of Taiwan. However, in retrospect, (as shall be seen in the next chapter) Johnson's language changes and Bradley's comments were significant harbingers of what would, in the next weeks, amount to a major reversal in Defense's previous thinking about Taiwan. But for the moment, State was given the green light to read Chiang Kai-shek the proverbial "riot act."

6.7 CHIANG IS PUT ON NOTICE

On October 27th, Dean Acheson sent orders to the field implementing the decision reached at the 47th meeting of the NSC. John

Macdonald, Consul General in Taipei since the 19th of July, was sent a copy of the modified *demarche* and told to deliver it to Chiang Kai-shek at the earliest opportunity. Macdonald was further informed that the NSC had decided to have the *demarche* read to Governor Ch'en Ch'eng and General Sun Li-jen after the Gimo received it. The next day, Acheson also sent a message to Robert Strong, *Chargé* at the U.S. Embassy in Chungking; the latest capital of an ever-retreating KMT on the mainland. Strong was likewise instructed to inform Li Tsung-jen of the contents of the *demarche* delivered to Chiang on Taiwan.[67] It was Acheson's reasoning that the more of the KMT's key players that understood the views of the United States toward Taiwan the better. Hopefully, Chiang's lieutenant's, as well as his rivals, would place pressure on him to face the realities of the situation if they too were aware of exactly what the Generalissimo was told by Washington.

Upon receiving his instructions, Macdonald cabled Butterworth. He argued that the interests of the United States would be better served if Ch'en Ch'eng were the recipient of the *demarche,* not Chiang. Macdonald believed that dealing directly with Chiang Kai-shek would only serve to underwrite the latter's claim that only he and Madam Chiang were capable of securing American support. Also, Macdonald relayed a rumor that a "locally plotted action" was in the works to remove Chiang "for China's good." If this were true, he reasoned to Butterworth, then an approach to the Gimo could foil the *coup* before it even got started. Finally, Macdonald offered that since Ch'en Ch'eng would ultimately be the man responsible for formulating and implementing reforms, he might as well be the one to whom the Consulate delivered Washington's notice. Moreover, Ch'en, Macdonald assessed, was very amenable to outside advice.[68]

Acheson responded to Macdonald's cable personally. He informed the Consul General that the decision to make Chiang the principal recipient of the *demarche* was that of the NSC's and could not be changed unilaterally by State. Moreover, it was in fact the view of the Department of State, "after careful consideration of all factors," that the Generalissimo should be the recipient. It was Chiang, all back in Washington agreed, who was in fact the genuine source of authority on Taiwan. Because Chiang was now clearly calling the shots on the island, it was feared, said Acheson, that having the views of the U.S. Government delivered to him by a third party would only result in those views being "distorted or watered down." Consequently, Macdonald was told once again to deliver the notice to Chiang, and to inform Sun and Ch'en as well.[69]

On the morning of November 3rd, Macdonald, accompanied by an FSO fluent in Chinese, delivered Washington's *demarche* to Generalissimo Chiang Kai-shek. When read the message the Gimo, according to Macdonald, evinced "an expression of displeasure" when statements about previous misgovernment on Taiwan were conveyed. As soon as the *demarche* was finished being read, Chiang asked one question: "to whom was this message addressed?" When Macdonald told Chiang that it was intended for him, he then seemed very pleased. Chiang then served tea in what was described as a friendly and cordial atmosphere. Chiang told Macdonald that he would like to study the message and would get back to him to offer his ideas for alleviating problems on the island. All in all, Macdonald related, he left with the impression that Chiang was "...highly pleased, perhaps not by the message we conveyed to him, but due to the fact that I was instructed to deliver it to him rather than someone else."[70]

Later on, K.C. Wu called on Macdonald to inform him of what occurred after the Consul General left the Gimo the day the *demarche* was delivered. Wu stated that Chiang immediately called a "special meeting" for all members of his headquarters to study the contents of the *demarche;* a meeting that lasted "late into the night." Wu related that Chiang was ecstatic that the message was delivered to him, and the Gimo declared to his headquarters staff that the United States was now willing "to deal with him again" and that "he had not been completely deserted by his old friend and ally." Wu then told Macdonald that he, Wu, warned Chiang that this was the Gimo's "last chance as far as the US is concerned" and that the Generalissimo had no choice but to agree to any terms that Washington demanded in exchange for assistance to Taiwan. After the meeting, Chiang left Taipei to meditate at a secluded mountaintop retreat. Wu adjudged to Macdonald that the administration on Taiwan would now do anything the U.S. asked of it; to include making changes in political positions from the governorship on down. "The Department's message to the Generalissimo," reported Macdonald, "has definitely given them the moral support for which they have been asking recently. In addition to giving them moral support, it has (been) interpreted, as the

Generalissimo mentioned to the members of his headquarters, that the US Government is willing to deal with him directly once again."[71]

On November 4th, the day after Chiang was delivered the *demarche,* Strong in Chungking apprised Li Tsung-jen of its contents. Li must have taken great delight in Washington taking a poke at his old nemesis. He told Strong that he agreed with the contents of the message and that Taiwan's only real hope rested with Sun Li-jen being placed in overall command of the island's defenses. Li then went on to point out to Strong Taiwan's great strategic significance to the United States. He suggested that the U.S. Navy use its ports to serve as a deterrent to an attack by the communists. The United States, Li proposed, could justify stationing military units on the island by declaring "right of conquest." Finally, Li told the *Chargé* that, were it within his power, he would establish a joint Sino-American administration over the island.[72]

Back in Taipei, Macdonald, on November 4th, called on Governor Ch'en Ch'eng to read him the contents of State's *demarche* and inform him that the Generalissimo had already received it. After being read its contents, Ch'en expressed "regret and shame" for the failures of the KMT on Taiwan. Ch'en then launched into a lengthy discussion about the problems he had encountered in governing the island when he first arrived. He claimed that he was unpopular with both the Chinese and the Formosans because he had attempted, and failed, to limit mainland immigration. Ch'en the proceeded to inform Macdonald of the great economic, military, and political accomplishments that were sure be carried out during 1950. He claimed that local elections would be held, Taiwanese would be brought into the provincial civil service, and that defense of the island was each day strengthening due to increased support from the populace. Ch'en assured Macdonald that Sun Li-jen would be given a responsible position in the island's military command. Only Sun's junior status to more senior generals kept him from realizing his potential, not his abilities which all recognized. Ch'en also made a plea for increased economic, technical, and military assistance. He told Macdonald that he welcomed his specific recommendations for improving the island's lot, and that Macdonald should "feel free" to tell Ch'en that which the Consul General might be reluctant to tell Chiang. Macdonald was impressed by Ch'en's forthright attitude. Furthermore, he cabled to State that he was quite amazed that the Governor spoke as if he really did have authority over the island, as opposed to being a lacky of Chiang's. Ch'en, Macdonald told State, seemed sincere and indicated "a great willingness to accept advice almost to the point of attempting to do anything we ask." Macdonald asked his superiors what he thought to be the salient question of the day: how many steps to improve the island's situation would the authorities on Taiwan be required to make before Washington deemed them acting in good faith and worthy of increased aid? Macdonald believed that Ch'en was "a rather good gamble" and his estimation of the Governor was growing each day.[73] Acheson maintained his silence.

Six days after being handed State's *demarche,* Chiang Kai-shek summoned Consul General Macdonald. With K.C. Wu acting as his interpreter, Chiang read to Macdonald an *aide-mémoire* of his own. The tone of the Generalissimo's response was not that of one who had been put on notice, but of a partner with Washington in a great crusade to save Taiwan. He took absolutely no personal responsibility for the problems on the island, and spoke of its administration, as well as its administrators, in a detached manner. He told Macdonald that he read the American *demarche* and "communicated its contents to the Chinese Government." He said that he attached great importance to the interest shown by the United States in the welfare of Taiwan and fully shared Washington's view that improving the welfare of its people would strengthen its security. Making no mention of previous misgovernment, Chiang assured Macdonald that the island's administration was making great progress in taking those steps which would benefit the people and enhance its defense. He went on to relay his conviction that at the current rate of progress being made in all areas, within a year, "a new and progressive Taiwan will be built up to satisfy the desires of its people and their sympathetic friends." In the meantime, "any concrete suggestions for further immediate political and economic improvement of the island from the United States Government will be received with the fullest appreciation and consideration by the administration of Taiwan." Chiang then made his pitch.

> At the present moment, however, Taiwan is facing the most serious menace of a full-scale Communist invasion. Its fate will be decided in the next few months. This is a fact which I cannot refrain from telling frankly to the United States Government whose concern over the island we appreciate. Besides facing economic difficulties, the administration of Taiwan is now profoundly anxious about the strength of its armed forces and must endeavour in every possible way to improve it.

This was the limit of the groveling Chiang was prepared to do personally. For in his *aide-mémóire,* he continued by stating that:

> Governor Chen Cheng of Taiwan has been asked by me to make a general statement on the Taiwan situation, outlining measures which his administration has already taken as well as those which it intends to take in the immediate future, and also stating the position of Taiwan in regard to American aid....It is hoped that the Governor's requests for American aid, including military assistance of a technical nature, will not be deemed to be outside the scope of the present policy of the US Government. And it is my firm belief that if the US Government decides to meet these requests, they can count on the fullest cooperation from the administration of Taiwan.[74]

Chiang, whom Macdonald described as being in "excellent spirits," then turned to Ch'en who delivered a lengthy review of recent accomplishments and future progress in political and economic reform. As his bottom line, Ch'en (read Chiang) asked the United States for an enlarged program of aid under the ECA and the JCRR as well as "some military assistance of a technical character." Ch'en (Chiang) specifically requested that "an American military advisory group be immediately sent to Taiwan, with whom we can assure close cooperation and for whose advice full appreciation and weight will be given."[75]

For his part, Macdonald suggested to Acheson that Washington agree to these requests "in principle," and begin to make plans for immediate implementation. "This is no time," he argued, "for indecision or pursuing a procrastinating policy if we really intend to make a last effort to deny the Communists Taiwan." He then informed Foggy Bottom that he would soon forward his recommendations for a military advisory group after consulting with his military attaches.[76]

Whether Consul General Macdonald did not appreciate the basis of Taiwan policy, was coopted momentarily by fine words, or merely determined to attempt a reversal of NSC policy is unknown. Nevertheless, on November 18th, Acheson broke his silence and sent Macdonald a lengthy cable which the Secretary hoped would insure that the Consul General understood Washington's views about the situation on Taiwan, and assist him "...in removing any misconceptions reference our attitude which may exist..." on the part of the Chinese authorities.

First, Acheson told Macdonald that the resources currently on Taiwan were deemed wholly adequate to save the island if the authorities now took "resolute steps" to use them effectively. That being the case, a commitment of U.S. aid at this time, said Acheson, would do no good. It would negate in the minds of the Chinese authorities the need to save the island through their own efforts. It would lead them to believe, mistakenly, that the United States was assuming an "active role" and taking "responsibility" for the salvation of Taiwan. Furthermore, Acheson went on, a large commitment of U.S. aid would be "costly" in terms of American resources and "prestige." Finally, U.S. aid to Taiwan could very possibly destroy Washington's chances of achieving its "political objectives on (the) mainland."

Acheson then addressed Macdonald's earlier question about how much change would be required for the KMT to prove worthy of assistance. He pointed out to Macdonald that while the Consul General's most recent cables painted a very optimistic picture of the situation on Taiwan, they represented a reversal of his earlier, pessimistic assessments. The Secretary cautioned Macdonald that until it was possible to gain a true and broad appreciation for conditions on the island, it would be premature to commit to the KMT on just how many steps they would be required to take until a show of good faith for future assistance was registered. Acheson was not prepared to develop a laundry list of reforms that Taipei had to enact as a *quid pro quo*. In Acheson's mind, the real signal of change would be less tangible. For as he told Macdonald:

> ...perhaps even more important than any specific measures is the need for some kind of spiritual regeneration (of the) Chinese leaders themselves which would lead them to lay aside self-aggrandizement and internal bickering and devote themselves with determination and patriotism to their cause and which would revitalize their followers. External aid cannot supply such leadership.

Acheson then addressed K.C. Wu's comments to Macdonald; comments which led the Secretary to believe that, perhaps, the entire point of the *demarche* was lost upon the Chinese. Acheson wanted Macdonald and the Chinese to fully understand that Washington's message to Chiang:

> ...was not opening gambit to be followed by specific 'terms' but was designed to place Gimo on notice that US had no intention of using its armed forces to defend Island and that responsibility for undertaking effective measures with respect internal and external security Formosa rested squarely upon him and Chi authorities who were appraised of this notification.

Acheson then instructed Macdonald to see K.C. Wu, C.K. Yen, and Sun Li-jen to insure that they, and through them the Gimo, were not confused on this fundamental point. He also told Macdonald to understand that the U.S. Government would under no circumstances place itself in the position of advising the Chinese authorities on political appointments. The United States would do nothing to "inferentially commit" its prestige to any Chinese leader.

Finally, and most important, Acheson told Macdonald to tell Chiang et. al. that the U.S. Government absolutely would not provide active-duty American military officers to serve as advisers to the Chinese authorities on Taiwan. For Macdonald's purposes, Acheson outlined the rationale. First, the presence of military advisers would become known and publicized. This in turn would be interpreted, incorrectly, as evidence of American intentions to "underwrite" the military defense of Taiwan. Second, Taipei would "undoubtedly" attempt to use the advisers "...as a channel to exploit for extraction of Amer aid rather than addressing their full efforts to the pressing problems which only they can solve." Third, the U.S. would suffer a great blow to its prestige if the island was lost to the communists through military action in spite of the presence of U.S. military advisers. Finally, the presence of American military advisers on Taiwan could very well place service attaches and private U.S. citizens still in communist areas on the mainland in danger. Acheson then warned Macdonald not to allow his attaches to place themselves in the position of advising KMT military officials if for no other reason than it would be "contrary to our world-wide practice respecting service attaches..."[77]

6.8 TAIWAN "ABANDONED"

With the *demarche* delivered to Chiang, the policy toward Taiwan as determined in NSC 37/8 was implemented. In effect, the KMT on Taiwan was "abandoned" by the United States; abandoned to its own devices.

Since January 1949, the Department of State had been seeking to find some way to save the island from communist domination. Direct military intervention, the only sure way to accomplish this objective, was ultimately rejected. With the fall of the mainland to the CCP, the greatest problem facing State in the Far East was the prospect that communist China would become "an adjunct to Soviet power." State

Department officials believed that military intervention in Taiwan would undermine the pursuit of Chinese Titoism on the mainland. But it is important to note that State was willing to subjugate political concerns to strategic necessary if the Department of Defense felt that Taiwan's fall would cause serious damage to national security. However, the Joint Chiefs of Staff, since December 1948, consistently refused to support military intervention in Taiwan. While they continually stated that Taiwan was strategically important, the Joint Chiefs argued that it was not so vital that the nation's limited military resources should be risked in a scenario which promised to escalate into a major military campaign. In any case, they argued, were general war to erupt, Taiwan could be easily secured. That being the case, State could cite no political reasons why the Joint Chiefs should be overruled and directed to intervene against their own judgment. Indeed, the assessment of the uniformed services allowed State to pursue its grand strategy for handling the newly proclaimed People's Republic of China (October 1, 1949).

At the same time, it appeared that on Taiwan the Nationalists already had both the economic and military resources to strengthen the island's economy and defend it from without for at least two years. If the Nationalist leadership could pull itself together and work for common salvation with the Formosans, there was no reason why they could not remain safely ensconced on Taiwan by dint of their own efforts. The purpose of the NSC's *demarche* was to shock Chiang into his senses; to let him know that no U.S. troops would come to his assistance. Hopefully, he would then set about the business of doing the many things which would keep Taiwan out of communist hands.

However, those who knew Chiang and had watched his mistakes on the mainland and on Taiwan did not believe for one moment that the Generalissimo and his lieutenants were capable of an eleventh hour metamorphosis. Few believed that the KMT could save itself. Almost no one believed that, in the absence of U.S. military intervention, Taiwan could be saved. As of 19 October, the CIA reported to the President that precisely because of the KMT's history and political weaknesses "...no amount of US aid, short of armed intervention and control of Taiwan, can ensure its indefinite survival as a non-communist area." Moreover, CIA judged that the Nationalist regime on Taiwan would not survive "...beyond 1950 except on Communist sufferance."[78] Certainly, no one at the Department of State believed that the Nationalists could save themselves. Merchant's time in Taiwan had convinced him that economic and diplomatic methods would not suffice. Kennan's bold scheme for intervention underscored his unwillingness to allow Taiwan's future—a strategic interest of the United States—to rest on the hopes of a rejuvenated KMT. Brainstorming by Rusk, Jessup, and Butterworth to use the United Nations to snatch Taiwan was another vote of no confidence to Chiang and the KMT.

On December 1st, Merchant wrote a memorandum to Butterworth referring to the fall of Taiwan as an "expected unhappy event" that would occur at "some uncertain date in the future." Merchant proposed that the time was now ripe to devise a series of military, economic, and political actions to take place on that day aimed at limiting the psychological damage in the Far East and bolstering the image of the U.S.[79] All were pulling for Chiang. But all felt that Taiwan's fall to the communists was only a matter of time. Abandoned to the KMT, Taiwan was as good as abandoned to the communists.

Notes

1. Office Memorandum, Merchant to Butterworth, U.S. Policy re Formosa, May 24, 1949, SDF:Reel 2, *Memorandum by Mr. Livingston T. Merchant to the Director of the Office of Far Eastern Affairs (Butterworth)*, May 24, 1949, FR:49:IX:337–341.

2. Blum, *Drawing the Line*, pp.44–46.

3. A reorganization of the State Department in 1949 elevated Butterworth's position, Director of the Office of Far Eastern Affairs, to the status of Deputy Secretary of State. Hence, Congressional confirmation was required.

4. *Congressional Record*, Volume XCV, 81st Congress, 1st Session (1949), p. 6306, as quoted in Tang Tsou, *America's Failure in China, 1941–50* (Chicago: The University of Chicago Press, 1963), p. 503.

5. The twelve-nation North Atlantic Treaty was signed in Washington on April 4, 1949 and ratified by the Senate on 21 July. On July 25th, Truman sent to Congress his proposal for $1.4 billion in military aid for the signatories of the treaty. Ultimately, the Act allocated $1.314 billion. For an good overview of the history of the Mutual Defense Assistance Act and the MAP program see Nelson, *History of the OSD*.

6. Public Law 329, 81st Congress (S. 2388, H.R. 5895). Italics added. HAS/Box 101. The various drafts of the Act may be found in Box 101 of the Papers of H. Alexander Smith, Seeley Mudd Library, Princeton University.

7. Blum's excellent work, *Drawing the Line: The Origin of the American Containment Policy in East Asia* (N.Y.: W.W. Norton & CO., 1982) makes a strong case that the origins of active United States involvement in Indochina

was a function of the Truman administration's frustration at not being able to be effective in stopping communism in China. Blum's Chapter 8, *Money for "The General Area of China,"* is one of the best available narratives on the origins and specifics of the Section 303 funds.

8. Throughout the spring and summer of 1949 members of the China Bloc and China Lobby bombarded the administration with suggestions on which KMT generals had the potential to continue the struggle, how they should be supported militarily, and what types of covert actions should be initiated to support them. Most reknown of these was the so-called "Chennault Plan" which can be found in RJCS:Reel 1, under JCS 1721/36, *Military Aid to China*, 10 September 1949.

9. Acheson, *Present at the Creation*, p. 303; Blum, *Drawing the Line*, pp. 88–89. Initially, the creation of the group of consultants was received positively by many administration critics. For example Senator H. Alexander Smith wrote to a close associate that, "The fact that we are definitely to reconsider our entire Far Eastern policy, and that we have men of the calibre of Philip Jessup to work this out for us is a big step forward. Frankly, I think this has been brought about by the agitation of those of us who have been insisting that our present policy is a failure and we are letting the Chinese slide after over half a century of intimate relationships with them..." Letter, H. Alexander Smith to Kenneth Twitchell, July 15, 1949, HAS/Box 98.

10. Acheson told the group in their initial instructions that the programs they ultimately suggest for the Far East should be based upon the understanding that it was a fundamental policy of the United States not to allow communism to spread in Asia beyond China. Michael Schaller, *The American Occupation of Japan: The Origins of the Cold War In Asia* (N.Y.: Oxford University Press, 1985), pp. 200–201.

11. Brigadier General Louis H. Renfrow served as Johnson's Special Assistant from 1949 until 1950, and is one of the few persons who has ever had anything positive to say about the former Secretary of Defense. Renfrow recounts that, "You've got to remember that between Johnson and Acheson there was absolutely no love. There was a constant fight between them, because neither one of them agreed with what the other one did...If Johnson would say, 'That's white,' Acheson would say, 'That's black'...and the dueling between them went on..." Transcript, BG Louis H. Renfrow Oral History Interview, March 12 and 15, 1971, Truman Library, pp. 129, 131.

12. Memorandum of Conversation with the President, July 14, 1949, Item No. 3, *Clearance of White Paper with NME*, DGA/MOC/Box 64/July 1949.

13. *Note by the Secretaries* to the Joint Chiefs of Staff on The China White Paper, 16 July 1949, RJCS:Reel 1.

14. Memorandum for the Secretary of Defense from the Joint Chiefs of Staff, 21 July 1949, HST/CF/Box 54/State Department White Paper on China. The JCS also clearly stipulated that release of the document in no way constituted their formal agreement with the judgments offered by State.

15. JCS 1721/32, 28 July 1949, RJCS:Reel 1.

16. Letter, Secretary of Defense Johnson to Secretary of State Acheson, 21 July 1949; Letter Secretary of State Acheson to Secretary of Defense Johnson, July 26, 1949, HST/CF/Box 54/State Department White Paper on China.

17. For background on the Ward affair see Blum, *Drawing the Line*, pp. 11, 55, 59, 63, 80, 144, 146, 162, and 164; Tucker, *Patterns in the Dust*, pp. 14–16; Stueck, *The Road to Confrontation*, pp. 125, 133, and 135; and Michael Hunt, "Mao Tse-tung and the Issue of Accommodation with the United States, 1948–1950," in Borg and Heinrichs, *Uncertain Years*, pp. 203–204, and 224.

18. Blum, p. 53.

19. Ibid., p. 50.

20. *The Ambassador in China (Stuart) to the Secretary of State,* April 26, 1949, FR:49:VIII:277–278.

21. *Selected Works of Mao Tse-tung,* Volume IV (Peking: Foreign Language Press, 1961), pp. 411–424, 425–432, and 433–440.

22. For background on the Stuart-Huang talks and the Chou *Demarche* see Blum, pp. 54–64. The meat of Chou's *Demarche* was condensed, and relayed to Truman. It can be found in HST/NAF/Box 21/May–Aug 1949.

23. Some, such as Shanghai Consul General Cabot, believed that recent anti-U.S. propaganda was mere lip service to Moscow and that the prospects for Titoism were good. *The Consul General in Shanghai (Cabot) to the Ambassador in China (Stuart),* April 20, 1949, FR:49:VIII:256–257 and, *The Consul General in Shanghai (Cabot) to the Secretary of State,* May 31, 1949, FR:49:VIII:355–357. Others, notably O. Edmund Clubb, were skeptical about the prospects for Titoism in China. While Clubb accepted that the CCP leadership might be split on the issue of taking economic aid from the U.S., he did not believe that those who favored such a move were any less committed to Moscow politically. He was quick to point out to that even if Chou En-lai was genuine, he commanded no troops. He also posited that Chou's approach might even have had the blessing of the highest councils of CCP leadership. Telegram, Peiping (Clubb) to Secretary of State, June 3, 1939, HST/PSF/Box 173/China 1949.

24. Four years later, Acheson was still convinced that in 1949 there was a "Russian wing of the Communist party." During the Princeton Seminars he maintained that "...it is quite clear that there were two groups within the Communist party in China, one which looked wholly to Russian guidance, and the other group which was more of an independent Chinese Communist group." DGA/Box 75/Princeton Seminars/Reading Copy, 22–23 July 1953/Folder II, p. 695.

25. National Security Council Progress Report by the Department of State on the implementation of U.S. Policy Toward China (NSC 34/2), August 19, 1949, HST/PSF/MNSC/Box 205/NSC Meeting #35.

26. Message, U.S. Embassy Moscow to the Secretary of State, June 10, 1949, SDF:Reel 1.

27. Message, Consul General at Tsingtao (Hawthorne) to the Secretary of State, July 28, 1949, SDF:Reel 1.

28. Message, Consul General at Tientsin (Smyth) to the Secretary of State, June 21, 1949, SDF:Reel 2.

29. Message, Nanking (Stuart) to the Secretary of State, June 10, 1949, SDF:Reel 1. Parenthetical comment added. The Cairo Declaration maintained that Taiwan was an integral part of China to be returned after the war against Japan.

30. Memorandum of Conversation, Dr. Kan Chieh-hou, V.K. Wellington Koo, The Secretary of State, and Fulton Freeman (Assistant Chief, Division of Chinese Affairs), July 1, 1949, DGA/MOC/Box 64/July 1949.

31. Message, Taipei (Edgar) to the Secretary of State, June 11, 1949, SDF:Reel 1.

32. Message, Taipei (MacDonald) to the Secretary of State, August 25, 1949, SDF:Reel 1. The residence of a member of the U.S. Consulate was broken into and robbed. The residence of an American businessman was taken over by soldiers. A British citizen was forced to buy towels and pencils from a KMT soldier at gunpoint. The Consulate began to issue placards to U.S. nationals to display on their property in an attempt to intimidate would-be looters.

33. Message, Taipei (Edgar) to the Secretary of State, June 28, 1949, SDF:Reel 2.

34. Message, Taipei (Edgar) to the Secretary of State, June 24, 1949, SDF:Reel 2.

35. Message, Taipei to the Secretary of State, July 12, 1949, SDF:Reel 3. The full text of Chiang's interview can be found in FR:49:VIII:412–416.

36. For details of military factionalism resulting from Chiang's reemergence see, Message, Taipei to the Secretary of State, August 25, 1949, SDF: Reel 2; Message, Taipei to the Secretary of State (Deterioration of Taiwan; eclipse of Sun Li-jen), August 30, 1949, SDF:Reel 2; and Message, Taipei to Secretary of State, August 31, 1949, SDF:Reel 2. General Chou Chih-jou, a founder of the KMT Air Force, served as Chief of Staff of the Air Force (1943–1952), Chief of the General Staff (1950–1957), and eventually as Governor of Taiwan (1957–1962). Boorman and Howard, *Biographical Dictionary of Republican China*, Vol I., pp. 389–391.

37. Department of State, *Summary of Telegrams*, July 14, 1949, HST/ NAF/Box 21/May–June 1949; Message, Taipei (Edgar) to the Secretary of State, July 18, 1949, SDF:Reel 1. The so-called Far East Union eventually came to naught.

38. Memorandum of Conversation, Governor Dewey, The Secretary of State, and Philip Jessup, September 21, 1949, DGA/MOC/Box 64/August– September 1949.

39. Office Memorandum, Merchant to Butterworth, U.S. Policy re Formosa, May 24, 1949, SDF:Reel 2; *Memorandum by Mr. Livingston T.*

Merchant to the Director of the Office of Far Eastern Affairs (Butterworth), May 24, 1949, FR:49:IX:337–341.

40. Office Memorandum, Butterworth to Rusk, June 3, 1949, SDF:Reel 2. This document contains Butterworth's memo to Rusk, the paper redrafted by Merchant, Kennan, Davies, Krentz, and Sprouse, as well as a draft statement on U.S. intentions toward Taiwan suggested for issuance by the Secretary of State at such time that the trusteeship issue is raised at the United Nations.

41. Office Memorandum, Krentz to Butterworth and Sprouse, June 8, 1949, SDF:Reel 2. Krentz added that the CIA was currently working hard to determine the validity of this report.

42. For the various arguments for and against the feasibility of U.N. action, and the lines of reasoning herein set forth against it see, Office Memorandum, Mr. Gerig (U.N. Division) to Dean Rusk, June 6, 1949, SDF:Reel 2; Office Memorandum, Mr, Harding F. Bancroft (U.N. Division) to Mr. Sandifer (U.N. Division) and Mr. Rusk, June 6, 1949, SDF:Reel 2; *Memorandum by the Director of the Office of Far Eastern Affairs (Butterworth) to the Deputy Under Secretary of State (Rusk)*, June 9, 1949, FR:49:IX:346; and Office Memorandum, Merchant to Butterworth, June 15, 1949, SDF: Reel 2.

43. Office Memorandum, Livingston T. Merchant to Mr. Butterworth, June 15, 1949, SDF:Reel 2. This document contains a cover letter by Merchant to Butterworth indicating that Dean Rusk added much of the language in this new iteration, and a copy of the draft to the NSC itself (dated 14 June).

44. Ibid.

45. PPS 53 can be found in three collections. See "United States Policy Toward Formosa and the Pescadores," July 6, 1949, SDF:Reel 1; *Memorandum by the Director of the Policy Planning Staff (Kennan)*, [PPS 53], FR:49:IX:356–364; and PPS/53, *United States Policy Toward Formosa and the Pescadores*, Nelson, ed. *The State Department Policy Planning Staff Papers*, Vol. III., pp. 63–74.

46. PPS 53 was written on June 30, 1949. According to the copy in the *FRUS* series (FR:49:IX:356) it was canceled as a formally submitted PPS paper on 6 July. In the SDF files, a handwritten note by Kennan, barely legible, was clipped to the document which read that "PPS-53 was recalled and canceled on 7-6-49. PPS views will be submitted to Secretary by personal views from Mr. Kennan." In the *PPS Papers*, PPS 53 has the following forward from Kennan to Acheson (dated 7 July): "Attached is a memorandum setting forth my personal views on the problem of Formosa. This is not written for possible transmission to the NSC. It is designed to state to you the issue as I see it. For purposes of record, I am making it a Policy Staff paper; but I wish to stress that it represents my personal view and not the consensus of staff opinion."

47. CIA, ORE 45–49, *Probable Developments in China*, 16 June 1949, HST/PSF/Box 173/China 1949.

48. NSC 37/6: A Report to the National Security Council by the Secretary of State on the Current Position of the U.S. with Respect to Formosa, August 5, 1949, HST/MNSC/Box 206/NSC Meeting #47. See also DNSC:Reel 1; and

Memorandum by the Department of State to the Executive Secretary of the National Security Council (Souers), FR:49:IX:369–371.

49. Note, Humelsine to Dean Rusk, August 4, 1949, SDF:Reel 2. Humelsine passed onto Rusk the Secretary's concern that the paper be drafted with the JCS in mind; that they be given "some leads" as to what was requested of them.

50. NSC 37/7: A Report to the National Security Council by the Secretary of Defense on The Position of the United States with Respect to Formosa, August 22, 1949, HST/PSF/MNSC/Box 205/NSC Meeting #35; DNSC:Reel 1; FR:49:IX:376–378; and J.C.S. 1966/17, *A Report by the Joint Strategic Survey Committee on The Position of the United States with Respect to Formosa,* 16 August 1949, RJCS:Reel 2.

51. Italics added.

52. Letter, LTG Albert C. Wedemeyer to Mr. George V. Allen (Assistant Secretary of State for Public Affairs), Subject: Current Situation with Respect to Formosa, 26 August 1949, SDF:Reel 2.

53. Memorandum, Adrian S. Fisher (Legal Adviser to the Department of State) to Mr. Jessup, Subject: Legal Status of Formosa, September 19, 1949, SDF:Reel 3.

54. Memorandum of Conversation, Dening (Foreign Office), Meade (U.K. Embassy), and Ford (First Secretary, U.K. Embassy) with Butterworth, Merchant, and Freeman, September 9, 1949, Subject: Formosa, SDF:Reel 2; and *Memorandum of Conversation, by the Assistant Chief of the Division of Chinese Affairs (Freeman),* [Washington], September 9, 1949, FR:49:IX:388–390.

55. NSC 37/8: A Report to the National Security Council by the Acting Secretary of State on the Position of the United States with Respect to Formosa, October 6, 1949, HST/PSF/MNSC/Box 206/NSC Meeting #47; DNSC:Reel 1; and FR:49:IX:392–397.

56. Italics added.

57. At this point in time, ECA aid consisted of small programs such as the importation of fertilizers, cotton yarn, medical supplies, and some foods. Also, some JCRR advisers were working with farmers to help increase staple agricultural yields. Finally, a few advisers from New York's J.G. White Engineering Corporation were permitted to be kept on retainer by Taipei to assist in infrastructural repairs required by wartime destruction. See National Security Council Progress Report by the Department of State on the implementation of NSC 37/2 and NSC 37/5, August 19, 1949, HST/PSF/MNSC/Box 205/NSC Meeting #35. The larger ECA program envisioned since the inception of the NSC 37 series consisted of a massive capital construction program.

58. Draft Statement to be issued by the Secretary of State, Memorandum for Merchant from Wilds, October 5, 1949, SDF:Reel 2.

59. The task of effecting internal State Department coordination and tracking extra-departmental issues related to Taiwan fell to Walter Wilds who,

since August 18th, headed an *ad hoc* Formosa "working group." Memo, Wilds to Rusk, August 18, 1949, SDF:Reel 1.

60. Memorandum, Fosdick to Jessup, October 6, 1949, SDF:Reel 2.

61. Memorandum, Charles Yost to Mr. Jessup, October 1, 1949, SDF:Reel 2.

62. Memorandum for Merchant from Wilds, October 5, 1949, SDF:Reel 2.

63. Letter, Merchant to Yost, October 6, 1949, SDF:Reel 2.

64. Memorandum for the President, Summary of Discussion at the 47th Meeting of the National Security Council, October 20, 1949, HST/PSF/Box 220/NSC Memos to the President, 1949. Discussions on Hong Kong (NSC 55/1 and NSC 55/2) remain classified as of 1982, and have been sanitized out of the document.

65. NSC 48 was Johnson's brainchild and will be discussed in detail in Chapter 7.

66. Specifically, Johnson recommended that the first sentence ("The U.S. has no designs on Formosa and seeks no military bases or special privileges of any kind on the island.") be dropped completely. He suggested that the second sentence ("The U.S. Government will not commit any of its armed forces to the defense of the island.") be changed to read, "The U.S. Government *does not intend* to commit any of its armed forces to the defense of the island." Italics added.

67. Office Memorandum, Butterworth to Acheson, October 27, 1949, SDF:Reel 2; *The Secretary of State to the Charge in China (Strong)*, October 28, 1949, FR:49:IX:401; Message, AMCONSUL Taipei from Acheson, October 28, 1949, SDF:Reel 1; and *The Secretary of State to the Consul General at Taipei (Macdonald)*, October 28, 1949, FR:49:IX:401–403.

68. *The Consul General at Taipei (Macdonald) to the Secretary of State*, October 31, 1949, FR:49:IX:403–404; Message, Taipei to the Secretary of State (For Butterworth—No Distribution), October 31, 1949, SDF:Reel 1.

69. *The Secretary of State to the Consul General at Taipei (Macdonald)*, November 1, 1949, FR:49:IX:404–405; Telegram, Acheson to AMCONSUL Taipei, November 1, 1949, SDF:Reel 3.

70. *The Consul General at Taipei (Macdonald) to the Secretary of State*, November 3, 1949, FR:49:IX:406–407; Message, Taipei to the Secretary of State, November 3, 1949, SDF:Reel 3; and HST/NAF/Box 21/Sep–Dec 1949.

71. *The Consul General at Taipei (Macdonald) to the Secretary of State*, November 6, 1949, FR:49:IX:411–412; Message, Taipei to Secretary of State, November 6, 1949, SDF:Reel 3.

72. *The Charge in China (Strong) to the Secretary of State*, November 4, 1949, FR:49:IX:407–408; *Summary of Telegrams*, Department of State, November 7, 1949, HST/NAF/Box 21/Sep–Dec 1949.

73. *The Consul General at Taipei (Macdonald) to the Secretary of State*, November 5, 1949, FR:49:IX:408–411; Message, Taipei to Secretary of State, November 5, 1949, SDF:Reel 3.

74. Message, Taipei to Secretary of State, November 9, 1949, SDF:Reel 3; The Consul General at Taipei (Macdonald) to the Secretary of State, November 9, 1949, FR:49:IX:415–416; *Summary of Telegrams*, Department of State, November 9, 1949, HST/NAF/Box 21/Sep–Dec 1949.

75. *The Consul General at Taipei (Macdonald) to the Secretary of State*, November 9, 1949, FR:49:IX:416–418; Message, Taipei to Secretary of State, November 9, 1949, SDF:Reel 3.

76. Ibid.

77. *The Secretary of State to the Consul General at Taipei (Macdonald)*, November 18, 1949, FR:49:IX:428–431; Message, Acheson to AMCONSUL Taipei, November 18, 1949, SDF:Reel 3.

78. CIA, ORE 76–49, "Survival Potential of Residual Non-Communist Regimes in China," 19 October 1949, HST/PSF/Box 257/ORE 1949, Numbers 76–87.

79. *Memorandum by the Deputy Assistant Secretary of State for Far Eastern Affairs (Merchant) to the Assistant Secretary of State for Far Eastern Affairs (Butterworth)*, December 1, 1949, FR:49:IX:431–433.

CHAPTER 7

December 1949:
NSC 48 and the Battle for Formosa

The even flow of policy formulation is filled with a good many whirlpools and hidden traps which are not often discussed, and perhaps not very often confessed. There are a great many of these—vagaries of human nature, occupational diseases of bureaucracy of which we ought to notice...[1]

Dean Rusk
October 1950

The decisions made during the 47th meeting of the National Security Council (October 1949), and the act of delivering the *demarche* to Chiang Kai-shek on November 3rd should have put to rest for the moment the question of administration policy toward Taiwan. It did not.

Those who hoped to save the island by active U.S. intervention had a major opportunity to reverse State's "hand off" policy in late December 1949. At that time the President and other members of the NSC were scheduled to finalize a policy paper that had been six months in the making; NSC 48, "The Position of the United States With Respect to Asia." The ambitious objective of this project was to develop an integrated policy for the Far East that would allow the United States to contain communism in the region. As part of the study current policy toward Taiwan would be reviewed, reconfirmed or changed.

Not surprisingly, the KMT, smarting from the November *demarche*, lobbied hard to save its hide. It did so by playing up to the China Bloc in Congress and making major personnel changes in the Taiwan provincial government which it hoped would ameliorate skeptics and hardliners in the State Department. At the same time, prominent American legislators from the China Bloc made trips to Taipei to show support for Chiang Kai-shek and attempted to persuade Secretary of State Acheson to do all that was possible to keep the island from going under. Neither the KMT or pro-Chiang Congressmen had much impact on State's thinking.

As it turned out, the most powerful force for reversing Taiwan policy was from within the administration itself. Although he was already signed up to the decisions engendered in NSC 37/8, Secretary of Defense Louis Johnson led an all-out offensive in December aimed at providing military assistance to the KMT on Taiwan. Johnson found a powerful ally in General Douglas MacArthur, who warned all who would listen that Taiwan's fall to the communists would rupture the American strategic perimeter in the Far East.

Ultimately, the decisive engagement in the battle for Formosa was the one waged by Johnson and Acheson during the last days of 1949 to win over President Truman. When the smoke cleared, the Pentagon lost its bid to provide military assistance to the KMT. The State Department emerged victorious, its Taiwan policy intact. Chiang would have to help himself.

7.1 NSC 48: A CHANCE TO "SAVE" TAIWAN

On June 10, 1949 Secretary of Defense Louis Johnson forwarded the following memorandum to Admiral Sidney W. Souers, Executive Secretary to the NSC:

> 1. I am becoming increasingly concerned at the course of events in Asia. The advance of communism in large areas of the world and particularly the successes of communism in China seriously affect the future security of the United States. I am aware that this critical situation is being watched closely in the several departments of the government, and I appreciate that the current problems are being handled as realistically as circumstances permit. It occurs to me, however, that this day-to-day, country-by-country approach may not develop a broad program in our best long-range interest.
>
> 2. A major objective of United States policy, as I understand it, is to contain communism in order to reduce its threat to our security. Our actions in Asia should be part of a carefully considered and comprehensive plan to further that objective. I therefore request that the staff of the National Security Council undertake as soon as practicable a study of the current situations in Asia to re-examine and correlate current policies and to appraise the commitments and risks involved in the various courses of action—political, economic and military—which might be undertaken in support of the broad objective and recommend for the

consideration of the National Security Council an appropriate plan of action outlining specific objectives to be achieved.[2]

Although couched in terms which raised concerns about the spread of communism in Asia, the memorandum was also a politically-charged document. It registered Johnson's deep displeasure with the administration's handling of policy in Asia and was a slap in the face of the State Department's Office of Far Eastern Affairs.[3] Nevertheless, the suggestion for the study, subsequently known as NSC 48, was approved.[4]

However, the task which Johnson levied upon the NSC staff was gargantuan in nature. The in-depth review of developments across all of Asia was itself a large undertaking. But the ultimate requirement to develop an integrated policy toward a region of the world so culturally diverse and comprised of nations differing so greatly in political and economic particulars was even more imposing. Consequently, the scope of the study was beyond the capabilities of the relatively small NSC staff and input from every policy-making body in government, as well as from the intelligence community, was requested.

Because of the magnitude of the project, it was not until the middle of October 1949 that initial drafts were being completed.[5] By that time Taiwan policy was controversial enough for the Secretary of Defense to grab hold of and use to complicate life for State. Moreover, by the autumn of 1949 the fact that NSC 48 was in the works was leaked all over Washington and the "friends of China" were quick to seize the opportunity the study presented to attempt to reverse what they considered to be State's death wish for Taiwan.[6]

7.2 CHIANG AND THE KMT: AN ELEVENTH-HOUR FACE-LIFT

The *demarche* that Consul General Macdonald delivered to Chiang in Taipei on November 3rd was initially viewed by the Gimo as a very positive development. It reconfirmed in his mind that the United States was still willing to deal with him.[7] However, the stern words in the missive were unsettling to Chiang. They indicated that in order to extract aid from Washington, especially military assistance, relatively drastic measures on his part were going to be required. However, Chiang first tested State's resolve by submitting multiple requests for military assistance.[8]

Typically, the requests for assistance that Chiang sent to U.S. Government officials throughout November and December had a dual character. On the one hand, they were couched in terms of demands rather than requests. At the same time, these communications included what the Gimo considered to be major concessions on his part. Some of these concessions underscored the degree of panic that Chiang and others in Taipei were now feeling. Nevertheless, Chiang never presented himself as a desperate supplicant; there were others to do that for him. Moreover, always present was the *quid pro quo*. The methods of approach and the tenor of the requests for assistance annoyed the State Department to no end.

A November 29th request for aid made in Taipei was typical. On that day the head of the Generalissimo's intelligence staff sent a runner to the Consulate's Assistant Army Attache, Captain Manning, with what was claimed to be an official communication from Chiang. Requested was the following: a public announcement of support from Washington, political and military advisors, financial aid to improve the welfare of KMT troops, and such military equipment as radars and patrol boats. In return for all of this, Chiang, Captain Manning was told, was willing to accept all political and military advice without question. Moreover, as a grand gesture to prove his "sincerity" in using military assistance wisely, Chiang also offered to turn over the command of his armies to an American.[9] This particular initiative, and others like it, elicited no response from the State Department. Consequently, Chiang and his lieutenants decided that a major gambit was in order.

On December 7th, K.C. Wu called on Consul General Macdonald to pass on important news. Wu informed Macdonald that the "Nationalist Government" (Chiang) had requested that Wu replace Ch'en Ch'eng and assume the governorship of Taiwan Province. Wu stated that he sent forward to Chiang a message of acceptance conditioned by four specific demands. Wu would accept the job only if he could: (1) establish a "truly democratic form of government," (2) "personally choose his officials," (3) "control all national and provincial organs," and (4) "attend all military conferences." Wu was certain, he told Macdonald, that the Generalissimo would accept his conditions. Then came the hook. Wu assured Macdonald that, once in power, he could foresee Sun Li-jen being given overall command of the island's defense forces "if US aid comes first." Furthermore, Wu stated that he hoped that the U.S. Government would look upon his impending appointment as Governor as a "first step" toward enacting the types of reforms that were mentioned in the November *demarche*. Finally, Wu offered that it would take months to enact "all necessary reforms" and that the reforms would not succeed if U.S. aid was not provided on a "step by step basis."[10] Macdonald dutifully relayed this back to Washington.

K.C. Wu may have been too confident that Chiang and his conservative advisers would accede to his demands. On the other hand, Wu and Chiang may have been staging a Peking Opera for the benefit of Macdonald and State. Whatever the case, on December 13th, one week after he had informed Macdonald of the Gimo's offer, Wu returned to the Consulate "in great agitation." He told Acting Consul General Donald D. Edgar (Macdonald was not in Taipei at the time) that Ch'en Ch'eng and Wang Shih-chieh had convinced Chiang to reject Wu's conditions for accepting the governorship. The Gimo's new offer to Wu was the title of Acting Governor. If within one month Wu could convince the U.S. to send aid to Taiwan, Chiang would then give him the title of Governor and acquiesce to Wu's original demands.

After passing on these developments, Wu proceeded to get down to the point of his visit. He asked Edgar point blank "whether he could expect US aid under such conditions and within one month." Edgar's response was one of scathing disapprobation. He told Wu that "...such decoy measures did not appear to meet [the] requirements of [the] recent *aide memoire*." So far as he knew, Edgar told Wu, "...the Chinese subsequent to receipt of that notice had taken no action toward [the] creation of efficient administration" on Taiwan. Furthermore, since delivering the *demarche* all the Consulate could see was the unnecessary arrival of more worthless troops and more "useless" government officials from the mainland. Edgar then delivered his *coup de grace*. He told Wu that Chiang "...appeared as usual more interested in US aid than in basic reform and preferring half measures to forthright facing of facts. Taiwan did not now need US material aid but US moral support and that the only way toward [the] latter was through drastic reform." Wu was quick to agree with Edgar's analysis. Wu, however, was a man with a mission. In spite of what he had just been told, Wu asked if Edgar would press the State Department to agree to provide aid if he promised "subsequent reforms." Edgar replied that he would not recommend that the State Department agree to such an idea. Moreover, he told Wu that he

"...doubted if [the] US Government would be interested in more Chinese promises." After being subjected to all of this Wu left, saying that he would reject the Gimo's latest offer.[11]

The very next morning, December 14th, Wu was back with more news. After leaving the Consulate the previous day, Wu told Edgar, he went to the Generalissimo to reject the offer of the governorship. This, according to Wu, precipitated a "heated debate" within the Nationalist Government which lasted throughout the night. Recalcitrant conservative leaders such as Wang Shih-chieh, Wu said, were won over to his side due to his "courageous stand." Chiang, who Wu claimed was always willing to support him and his *provisos,* was able to prevail over the forces of opposition. As a result, Wu was to be the Governor of Taiwan and his original four conditions were accepted. He told Edgar that he was now preparing to launch into the business of reforming rule on Formosa and that he was in the process of selecting a number of Taiwanese to serve as high-ranking provincial officials. Before taking his leave, Wu admitted to Edgar that he doubted that he would have any real influence in the arena of military reform.[12]

The next day, December 15th, General Sun Li-jen summoned Edgar to a meeting. He asked the Acting Consul General if State had replied to the request for military advisers; presumably the approach to Captain Manning two weeks earlier. Edgar offered that there was no action on the request, adding that he and the Consulate's Attaches "could see no evidence of Chinese efforts toward military reorganization." According to Edgar, Sun "...begged that some move be made by the US." Sun told Edgar that he had a "1 hour's conference" with Chiang on December 14th during which Sun "spoke frankly" of the need for military reform. Sun appealed to Edgar, saying that there were no reform-minded military leaders upon whom he could prevail to join him in pressuring the Generalissimo for military reform. Sun argued that only the United States could now pressure Chiang into making changes throughout the military. It was incumbent upon Washington to support Sun's appeal to Chiang. Otherwise, Sun warned, the "...old generals will continue to control policy." Sun further stated that he was heartened by the prospects for civil reform now that K.C. Wu was to be Governor. However, Sun pointed out that without concomitant military reforms, changes in the civilian sector would mean nothing. Wu, said Sun, had been told to keep his nose out of military affairs. Sun further stated his belief that the KMT military could hold out for another six months, but thereafter outside military assistance would be required if Taiwan was to survive. Interestingly, the General then made the same suggestion that K.C. Wu had made a few days earlier. He recommended that the United States provide military aid to the KMT on a "step by step" basis. This meant that for every positive reform enacted, Taipei be rewarded with some form of assistance. While Sun (and K.C. Wu) suggested that this form of diplomatic behavior modification could be used by State to encourage reform, State saw this in a rather different light; the U.S. would have to pay Taipei to reform. Consequently, Edgar told Sun that Washington "...would probably make no positive move prior to evidence of Chinese willingness to face facts and reform in accordance with realities of [the] current desperate situation."[13] The next day it was learned that Sun was placed in command of the island's defenses.[14]

Within one week, then, two of Nationalist China's premier "reformers" and U.S. favorites appealed to Washington to help them in an alleged battle to defeat conservative elements within the KMT. While Wu and Sun were legitimate forces for reform, Chiang Kai-shek, more than likely, was using them to gain leverage over the United States. Wu and Sun had a degree of credibility which Chiang did not. As savvy observers of American politics, the KMT may have been attempting to draw out U.S. economic and military assistance by having Washington believe that in doing so it would not necessarily be helping the much-despised Gimo, but strengthening the hand of reformist elements within the Nationalist Government. This is certainly how the Western press in Taipei viewed these events. For example, when official announcement of Wu's impending governorship was made the Associated Press (AP) talked in terms of "...an attempt to win US aid in the war against Communism in the orient" and "...an obvious move to woo United States aid for Nationalist China."[15] This interpretation was shared as well by State Department officials back in Washington.

The conversations that Walton Butterworth and Fulton Freeman (CA) held with John L. Sullivan in December 1949 reveal that State was highly skeptical about the motives behind Wu's appointment. The conversations reveal as well how the KMT was able to use prominent intermediaries with access to the highest reaches of government to plead their case.

Sullivan, former Secretary of the Navy, had resigned from office in mid-1949 during the "Revolt of the Admirals" and was back in private legal practice. In December 1949, as Sullivan told it, he was providing legal counsel to a public relations group representing the Bank of China in New York. In reality, Sullivan was advising Madame Chiang Kai-shek who was still residing in Riverdale, New York.[16] Nevertheless, Sullivan also offered to help State by advancing the Department's messages and thoughts to his "clients" (Madame Chiang) in an unofficial capacity.

On the 12th, 14th, and 20th of December Sullivan met with Butterworth. The message he carried from Riverdale was, "(1) that the Chinese would be willing to accept and carry out any program of political, economic and social reform for Formosa which the U.S. Government would be willing to propose; and (2) that the Chinese would be willing to approach General Eichelberger or some other prominent retired American general with the request that he assume complete command of the defense of Formosa." Sullivan admitted to Butterworth that these offers constituted "death-bed repentance" but that they seemed to him to be genuine and deserved State's consideration. To these proposals Butterworth offered a lengthy discourse on why the U.S. would not propose specific political and economic reforms. The bottom line was that Butterworth and others at State believed that the Chinese already knew what they had to do to make Taiwan viable and gain the support of the Formosans. What State was looking for was the "substance" of KMT reforms, not merely "form." On the matter of a retired U.S. general being given command of KMT forces, Butterworth believed this to be an "old story" and recounted to Sullivan the trials and tribulations of Generals Stilwell and Wedemeyer and the frustrations of General David Barr, former commander of JUSMAGCHINA. Butterworth offered that the U.S. had suffered a terrible blow to its prestige by its "tragic failure in China," and that now that the United States was finally disengaged from the civil war it would be folly to fully commit American prestige in the Far East once again to "...any given cause in China..." Referring to K.C. Wu's appointment as Governor, Sullivan asked Butterworth "...whether this did not appear to be a step in the right direction." Butterworth remarked that State had the greatest confidence in Wu's personal abilities. However, Butterworth divulged to Sullivan the fact that Chiang originally offered Wu the position only if he could produce U.S. aid within one month. As Fulton Freeman explained to Sullivan, "...the incident was revelatory of the Generalissimo's attitude that reform was not of itself necessary to strengthen the Chinese Government's position but rather a necessary step to obtain further U.S. aid." At the close of their conversations, Butterworth, Freeman, and Sullivan agreed to have the latter deliver the following message to Madame Chiang:

> K.C. Wu, a man in whom the Department of State has great confidence, has now been made Governor. In view of his long and successful experience in administering Chinese provinces and large municipalities, it would be superfluous for the U.S. to suggest any specific program of reform—a matter in which K.C. Wu is much more competent to judge than any group of Americans. The U.S. will, however, watch with considerable interest the scope of authority which Wu will be permitted to exercise and the extent to which he is permitted to implement his own recommendations regarding political, economic, and social reforms.[17]

On December 23rd, Butterworth had the opportunity to deliver to Ambassador V.K. Wellington Koo the same message he sent to Madame Chiang through Sullivan. On that day Koo called on Butterworth and Merchant at State. He brought with him, to be forwarded to Acheson, an official communication from his government requesting military equipment, economic aid, and military and political advisers. Koo told Butterworth that K.C. Wu's appointment as Governor was already yielding results; Formosans were now included in the Provincial administration and General Sun Li-jen had recently been given command of the island's defenses. After Koo's review of recent events Butterworth underscored the great confidence that State had in Wu's abilities. However, he told Koo, "the test would be the extent of the powers granted him..." Butterworth then reviewed for Koo all the problems Wu had encountered in his attempts to reform Shanghai before its collapse simply because he did not control the military. The same situation, Butterworth offered, now faced Wu on Taiwan. As for Sun's new command, the Assistant Secretary remained skeptical; confused lines of military authority still existed on the island. Butterworth then emphasized the hope that reforms on Taiwan were not being made simply because it was perceived that the United States desired them. Moreover, Koo was reminded that Washington "...had no intention of using American troops to defend the island."[18]

And so it went. Chiang attempted to put a new face on Taiwan and seek assistance from Washington. However, overt approaches for aid did no good. State's attitude had hardened to the point that only successful and sustained reform would be acknowledged as deserving of U.S. assistance. By the time such conditions were met Taiwan could well go under to the CCP. Moreover, and in all fairness to Taipei, State had now levied a much more nebulous prerequisite for assistance. Reform also had to be the result of proper motivation. Consequently, Chiang and the KMT also attempted to pressure the administration into offering aid by calling upon and manipulating the China Bloc in Congress for help.

7.3 THE CHINA BLOC: H. ALEXANDER SMITH

Although Senator William Knowland (R. California), known as the "Senator from Formosa," made much noise about the administration's Taiwan policy, his counsel was never welcomed by State. Indeed, of all the Republicans who comprised the China Bloc, only Senator H. Alexander Smith of New Jersey was ever taken seriously by Acheson and his advisers. Even though the Secretary and the Senator disagreed on many issues, the two men maintained a mutual respect and conducted themselves in a gentlemanly fashion which facilitated dialogue.[19]

A leading member of the Senate Foreign Relations Committee, Smith took a keen interest in Far Eastern Affairs in general and China policy in particular.[20] His complaints in this area were substantial. He argued that although State's foreign policy toward Europe was developed in close consultation with the Congress, the legislative branch was "definitely not" being consulted on policy toward Asia. Also, Smith was "frustrated" by the feeling that there was no overall policy toward Asia at all. Finally, the administration seemed to be doing nothing to help China in its hour of need. Smith rejected the notion of "waiting until the dust settles" and believed that somehow there were still ways in which China could "be aided and rebuilt on sound foundations..."[21]

While these were the same complaints lodged by most members of the China Bloc, Smith was definitely not among those politicians who were using China problems for personal or partisan reasons. He once remarked that the men in Congress fighting the administration's Far Eastern policies were a "strange combination" of individuals. Congressman Walter Judd, he felt, was too "emotional" to have any impact on policy. He thought Senator McCarren's motives were suspect; especially the Nevada legislator's scheme to loan silver to the Chinese. Senators Owen Brewster and Styles Bridges, lamented Smith, were determined to use China policy as strictly a partisan issue. None of this appealed to Smith. He believed that there were only two paths which could be taken in attempting to change China policy: "To blast the State Department publicly on the floor of the Senate and in the press..." or attempting to "...organize the pro-China group into a bipartisan attitude of cooperation and insistence that our present policy be changed..." Smith wanted "to get the State Department leadership to work with us rather than against us."[22] He genuinely attempted to work toward that end.[23]

Smith had helped Knowland in his fight to include the Section 303 funds into the Mutual Defense Assistance Act; the $75 million discretionary fund which the China Bloc hoped would be used to help the KMT. However, by the autumn of 1949 it became apparent to Smith that the Nationalist cause on the mainland was doomed. He concurred with others who by then believed that sending more military aid to help the KMT beat back the communists would be "money poured down the 'rat hole'."[24] Consequently, the Senator began to focus his attention and concern on the issue of saving Taiwan.

Smith believed that U.S. strategic interests would be threatened if the island fell to the CCP. Moreover, he felt that a communist takeover of the island would be a devastating blow to American prestige in the region. Furthermore, if the KMT could make Taiwan a model province, it would be an inspiration to those on the mainland determined to resist the CCP. At the same time, Smith was genuinely concerned about the welfare of the Formosan people, learning of their troubles from correspondence with Thomas Liao of the FLR.[25] He was aware that native Taiwanese were thoroughly alienated by the KMT due to what Smith termed "...the inept handling of the island by the Nationalists since they have taken control."[26] On each of these counts, he and State were in general agreement. Nevertheless, he was not convinced that the administration was doing anything to act upon these concerns or accomplish these objectives. He felt that an aggressive policy of assistance to the island was in order. However, just what should be done was unclear to Smith. Consequently, in order to find a solution to the thorny problem of Taiwan (and other Asian policy issues), the Senator embarked on a fact-finding tour of the Far East during September and October of 1949.

In the course of his weeks in the Far East, Smith visited Japan, Okinawa, the Philippines, Hong Kong, Korea, Guam, Hawaii, and Taiwan. In each country or territory he spoke with United States and local national officials, military and civilian, learning about conditions and entertaining suggestions for U.S. policy. The burning issues, of course, centered upon finding ways in which the United States could stem the tide of communism throughout Asia, as well as a proper policy toward China and Taiwan.

Smith's first stop was in Tokyo where he conferred with MacArthur; his official host for the trip. His subsequent destinations were arranged by SCAP headquarters, which provided intra-theater transportation and escorts. Indeed, on almost every leg of his journey, Smith was accompanied by a member of MacArthur's staff.[27] Even when the Senator met with Chiang Kai-shek in Taipei a member of SCAP's Government Section, Colonel Herbert B. Wheeler, was present.

Smith was thrilled to have the "privilege" of lunching with MacArthur on September 26th. He was treated to a briefing on the successes of the Japanese occupation, the general's views on the situation in the Far East, as well as MacArthur's assessment of Chiang Kai-shek. Smith was impressed, recording that MacArthur "...obviously understands the psychology of the [Asian] people." As for Taiwan, MacArthur told Smith what the Senator already believed; the island must never be allowed to fall to the communists. The Senator came away from his meeting knowing that MacArthur "...is a believer in Chiang Kai-shek..." even though he recognized "his faults and weaknesses." MacArthur also lectured Smith that Washington "misunderstood" the Gimo, and had "permitted a smear campaign to get underway in the United States, which had much to do with undermining him in China."[28] MacArthur appealed to Smith to help in procuring assistance for Chiang.[29]

The royal treatment that Smith received in Tokyo was second only to the reception he got in Taipei. While on Taiwan Smith was feted by K.C. Wu, Sun Li-jen, Ch'en Ch'eng, and other KMT notables. The highlight of the trip to Taipei should have been Smith's audience with Chiang Kai-shek. However, the Senator did not leave his conference with the Gimo overly enthused.[30] For example, Smith asked Chiang what programs the KMT had developed to counter the CCP's "vicious" anti-American propaganda and communist promises of agrarian reform on the mainland. The Senator also asked Chiang what the KMT was doing to improve conditions on Taiwan. According to Smith, Chiang talked in generalities about the KMT being the only force which could change the mainland and about his determination to hold out against the CCP in southwest China. Chiang vowed to his guest that even if driven off the mainland completely, he would continue the fight from Taiwan. As for his political reform program, the Gimo philosophized about the ideals of Sun Yat-sen. After addressing Smith's questions in a fashion, Chiang then told the Senator that he was "discouraged" by the present policy of the United States toward Taiwan. He did not know what the U.S. proposed to do to help the island, if anything. Overall, Smith confided to Knowland that he found Chiang to be "disappointingly vague."[31] So much for Smith's meeting with the leader of Free China.

Although Chiang may have proven disappointing, Smith was heartened and extremely enthused by his meetings with K.C. Wu. The two Princeton alumni (Smith '01; Wu,'25) seemed to develop an instant rapport. After his return to the United States, Smith and Wu maintained a personal correspondence in which each apprised the other of developments of mutual concern.[32] Moreover, Smith was elated when Wu, whom he proudly described to others as "an American educated Chinaman of real ability and broad vision" or "most able" and "most reliable," was made Governor of Taiwan later in December. During his stay in Taipei, Smith talked with K.C. Wu, not Chiang, about the issues of U.S. economic and military aid for Taiwan.[33]

While still in the Far East, Smith began to publicly air his views about Taiwan. Whether by design or coincidence, he gave an interview on October 10th (the anniversary of Sun Yat-sen's 1911 revolution) to the *Pacific Star and Stripes,* the SCAP-controlled newspaper of the U.S. Far Eastern Command. Smith was quoted as saying that he considered it "vitally important for the United States not to let Formosa get into Communist hands." He further stated that the KMT could hold the island (described by the reporter as being "astride the U.S. Pacific base chain") if they were permitted to buy military equipment using the $75 million allocated by Section 303 of the Mutual Defense Assistance Act. The article also attributed to Smith the statement that helping the Nationalists to save Taiwan would not entail risking war with the Soviets.[34]

Upon his return to the United States, Smith began his campaign to save Taiwan. Throughout November and December he had meetings with Acheson, Jessup, Fosdick, Kennan, and Rusk; attempting to goad them into positive action to assist Taipei.[35] He briefed Senator Knowland, about to make his own celebrated sweep through the Far East, on his ideas for supporting Taiwan.[36] Moreover, Smith took to the radio to talk to the American public about the situation in Asia.[37] He established a correspondence with MacArthur's headquarters in Tokyo to keep the general apprised of developments in Washington.[38] Also, the Senator talked with members of the Joint and Navy staffs about the strategic importance of Taiwan and what should be done to deny it to the CCP.[39] Finally, Smith delivered to the Senate, both in writing and orally, a report on his trip and his recommendations for U.S. policy.

In his discussions with State, Smith's bottom line was straightforward; Taiwan should not be allowed to fall into communist hands. On this fundamental point Smith and State were in full agreement. Where they differed was in how to do it. Acheson and his advisers were all for denying Taiwan to the CCP. However, State was prepared to subordinate Taiwan's salvation to the larger policy objective of fostering Titoism on the mainland. Moreover, all evidence indicated that Chiang and the KMT already had the military and economic wherewithall to survive; it was just a matter of Chinese leaders using their assets wisely. Smith, on the other hand, told Acheson that he "could see no possibility whatsoever of any Titoism developing in China."[40] Consequently, the Senator felt that there was no reason why worries about CCP sensitivities should preclude at least economic aid to Taipei. In any case, Smith argued to the Secretary that the security implications of a CCP-dominated Taiwan transcended all other considerations. The "many military authorities" with whom Smith spoke during his trip, he told Acheson, "regarded the retention of Formosa as of the utmost strategic importance to the United States." He told the Secretary that it was in the "compelling interest" of the nation "to hold on to the island by any means short of actual war." While Smith preferred a U.N. Trusteeship to snatch the island from Mao, Smith realized that this would probably not be possible. Consequently, the Senator recommended to Acheson that a unilateral military occupation by the United States be considered. Acheson explained to Smith that both courses of action had already been explored. He also pointed out that among the military authorities in Washington there was "some difference of opinion" about the strategic importance of the island.[41] The two men also parted ways on the issue of the utility of Chiang Kai-shek's continued leadership. Acheson felt that the Gimo was a political liability. Smith admitted the Generalissimo's many faults as well and felt that K.C. Wu would ultimately be the man to reform Nationalist rule on Taiwan. However, the Senator still saw Chiang as the only man around whom the Chinese could rally. He believed the Gimo still possessed invaluable symbolic importance.[42] Neither man swayed the other on any of these points.

Smith went public on December 1st. On that day his trip report was released with much fanfare. Besides a press release from his own office, the *New York Times* reported on Smith's recommendations. The actual report, which covered all aspects of Far Eastern policy, was twenty pages long. It was written in surprisingly objective terms, relatively free of polemics and inflammatory language.[43] However, the *New York Times* article was a political blockbuster. Titled "Senator Urges U.S. To Take Formosa," it highlighted Smith's recommendation that the U.S. occupy Taiwan, associated General MacArthur with that course of action, and implied that General Bradley was not in favor of saving the island.

> WASHINGTON, Dec.1—A recommendation that the United States send troops into Formosa to occupy it indefinitely was made today by a Republican member of the Senate Foreign Relations Committee, Senator H. Alexander Smith of New Jersey...
>
> ...Senator Smith said in effect that his proposal had the support of General of the Army Douglas MacArthur and other military and naval authorities in the Orient, although probably not of high officers in the United States...
>
> ...Discussing Formosa, Mr. Smith made it plain that the island had been the subject of much anxious speculation among high United States officers in the Orient during his visit there.
>
> "The feeling I got from MacArthur and the admirals was that they were unwilling even to assume that we would consider letting Formosa fall into hostile hands," he said. "I got the impression that there was some

difference of opinion in the Pentagon here; there is an understanding among some that General [Omar N.] Bradley [chairman of the Joint Chiefs of Staff] doesn't think that holding Formosa is necessarily so vital."[44]

Smith's good intentions backfired. His trip report, his recommendations, and the publicity he generated only served to alienate State and undermine the close cooperation he sought with Foggy Bottom on the Taiwan issue. In effect, he opened the administration's Taiwan policy to public scrutiny and urged a policy option that had already been rejected. Ironically, Smith's report also gave plenty of ammunition to those in Congress determined to make Taiwan a partisan issue; something the Senator wished to avoid at all costs. Moreover, given the politics of the day, inferring that General Bradley was not in favor of defending Taiwan was tantamount to character assassination. Finally, invoking MacArthur's name must have been as irksome to most military officials in Washington as it was to State.

7.4 DOUGLAS MACARTHUR: SCAP WEIGHS-IN

George Kennan once wrote that "any great military occupational government at once takes on certain aspects of a sovereign government."[45] This was certainly true of General Douglas MacArthur, his staff, and the occupation government that ruled Japan from Tokyo's *Dai Ichi* building. MacArthur had enormous powers and responsibilities. He was the Supreme Commander Allies Pacific (SCAP); an international post which authorized him to preside over the Japanese occupation on behalf of the victors of the Second World War. At the same time, he was Commander-in-Chief, Far East (CINCFE); commander of all U.S. forces in the Pacific. Except for China (which was a Navy theater) MacArthur had operational responsibility for all of Asia. When the Korean War erupted, he would add to these posts another; Commander-in-Chief, United Nations Forces, Korea (CINCUN-K).[46]

A power unto himself, MacArthur remained as detached as possible from the government whose uniform he wore. Whether he was friend or foe was strictly a function of the issue at hand. He was as apt to align himself with State against the Pentagon as he was to support the Department of Defense in its battles against the diplomats.[47] Indeed, there was no love lost between the general and the Joint Chiefs of Staff. To MacArthur, JCS Chairman Omar Bradley personified the "Europe First" strategy of the Second World War which relegated his Pacific theater to secondary importance in obtaining much needed manpower and supplies. Furthermore, the men in the Pentagon were junior to MacArthur in both grade and time-in-service. More immediately, in 1949, MacArthur's Far Eastern Command (FEC) suffered the transfer of naval and air assets to Europe, and the general was known to rant and rave about the "atlantic mentality" of the National Military Establishment and their determination to "scuttle the Pacific."[48]

However, MacArthur was no friend of Foggy Bottom's. The Department of Śtate was equally guilty in his eyes of subordinating Asia to European concerns. In particular, MacArthur railed incessantly about State's China policy, equating its non-support for the KMT with abetting the roll of the red tide through Asia. Prior to the Korean War he made the issue his *cause celebre*, making him the darling of the China Bloc in Congress. On two occasions, once in 1948 and again in 1949, members of Congress invited MacArthur back to Washington to testify on a proper policy toward China. On both occasions he declined citing "the pressure of my operational duties..." Yet, even in declining these invitations, and reminding all that China was technically outside his area of operational control, MacArthur was able to take a swipe at State. "The international aspect of the Chinese problem," he wrote to the House Committee on Foreign Affairs, "unfortunately has become somewhat clouded by demands for internal reform. Desirable as such reform may be, its importance is but secondary to the issue of civil strife now engulfing the land, and the two issues are as impossible of synchronization as it would be to alter the structural design of a house while at the same was being consumed by flame."[49]

Amazingly, as late as the summer and fall of 1949, as the Nationalist armies were marching from one defeat to another, MacArthur was still arguing that an ultimate KMT victory in the civil war was possible. For example, on August 30, 1949, MacArthur told David Sentner, in a newspaper interview for the *New York Journal American,* "That China was not gone," and "That China was now more a military than a political problem." He judged that "the Chinese Red Army is not as good as the Japanese Army which the Nationalist forces held off and pushed back." In the same article MacArthur declared his resounding support for Chennault who claimed that with "a few hundred million dollars" from the United States, "China could turn the tide against the Reds."[50] MacArthur passed along the same message to a visiting Congressional delegation in September 1949. He told the legislators that "Relatively little effort will be required now to turn the tide in China," and that the red army was "grossly overrated." The general also took the opportunity to make excuses for Chiang's weaknesses as well as underscore his positive points. "Chiang," said MacArthur, "is surrounded by corrupt officials including corrupt generals. The Generalissimo is a highly intelligent individual but knows nothing of the art of war." However, MacArthur pointed out, the Gimo has "a driving determination and strength of character which makes him a natural leader." The general then told the congressmen that if four things were done immediately, "the situation can be saved." These four actions were:

> a. Make a ringing declaration that the United State will support any and every one who is opposed to communism; b. Place 500 fighter planes in the hands of some "war horse" similar to General Chennault; c. Give volunteers the right to join such a fighting force without penalty; d. Assign surplus ships to the Chinese Navy sufficient to blockade and destroy Chinese coastal cities.[51]

Needless to say, these types of statements appalled State Department officials.[52] Moreover, MacArthur's claims that the KMT could still win the civil war if given U.S. aid at this late date flew in the face of assessments made by every American military official who had first hand experience on the mainland, to include Marshall, Wedemeyer and, most recently, General Barr. Consequently, MacArthur's wild claims either revealed just how out of touch he was with battlefield realities in China, or exposed him as consciously attempting to embarrass the administration for political reasons. Perhaps both explanations are valid. In any event, his bombast only served to debunk the thesis underlying State's *White Paper* and gave powerful ammunition to those who would reinvolve the United States in the Chinese civil war.

MacArthur was as opinionated on the issue of Taiwan as he was in his calls for supporting the KMT on the mainland. Those who asked for his thinking on the matter found that MacArthur "needed no urging," and that the matter was "close to his heart and mind."[53] It was a subject which moved MacArthur to eloquent soliloquy.

Ultimately, the general's concerns about Taiwan were, he claimed, purely strategic in nature. And there was one message which he delivered time and again, as if rehearsed, to all who would listen: Formosa must not fall! The following lecture, which MacArthur delivered to Max W. Bishop (head of State's Northeast Asian Affairs Division) in February 1949, is representative of the general's views. When asked by Bishop what impact the fall of Taiwan would have upon U.S. security, MacArthur's reaction "...was immediate and vehement." According to William Sebald, who recorded the discussion, MacArthur:

> ...said that if Formosa went to the Chinese Communists our whole defensive position in the Far East was definitely lost; that it could only result eventually in putting our defensive line back to the west coast of the continental United States. He said that he felt there could be no question but that if Formosa were in the hands of the Chinese Communists it would be available to the USSR as a base at any time the latter desired. He pointed out that Formosa was astride the line of communications between Okinawa and the Philippines, that it outflanked our position on Okinawa and, in the hands of the Chinese Communists, broke through the island wall which we must have along the Asiatic 'littorals' in order to maintain in a strategic sense a defense line in the western Pacific...Referring again to the vital importance of Formosa and to the fatal consequences of its loss, General MacArthur emphasized that as long as we had superior air and naval forces in that part of the world we could prevent a launching from Asia of an attack on the United States, but that without holding solidly this Asiatic fringe of islands, with Japan as a neutralized area, our defense position would be forced back to the west coast of the continental United States.[54]

In the last months of 1949, MacArthur became more aggressive in lobbying for a policy which would ensure that Taiwan was not allowed to fall to the CCP. Congressional delegations which travelled through Tokyo were prime targets. Senator Smith's trip and the publicity surrounding it was a great boon to the general's cause. Moreover, MacArthur pressured the Joint Staff in the Pentagon to remove the ambivalence in their analysis of Taiwan's strategic importance. In November, MacArthur dispatched a member of his staff, Colonel C. Stanton Babcock, to the Pentagon to discuss issues related to the Japanese peace treaty. Babcock's other mission was to lobby MacArthur's concern about Taiwan. Babcock dutifully related to a group of DoD and State Department officials that "General MacArthur considers it of the greatest importance that Formosa not fall under Communist control. He does not believe it essential that we control the island, but believes that 'by hook or by crook' we must keep it out of Communist hands." The General further believed that "rather than permit Formosa to go to the Communists, it would be better to return it to Japan."[55]

The records are still not definitive about whether MacArthur may have taken actions to bolster the KMT on Taiwan without the administration's knowledge ('by hook or by crook') prior to the Korean War. Nevertheless, there is some reason to speculate that the general was probably dabbling on the island in 1949. General Sun Li-jen made at least one trip to SCAP headquarters in Tokyo that year, the purpose of which remains unknown.[56] In mid-November MacArthur dispatched a team of American military officers to Taiwan without requesting country clearance from State. The mission of the team was never revealed to State Department officials in Taipei or Washington.[57] Scholar Michael Schaller, citing declassified intelligence documents obtained under the Freedom of Information Act, offers that in November 1949 the Central Intelligence Agency was surprised to discover that MacArthur was allowing former pilots from the Japanese Imperial Army to travel to Taiwan to assist the KMT Air Force.[58] In December, one Taipei newspaper, *New World,* carried a story that claimed the recent "rumor" that "...Japanese volunteers arrived in Taiwan to join the Nationalist forces has received official confirmation." The article also reminded its readers that "Without the permission of the SCAP, it is next to impossible for Japanese soldiers to come to Taiwan."[59]

Whether based upon wishful thinking, or grounded in some truth, Taiwan was awash with rumors that MacArthur was making plans to save the island in late 1949. In September, the Consulate in Taipei was besieged with requests for confirmation of the news that American intervention was at hand, set for the fifteenth of the month.[60] In November, a local paper reported that the KMT's Ministry of National Defense disclosed that a representative from Tokyo had met with Chiang and the Military Council in Tso-san to work out details for MacArthur assuming responsibility for the defense of Taiwan.[61] Also in November, officials from the Consulate in Taipei were being told by local nationals and foreign missionaries that SCAP had in fact been given authority by Washington to defend Taiwan, that the $75 million was going to be allocated for assistance to Taipei, that MacArthur was personally conferring with mainlanders and islanders about the future political system to be established under his auspices, and that Chiang Kai-shek would leave Taiwan for good.[62]

The rumors, the unannounced visits from Tokyo, MacArthur's statements to visiting congressmen, and his attempts to pressure the Pentagon to reverse its assessment of Taiwan's strategic significance all worked to counter State's objectives and its policies toward Taiwan. In December, MacArthur would provide Louis Johnson with a potentially powerful weapon with which to fight against State's recommended policy toward the island as NSC 48 came under review.

7.5 PENTAGON PRESSURES

As mentioned earlier, NSC 48 was Louis Johnson's brainchild. And it was clear from the very inception of the study back in June that the Secretary of Defense was determined to make it an unpleasant affair for Foggy Bottom; even to the point of denying Acheson's request that a general officer from DoD be seconded to State to give informal advice on the military aspects of the Asian situation.[63]

By the autumn of 1949, it was also apparent that Johnson planned to use the study to attack State's policy of non-intervention in the Chinese civil war. Initially, the Secretary of Defense focused on trying to reopen the issue of supplying KMT elements on the mainland with military assistance with which to fight the red army. The passage of the Mutual Defense Assistance Act, with its $75 million for the "general area of China," presented Johnson with an opportunity to do just that. On September 15th, even before the the Act was formally passed into law, Johnson ordered the JCS to begin making plans to provide assistance to the KMT in China. "The inclusion of $75,000,000 for aid to China makes it imperative," read Johnson's OSD directive, "that immediate action be taken to study the military problems involved in aiding China and the determination of a plan and program for that aid." It was ordered that, "...the Joint Chiefs of Staff undertake this study at the earliest possible date."[64]

Much to Johnson's consternation, however, the military planners on the Joint Staff were extremely skeptical that any amount of money or military equipment could reverse the inevitable defeat of the KMT on the mainland at that late date. For example, the Joint Strategic Survey Committee (JSSC) agreed with State that the famous "Chennault Plan" for helping the KMT to hold southwest and western China was unworkable. In October 1949, they reported to

Johnson and the NSC that the plan was based on a major assumption which the JSSC believed incorrect; that "unified resistance" to the CCP existed in unoccupied areas of China. Moreover, military planners did not believe that there was any way in which assistance in areas such as Sinkiang or Tibet could be reasonably sustained.[65] However, ordered to conduct their own study, the JSSC proceeded.

In the course of its preliminary assessment, the Joint Staff found itself in fundamental disagreement with MacArthur's assertion that all was not lost. Finding ways to assist the KMT on the mainland was a military planner's nightmare. And although the logistical aspects of assistance were workable to a certain degree, JSSC planners found that the political and human factors were the greatest hindrance to successful military assistance to the Nationalists. They noted that KMT control even over non-communist areas was "so weak that it is now little more than nominal." They pointed out that the KMT was "itself divided into two major political factions..." While intelligence indicated that some areas of communist-occupied China were experiencing peasant uprisings, it was judged that "...there is no evidence that civil disturbances in rear of the Communist troops have yet affected plans for Communist military advances." JSSC planners assessed that the KMT troops were riddled with defeatism and that Nationalist generals were political hacks, not trained professionals capable of using aid wisely. In short, "based on purely military grounds," it was judged that the KMT would not be able to recover any ground lost to the CCP. "Military aid alone," they believed, "regardless of the amount, cannot halt the advance of the Communists in the immediate future."[66]

The Joint Chiefs did not respond to Johnson's September request until December. The best that the military planners could come up with was a strawman program using 303 funds to assist non-communist forces still fighting and for "special operations" that might "effectively interfere in communist control of China." Moreover, the final study (J.C.S. 1721/37) was forwarded to the Secretary of Defense without the formal endorsement of the Joint Chiefs of Staff, who believed that the study would better serve Johnson if it were considered "background material."[67]

In putting off Johnson on this particular issue, the JCS hid behind the very valid (and convenient) excuse that without a policy decision authorizing military aid to the mainland, planning was pointless.

In considering the problem of determining a plan and program for furnishing United States military assistance to China primary consideration should be given to the over-all United States policy in China and Asia as a whole. If such a policy were now available to the Joint Chiefs of Staff, they could proceed with confidence in this matter. In the absence of such a policy they must exercise unusual caution in order not to place themselves in a position of dictating, even by indirection, the course of our national policies in China and Asia. Although the Joint Chiefs of Staff should stand ready at all times to give military advice, in this case the advice would of necessity be predicated upon assumptions which may or may not prove to be valid. Proceeding further with the development of the military guidance, new and potentially even less valid assumptions would have to be made. The end result would be guidance based on compounded conjecture.

...Pending completion of studies now under consideration in the National Security Council and the Department of State with respect to United States policy in Asia and China [NSC 48], any determination at this time of a plan or program for furnishing assistance to China would probably be unacceptable.[68]

With his own military advisers reluctant to embroil the Pentagon in a crusade to assist the KMT on the mainland, Johnson, in December, turned instead to the issue of Taiwan. On this matter, the JCS did not feel constrained by the fact that NSC 48 was not finalized or that current policy did not authorize military assistance. Here was an issue ripe for further exploitation.

Even though the Joint Chiefs felt that global requirements precluded a major commitment to the island they had judged all along that its capture would be a strategic loss. However, as Dean Acheson pointed out to Senator Smith, within the JCS there was "some difference of opinion" as to how vital Taiwan really was to U.S. security.[69] Not all DoD officials believed that a major military effort to save the island was justified.[70] Among those who had always supported positive action was Secretary Johnson and the civilian and uniformed leadership of the Army.

As soon as the Mutual Defense Assistance Act was passed into law General J. Lawton ("Lightning Joe") Collins, Army Chief of Staff, set his Plans and Operations Division to work planning potential uses for the $75,000,000. By early November 1949, Major General Charles L. Bolte (Collins' Deputy Chief of Staff for Plans and Operations) produced a hypothetical breakout of the funds which allocated $20 million for Taiwan. Also in mid-November, Army Secretary

Gordon Gray was pressuring the Joint Staff to find some way to give assistance to Taipei.[71] But, without a consensus among themselves, the Joint Chiefs were not prepared to raise the issue in the NSC again or buck State on the matter.

However, in December, those in DoD who always desired a positive policy of assistance, especially the Army, found that the time was right to launch a new Taiwan offensive. The catalyst for their renewed initiative to reopen the matter appears to have been the visit to Tokyo by Under Secretary of the Army Tracy S. Voorhees and Major General Alfred M. Gruenther (Director of the Joint Staff) for talks with MacArthur on the situation in the Far East during the first days of December.

As Voorhees told Acheson upon his return, MacArthur gave him and Gruenther "his military views...in his military capacity as CINCFE." Voorhees also told the Secretary of State point blank that SCAP offered his political views as well, but requested that Voorhees not share them with State; a request the Army Under Secretary honored with relish.[72] Apparently, MacArthur treated his visitors to one of his lectures on Taiwan, for Voorhees took notes which summarized MacArthur's views on the topic. The general's message was familiar: allowing Taiwan to fall to the CCP would be "fatal" to the U.S. line of defense in the Far East; a "large part of the $75,000,000" should go to the KMT to bolster their defense; and the U.S. should declare that an attack on Taiwan would be considered an act of war by Washington. However, MacArthur did not suggest the occupation of the island by U.S. troops. All that was needed, he argued, was to deny it to the enemy.[73]

Voorhees' trip and his return coincided with a spate of DoD activity on the Taiwan issue. As OSD historian Steven Rearden points out, in early December, Secretary of Defense Johnson "asked the Joint Chiefs for 'an opinion as to whether there was anything the Military Establishment ought to be doing [on Formosa] that affected the security of the United States, regardless of what might be the Government's political objectives.'"[74] On December 1st, General Bolte on the Army Staff wrote General Collins that "the moment is psychologically right for public opinion and the Congress to support positive measures with respect to Taiwan."[75] On December 7th, General Collins sent a memorandum to the JCS stating most emphatically, that he considered it necessary "to reexamine and reappraise the strategic importance of Taiwan and U.S. policy toward Taiwan as a matter of priority in order to permit determination of a prompt, positive U.S. course of action which would be practicable from a military point of view to prevent Chinese Communist domination of Taiwan."[76] On December 14th Voorhees personally briefed the JSSC on MacArthur's views on Taiwan.[77] By the 15th of December, the Joint Staff was at work drafting a paper for the NSC which would argue for military assistance to Taiwan![78]

General Omar Bradley, JCS Chairman, probably felt uneasy about supporting such a politically-charged initiative. Bradley was one of the finest battlefield generals of the Second World War. But his memoirs leave one with the distinct impression that he was not happy with his lot in Washington. The political machinations and bureaucratic in-fighting frustrated him. Moreover, Bradley was uncomfortable in the NSC when asked to offer anything other than the military aspects of a problem. Bradley's reluctance to offer opinions on geo-political issues frustrated Acheson. At one of their first meetings Acheson recalls that Bradley continually prefaced his remarks with the caveat, "from the purely military point of view." The Secretary of State told him, "General Bradley, would you mind just not having that phrase come in. We aren't going to talk about 'from the purely military point of view,' I am not going to say 'from the purely diplomatic point of view.'"[79] Furthermore, Bradley did not care for Secretary Johnson and certainly would not have supported the Taiwan relook to curry favor with him. As Bradley wrote years later:

> Louis Johnson, fifty-eight, was a big 250-pound bear, whose major goal was to work a miracle in the Pentagon. That is, bash heads, cut budgets, stop the interminable wrangling and truly unify the services. He was the direct opposite of the shy, introverted, intellectual, apolitical Forrestal. Johnson was flamboyant, outspoken, and rumor had it, had his eyes on the White House...I doubt seriously if Johnson knew much about military strategy or weapons systems. He was probably the worst appointment Truman made during his presidency.[80]

Nevertheless, the paper, later designated NSC 37/9, could not have gotten started if Bradley had opposed it. Johnson, MacArthur, Voorhees, and Army Secretary Gray were applying pressure on the JCS to take positive action; combined pressure that Bradley probably felt was too great to resist. Moreover, Bradley trusted Collins' judgment. The latter was a wartime subordinate whom Bradley had known since the two served on the faculty at Fort Benning in the 1930's. The Army Chief of Staff's suggestion that Taiwan should be assisted by military measures "short of the dispatch of a major military force" appealed to Bradley who was not prepared to commit to a major military effort to save Taiwan, but who always agreed that the island's loss would engender serious strategic liabilities for the U.S.[81] Finally, even Bradley must have been sensitive to the political winds rising in favor of action to save Taiwan. His name being dragged through the newspapers as judging Taiwan not to be vital to U.S. security must have annoyed him to no end. Consequently, work proceeded in the Pentagon. The military would try to reverse policy on Taiwan at the end of the month when NSC 48 was to come into final review.

7.6 STATE STANDS FIRM

State's input to NSC 48 on the Taiwan issue was made in late October. Foggy Bottom held firm to the courses of action agreed upon at the 47th meeting of the National Security Council and submitted NSC 37/8 as its recommended policy toward the island.[82] The objective remained keeping Taiwan from falling to the CCP. It was assessed that Chiang had all the military equipment he needed to provide for the island's defense. Further economic aid would be dependant upon real political and economic reforms, and Taipei was put on notice that the U.S. would not intervene with military force to save the island. The U.S. would seek to avoid making Taiwan an issue which would push the Chinese communists into the Soviet camp. There was no further debate within State about the correctness of this policy. Its correctness was predicated upon two points. First, the defense establishment, after being queried several times, refused to declare Taiwan so vitally important to U.S. national security that it was willing to mount a major military effort to defend it should the CCP invade. Second, and most fundamental, the course of action toward Taiwan articulated in NSC 37/8 fit hand-in-glove with State's vision of how to cope with the revolutionary situation in post-war Asia.

State Department officials took Johnson at his word that NSC 48 should result in a comprehensive strategy for the containment of communism throughout all of Asia. The diplomats agreed with the Secretary of Defense that a "day-to-day, country-by-country

approach" would not result in achieving the overall objective of halt-
ing the advance of communism in the East. The specific policies to be
developed for each country in Asia, it was felt, should contribute to a
regional strategy as yet developed or articulated. Consequently,
throughout the fall and early winter of 1949, State's Office of Far
Eastern Affairs directed its energies toward arriving at such a formulation. Assisting Butterworth and his subordinates in FE were the
"Wise Men"; consultants Jessup, Case and Fosdick.

The "consultants" most certainly brought their own intellectual
baggage with them to State. Nevertheless, they took care to cast a
wide net in studying the situation in the Far East and in coming to conclusions as to just what the U.S. approach should be. They continually
conducted polls of academics, former government officials, and business organizations such as the National Foreign Trade Council.[83]
One of the premier events of their tenure was a round table discussion on China and Southeast Asia which brought together some of the
foremost Asian specialists of the day, informed business persons,
intelligence analysts, and State Department officials. For three days
in October, 1949 such notables as John K. Fairbank, Edwin O.
Reischauer, Owen Lattimore, Joseph Ballentine, George Marshall,
Phillips Talbot, Nathaniel Peffer, and Lawrence Rossinger among
others discussed, debated, and argued how U.S. policymakers should
cope with the situation in Asia.[84]

Exposed to official thinking in State, and benefiting from the
opinions of experts in the private sector, Fosdick and Case developed
very concrete ideas about the nature of the regional problems
confronting the U.S. in Asia and how Washington should approach
them. Of the two men, Fosdick maintained the higher profile. He
constantly wrote down his thoughts and passed them to Jessup who
acted as the other men's immediate point of contact into the State
Department bureaucracy and the channel through which they communicated with Acheson. Fosdick's analysis is worthy of some attention because it heavily influenced the various reports that the
consultants offered to the Secretary as the collective ideas of all
three.

Asia, Fosdick believed, was in revolution. "Vast social forces"
were at work moving every country in the region. In that part of the
world were countries formerly or currently ruled by colonial powers
which were striving for independence, internal political reform, and

an ascent out of perpetual poverty. Fosdick offered that the major manifestation of this revolution was ardent nationalism. The forces impelling this new Asian nationalism, he believed, were so strong that it was "idle" to think that the United States could control them. Although the forces of nationalism and revolution could not be controlled or reversed, they could be guided and influenced. The failure of the United States in the region since the war, he argued, was that America had failed to become associated with these forces in a positive sense. The Soviets, on the other hand, armed with communist ideology, were able to pose as the friend of change and revolution. The U.S. would have to recapture the revolution in progress if it was to counter communism. To do so, Fosdick suggested that arms and money alone would prove futile. The U.S. would have to fight ideology with ideology, and use propaganda as effectively as the communists.[85]

In a sense, the American dilemma in China was representative of the U.S.'s problem in Asia as a whole. In China, Fosdick offered, Washington aligned itself with the forces of reaction as opposed to revolution. He lamented that, "We are associated with a regime that is hated from one end of China to the other." He pointed out the "bankruptcy" of the KMT, the fact that its armed forces had disintegrated, and that it had "lost the confidence of all classes of people in China." The best that could now be hoped for in China was to attempt to wean Peking away from the Soviet orbit. Moreover, Fosdick believed that whatever policy the U.S now adopted toward China would have broad regional significance; it would affect how the rest of nationalistic, revolutionary Asia would come to view Washington. The solution seemed clear. Only by getting out of the Chinese civil war, and staying out, he told Jessup, would the U.S. have a chance to "rebuild our standing in the Far East." Further assistance to the KMT would alienate whatever "liberal elements" remained in China. Furthermore, continued aid to the KMT would also alienate those liberals in other Asian countries who, although not inclined to accept communism, identified with the Chinese revolution and its aims. The liberal elements in China and the rest of Asia, Fosdick argued, were not yet necessarily wedded to communism. It was these people around whom the U.S. would have build a long-range policy. The United States would have to become the champion of their aspirations.[86]

Given these general views, it is not surprising that Fosdick, like Acheson, was not well-disposed to intervene in Taiwan to save the KMT. However, whereas the motive force behind Acheson's "hand off" policy toward Taiwan was the encouragement of Titoism on the mainland, Fosdick saw much broader regional implications should the U.S. actively assist Taipei. Fosdick reasoned to Jessup that:

> In the opinion of the Joint Chiefs of Staff, the loss of the island would not vitally affect our national security. Military or economic intervention on our part to save it from the communists would arouse Chinese nationalism and anti-American sentiment to white heat. *Nothing that we could do would so effectively solidify the Communist position in China, or inflame the suspicions and smoldering animosities of India and Southeast Asia against "American imperialism."* Formosa is properly part of China; we have so indicated not only by our pledged word at Cairo, but by the swift turnover of the island to the Chinese Government after VJ-Day. It is too late now to try to hide behind a legal technicality that ties the disposition of Formosa to the Japanese Treaty.[87]

The original mandate of the consultants, to study the situation in the Far East and recommend an appropriate U.S. approach, was fulfilled in the early days of November. After two widely attended conferences with all relevant State Department officials, the consultants and the Foreign Service professionals arrived at a consensus of what that approach would be. In the case of China, what emerged was a revalidation of previous State policy.

The cornerstone of U.S. policy toward communist China would remain waiting for and encouraging the Titoist regime in Peking which all were convinced was destined to emerge from the ashes of revolution. Strains between Moscow and "Peiping" were sure to develop. "These strains," it was argued, "would not only work to our advantage but would contribute to the desired end of permitting China to develop its own life independently rather than as a Russian satellite." There was no reason that the U.S. should go out of its way "to create difficulties" for the CCP. This would only backfire and drive the communists "more firmly into the arms of the Kremlin..." Indeed, the wiser course was to recognize the various reasons why strains were destined to develop and "allow these ingredients full opportunity to operate." Consequently, it was agreed that overt or covert aid to KMT armies on the mainland "would be futile" and "recoil to our disadvantage." Those who advocated aid to non-communist areas of China would shoulder the "burden of showing that such assistance would be effective..." It was further agreed that U.S. Government financial assistance, such as Point IV aid, for the communist regime was out of the question, and that Washington would not encourage loans to increase American investment on the mainland. However, those private businesses already operating in China should be allowed to continue so long as no strategic materials were involved. Eventual recognition of the communist regime was not deemed out of the question. However, recognition would not "...be regarded as a major instrument for showing our interest in the Chinese people or for winning concessions from the Communist regime. Our attitude on this question should not be an eager one, but should be realistic."[88]

As for policy toward Taiwan, the consensus reached was that active U.S. measures to snatch the island from the CCP would engender unjustifiable political costs. It was decided that:

> We should not seek to detach Formosa from the Communist-controlled mainland either by the application of force or by seeking jurisdiction over the island through a trusteeship arrangement on behalf of Formosan self-government, since such actions on our part would outrage all Chinese elements and as a resort to naked expediency would destroy our standing with the smaller countries of the world.[89]

This course of action reconfirmed prior thinking in State. However, it was now placed into a regional and even global context. Consequently, previous decisions not to intervene with force, unilaterally occupy the island, or turn it over to the United Nations made even more sense. Although this decision flew in the face of every suggestion made by China Bloc legislators such as Senator Smith, and completely ignored MacArthur's warning that such a policy would be fatal to U.S. national security in the Far East, State was prepared to stand firm. Nothing would please Foggy Bottom more than seeing non-communist Taiwan survive by dint of its own efforts. However, State would not sacrifice its regional goals to save an island the Pentagon had yet to declare vital to national security.

By November 16th, these ideas and others, which espoused what was now being referred to as the consultants' "area approach" to Asia, were prepared in a report for President Truman.[90] On the 17th of November Acheson, Jessup, Fosdick and Case spent the morning in the White House with the President. At that time the consultants gave Truman their views in person. Acheson recorded that the President considered the discussions "tremendously helpful," claiming "new insight into the reasons for the Communist success in China" and "a better understanding of the whole situation." He now "found himself thinking about it in a quite new way."[91] The session ended with Acheson summing up for Truman the basic policy decision the President would have to make toward China.

> Broadly speaking, there were two objectives of policy: One might be to oppose the Communist regime, harass it, needle it, and if an opportunity appeared to attempt to overthrow it. Another objective of policy would be to attempt to detach it from subservience to Moscow and over a period of time encourage those vigorous influences which might modify it. I pointed out that this second alternative did not mean a policy of appeasement any more than it had in the case of Tito. If the Communists took action detrimental to the United States it should be opposed with vigor, but the decision of many concrete questions would be much clarified by a decision as to whether we believed that we should and could overthrow the regime, or whether we believed that the second course outlined above was the wiser. I said the Consultants were unanimous in their judgment that the second course was the preferable one.

The President responded by telling Acheson that "in the broad sense" he concurred with the analysis of the consultants, and would seek a "thorough understanding of all facts in deciding the question." He also mentioned again that the meeting had helped him greatly.[92] The Secretary must have been pleased.

7.7   STATE AND DEFENSE SQUARE OFF

The final offensive in the battle for Formosa began in earnest on December 15th, almost one month after the consultants briefed the President, and the day K.C. Wu became Governor of Taiwan. Louis Johnson fired the first salvo. On that day he sent to Truman, then at the presidential retreat at Key West, a memorandum which indicated that the Defense Department was now inclined to take positive measures, short of the dispatch of U.S. troops, to defend Taiwan. He reminded Truman that NSC 48 was being finalized and that "Formosa is one of the important questions involved." He informed the President that the Joint Chiefs and the service staffs now generally agreed that "efforts should be continued and perhaps increased to deny Formosa to the Communists" and that the details of an appropriate program of military assistance was currently being worked on.[93]

Along with the basic memorandum, Johnson attached two items. The first was a letter from Senator Homer Ferguson, a respected colleague of Truman's (recently returned from Taiwan) who expressed great concern over the future fate of the island. The second was a memo from Tracy Voorhees.[94] In his memo, the Under Secretary of the Army relayed to President Truman the views of General MacArthur about Taiwan as given to him the previous week in Tokyo. SCAP's message was as follows:

> It would be fatal to our littoral island defense for Formosa to fall into predatory hands. It can be denied to the Communists with very little effort.
>
> Formosa remains legally a part of Japan until a treaty of peace. At Potsdam, it was agreed that Japanese areas other than the four main islands should be assigned respectively to certain of the Allies for control until a treaty could be made. Under this plan Formosa was assigned to China. While it was understood generally, although not written in the agreement, that such assignment—like others—was made in the expectation that it would be in accordance with future ownership, until there is a treaty of peace the Nationalist Government of China is merely a custodian representing the Allies. As such custodian, it has certain obligations. If Formosa is threatened, it is the duty of all the Allies to defend it. Such a defense could be made without the necessity of committing U.S. troops, merely by a declaration under the Potsdam Agreement that the U.S. would treat any attempt to invade Formosa as an act of war, and similarly that it would be treated as an act of war for the Nationalist Government itself to use Formosa as a base to launch an attack against China.
>
> We could contend in the peace negotiations that conditions have so changed since the Yalta Agreement that it would not be obligatory to give Formosa to the Nationalist Government of China, but that it should be set up as an independent self-governing nation. Formosans are now neither truly Japanese nor Chinese but a distinct race of their own.
>
> If necessary a large part of the $75,000,000 recently appropriated to be used in connection with Chinese matters should be employed for the protection of Formosa.
>
> It would be fatal to split the U.S. line of littoral bases by letting the Communists put an air force on Formosa thereby threatening both Clark Field in the Philippines and our fields in Okinawa. However, placing U.S. forces on Formosa is not favored.[95]

Evidently, Johnson hoped that the letter from Ferguson and the powerful words of MacArthur would help sway the President to his side in attempting a reversal of the standing policy toward Taiwan as NSC 48 came under review. State, however, soon launched its own counter-offensive.

FE and CA at State anticipated such a move on Johnson's part and were aware of the study being finished by the Joint Staff. On

December 16th Butterworth sent to Acheson a memorandum which warned that "There is some reason to believe that the National Military Establishment may be reconsidering its previous opinion regarding the desirability of the use of American forces..." on Taiwan. Consequently, he provided Acheson with a sixteen-page paper reviewing the history of the NSC 37 series of policy papers and the Pentagon's previous statements about Taiwan since the beginning of the year.

Butterworth also included for Acheson comments and analysis that would support the State Department position and undercut DoD's new stance. He began by providing talking points with which to debunk the Pentagon's argument that if Taiwan fell it would do irreparable damage to the strategic position of the United States in East Asia. He pointed out that CCP bases on the island would only bring the communists forty miles closer to Okinawa and 160 miles closer to the Philippines relative to points on the south China coast already held by the CCP. Given the capabilities, or lack thereof, of the red army at the moment, this did not make so great a difference. In any case, he argued, hostile forces on Taiwan would be equally vulnerable to attacks from U.S. bases. Moreover, with the American naval presence in Japan and the Philippines, the communists would not be able to protect their own internal sea lanes of communications between the island and the mainland; they could be easily interdicted. Butterworth then quoted to Acheson remarks made by MacArthur in March 1949 to Kenneth Krentz, former Consul General in Taipei. MacArthur told Krentz that "There is no earthly military reason why we should need Formosa as a base. It would be no earthly use to us against our only possible major enemy and certainly they could not utilize it against us." Butterworth also provided the various statements of the JCS to the NSC that Taiwan was not considered so vital to U.S. national security that its defense warranted the use of American military forces. Butterworth next reviewed for Acheson various requests from the KMT that had recently been received for a military advisory group. He reminded the Secretary that the Nationalists already had the military wherewithall to make a stand and listed in general terms the type of equipment on hand and the amount of U.S. assistance Taipei had in fact received during 1949 as part of Washington's obligation to deliver the last of the equipment owed the KMT under the provisions of the original China Aid Act. Butterworth told Acheson in no uncertain terms that renewed military assistance would be an unqualified mistake. "We simply cannot afford to be directly associated with another failure in China," he argued, "and there is present little reason to believe that the provision of U.S. military advisers would in itself correct the basic weaknesses or contribute substantially to the defense of Formosa." Based on past experience, the military advisers would be coopted and manipulated by Taipei to engineer aid for the KMT. They would provide a "wedge" with which to "obtain further commitments" from the U.S. Butterworth buttressed this point by recalling for Acheson that K.C. Wu had himself admitted to Edgar in Taipei that his mandate from Chiang Kai-shek was to obtain assistance from Washington within one month or lose the governorship! Butterworth also argued that it was now too late even for a U.S. occupation of Taiwan with the consent of the KMT. With the recent relocation of the Nationalist capital to Taipei, Chiang's consent to placing Taiwan under SCAP authority, or allowing a U.S. occupation, would be "so obviously the act of a government *in extremis* which had entirely lost its claim to speak for the Chinese people as to deprive it of moral force." The CCP had already established a regime in Peking which claimed to speak for the Chinese people. The Soviets recognized that regime. The U.K. and other allies would probably soon recognize Peking as well. None of America's allies, submitted Butterworth, would risk future relations with the CCP by supporting Washington's bid to detach Taiwan from China. Moreover, such a move on the part of the U.S. would render hypocritical recent resolutions introduced into the U.N. General Assembly by the American delegation which called for all nations to respect the sovereignty of China; resolutions which were meant to expose Soviet aggression in Manchuria and the northwest. "While we might assert that Formosa is a part of the Japanese Empire pending the signing of a Japanese peace treaty and not a part of China," Butterworth continued, "such legalistic acrobatics would come with particularly bad grace from the U.S. in view of the Cairo and Potsdam declarations and our tacit support until now of the exercise of Chinese sovereignty over the Island." In the final analysis, Butterworth deemed an occupation of the island too costly politically to the entire U.S. position in Asia, and the future of relations with mainland China.

By occupying Formosa we would create an irredentist cause about which the Chinese Communists could rally almost universal support within China. At the same time, we would largely nullify one of our major political weapons, namely, exploitation of Soviet encroachment from the north. We would create an enduring issue of major proportion between this country and the Chinese Communist regime, an issue in which that regime would enjoy complete support of the Chinese people and from which neither we nor the Chinese Communists could back down without an almost impossible loss of prestige. The political cost within China of U.S. occupation of Formosa are of such magnitude as to require, should occupation be undertaken, a most careful review and possibly revision of our whole attitude toward Communist China.

Butterworth passed these ideas on to Acheson hoping that they "...might be helpful to you in the event that you discuss this subject with the President."[96] On December 20th Acheson did in fact meet with Truman. The purpose of the meeting was to have the Secretary of State review for the President the inclinations of other countries toward recognizing the People's Republic. However, Acheson took the opportunity to also discuss State's position on NSC 48.[97] Undoubtedly, the Taiwan issue would have come up. Acheson was well prepared to counter the arguments being fed to Truman by Johnson, MacArthur, and the Pentagon; and it must be assumed that he did.

Two days later, on December 22, Bradley and the service chiefs gave final approval to the Joint Staff's Taiwan paper; "Possible United States Military Action Toward Taiwan not Involving Major Military Force."[98] It was forwarded and addressed to Johnson the next day.

The Joint Chiefs of Staff have assessed the military measures, short of the dispatch of a major military force, which might be undertaken with respect to Taiwan in furtherance of United States political, economic and psychological measures now underway.

The following are the major conclusions arrived at as a result of their study:

a. A modest, well-directed, and closely supervised program of military aid to the anti-communist government in Taiwan would be in the security interest of the United States; and

b. A modest program of military aid to the Chinese Government in Taiwan should be integrated with a stepped-up political, economic, and psychological program pursued energetically in extension of present United States programs there.

The Joint Chiefs of Staff will, subject to your concurrence:

a. Direct the Commander in Chief, Far East, with the assistance of the Commander, 7th Task Fleet, to make an immediate survey of the nature and extent of the military assistance required in Formosa in order to hold Formosa against attack; and

b. Based on the results of the survey, make recommendations to you as to the military program.

The Joints Chiefs of Staff desire to point out that the recommended action with respect to Formosa is part of the overall problem of resisting the spread of Communist domination in East Asia. It is recognized that this is a piecemeal approach as is their recommendation with respect to assistance to Indonesia forwarded to you on 22 December 1949, but it is likewise a matter of urgency. These separate but related projects point up the necessity of early determination of an overall program for the solution of the major problem.[99]

On December 23rd, Johnson forwarded the paper to the National Security Council for inclusion into NSC 48 and for discussion during the upcoming 50th Meeting of the NSC scheduled for December 29th. However, the previous day, the Defense Secretary already knew that the battle was lost.

On December 22nd Johnson had lunch with President Truman at the White House and Taiwan was discussed. Evidently, Truman informed Johnson that he would not support active military measures to help defend the island. Testifying during the MacArthur Hearings in 1951, Johnson recalled that Truman agreed with the Pentagon that Taiwan was militarily important. However, Johnson said, "I was told, without quoting him directly, that he wasn't going to argue with me about the military considerations but that on political grounds he would decide with the State Department." On December 23, after forwarding the JCS paper to the NSC, Johnson left Washington for vacation in Florida. He decided not to attend the upcoming NSC meeting (to be chaired by the President) which would discuss NSC 37/9 and his own pet project NSC 48![100] Even more bizarre is the contention of Steven Rearden, author of the official history of the OSD, that Johnson never bothered to tell Bradley that Truman had already made up his mind on the issue.[101] If this is true, then the JCS Chairman was set up by Johnson to walk into a minefield at the upcoming NSC meeting.

By December 23rd, there was no longer a doubt that the NSC meeting would be a contentious one and that Taiwan would be the hot issue. On that date, the staff of the National Security Council circulated its draft of NSC 48 (designated NSC 48/1) for review by the principles and their staffs. Only on policy toward Taiwan was there dissension between State and DoD on how to deal with the situation in Asia. The NSC Staff was obliged to incorporate into the draft both State's recommendation that the policies outlined in NSC 37/2, 37/5 and 37/8 be continued as well as DoD's recommendation for a moderate program of military assistance to Taipei, an advisory group and a general review of the appropriateness of previous policy toward the island.[102]

In the days leading up to the NSC meeting communist propaganda and more bad blood between State and DoD added to tensions over Taiwan policy.

It became common knowledge that a major decision about Formosa was about to be made. On December 23rd, the CCP-controlled *Kwang Ming Jih Pao* carried an article accusing the U.S. of preparing to occupy Taiwan. The dispatch claimed that "Formosa has become problem of imperative urgency to American State and Defense Departments" and that the issue was going to be brought to the NSC. It recounted trips to Taiwan by Senators Smith and Ferguson and attributed to them statements urging MacArthur to take over the island.[103] Previous CCP newspaper articles had already seized upon the recent trip to Tokyo by Voorhees and Gruenther (*Ke Lu Te*) as proof positive that a MacArthur-led invasion was in the offing.[104] The Soviets also stirred the pot of speculation about U.S. Formosa policy. On December 25th, the U.S. Embassy in Moscow reported a piece in *Izvestia* which had as its headline "Rumors of US Intention Occupy Formosa." The article alleged that a decision had been made to declare Taiwan Japanese territory.[105] These types of articles exemplified the very fears that State had been voicing all along; that the Taiwan issue was one which the CCP could use to rally Chinese against perceived American imperialism and allow the Soviets to deflect criticism of their own actions toward China onto the U.S.

At the same time, inter-departmental relations hit an all-time low. It was bad enough that Johnson was attempting to reverse Taiwan policy and that the Joint Chiefs appeared to be reneging on statements about Taiwan's strategic importance. What was worse was that State was convinced that the Pentagon was leaking information to the press and the Nationalists to discredit Foggy Bottom's policy and give the KMT an edge in lobbying for assistance.

It is to be recalled that in late August, General Wedemeyer wrote State suggesting that it should formulate and keep at the ready a public affairs campaign aimed at lessening the demoralizing effect the fall of Taiwan might have on U.S. allies in the region.[106] On December 1st, Livingston Merchant came to the same conclusion and suggested to Butterworth that public affairs guidance be prepared immediately which would soften the blow of Taiwan's fall not only on allies, but on the Congress and American people as well.[107] On December 23rd, such a public affairs guidance paper was completed and sent out to all U.S. embassies. American officials were instructed to downplay the strategic importance of Taiwan, argue that its fall was not a major setback to U.S. strategic security, and assert that Taiwan is legally a part of China and the U.S. has never sought special interests or concessions on the island.[108] In MacArthur's headquarters the paper, classified as confidential, was mistakenly placed in a box of outgoing press releases and before it could be recalled portions of it were being quoted in the press. As Acheson remembers, "Congress burst into an uproar," and Senator Knowland demanded that the entire paper be released and that he be handed the names of the State Department officials who worked on it. In his memoirs, Acheson left little doubt that he believed that the paper was intentionally leaked by MacArthur's people. "One is left wondering," Acheson mused in his typically sarcastic way, "whether this windfall for Messrs. Knowland and Smith flowed from a mere lucky combination of coincidence and stupidity."[109]

Equally ugly was State's belief that Johnson and the OSD were leaking inside information about Taiwan policy to the Chinese Embassy in Washington. On December 23rd, during a meeting with Acheson, Butterworth and Merchant, Ambassador Koo presented an *aide memoir* from his government asking for military advisers and certain equipment.[110] A few days later, after reviewing the JCS proposal for Taiwan (also dated December 23rd), Butterworth, very agitated, wrote the Secretary of State that:

> The latest Joint Chiefs of Staff recommendation with regard to Formosa is understood to call for stepped-up economic and diplomatic aid and, even more important, military advisers and the gift of military equipment and supplies. *It parallels with extraordinary fidelity the request for increased*

assistance from the Chinese National Government received on the same date.[111]

Butterworth's instincts may have been correct. Scholars who have studied the papers of Ambassador V.K. Wellington Koo assert that Johnson's deputy, Paul Griffith, was responsible for maintaining liaison with Koo. Moreover, the Koo papers are said to indicate that on a number of occasions Johnson and Griffith met with the Ambassador to coordinate ways to influence administration policy toward Taiwan, undermine the State Department's China policies, and even pass intelligence to the Chinese Government.[112]

Acheson and Butterworth were hopping mad. The JCS appeared to be reversing their previous stand. There were strong indications of Pentagon collusion with the KMT. Johnson was out of town, and on December 27th Senator Smith was calling for a U.S. occupation of Taiwan with the consent of the KMT![113] All of this made for a very acrimonious meeting between the Joint Chiefs and Acheson, Rusk, Butterworth and Merchant on the morning of December 29th; just hours before the 50th meeting of the NSC scheduled for two-thirty that afternoon.

The meeting between the State crew and Bradley and his service chiefs took place in Acheson's office at the Secretary of State's request. Bradley opened the conference by stating that he assumed that the meeting was being held because Acheson desired the views of the Joint Chiefs on the strategic situation in the Far East. Acheson replied that the meeting was being held to specifically discuss their views about the strategic significance of Taiwan. Acheson stated that it was his understanding from previous JCS pronouncements that "the strategic importance of Formosa was insufficient to warrant the use of United States armed forces." He pointed out that because of previous JCS appraisals, State was charged by the NSC to employ economic and diplomatic means to save the island. Moreover, he reminded the Joint Chiefs that as early as last summer State reported to the Council that such measures alone were doomed to fail. Acheson then told Bradley that the latest JCS memorandum "appeared to give a different view or weight to the matter" of Taiwan's strategic importance. According to State's transcript of the meeting, General Bradley "denied that there had been any change in the position of the Joint Chiefs." He argued that their previous statements had been consistent in stating that Taiwan was strategically important.

Bradley reminded Acheson that in February of 1949 the JCS recommended basing a small naval presence on Taiwan as a deterrent to CCP invasion but that the recommendation was overturned by the NSC. The Joint Chiefs, according to Bradley, were always in favor of military assistance to the KMT on Taiwan. However, prior to the passage of the Mutual Defense Assistance Act no funds were available to support such aid. Bradley insisted that the suggested policy in NSC 37/9 "was based on the existence of funds under Section 303 of the Military Assistance Act and on the estimate that in the recent past the situation had changed on Formosa." Admiral Sherman agreed, when asked by Bradley, that the Chairman had adequately stated the position of the Joint Chiefs. Sherman also offered that K.C. Wu's recent selection as Governor was an example of some of the positive developments that had recently taken place on the island. At that point General Collins "interjected" that the military's intelligence estimate of the Nationalist's survivability was going to be changed and "the Joint Chiefs' views were that by comparatively small expenditures Formosa might be placed in a position where it would hold out longer than otherwise, with a consequent significant effect on the ability of the Chinese Communists to consolidate their regime." Collins then spoke to the "diversionary value" of Taiwan. It was imperative, said the general, to prevent the communists from dominating Indochina, Burma and Siam. He argued that "Chinese Communist expansion to the south might be deflected so long as they had Formosa to contend with or subdue." Rusk and Butterworth responded to the rationale of the Joint Chiefs by stating that there seemed to be "an element of pre-judgment in the JCS paper in that it stated that it was in our security interests to give military aid to Formosa and then suggested sending a team in to ascertain what that need was." When asked what type of aid they envisioned, government-to-government sales or the establishment of a JUSMAG, the service chiefs stated that they would defer to State on how best to manage such military assistance. However, they all agreed that military retirees would be preferable to active duty officers should a decision be made to send in a team of advisers. They reiterated MacArthur's views that Taiwan must not be allowed to fall, but that U.S. troops need not be employed to defend the island.

At this point in the meeting Acheson took the stage and offered a lengthy analysis of the problem at hand. The Secretary stated that it was important to decide whether the problem was that of checking the spread of communism throughout all of Asia, or arguing the relative strategic importance of Taiwan. He offered that communist control of China was now a fact of life. Moreover, there was no longer any real resistance to the CCP which might change that state of affairs. Also, it was certain that the CCP would now attempt to spread its revolution and control throughout Southeast Asia. At this point, he suggested, the mission was to check the spread of communism to China's neighbors. To do that in the region the U.S. would have to insure domestic stability, raise the standard of living, and realign itself with the forces of nationalism that were thriving now that "the dead hand of European colonialism" had been removed. The U.S. would have to fill the void in assistance to these nations before the communists could step in and subvert their revolutions. Acheson then argued that the Chinese are true Marxists "who regard the Soviet Union as their great and only friend." However, the United States would have to take the "long view not of 6 or 12 months but of 6 or 12 years." Inevitably, frictions between the Soviets and Chinese would develop. "Mao," said Acheson, "is not a true satellite in that he came to power by his own efforts and was not installed by the Soviet Army." That fact, he argued, "is our one important asset in China and it would have to be for a very important strategic purpose that we would take an action which would substitute ourselves for the Soviets as the imperialist menace to China." This was the reason, he explained, that State opposed economic warfare against the CCP. While the U.S. would not allow China to receive material of strategic value, neither would Washington give the communists the propaganda weapon to cause them to decry us as their eternal enemy. Besides, Acheson said, the well being of Japan was at stake as well. China remained Japan's natural trade partner and the U.S. could not shoulder the burden of underwriting that country indefinitely. It was against this rationale, Acheson told the Joint Chiefs, that policy toward Taiwan must be made. Taiwan, he argued, is doomed to fall from internal decay. "With a hostile population, overrun by refugees, a corrupt government even though K.C. Wu has been brought forward as scenery, it seems likely we will see a continuation of the process which lost the mainland." If we follow the recommendations in NSC 37/9, he continued, and the fall of Taiwan can be postponed for a year, "we must ask what price do we pay for this delay." The U.S., said Acheson answering his own question, will once again commit its prestige to a lost cause. The U.S. will incur the wrath of all the Chinese people. The Soviets will be able to denounce Washington in the U.N. and act as the champions of Chinese sovereignty. And finally, the U.S. will come to represent a reactionary force to the highly nationalistic nations now emerging in Asia. "If at this price we acquire an island essential to the defenses of the United States then it might be worth the price but there does not appear to be demonstrated a claim that the loss of Formosa really breaches our defense."

After Acheson ended his tutorial, General Bradley demurred that the Secretary's arguments were political. The Joint Chiefs, he said, "were only giving the military view" and accepted that at times political views must prevail over military reasoning. Bradley then stated that he understood Acheson to be saying that the Secretary "had decided it was better to let Formosa go for political reasons." Acheson confirmed that Bradley's understanding was correct. He told the General that "unless the Joint Chiefs could offer strategic reasons beyond those adduced," he was "inclined to regard the political price as too high to pay for the purchase of some additional time." Rusk then asked Collins to compare the relative strategic importance of Taiwan and Korea to the U.S. position in Asia. "General Collins admitted," according to the transcript of the meeting, that Korea was much more important as a potential threat to Japan than Taiwan if overrun by hostile forces. As for Okinawa, Collins further stated that "there was little difference in terms of exposure...between hostile air bases on the China Mainland and on Formosa." Admiral Sherman, sensing defeat, pointed out that plans should be made to remove planes and other strategic assets from Taiwan before they fall into Communist hands. Bradley closed the meeting by reiterating that the Joint Chiefs had merely offered the military view of the situation and accepted "that political considerations might override their views."[114] The Joint Chiefs were completely beaten down.

A few hours later the National Security Council convened. President Truman presided and NSC 48 was the topic at hand. For the most part, the conference was anti-climactic. The paper had been worked and reworked so many times that there was little left that remained in contention. The study did fulfill its mandate in that it articulated basic U.S. objectives in the region, and outlined the various ways that Washington would pursue those objectives.

It was decided that in Asia, the "basic security objectives" of the United States required: (1) the development of stable and self-sustaining nations, (2) the employment of sufficient military power "in selected non-Communist nations to maintain internal security and to prevent the further encroachment of communism," (3) a reduction in Soviet power and influence in the region, and (4) the prevention of the formation of alliances that might threaten U.S. or allied security. To realize these objectives, NSC 48 offered an array of measures that included the encouragement of regional associations among non-communist nations, strengthening the U.S. military posture in the Philippines, Okinawa, and Japan, offering military assistance to selected nations, providing Point IV aid to most, and encouraging U.S. trade and investment where it would bolster local economies. Above all, it was determined that all programs should be carried out in such a manner that the United States would become associated with the positive forces of regional nationalism and pre-empt Soviet domination of the forces of change.

While NSC 48 did provide the blueprint with which to guide U.S. policy in the region, it did not result in radical changes to the basic policies toward individual countries already in motion. In fact, the study merely reconfirmed what had been formulated in the past, to the point that previous NSC papers, such as those for China and Korea, were cited. Significantly, the NSC 34 series of papers on China were revalidated as was the concept of pursuing a policy toward the mainland which would result in Titoism.[115]

Only on the issue of policy toward Taiwan was a formal decision required to be made by the President. As Acheson pointed out to the Council members, State's and DoD's conflicting recommendations remained in the draft. General Bradley, directing his remarks to Truman, stated that "the Department of Defense version on Formosa was preferable from the military point of view" because it made an early start in "resisting the spread of communist domination in Asia." Acheson then launched into a discourse which followed closely the remarks he made earlier that day to the Joint Chiefs.

The Secretary of State pointed out that he understood that the Joint Chiefs were not recommending the employment of military forces on Taiwan. Nevertheless, he told the group that State and Defense "were agreed" that the program in NSC 37/9 "would not prevent the fall of Formosa, but might at best only lengthen the time remaining before it falls." The question then, asked Acheson, was "what will it cost us to buy some more time and is what we will get worth the price?" The Secretary went through his by now familiar litany on the need to take no action which "would deflect Chinese xenophobia from Russia to ourselves." Soviet aggression in northern China and forced collectivization would "eventually" cause frictions between Moscow and Peking which would work to the advantage of Washington. "U.S. military assistance enabling the Chinese National Government to continue the fight from Formosa," he argued, "would turn Chinese anti-foreign feeling against us and also place us in the position of subsidizing attacks on a government which will soon be generally recognized." Furthermore, military aid to Taiwan would undermine the position of the U.S. in the rest of Asia "where we wish to be on the side of nationalist movements and avoid supporting reactionary governments." "Formosa," he said in closing, "though important to the U.S. was not vital. Military assistance with respect to Formosa would buy only a little time at the risk of losing the influence we have left in Asia."

Bradley countered by offering that both the State and Defense Departments desired to preserve Taiwan from CCP domination. It was only the wish of the Joint Chiefs to supplement economic and diplomatic means with "modest military assistance." However, Bradley conceded once again that, "if for political reasons it was desired to drop support of the current Nationalist Government, then perhaps the JCS proposal went too far." Acheson chimed in one more time declaring that "we had now extricated ourselves from the Chinese civil war and it was important that we not be drawn into it again." However, he said that he would have no problem with the Nationalists purchasing small arms and military supplies from the United States "by using their large gold reserves."

President Truman, after hearing the arguments, formalized the decision he made on December 22nd. He approved the course of action recommended by State "for political reasons."[116] The next day, NSC 48 was changed to reflect the President's decision.[117]

The battle for Formosa within the administration had ended. The policy toward Taiwan promulgated in the NSC 37 series of papers would hold. Chiang would have to fend for himself.

Notes

1. "The Formulation of Foreign Policy," a speech by Dean Rusk, given to students at the National War College, October 3, 1950, LTM/Box 20.

2. Memorandum for the Executive Secretary of the National Security Council from the Secretary of Defense, June 10, 1949, DNSC:Reel 2.

3. More subtle, but perhaps of greater long-term significance, Johnson's suggestion that the NSC staff develop and recommend policy to Council members was an attempt to give the staff of the NSC (hitherto merely an inter-departmental coordinating body) a policy-making role in the executive branch; thereby undermining State's mandate for policy formulation.

4. NSC 48 touched on United States policy toward every country in Asia. However, this study shall confine its treatment of NSC 48 to the portions relevant to Taiwan and China. The two best published treatments of the regional implications of NSC 48 and the bureaucratic battles that an NSC staff-generated paper caused can be found in Schaller, *The American Occupation of Japan* (Chapter 11, "NSC 48 and the Renewed Debate over Asian Communism," pp. 195–211), and Blum, *Drawing The Line* (Chapter 10, "Policy Showdown: NSC-48," pp. 160–177).

5. Schaller, *The American Occupation of Japan*, p. 203. The reader can gain an appreciation for the broad scope of issues that were considered from the following partial list of studies that were fowarded to the NSC staff for inclusion into NSC 48: SANACC 360/14, "Appraisal of U.S. Interests in South Asia," (Defense); "Implications of a Possible Full-Scale Invasion from North Korea Subsequent to the Withdrawal of U.S. Troops from Korea," (Defense); NSC 49, "Current Strategic Evaluations of U.S. Security Needs in Japan," (Defense); NSC 51, "U.S. Policy Toward Southeast Asia," (State); NSC 55, "Implications of a Possible Chinese Communist Attack on Foreign Colonies in South China," (Defense); Intelligence Memorandum No. 254, "Regionalism and Orientation Trends in Asia," (CIA); National Security Council Status of Projects, August 31, 1949, HST/MNSC/Box 206/NSC Meeting #50; J.C.S. 1330/54, 26 July 1949, RJCS:Reel 1; and HST/NSC/CIA/Box 2/December 48–December 49.

6. Even Kan Chieh-hou, Li Tsung-jen's personal representative in the United States, had knowledge that a study was underway. On October 30th Kan wrote directly to President Truman on Li's behalf. He stated that he had received a "perturbing report" that the U.S. Government was planning to write off China completely in its overall plan for Asia, while increasing aid and support for India, Australia, and the Philippines. Kan enjoined Truman not to abandon China. Letter, Kan Chieh-hou to President Truman, October 30, 1949, HST/PSF/Box 173/China 1949.

7. See Chapter 6.

8. Although Chiang met with visiting dignitaries from the U.S. sympathetic to his cause, at no point did he personally appeal to administration officials for help; this would have been too great a loss of face. Consequently, his

modus operandi, typically Chinese, was to send personal messengers to convey his wishes, table bargaining positions, and test the waters of diplomacy. More-over, Chiang sent his vetted messages to various officials of the U.S. Govern-ment simultaneously. At the same time, his representatives in the U.S. mobilized the powerful China lobby and China Bloc in Congress to pressure the administration into changing its policy toward Taiwan. An accounting of the activities of the China lobby is obviously well beyond the scope of this study. For a fascinating look at the KMT's vast network of supporters in the United States see Ross Y. Koen, *The China Lobby in American Politics* (N.Y.: Octagon Books, 1974).

9. Message, Taipei (Macdonald) to Secretary of State, November 29, 1949, SDF:Reel 3. In the comments section of this message Macdonald relayed that, "Similar requests for moral support and advisors have been made to me by such civil and military authorities as K.C. Wu, Wang Shih-chieh, Governor Chen Cheng and General Sun Li-jen."

10. Message, Taipei to Secretary of State, December 7, 1949, SDF:Reel 3; *The Consul General at Taipei (Macdonald) to the Secretary of State,* December 7, 1949, FR:49:IX:441. Wu also passed this information to ECA Taiwan repre-sentatives Craig and Moyer on December 14th. Wu stated that he was confi-dent that he would be able to handle civil reform. However, warned Wu, Sun Li-jen would need U.S. military assistance to strengthen his hand if he was given the chance to command the island's defenses. Letter, John B. Nason (Director, ECA China Division) to Livingston Merchant, December 27th, 1949, with attachment, "Memorandum of Conversation with K.C. Wu on December 14, 1949 Just Prior to Announcement of his Appointment as Governor of Taiwan," SDF:Reel 3.

11. Message, Taipei to Secretary of State, December 14, 1949, SDF:Reel 3; *The Consul at Taipei (Edgar) to the Secretary of State,* December 14, 1949, FR:49:IX:445. Parenthesis added. Although I have not been able to document the exact response of key State Department officials to Wu's December 7th news that he might be made Governor, it is safe to assume that Edgar's response to Wu on the 13th was made as a result of instructions from Washing-ton. In the message of December 7th, Macdonald warned State that he be-lieved that a request for aid was imminent (ibid., footnote 10). Also, it would have been extraordinary for a mid-level FSO to make such a strong represen-tation on what the U.S. Government would or would not be in favor of without prior guidance. Finally, later statements made by Acheson and Butterworth on the issue of Wu as Governor are consistent with those ideas conveyed by Edgar.

12. *The Consul at Taipei (Edgar) to the Secretary of State,* December 14, 1949, FR:49:IX:446; *Summary of Telegrams,* December 15, 1949, HST/NAF/Box 21/September–December 49. It is uncertain whether there was in fact a great internal KMT debate on the issue of accepting Wu's conditions or whether, as Wu alleged, Chiang Kai-shek was hamstrung and unable, initially, to make such a decision unilaterally. It is not an unreasonable proposition that

KMT factional politics had to play itself out before such a major move was made. If that was the case, then the players came to a consensus in rather short order—less than twenty-four hours. One is left wondering if Edgar's harsh words catalyzed the consensus-building process or whether the Gimo always had the power to have the final word. In any case, Wu's allegation that Wang Shih-chieh was a major opponent is curious. Wang, a close associate of the Generalissimo's, was a career KMT diplomat quite sensitive to U.S. concerns. See Boorman and Howard, *Biographical Dictionary of Republican China*, Vol. III, pp. 395–397.

13. *The Consul at Taipei (Edgar) to the Secretary of State*, December 16, 1949, FR:49:IX:446. Parenthesis added.

14. Message, Taipei to Secretary of State, December 16, 1949, SDF:Reel 3. Wu told Edgar that he doubted that Sun's appointment was going to mean very much. Chiang was still reluctant to allow Sun to command troops other than those in his old training command. Only U.S. military advisers, said Wu, would help Sun to make a difference in military reform. Edgar replied that U.S. advisers doing Chinese "dirty work" would not set well in Washington.

15. Message, Taipei to Department of State, December 27, 1949, "The Local Press on Appointment of K.C. Wu as Governor of Taiwan," press reports from December 16, 1949, SDF:Reel 3.

16. The role of the Bank of China in the United States as a front for lobbying activities can be found in Koen, *The China Lobby in American Politics*, pp. 38–41 and Sterling Seagrave, *The Soong Dynasty* (N.Y.: Harper & Row Publishers, 1985), pp. 435, 444, 446, and 450–451. According to both Koen and Seagrave, the New York public relations firm used by the Bank of China was David B. Charney's Allied Syndicates, Inc. It was Allied which apparently hired Sullivan, then with the Washington law firm of Sullivan, Bernard, and Shea. Caution should be exercised in using both Koen and Seagrave. Both have an anti-KMT ax to grind. Of the two, Koen's is much better researched and documented, but probably more politically motivated. Originally published in 1960, the study was reissued in 1974 by the Committee of Concerned Asian Scholars. Seagrave (son of Dr. Gordon Seagrave) has written a work which is informative but not one of serious scholarship.

17. Memorandum of Conversation, December 14, 1949, Chinese Proposals Regarding Formosa, Mr. John L. Sullivan, Mr. Butterworth, Mr. Freeman, SDF:Reel 3; Office Memorandum, Butterworth to Acheson, Proposals re Formosa Communicated by Mr. John L. Sullivan, December 15, 1949, SDF:Reel 3; Memorandum of Conversation, December 20, 1949, Chinese Proposals Regarding Formosa, Mr. John L. Sullivan, Mr. Butterworth, Mr. Freeman, SDF:Reel 3.

18. Memorandum of Conversation, Dr. V.K. Wellington Koo, W. Walton Butterworth, and Livingston T. Merchant, December 23, 1949, SDF:Reel 3; *Memorandum of Conversation, by the Assistant Secretary of State for Far Eastern Affairs (Butterworth)*, December 23, 1949, FR:49:IX:456–457.

19. Acheson and Smith conferred often; usually at the senator's request to discuss specific points of policy. Their discussions were usually frank and to the point, but rarely confrontational in nature. Acheson realized that he was not able to change Smith's mind when they were in fundamental disagreement. However, on some occasions their discussions, according to Acheson, resulted in Smith being "somewhat talked down." For example, see Memorandum of Conversation with Senator Smith with Reference to China, July 14, 1949, DGA/Box 64/July 1949.

20. Smith had a variety of non-governmental sources which kept him informed of developments in Asia. Among others with first-hand information was Smith's cousin, Burton Crane, Far Eastern correspondent for the *New York Times*, who worked out of Tokyo. The relationship between the two men is established in the letter, Crane to Smith, 19 February 1950, HAS/Box 100.

21. Office of Senator H. Alexander Smith, press release, June 30, 1949, "Senator Smith Calls for Positive U.S. Policy to Help 'Rebuild' China," HAS/Box 98.

22. Letter, Smith to H. Kenaston Twitchell, August 15, 1949, HAS/Box 98. Twitchell was Smith's son-in-law.

23. For example, Smith privately lambasted the *White Paper* as "...an attempt to alibi the United States' bankrupt Far Eastern policy..." However, his public criticism was mild. He termed it "disappointing" and called on the administration and the congress to move beyond past problems and concentrate on working together on a future course of action in Asia. Ibid.; and "Statement by HAS re China," August 9, 1949, HAS/Box 98.

24. Letter, Smith to H. Kenaston Twitchell, August 15, 1949, HAS/Box 98. Interestingly, in this letter Smith told Twitchell that "Everyone here, including Wedemeyer, Chennault, and others who are supporting the China cause..." were "virtually agreed" on the pointlessness of further military aid to the KMT. Smith even went one step further; he opined that Chiang Kai-shek "...has lost his prestige to the extent that it would be unwise for United States intervention to back him personally."

25. Copies of correspondence between Smith and the FLR's Thomas Liao can be found in HAS/Box 98.

26. "Far Eastern Problems Facing The United States: Report of Visit to the Far East September and October 1949," by H. Alexander Smith, Draft of November 21, 1949, HAS/BOX 98.

27. United States Senate, MEMORANDUM NO. 2 (by H. Alexander Smith), HAS/Box 98; Letter, Smith to Knowland, October 24, 1949, HAS/Box 98.

28. United States Senate, MEMORANDUM NO. 2 (by H. Alexander Smith), HAS/Box 98. Parenthesis added. Apparently MacArthur's allegations about attempts in Washington to undermine Chiang had a great impact upon the Senator. On October 24th he wrote Senator Knowland, about to make his own trip to the Far East, that, "I am convinced that for some years there has been a group in the State Department with representatives in China, who have

tried to defend the communist philosophy for China, and who correspond-ingly have tried to 'smear' the Gimo and his attempts at the unification of China. I think it was this group that had a lot to do with Stillwell's (sic) negative attitude, and also the attempt to force Marshall to the point of bringing the commies and the Nationalists together in a coalition government, which was impossible from the beginning." Letter, Smith to Knowland, October 24, 1949, HAS/Box 98.

29. Michael Schaller, *Douglas MacArthur: The Far Eastern General* (N.Y.: Oxford University Press, 1989), p. 170.

30. It is uncertain what expectations the Senator had for his meeting with Chiang. In addition to MacArthur's hype about the Gimo, Smith was also treated to negative appraisals of Chiang during his trip. Interestingly, General Chu Shih-ming, the KMT's representative to occupation headquarters in Tokyo was "fairly critical" of the Gimo in discussions with the Senator. In the Philippines, Admiral Berkey, who had recently replaced Oscar Badger as Commander of U.S. Naval Forces Western Pacific, appeared to Smith to be "definitely against the Gimo." Letter, Smith to Knowland, October 24, 1949, HAS/Box 98.

31. Letter, Smith to Knowland, October 24, 1949, HAS/Box 98.

32. Smith began writing to Wu after his return to the U.S. After only one meeting in Taipei Smith was addressing Wu as "My dear K.C.," and writing to him "as one Princeton man to another." Letter, Smith to Wu, December 10, 1949, HAS/Box 98.

33. Letter, Smith to Colonel Herbert B. Wheeler, December 21, 1949, HAS/Box 98; Letter, Smith to Knowland, October 24, 1949, HAS/Box 98. As an interesting aside, during one of Smith's luncheons with Wu, a native Taiwanese waiter took the opportunity to tell the Senator just how rotten KMT rule on the island was and of the plight of the Formosans.

34. *Pacific Star and Stripes,* October 10, 1949, HAS/Box 92. Also in the article, Smith expressed his displeasure once again with what he described as State's "let the dust settle" policy toward the Far East. Moreover, Smith related that MacArthur "had assured" him "that the American investment in South Korea was secure" and that "Unless Russia itself launches an invasion, South Korea can hold its own."

35. *Letter, Senator H. Alexander Smith to the Secretary of State (Acheson),* November 5, 1949, FR:49:IX:173; Memorandum of Conversation, Smith, Fosdick, and Jessup (November 22nd), November 28, 1949, SDF: Reel 3; Memorandum of Conversation, "Senator Alexander Smith's Observations re Far Eastern Developments," Smith and Acheson, November 30, 1949, DGA/Box 64/October–November 1949; Letter, Smith to Acheson, December 27, 1949, HAS/Box 98.

36. Letter, Smith to Knowland, October 24, 1949, HAS/Box 98.

37. "Statement for NBC on China," (no date given, but after return from trip), HAS/Box 98.

38. Letter, Smith to Colonel Wheeler, SCAP Government Section, December 21, 1949, HAS/Box 98. Smith communicated with MacArthur through Wheeler. As Smith wrote Colonel Wheeler, "I am sending this letter to you confidentially so that you can determine what parts of it should be taken up with the General and to the end that the General may not in any way be embarrassed by direct correspondence with me."

39. Letter, Smith to Wheeler, ibid.

40. Memorandum of Conversation, Acheson and Smith, November 30, 1949, DGA/Box 64.

41. Memorandum of Conversation, Acheson and Smith, November 30, 1949, DGA/Box 64.

42. Press Release, Office of Senator H. Alexander Smith, "Continued Support of Free Chinese Urged by Smith After Far East Tour," December 1, 1949, HAS/Box 98. Smith publicly called for an end to the practice of "making Chiang Kai-shek and other Nationalist leaders 'political lepers.' With all their alleged mistakes they merit our interest and help. They can help build the New China."

43. Both the draft report of November 21 and the final version (December 1st) can be found in the Smith Papers, Box 98. Smith was fairly critical of Chiang and the KMT in his draft but toned down some of the Gimo's faults in the final version. Nevertheless, the final report did not relieve the Gimo of some responsibility for his defeat on the mainland and his problems on Taiwan.

44. "Senator Urges U.S. To Take Formosa," *New York Times*, December 2, 1949, p. 15.

45. George F. Kennan, *Memoirs: 1925–1950* (Boston: Little, Brown & Co., 1967), p. 371.

46. Biographies of MacArthur are plentiful. The most comprehensive, of course, is D. Clayton James' trilogy, *The Years of MacArthur*. Michael Schaller's recent interpretive biography, *Douglas MacArthur: Far Eastern General* (1989) deserves reading. It is outstanding for its concise analysis of the General's views on the the Far East and the very fallible quality of his real knowledge about Asia.

47. For example, in 1949 both MacArthur and State were in favor of concluding an early peace treaty with Japan and embarking on a military build-up of Okinawa. The Pentagon objected to both courses of action.

48. *Memorandum of Conversation, by the Chief of the Division of Northeast Asian Affairs (Bishop)*, February 16, 1949, FR:49:VII:Pt.2:656; Memorandum of Conversation With General Douglas MacArthur, December 7, 1948, SDF:Reel 3.

49. Letter, MacArthur to Congressman Charles A. Eaton, Chairman, House Committee on Foreign Affairs, 3 March 1949, DM/RG 6/FECOM/ Formosa File; Message, MacArthur to Senator Millard E. Tydings, Chairman Senate Armed Services Committee, 22 February 1949, DM/RG 6/FECOM/ Formosa File.

50. "World War 3 Seen If U.S. Fails to Act," *New York Journal American*, August 30, 1949, pp. 1 and 2.

51. *Memorandum of Conversation, by Mr. Allen B. Moreland, Department of State Representative With the Huber Congressional Committee on Far Eastern Tour,* [Tokyo] September 5, 1949, FR:49:IX: 544–546. MacArthur admitted to a concerned delegation member that the four actions he proposed did in fact entail "a certain amount of risk" of precipitating "a general war with the Soviets..." However, the general was confident that the Soviets were in no shape at the moment for a war with the U.S. Also of interest, MacArthur assured the congressmen that "South Korea is in no danger of being overrun by North Korea."

52. For State's reaction to MacArthur's meeting with the Huber delegation see *Memorandum by the Director of the Office of Chinese Affairs (Sprouse) to the Assistant Secretary of State for Far Eastern Affairs (Butterworth),* October 20, 1949, FR:49:IX:558–561.

53. *Memorandum of Conversation, by the Counselor of Embassy in the Philippines (Flexer),* December 7, 1948, FR:49:IX:263–265; Memorandum of Conversation with General Douglas MacArthur at Tokyo, December 7, 1948, 11:00–12:10, SDF:Reel 3.

54. *Memorandum of Conversation, by the Chief of the Division of Northeast Asian Affairs (Bishop),* February 16, 1949, FR:49:VII:Pt.2:655–658. In briefing visiting dignitaries on the importance of Taiwan, MacArthur's G-2, Major General Charles Willoughby, parroted SCAP's points. On at least one occasion, Willoughby included Taiwan in the island defense chain but conceded that its "effective incorporation" into the defensive line "was contingent upon political factors and decisions outside the scope of the Far East Command." *The Acting Political Adviser in Japan (Sebald) to the Secretary of State,* September 9, 1949, FR:49:VII:Pt.2:857. For an excellent analysis of the origins of the island-chain defense concept see John Lewis Gaddis, "The Strategic Perspective: The Rise and Fall of the 'Defensive Perimeter' Concept, 1947–1951," in Borg and Heinrichs, eds. *Uncertain Years: Chinese-American Relations, 1947–1950* (N.Y.: Columbia University Press, 1980), pp. 61–118.

55. *Memorandum of Conversation, by Mr. Robert A. Fearey, of the Office of Northeast Asian Affairs,* November 2, 1949, FR:49:VII:Pt.2:890–894.

56. Desk note, McDermott (State) to Butterworth and Rusk, March 11, 1949, SDF:Reel 2.

57. Message, Taipei to Secretary of State, November 16, 1949, SDF:Reel 3; *The Consul General at Taipei (Macdonald) to the Secretary of State,* November 16, 1949, FR:49:IX:428; and *The Secretary of State to the Consul General at Taipei (Macdonald),* November 15, 1949, FR:49:IX:427.

58. Schaller, *Douglas MacArthur: The Far Eastern General,* pp. 167, 170. Schaller cites "report of a meeting between Gen. MacArthur and Chennault, November 21, 1949, NLT-12, CIA, FOIA." Schaller further states (p. 170) that MacArthur "encouraged the efforts of American entrepreneurs such as

Chennault, Preston Goodfellow, William Donovan, and William Pawley to sell weapons to the Nationalists."

59. Message, Taipei to the Secretary of State, December 13, 1949, SDF:Reel 2.

60. Message, Taipei to Secretary of State, September 6, 1949, SDF:Reel 2.

61. Message, Taipei to Secretary of State, December 13, 1949, SDF:Reel 2.

62. Political Report, Taipei to Secretary of State, November 25, 1949, SDF:Reel 1.

63. Rearden, *History of the OSD*, p. 234.

64. Memorandum from the Office of the Secretary of Defense to the Joint Chiefs of Staff, 15 September 1949, RJCS:Reel 1.

65. *Memorandum by the Executive Secretary of the National Security Council (Souers) to the Council*, "Study of Chennault Plan by Joint Chiefs of Staff," October 19, 1949, FR:49:IX:556–558.

66. *Memorandum by Mr. Max W. Bishop, Special Assistant to the Deputy Under Secretary of State (Rusk), to the Deputy Under Secretary of State (Rusk)*, October 21, 1949, FR:49:IX:561–567.

67. J.C.S. 1721/40, Report by the Joint Munitions Allocation Committee in Collaboration with the Joint Strategic Plans Committee and the Joint Logistic Plans Committee to the Joint Chiefs of Staff on *Aid For China*, 6 December 1949, RJCS:Reel 1.

68. Ibid. Parenthesis added.

69. Memorandum of Conversation, Senator Smith and Secretary Acheson, November 30, 1949, DGA/Box 64.

70. As a compromise among themselves, the JCS tried to convince the NSC to station "minor fleet units" on the island as a deterrent to CCP attack when Taiwan policy was initially being formulated in January and February of 1949. (NSC 37/3).

71. Stueck, *Road to Confrontation*, p. 138.

72. Memorandum Of Conversation, Mr. Tracy S. Voorhees, Secretary Acheson, Mr. Jessup, Mr. Butterworth, Mr. Humelsine, December 15, 1949, DGA/Box 64. The only reason Voorhees took the time to debrief State at all was to give Acheson MacArthur's views on the Japanese Peace Treaty. No other discussions of substance took place. Apparently it was a chilly session. Voorhees accused State of leaking news of his visit to the press, and declared that DoD and SCAP would no longer allow State to solicit MacArthur's views by going through William Sebald (State's political adviser on SCAP's staff). In the future, Voorhees told the group, requests for information from MacArthur would have to come through the Pentagon.

73. Memorandum for the Secretary of Defense, Tracy S. Voorhees, 14 December 1949, DM/RG 6/FECOM/Formosa.

74. Rearden, *History of the OSD*, p. 236.

75. Stueck, *Road to Confrontation*, p. 139.

76. Memorandum by the Chief of Staff, U.S. Army, for the Joint Chiefs of Staff, 6 December 1949, on *Strategic Importance of Taiwan*, J.C.S. 1966/22, RJCS:Reel 2.

77. Memorandum of Conversation, Voorhees, Acheson, Jessup, Butterworth, and Humelsine, December 15, 1949, DGA/Box 64.

78. Rearden, *History of the OSD*, p. 236.

79. DGA/Box 75/ Princeton Seminars/ Reading Copy I, October 10–11, 1953/Folder 1/p. 791.

80. Omar N. Bradley and Clay Blair, *A General's Life* (N.Y.: Simon & Schuster, 1983), pp. 501–502.

81. Memorandum by the Chief of Staff, U.S. Army, for the Joint Chiefs of Staff, 6 December 1949, on *Strategic Importance of Taiwan*, J.C.S. 1966/22, RJCS:Reel 2; Bradley, *A General's Life*, p. 527 and Bradley's statements during NSC meetings on the subject in previous chapters of this study. Bradley has said of Collins that, "Joe was not a deep thinker or strategist. He was a 'doer,' an action man; and on occasion he was all too apt to live up to his nickname, 'Lightning,' and go chasing off as if he were still commanding VII Corps in ETO. But on the whole, he was an excellent executive, and [when Bradley was Chief of Staff of the Army] I let him handle most matters with complete confidence that he would make the right decisions." Bradley, ibid., p. 472. Parenthesis added.

82. Memorandum for the President, Summary of Discussion, 47th Meeting of the NSC, October 20, 1949, HST/PSF/MNSC/Box 220/NSC Meetings 1949. It is noted that NSC 37/8 would be forwarded to the NSC staff to be included as State's input to NSC 48.

83. Additional Statements from Far East Specialists: Summary of National Foreign Trade Council's Recommendations on China Policy, November 10, 1949, RBF/Box 9.

84. Transcript of Round Table Discussion on American Policy Toward China Held in the Department of State, October 6, 7 and 8, 1949, HAS/Box 98. The entire transcript can be found in the Smith papers. How he came to be in possession of them is not noted. The marginalia on Smith's copy indicates that he read the transcript. Smith went down the list of participants and annotated which were affiliated with the Institute of Pacific Relations. Except for the notable exception of Governor Harold Stassen, the participants decided the U.S. had no choice but to recognize the People's Republic of China. What remained unresolved was the timing and conditions of recognition, and what to do about the Nationalist regime on Taiwan.

85. *Memorandum to the Secretary of State*, from Fosdick, Case, and Jessup, August 29, 1949, FR:49:VII:Pt.2:1193–1195; Memorandum, Fosdick to Jessup, August 29, 1949, RBF/Box 9; Memorandum, Fosdick to Jessup, October 25, 1949, RBF/Box 9. Fosdick's conceptualization of the problem of asian nationalism was very much in consonance with Owen Lattimore's ideas in, *The Situation in Asia* (Boston: Little, Brown and Company, 1949). Over forty years after its publication, Lattimore's work is still an excellent read.

86. Memorandum, Fosdick to Jessup, "Some Notes on an Approach to China," August 29, 1949, RBF/Box 9; Memorandum for Mr. Jessup, November 8, 1949, RBF/Box 9.

87. Memorandum for Mr. Jessup, October 25, 1949, RBF:Box 9. Emphasis added.

88. *Memorandum by Mr. Charlton Ogburn, Jr., of the Bureau of Far Eastern Affairs*, "Decisions Reached By Consensus At The Meetings With The Secretary And The Consultants On The Far East," November 2, 1949, FR:49:IX:160–162.

89. Ibid.

90. *Memorandum by the Ambassador at Large (Jessup) to the Secretary of State*, with attachment, "Outline of Far Eastern and Asian Policy for Review with the President," November 16, 1949, FR:VII:Pt.2:1209–1215.

91. Conversation with the President, *Item 1 – China and the Far East*, November 17, 1949, DGA/Memoranda of Conversations/Box 64/ October–November 1949.

92. Ibid.

93. Memorandum for the President, The Secretary of Defense, 15 December 1949, DM/RG 6/FECOM/Formosa File.

94. Memorandum for the Secretary of Defense from Tracy Voorhees (Under Secretary of the Army), 14 December 1949, DM/RG 6/FECOM/ Formosa File; Rearden, *History of the OSD*, p. 236.

95. Letter, Voorhees to MacArthur, 17 December 1949, DM/RG 6/FECOM/Formosa File. It appears that MacArthur and Voorhees decided during the latter's visit to Tokyo the previous week that SCAP's views should be given to Truman at the soonest possible time. On December 17th, Voorhees sent MacArthur an information copy of the entire packet that was sent to Truman two days earlier with no other comments than "For your information." Memorandum For The Secretary Of Defense, From Tracy S. Voorhees, 14 December 1949, DM/RG 6/FECOM/Formosa File. "The following summarizes General MacArthur's views about Formosa."

96. Butterworth to Acheson, "Memorandum Respecting Formosa," December 16, 1949, SDF:Reel 3.

97. Meeting With The President, Item 5. *US Policy Toward the Far East*, December 20, 1949, DGA/Box 64.

98. JCS 1966/24, 22 December 1949, MJCS:Reel 1.

99. Memorandum For The Secretary of Defense from the Joint Chiefs of Staff, "Possible United States Military Action Toward Taiwan not Involving Major Military Forces," 23 December 1949, HST/MNSC/Box 206/NSC Meeting #47; DNSC/Reel 1; *Note by the Executive Secretary of the National Security Council (Souers) to the Council*, NSC 37/9, December 27, 1949, FR:49:IX: 460–461. The paper was signed by Bradley.

100. Rearden, *History of the OSD*, pp. 236–237. Rearden quotes Johnson from transcripts of his 14 June testimony (p. 2577) found in *Military Situation in the Far East: Inquiry Into the Military Situation in the Far East and the Facts*

surrounding the Relief of General of the Army Douglas MacArthur From His Assignments in that Area, 5 Vols. (Washington, D.C.: Government Printing Office, 1951). Further references to this work will be cited as MSFE.

101. Rearden, *History of the OSD,* p. 237.

102. NSC 48/1: A Report To The National Security Council by the Executive Secretary on The Position Of The United States With Respect To Asia, December 23, 1949, HST/MNSC/Box 206; and DNSC:Reel 2.

103. Message, Peiping to Secretary of State, December 23, 1949, SDF:Reel 3.

104. Message, Peiping to Secretary of State, December 13, 1949, SDF:Reel 1. Cites NCNA article in *Jen Min Jih Pao* entitled, "American Imperialism Plans Direct Occupation of Taiwan."

105. Message, Moscow to Secretary of State, citing a December 25th *Izvestia* dispatch, December 28, 1949, SDF:Reel 3.

106. Letter, LTG Albert C. Wedemeyer to Mr. George V. Allen (Assistant Secretary of State for Public Affairs), 26 August 1949, SDF:Reel 2. (See Chapter 6)

107. *Memorandum by the Deputy Assistant Secretary of State for Far Eastern Affairs (Merchant) to the Assistant Secretary of State for Far Eastern Affairs (Butterworth),* Subject: If Formosa Falls, December 1, 1949, FR:49:IX:431-433.

108. The paper, "Special guidance No. 28, December 23, 1949, Policy Information Paper-Formosa," is found in Appendix A (pp. 218-220) in Koen, *The China Lobby,* and MSFE, pp. 1667-1669.

109. Acheson, *Present at the Creation,* p. 350. For more on this affair see DGA/Box 75/Princeton Seminars/Reading Copy, 22-23 July 1953/ Folder 2/pp. 655-658. The leak, "...may have been a clerk's error," recounted Acheson, "but there were an awful lot of errors of this sort coming out of Tokyo, and this one was one which was so very embarrassing to us..."

110. Memorandum Of Conversation, Koo, Acheson, Butterworth, and Merchant, December 23, 1949, SDF:Reel 3.

111. Memo, Butterworth to Acheson, "Formosa and the December 23, 1949 Joint Chiefs of Staff Proposal," December 28, 1949, SDF:Reel 3. Emphasis added.

112. Rosemary Foot, *The Wrong War: American Policy And The Dimensions Of The Korean Conflict, 1950-1953* (Ithica, N.Y.: Cornell University Press, 1985), p. 51; Schaller, *Douglas MacArthur: Far Eastern General,* p. 284, footnote #32; Tucker, *Patterns in the Dust,* p. 187. In 1951, during the controversy over the relief of MacArthur, Drew Pearson of the *Washington Post* alleged that Johnson had served as H.H. Kung's "personal attorney" before serving in the Truman administration. "China Lobby Aims at U.S. Policy," *The Washington Post,* June 18, 1951.

113. Letter, H. Alexander Smith to Acheson, December 27th, 1949, SDF:Reel 3. Copies of the letter calling for a unilateral American occupation were sent as well to Butterworth and Kennan. Butterworth's hackles were definitely raised by all of this and he vented his spleen in a memorandum to

Acheson ripping apart NSC 37/9. Memorandum, Butterworth to Acheson, "Formosa and the December 23, 1949 Joint Chiefs of Staff Proposal," SDF:Reel 3.

114. Memorandum of Conversation, General Omar N. Bradley, General Lawton J. Collins, Lt. General Lauris Norstad, Admiral Forrest Sherman, Secretary Acheson, Dean Rusk, W. Walton Butterworth, and Livingston T. Merchant, December 29, 1949, SDF:Reel 3; and FR:49:IX:463–467.

115. NSC 48/1, The Position of the United States With Respect to Asia, DNSC:Reel 2; and HST/MNSC/Box 206/NSC Meeting #50/12–29–49.

116. Memorandum for the President, Summary of discussion at the 50th meeting of the National Security Council, December 30, 1949, HST/PSF/Box 220/NSC Memos to the President, 1949.

117. The draft discussed at the meeting was NSC 48/1. The final paper approved by the President on December 30th, was redesignated NSC 48/2. For the final version see NSC 48/2: The Position Of The United States With Respect To Asia, December 30, 1949, DNSC:Reel 2; and FR:49:VII: Pt.2:1215–1220.

CHAPTER 8

Taiwan Policy Besieged: January–June 1950

> I have not favored the general tone of the Department's approach to Congress. I hate to see it appear in a defensive and apologetic posture, or as a supplicant in the national interest. I would like to see Congress held firmly to its own responsibilities before the public, which is certainly no less than that of the Executive. I do not really know what a bi-partisan foreign policy means, nor do I know of any means of assuring the support of an antagonistic legislative body other than by policies so sound and so vigorously and persuasively put forward that people will be afraid to vote against measures that support it.[1]

> George F. Kennan

The State Department had little time to gloat over its victory in the National Security Council. News of the "hands off" policy toward Taiwan in NSC 48 unleashed a wave of Republican attacks against Foggy Bottom that lasted for months. The domestic political repercussions were tremendous. Truman and Acheson were forced to defend the futility of intervening in the Chinese civil war. In the process bipartisanship in foreign policy was all but destroyed. When Senator Joseph McCarthy joined forces with the China Bloc, and the attack of the "primitives" began in earnest in February 1950, State's Office of Far Eastern Affairs was placed squarely in the crosshairs of the Wisconsin Senator's communist-baiting shotgun. The first major casualty was Walton Butterworth, whom Acheson was forced to replace in March lest his career be ruined. In spite of the Congressional uproar Acheson never wavered in his belief that it would be a grave mistake to intervene with armed force to save Taiwan from an invasion which, it was believed, could take place as soon as June, 1950. Neither did the mounting hostility of the Chinese communists toward the United States shake Acheson's confidence in the policy toward

Peking which sought to encourage and patiently await a Titoist regime. Although Dean Rusk began to have grave doubts about the wisdom of sacrificing Taiwan, the "hands off" policy toward the island remained in effect.

8.1 FUROR OVER FORMOSA

The weekend holiday bringing in the new year offered no respite to Truman and the State Department. Almost as soon the NSC adjourned on December 29th, news that a Taiwan policy had been decided was leaked all over the press. On December 30th the *New York Times* carried an article declaring "Truman's Top Aides Divided On What to Do About China." James Reston informed his readership that the NSC had met the previous day to decide "...what to do about China in general, and with Formosa in particular..." Reston's account had MacArthur and Johnson in support of active measures to save Taiwan. State and General Bradley were reported as believing that "...the cost and consequences of holding Formosa for the Nationalists might very well outrun the advantages." Acheson, wrote Reston, while not in favor of recognizing the communists, was not prepared to support a "..really bold effort to save Formosa..." because it would undermine "...efforts to build a new policy in the wider area of South Asia..."[2] Most troubling, on January 1st, Reston wrote another article which disclosed some of the recommendations in NSC 48/2.[3]

The China Bloc quickly went into action. Congressman Walter Judd telephoned Truman on December 30th recommending military aid for Taipei. His words fell on deaf ears.[4] On December 31st, the *New York Times* carried statements by Senator Knowland calling for the dispatch of a military mission to Taiwan.[5] On January 3rd Knowland solicited and released to the *New York Times* a letter from Herbert Hoover. The former president called for continued recognition of the KMT, and providing "...naval protection to the possessions of Formosa, the Pescadores and possibly Hainan Island." That same day Senator Taft (R, Ohio), Chairman of the Senate Republican Policy Committee, held a news conference declaring that "...we should take steps to see that the communists do not cross over into Formosa, and I would use the Navy to keep them out if necessary."[6] Later that evening, Knowland publicly demanded that the State Department produce the December 23rd public affairs guidance paper which had been mistakenly released, then recalled, in Tokyo.

Senator Smith chimed in by declaring that the U.S. should immediately adopt "an aggressive policy" in the Far East and "find a formula for occupying Formosa."[7]

The KMT and CCP added their voices to the tumult over Taiwan as well. In Taipei, KMT sources were confidently predicting to the Associated Press that within six to eight weeks funds for military assistance would be programmed for Taiwan and that U.S. advisers would be sent to supervise its use. In Hong Kong United Press dispatches, quoting Nationalist sources once again, claimed (falsely) that Washington had already dispatched thirty-two retired U.S. Army and Navy officers to Taiwan to make a survey of Chiang's military needs in order to assist in the island's defense; a claim which the Consulate in Taipei publicly denied. In Peking *Hsinhua* accused the U.S. of concluding a "secret agreement" with Taipei whereby the KMT would soon receive "sixteen naval vessels, arms and equipment for five divisions, radar installations, and spare parts and repair equipment for military aircraft."[8] Even Tokyo joined in this Formosa free-for-all. Incredibly, the Associated Press reported on January 4th that a "responsible source" in SCAP headquarters, "predicted" that "...a final decision on United States policy toward Formosa would emerge from a visit of the Joint Chiefs of Staff to Japan next month."[9] The clear implication of this statement was that MacArthur had yet to give his imprimatur to any Taiwan policy made in Washington.

At this point, not only was the administration's Taiwan policy under attack by irate China Bloc leaders, but there was obviously confusion at home and abroad about just what the policy was. Acheson immediately set out to address both of these problems by having the president issue a policy statement and by attempting to deal with the concerns of Congress.

In an attempt to assuage congressional critics, Acheson went to Capitol Hill late on the afternoon of January 4th. He asked Tom Connally to call the Senate Foreign Relations Committee into session the next week in order for him to explain administration Far Eastern policy.[10] Acheson also called upon Congressman John Kee, Chairman of the House Foreign Affairs Committee, to explain why Taiwan required no military assistance and to ask to speak to Kee's committee after addressing Connally's group. Judge Kee was receptive to the Secretary's arguments that Taiwan already had sufficient military arms, the CCP did not have the capability to invade, and that if

Formosa fell it would be due to internal collapse. Kee pledged his support to the administration's policy and agreed to call his committee into session to hear these arguments.[11] Acheson's scheduled meetings with the two committees would take place on the 10th and 11th of January. At that time he would try to bring his critics around.

The next day, January 5th, Acheson planned to have President Truman release his famous statement on Taiwan policy. As Acheson recalled it during the Princeton Seminars (1953), he went to the White House on the afternoon of January 4th to see President Truman before calling on Connally and Kee. According to his account, he and the President discussed the fact that "all sorts of things were being leaked from within the Administration," that Taiwan was becoming a partisan issue, and that Truman had already made his decision on Taiwan policy when he signed NSC 48. Acheson recollected that he recommended to Truman, and that the president agreed with him, "...that he (Truman) had to come out very clearly and firmly and put his foot down and say this is the end of the thing, and this is what we are going to do, and there isn't going to be any more argument about it..." Therefore, claimed Acheson, "together we drew up a statement he would give the next day, January 5th."[12] The full text of the original statement read as follows:

> The United States Government has always stood for good faith in international relations. Traditional United States policy toward China, as exemplified in the Open Door policy, called for international respect for the territorial integrity of China. This principle was recently reaffirmed in the UN General Assembly resolution of December 8, 1949, which, in part, calls on all states
>
> To refrain from (a) seeking to acquire spheres of influences or to create foreign controlled regimes within the territory of China; (b) seeking to obtain special rights or privileges within the territory of China.
>
> A special application of the foregoing principles is seen in the present situation with respect to Formosa. In the Joint Declaration at Cairo on December 1, 1943, the President of the United States, the British Prime Minister and the President of China stated that it was their purpose that territories Japan had stolen from China, such as "Formosa," should be restored to the Republic of China. The United States was a signatory to the Potsdam Declaration of July 26, 1945, which declared that the terms of the Cairo Declaration should be carried out. The provisions of this Declaration were accepted by Japan at the time of its surrender. In keeping with these declarations, Formosa was surrendered to

Generalissimo Chiang Kai-shek and for the past four years the United States and the other Allied Powers have accepted the exercise of Chinese authority over the Island.

The United States has no predatory designs on Formosa or on any other Chinese territory. The United States has no desire to obtain special rights or privileges or to establish military bases on Formosa. Nor does it have any intention of utilizing its armed forces to interfere in the present situation or detach Formosa from China. The United States Government will not pursue a course which will lead to involvement in the civil conflict in China.

Similarly, the United States Government will not provide military aid or advice to Chinese forces on Formosa. In the view of the United States Government, the resources on Formosa are adequate to enable them to obtain the items which they might consider necessary for the defense of the Island. The United States Government proposes to continue under existing legislative authority the present ECA program of economic assistance.[13]

Obviously, this statement was not just for a domestic audience. By issuing this statement, Truman and Acheson were sending important messages both to the CCP and the KMT. Because it was known that Mao was in Moscow visiting Stalin, Truman made it clear that it was not the United States that had predatory designs on Chinese territory, but, by implication, the Soviets. Furthermore, Peking was assured that the U.S. had no intention of intervening in the Chinese civil war and would not attempt to bring down the communist regime by force. To clear up any possible confusion about U.S. policy toward Taiwan, Peking was told that the U.S. was not about to occupy Taiwan, or even send military equipment to the KMT. All of this was consistent with the policy of encouraging Titoism on the mainland. As for the Nationalists, the president made it painfully clear that the *demarche* of November continued to be the basis of United States policy toward Taipei. It was pointless for the KMT to continue to ask Washington for government-to-government military assistance. Taipei had what it needed or could buy with its own funds other military equipment it desired. The most that Taipei could expect was continued economic aid. For their congressional critics, Truman and Acheson let it be known that the U.S. had honored its wartime pledge of returning Taiwan to China but that the KMT had made a mess of things, that the island was not worth becoming involved militarily in the Chinese civil war, that Taiwan had what it needed to defend itself, but that the administration would provide economic assistance.

As it turned out, this statement caused great consternation within the administration and ultimately confusion without. Moreover, Acheson's account about whose idea it was to issue the statement and whether Truman helped him draft it may not be completely accurate.

According to a memorandum written on January 6, 1950 by George M. Elsey (Truman's administrative assistant) Acheson, on January 4th, brought to the White House a statement which was already drafted for the President. After Acheson took his leave (probably to go to Capitol Hill), Truman, said Elsey, held a meeting with Clark Clifford and Charles S. Murphy (White House special counsels), Admiral Souers (NSC), and James Lay (NSC) to discuss the proposed draft. Elsey contends that the "unanimous advice" of Truman's staff was *not* to release the statement. The President asked Admiral Souers to get Defense Secretary Johnson's advice. Johnson "felt very strongly that the statement should not be issued." The President then decided against releasing the statement and there was no further discussion of the draft that day by the group, for it was assumed to be a dead issue. However, according to Elsey, later that evening Truman and Acheson spoke to each other on the telephone and the president "was persuaded by Mr. Acheson that the statement should be handed out Thursday morning January 5 at the President's press conference."[14]

Early on the morning of January 5th, Truman had Admiral Souers call Defense Secretary Johnson and General Bradley to inform them that the President had decided to issue the statement at his 10:30 A.M. press conference after all. The next to last paragraph in the statement bothered Bradley. He asked that the phrase "...or detach Formosa from China" be deleted, arguing that in case of general war the U.S. might in fact desire to occupy the island. Moreover, Bradley asked that three words, "at this time" be added to the sentence which declared that the U.S. had no desire to establish military bases on Formosa. The President agreed to both changes and told Souers to inform Acheson. At 10:00 A.M. Acheson was told of Bradley's request to delete the phrase about detaching Formosa from China and reluctantly agreed. However, Souers apparently forgot to mention to Acheson the addition of the three words "at this time". Moreover, no one informed the White House press office about the changes to the draft. Consequently, prior to Truman's 10:30 A.M.

press conference copies of the original statement were released to the press corp. When Truman read the statement, the press was surprised that it did not conform to the copy released, and Acheson was surprised that the three-word phrase was added. Copies of the original statement issued to the press were recalled immediately after the conference and corrected versions were distributed. Acheson rushed to meet with Truman to ask how the extra phrase found its way into the statement. The president explained Bradley's concerns. However, it was too late. The discrepancies in the two versions were already noted by the press corp. It was decided by Truman and Acheson that the latter would hold a press conference later that afternoon to discuss the intent of Truman's statement and to explain away the differences between the two versions.[15] In the meantime, all the involved parties in the administration were seething at the way the entire affair was handled. As Elsey told it, Johnson was "angry" that the statement was issued at all. Acheson was "angry" about the insertion of the phrase, "at this time." Clark Clifford was "annoyed" at Acheson's "pressure tactics" in having Truman reverse his decision the day before not to issue the statement. All in all, observed Elsey, "Everyone seems upset!"[16]

Needless to say, the China Bloc was also very upset. After the president's press conference, Acheson had to contend with Senators Knowland and Smith who rushed into the Secretary's office to voice their opposition to and disappointment with such a policy. In a meeting which lasted over ninety minutes, Secretary Acheson attempted to explain the rationale behind the administration's policy. He expounded the very themes and arguments that had been gone over time and again within the NSC. He talked about the need to encourage Titoism on the mainland, the ultimate goal of keeping Peking out of the Soviet orbit, a desire not to act like imperialists before the eyes of other emerging Asian nations, that the U.S. could not morally hide behind the legalities of a Japanese Peace Treaty to occupy Taiwan having committed itself to return it to China, the fact that Taipei had all it needed to survive if it could just muster the will, and the need to detach the prestige of the United States in Asia from the fate of Chiang and the Nationalists. Acheson also made sure to inform the senators that the Joint Chiefs of Staff refused to deem Taiwan of vital importance to national security. He argued that only by being prepared to go to war over Taiwan could the United States guarantee the island's survival. This was a commitment, Acheson told the two senators, he was not willing to make. Knowland and Smith were not moved by these arguments. Both pointed out that morale on Taiwan was better than Acheson thought it to be, and they both cited their respective trips to Taiwan and their impressions. Furthermore, they could not fathom why Acheson and the Joint Chiefs viewed Taiwan less important strategically than General MacArthur and Admiral Radford; both of whom considered it a vital asset. Acheson and Knowland also went around on the public affairs press release paper which had been leaked in Tokyo. Acheson told Knowland that the paper was prepared as a contingency, not one outlining a policy to be followed before the unhappy event of Taiwan's fall came to pass. The senator, Acheson assured Knowland, was reading only snippets of the paper and out of context from the whole at that. Knowland remained unmoved and deemed it typical of State's defeatist attitude toward Taiwan. Smith told Acheson how disappointed he was that the Senate was not consulted before a Taiwan policy was determined. He warned that he would now have to rethink his previous inclinations to work for bipartisanship in foreign policy. Knowland was more direct. He intended to make Taiwan a partisan issue. He warned that State was now "pursuing a policy of grave danger to the American people and that he considered the issue to be one of paramount importance." Knowland told Acheson that he now felt it "his conscientious duty to endeavor to acquaint the American people with what he regarded to be a fatal policy" which State "would live to rue and regret."[17] Knowland made good his threat. Upon returning to Capitol Hill, he initiated a five-hour debate in the Senate in which he accused a "small group of willful men in the Far Eastern Division who had the backing of their superiors" of being responsible for the China debacle.[18]

At 2:30 P.M. that same afternoon Acheson met with the press, as he informed them, "at the request and at the direction of the President for the purpose of going into the background of the statement which he made this morning on the subject of Formosa." He offered that too much confusion about U.S. policy toward the island had recently resulted from incorrect speculation in the foreign and domestic press. Consequently, "...it was the President's desire to clarify the situation." Although the administration would have liked to have consulted the Congress first, the president felt that to wait any longer to make a definitive statement of policy would have been detrimental to the interests of the United States. Taiwan was but "a small part of the great question of the Far East," he argued, and the kind of "amateur military strategy indulged in" by many of late obfuscated the rationale behind the administration's policy. Quite simply, Acheson told the press that the United States had always been committed to the fact that Taiwan belonged to China. Although it was highly regrettable that the Nationalists no longer controlled the mainland, the U.S. was not now going to go back on that commitment to principle or "quibble on any lawyer's words" that the final disposition of Taiwan would have to await the conclusion of a peace treaty with Japan. To do so would undermine the credibility of the United States Government in the eyes of the rest of the world. Acheson reminded the group that no legal objections were raised when the Nationalists made Taiwan a province of China in the absence of a peace treaty immediately after the war ended. As for the decision not to grant military assistance to Taipei, Acheson pointed out that plenty of military assistance had been made available to the KMT after the war and plenty of equipment was currently available on Taiwan. However, he pointed out, military equipment is not the solution to the island's predicament. "The trouble," he said, "lies elsewhere..." The United States cannot "furnish a will to resist..." The KMT must provide that themselves. Finally, as for the addition of the phrase "at this time," Acheson lectured the group that:

> That phrase does not qualify or modify or weaken the fundamental policy stated in this declaration by the President in any respect. It is a recognition of the fact that, in the unlikely and unhappy event that our forces might be attacked in the Far East, the United States must be completely free to take whatever action in whatever area is necessary for its own security.[19]

The reaction of the domestic press to Truman's statement and Acheson's press conference remarks were mixed. the *New York Times* and the *Washington Post* printed editorials which were generally favorable. The *Times* declared that "a majority of Americans will agree that this decision is well taken." The *Post* commented that "The statement is pithy, full of point, and compact with common sense; and it should clear the air all over the world about American intentions." More neutral, Eric Sevareid of CBS commented that "Wise or foolish, the President's decision at least prevents the curious situation of America helping Chiang fight the Communists while our important allies around the world recognize and continue to do business with the Communists." The *Philadelphia Inquirer* came out against the policy, charging that Truman now "gave the Communists the green light" to invade Taiwan. *The Herald Tribune* called upon the administration to enlist Republicans in formulating Far Eastern policy and give up its go-it-alone style. All major newspapers, even those in favor of the Taiwan decision, pointed out that the administration was following a generally negative policy in the Far East and called upon the president and State to take positive actions in the region to secure United States interests.[20]

In the foreign media there was approval for Truman's statement in London, Paris, and Manila. The British had been very concerned that U.S. support for Taiwan would ultimately endanger their position in Hong Kong politically by association and militarily by providing the CCP with an excuse to attack the crown colony. For its part, Manila feared that the expansion of hostilities into the South China Sea would incite communist insurgencies at home. The president's statement was met "with considerable relief" in New Delhi as India was trying to walk a diplomatic tightrope by staying in good graces with both Peking and Washington. The American Embassy in Saigon reported that the Vietnamese were also pleased with the policy toward Taiwan because an American occupation, said a local official, would have been met with popular charges of U.S. imperialism, resulting in a great embarrassment for the government. In Taipei, understandably, KMT radio expressed "regret" and "bewilderment" at the president's statement. In Seoul, Syngman Rhee denounced it. The Soviets and Chinese communists virtually ignored the statement, for it pulled the rug out from under Moscow's and Peking's recent propaganda blitz which claimed that the United States was intent upon invading the island. The best that the communist press could do was to counter the president's words with the well-known sentiments of Douglas MacArthur and claim that Truman was concealing his true intentions.[21]

In the Senate, the debate over Taiwan policy initiated by Senator Knowland on January 5th continued in a most heated manner for four more days.[22] The debate took on increased momentum on January 6th with London's announcement that it had recognized the communist government in Peking. More fuel was added to the fire on January 8th when Madame Chiang Kai-shek bid an impassioned farewell to

America as she ended her long stay in the United States. With ample coverage from the newsreels, radio, and the press, Madame Chiang, exuding the same mix of eloquence and stoicism that made her America's darling during the war, thanked the many friends of China for their help throughout the years. She concluded dramatically by stating that:

> I can ask the American people for nothing more. At such a time no pleading can be made with dignity. It is either in your hearts to love us, or your hearts have turned against us. It is either in your mind and will to aid China in her struggle for liberty, or you have abandoned liberty.[23]

The abandonment of liberty was exactly what some China Bloc leaders accused the administration of in their oratory during the senate debate. Knowland denounced the president's Taiwan decision as "a bankrupt policy which now stands revealed in all of its sorry detail."[24] He called for the dismissal of the men in State's Office of Far Eastern Affairs, giving MacArthur responsibility for formulating Far Eastern policy, and sending a military assistance mission to Taipei headed by General Wedemeyer. Senator Joseph McCarthy used the debate to revive allegations that John Service was sympathetic to the communist revolution in China.[25] Senator Homer Ferguson attacked the policy as well, and lamented that it "kicks the bipartisan policy right out the window."[26] But in spite of the noise made by the China Bloc, Democratic Senators such as Connally, Humphrey, McMahon, and Lucas were prepared to support the president's decision. Connally asked his colleagues if there was one among them that wished to send an army to Taiwan. Who, he asked, would rise on the senate floor and say, "I favor sending an army to Formosa."

> I want to know who the Senators are, and I shall revive the question from time to time, who want to plunge this country, not directly, but possibly, into World War III, in the name of Formosa, but principally in the name of a bitter attack upon the President of the United States and upon the Department of State.[27]

Connally's challenge to the call for military intervention in Taiwan was so effective that he literally brought an end to the debate on January 9th. But the end of the senate debate was by no means the last of the China Bloc's criticism. During the next two days, January 10th and 11th, Acheson went before the Senate Foreign Relations Committee and the House Foreign Affairs Committee as previously scheduled. During these closed hearings the Secretary of State attempted to explain the administration's grand strategy for containing communism throughout Asia and place policy toward Taiwan in that larger context. However, Acheson's critics, especially Taft, Knowland, and McCarthy, continued to harass him. They focused their attacks on the administration's failure in China, resurrected Patrick Hurley's allegations about the suspect political motives of certain Foreign Service Officers, and attempted to further embarrass Acheson by bringing up the public affairs guidance paper on the fall of Taiwan. Although Vandenberg and Smith began to fall off of the idea of a unilateral military occupation, distancing themselves from Taft and Knowland, they still demanded that State find some legal formula for separating Taiwan from China.[28]

Overall, Acheson's two days on Capitol Hill were unsuccessful. He was unable to quiet criticism over Taiwan policy. Moreover, because he was immediately put on the defensive, he was not able to use the hearings to explain the fundamental premises upon which the administration was building its policy of containment in Asia; the original purpose for which the two sessions were scheduled. Consequently, Truman and Acheson took their case to the American public.

On January 12th, Acheson delivered his well-known speech to the National Press Club in Washington. The timing of the speech could not have been better. Acheson had received the invitation to speak in late December. On January 5th, the day of the president's statement on Taiwan, Acheson asked Truman if he thought it would be a good idea to accept the engagement. Truman endorsed the idea and, according to Acheson's memorandum of the meeting, the president agreed that a "hard-hitting speech at this time" on Far Eastern policy was in order.[29]

The speech, *"Crisis in Asia*-An Examination of U.S. Policy," is universally acclaimed as Acheson's most memorable address. Primarily, it is remembered for the controversy it raised when he outlined the strategic defense perimeter of the United States in the Far East.[30] Ironically, Acheson's primary purpose in delivering the talk was not to discuss the military aspects of U.S. security in Asia.[31] The purpose of the speech was to explain to the American public the fundamental analysis upon which the administration's China policy was based. In the course of his talk, Acheson expounded upon three major concepts; the revolutionary situation in Asia, the fact that Russian imperialism in China would eventually work to the benefit of the United States, and the limits of American aid and assistance.

Before one could understand the situation in China, argued Acheson, one had to grasp the great changes underway in Asia. The end of the Second World War destroyed the old political relationships between the East and the West. Since that time, he pointed out, over half a million people had gained their independence and seven new nations had been founded. Asian nationalism, the common expression of the desire "both of freedom from foreign domination and freedom from the tyranny of poverty and misery" was now a fact of life in the Far East. The people of Asia were now determined to take their fate into their own hands; to make their own decisions and make their own mistakes. The phenomenon of Asian nationalism was not a threat to the United States. To the contrary, Acheson offered, this desire for independence was in perfect consonance with the fundamental democratic traditions of the U.S. Moreover, an Asia unfettered by foreign domination had always been considered in America's best interests. This was articulated in the Open Door Notes. The threat to the U.S., argued the Secretary, was that communism, "the most subtle instrument of Soviet foreign policy that has ever been devised...the spearhead of Russian imperialism" was threatening to subvert the national revolutions occurring in the Far East. Moscow was determined to ride upon the crest of legitimate revolution to shackle the peoples of Asia as surely as did the imperialist nations of the nineteenth century. This was the development that the United States would have to counter, not the changes underway within the nations of the Far East. In doing so, the interests of the peoples of Asia and those of the United States were "parallel." But in doing so, Acheson warned, Washington would have cooperate with, not dictate to, the nations of Asia.

Understanding the revolutionary nature of Asia, said Acheson, gave more insight into the reasons for the collapse of the *Kuomintang* than any theory of conspiracy, bungled, or inadequate U.S. aid. Chiang Kai-shek had the armies. He had the military equipment, and he had international recognition. What he did not have, said Acheson, was the solution to the misery of the people of China. This, coupled with "the grossest incompetence ever experienced by any military command," cost him the confidence of his own people. The people of China "completely withdrew their support from this government" and the whole Nationalist regime collapsed.

> The communists did not create this. The communists did not create this condition. They did not create this revolutionary spirit. They did not create a great force which moved out from under Chiang Kai-shek. But they were shrewd and cunning to mount it, to ride this thing into victory and power.

In effect, Acheson argued that there was nothing that the United States could have done to preclude the *denouement* on the mainland. The argument, previously stated in the *White Paper,* was that Washington gave Chiang everything he needed, but could not supply the support of his own citizens.

But the good news was that all was not hopelessly lost. The same revolutionary nationalism which snatched China from Chiang could very well take the mandate of heaven from the communists. Communism was merely a modern expression of traditional Russian aggression, argued Acheson, and the fact that Moscow was in the process of detaching Manchuria, Mongolia and Sinkiang was proof of the assertion. Sooner or later the people of China would see their folly if the United States was patient and did nothing to divert the anger of Chinese people from Soviets.

> I wish to state this and perhaps sin against my doctrine of non-dogmatism, but I should like to suggest at any rate that this fact that the Soviet Union is taking the four northern provinces of China is the single most important fact, in the relations of any foreign power with Asia.
> What does it mean for us? It means something very, very significant. It means that nothing that we say must be allowed to obscure the reality of this fact. All the efforts of propaganda will not be able to obscure it. The only thing that can obscure it is the folly of ill-conceived adventures on our part which easily could do so and I urge all who are thinking about these foolish adventures to remember that we must not seize the unenviable position which the Russians have carved out for themselves. We must not undertake to deflect from the Russians to ourselves the righteous anger and the wrath and the hatred of the Chinese people which must develop. It would be folly to deflect it to ourselves. We must take the position that we have always taken that anyone who violates the integrity of China is the enemy of China and is acting contrary to our own interest. That, I suggest to you this afternoon, is the first and greatest rule in regard to the formulation of American policy toward Asia.

Next, Acheson, by inference, explained why the president's statement on Taiwan was necessary and why arguments about using the absence of a peace treaty with Japan to detach Taiwan from the mainland could come to no good.

> I suggest that the second rule is very like the first. That is to keep our own purposes perfectly straight, perfectly pure and perfectly above-board and do not get them mixed up with legal quibbles or the attempt to do one thing and really achieve another.

Using this discussion of Soviet transgression in China, Acheson proclaimed that time was on the side of the U.S. and implied that Peking would eventually go the way of Tito, or the CCP would lose its newly won mandate.

> The consequences of this Russian attitude and this Russian action in China are perfectly enormous. They are saddling all those in China who are proclaiming their loyalty to Moscow, and who are allowing themselves to be used as puppets of Moscow, with the most awful responsibility which they must pay for. Furthermore, these actions of the Russians are making plainer than any speech or any utterance or any legislation can make throughout all of Asia what the true purposes of the Soviet Union are and what the true function of Communism as an agent of Russian imperialism is. These I suggest to you are the fundamental factors, fundamental realities of attitude out of which our relations and policies must grow.

Finally, Acheson propounded what might be called the "Missing Component Doctrine." The United States, said Acheson, had the administrative, agricultural, and technical skills to assist the people of Asia secure their political independence and better their quality of life. "If we can help that development, if we can go forward with it, then we have brought about the best way that anyone knows of stopping this spread of communism." The challenge to U.S. policymakers was to recognize that American help could not be imposed upon the new nations of Asia against their will. When requested, the U.S. would provide assistance. But Secretary of State Acheson pointed out that the limits of "effective American assistance" had to be recognized.

> American assistance can be effective when it is the missing component in a situation which might otherwise be solved. The United States cannot furnish all these components to solve the question. It can not furnish determination, it can not furnish the will and it can not furnish and it will not furnish the loyalty of a people to its government. But if the will and if the determination exists and if the people are behind their government, then, and not always then, is there a very good chance. In

that situation American help can be effective and it can lead to an accomplishment which could not otherwise be achieved.[32]

The reaction to the speech, as would be expected, was mixed. The China Bloc rejected Acheson's arguments, some dismissing it as a cover for a policy of inaction and others decrying it as an outright sell out of the KMT. At the same time, those columnists generally friendly to the administration gave the Secretary high marks. Walter Lippman, in an article entitled "Acheson Takes Long View Of the Revolution in Asia," offered the loudest accolades. "Now we can see in broad outline the working hypotheses to which their (State's) thinking had led them," he wrote. Mao, said Lippman, would find out "as Tito has found out...that the Cominform tail does not wag the Russian bear." The recognition of the inevitability of Sino-Soviet tensions and that "the crucial area is not in Formosa...*is* a China policy."[33] In the *New York Times* Arthur Krock predicted that the insistence of some G.O.P. members to attack Taiwan policy "before knowing all the facts leading up to the decision" would hurt the Republican cause. Had Taft, Knowland and Smith been aware of the reasoning that had gone into Truman's and Acheson's "hands off" policy toward Taiwan, said Krock, they "would have more carefully defined the military aspects of their proposals."[34]

Regardless of the effectiveness of the speech or the soundness of its arguments the talk represented a genuine effort by Acheson to explain the Department's approach to China policy. It was true to the analysis that Acheson's advisers had brought to the problem throughout 1949. The concept of Asian nationalism was contributed by Fosdick, Case, and Jessup. The failure of the KMT to address China's problems on the mainland and Taiwan showed the influence of Butterworth, Merchant, and Davies. Communism as a form of Russian imperialism was classic Kennan. Moreover, the concept of the "missing component" in predicting the effectiveness of U.S. foreign assistance was apparently Kennan's as well.[35]

Over the next few weeks, the Department continued its campaign to educate the American public about Asian realities and China policy. Of particular note, Livingston Merchant took on the role of State Department spokesman at a variety of engagements. Merchant spoke at the White House to leading members of the Advertising Business Council, at the Institute for World Organization, and the Minnesota World Affairs Center. In these speeches he drove home the following points: the U.S. *was* supplying large amounts of foreign aid to most of the countries in the Far East (almost $6 billion worth, especially in Southeast Asia); Soviet imperialism in China was real; the prospects for Titoism were good; and no foreign aid could be effective without the "missing component."[36] Raymond Fosdick, no longer with State as a consultant, went public as well in a feature article in *The New York Times Magazine* entitled, "Asia's Challenge to Us-Ideas, Not Guns."[37] In his piece, Fosdick presented to the public many of the concepts that he had articulated to Acheson and Jessup during his tenure at State. He described the "vast revolutionary forces" at work in Asia. He offered that Chiang had lost his government for failing to address the economic plight of China; in effect forfeiting his original revolution to the communists. Unlike Acheson, however, Fosdick, who had none of the Secretary's political constraints, publicly advanced the bold thesis that the United States had a large hand in the communist victory. This, he argued was because of a misplaced reliance on military assistance to Chiang instead forcing the Gimo to enact social and economic reforms (an indictment of the Congress), continuing to support the KMT when it became clear that it was a reactionary force, and finally a failure of the West in general to fight the ideological battle against Moscow. "Communism," said Fosdick, "has sold China a copy of our ideals. We must prove that ours are the genuine thing." Except for Fosdick's bolder statements about the loss of China, his article and Acheson's Press Club speech were absolutely complimentary and in some cases almost identical in reasoning. Indeed, the *Times* article leaves the striking impression that Acheson was much more influenced by Fosdick's analysis of the situation in Asia and the problems in China than may have previously been thought. Whereas most works on this period often mention the existence of the Far Eastern consultants (Jessup, Fosdick, and Case), none seem to give the group, especially Fosdick, their due for having influenced Acheson's (and Truman's) thinking about Asia.

Interestingly, neither in Acheson's speech, Merchant's various talks, or even Fosdick's blunt article was there ever any direct reference to the situation on Taiwan or administration policy toward the island; the immediate reason that a publicity blitz was required. Why? First, Truman already made an unequivocal statement about U.S. Taiwan policy on January 5th. By not attempting to defend that policy directly the administration was sending the message that it was not about to change it due to congressional pressures. Second, the examination of Chiang Kai-shek's failures on the mainland in Acheson's speech and Fosdick's article were an indirect attack on the argument that the Gimo would do much better on Taiwan. This indirect approach would not give congressional critics another specific excuse to attack Taiwan policy. Finally, and most important, the administration hoped that by explaining the broader problems the U.S. faced in Asia, and how it was attempting to deal with them, the public would see that the issue of Taiwan was a relatively minor portion of a larger problem. The pronounced policy toward the island would come to be seen as part of a larger strategy addressing broader U.S. interests. In the final analysis, the administration argued, the problem facing the U.S. in Asia was not whether the KMT on Taiwan could survive, but the fact that the Soviets were exploiting revolutionary regional nationalism to their benefit and to the detriment of the United States. The advance of Soviet-inspired communism throughout Asia was that threat which the U.S. had to counter. That was the prime interest of the U.S. in Asia, not helping the KMT to defend against the CCP on Taiwan; especially since Chiang could do that himself if he mustered the will.

Regardless of how well the public, some media notables, and Democrats in Congress received the public defense of Truman's and Acheson's Asia policy, administration critics in the legislature were not placated. On January 19th, administration officials were shocked when a bill (HR 5330) authorizing $60 million in economic assistance for Korea was defeated in the House of Representatives by one vote. As Tang Tsou points out, the initial defeat of the Korean Aid Bill was the first major foreign policy defeat for the executive since the end of the Second World War! Isolationist legislators and those who desired to cut government spending in general were already known to be against more foreign aid expenditures. However, what clinched the vote killing the resolution was the added weight of China Bloc congressmen who reacted to Truman's pronounced policy toward Taiwan. "What kind of policy for the Far East," asked Donald L. Jackson (R., California), "would put economic aid into Korea, which bears no relationship to our national defense, and at the same time refuse a request to put aid into Formosa?" Equally shocked by this turn of events were China Bloc senators Smith, Judd and Knowland who argued with their colleagues in the House that they were cutting their nose to spite their face. As it turned out, a compromise was eventually worked out. The Korean Aid Bill was eventually passed only after the expiration date for using residual funds allocated in the China Aid Act (due to expire on February 15, 1950) was extended once more until June 30th. Although relieved that the Korean Aid Bill was finally pushed through, Knowland took the opportunity to warn Acheson that he would continue to have problems in all foreign policy initiatives if the administration continued to pursue a policy of writing off Taiwan.[38]

Acheson believed, as he told the Joint Chiefs, that the U.S. would have to take "the long view not of 6 or 12 months but of 6 or 12 years" if the overriding objective of fostering a Titoist China (the only real option he felt was now left open to Washington) was to succeed.[39] He rested this policy, as Walter Lippman said, "on an estimate of historical forces at work in Asia" that would have to be viewed "in a longer perspective than tomorrows headlines" and "not wait tensely for news that Mao has defied Stalin and is hurrying back to Peking" in the "next week, next month, or next year."[40] Unfortunately for the administration, many in the Congress were not willing to wait that long for the United States to see the fruition of its estimates. Consequently, over the next few months State was forced to continue to defend its policy to an increasingly hostile legislature. At the same time, State had to cope with the immediate challenges posed by an increasingly hostile CCP and a troublesome regime in Taipei.

8.2 JANUARY–MARCH: PROBLEMS WITH PEKING, TROUBLE WITH TAIPEI

While the Congressional clamor over China continued, State, in January 1950, began in earnest to develop concrete policies to achieve the overriding objective of NSC 48; stemming the advance of communism in Asia. With China already under CCP rule, and the fall of Taiwan considered inevitable, the State Department's Far Eastern specialists focused their energies on the countries of Southeast Asia. Here was a region where there was still time to halt the spread of Soviet-inspired communism. Here was an opportunity to put American assistance, especially economic aid, into programs which would produce the desired result. It was during this period that Philip Jessup and Allen Griffin made their respective trips throughout the region. Jessup conducted a fact-finding mission to fourteen Asian countries which began in mid-December 1949 and lasted until mid-March 1950. The most important event of his journey was the Bangkok Conference of United States Chiefs of Mission in the Far East (13–15 February). Jessup was joined by Walton Butterworth who flew out to attend the conference. The two architects of current policy presented State's grand strategy for Asia to the assemblage of nineteen Ambassadors, Consuls General, and political advisers. For their part, the diplomats presented overviews of conditions in their host countries. While there was considerable debate about the wisdom of committing U.S. military assistance to the area at that time, there was consensus that Southeast Asia required immediate economic aid as a prophylaxis to the spread of communism.[41] It was within this context that the "Griffin Mission" was dispatched to Southeast Asia. From February until May, Griffin (Director of ECA Programs for the Far East) visited Singapore, Rangoon, Saigon, Bangkok, and Jakarta. The purpose of the trip was to study local conditions and assist the State Department in developing "a program of economic assistance on an emergency basis which would remove impediments to economic development in Southeast Asia and strengthen the governments there by making it possible for them to assist their peoples in economic rehabilitation."[42] The programs of assistance developed for the region were further steps down America's road to war in Indochina.

Although State's focus had clearly shifted to Southeast Asia, the China-Taiwan problem did not go away. If anything, handling relations with the two China's, especially with the communist regime, became more difficult. On January 6th, the British announced their intention to grant Peking recognition. London's lead was followed in turn by Norway, Ceylon, Denmark, Israel, Afghanistan, Finland, and Switzerland.[43] The Soviets had recognized the communist regime on the day the PRC was declared (October 1, 1949), and in January 1950 the United Nations Security Council was scheduled to vote upon a resolution introduced by Moscow to expel the KMT representative from the world organization. In Peking, also on January 6th, communist officials gave notice to Consul General O. Edmund Clubb that the People's Central Government intended to nationalize portions of the Consulate that had previously served as military barracks. Clubb was told to vacate these facilities by January 13th.[44] Throughout China, in fact, U.S. Consulates began to operate under increasingly hostile conditions. Moreover, in mid-February Peking and Moscow finally came to accords and signed their Treaty of Friendship, Alliance, and Mutual Assistance.

In retrospect one can argue that during the first weeks of 1950 events on the mainland and in international diplomacy were moving faster than Washington's passive "Titoist" policy could accommodate. Nevertheless, Acheson and his advisers did not view these events as the failure of their approach to the China problem. To the contrary, they viewed these events more or less as expected developments. In the calculus of State's Soviet and Far Eastern experts the questions of recognition for the PRC, Taipei's status in the U.N., and the Sino-Soviet alliance were mutually dependant variables in the same Titoist equation. If manipulated correctly, these developments, it was felt, could work to the benefit of the United States. Central to this calculus were three assumptions.

The first assumption was that the CCP leadership was not monolithic. Along with a pro-Moscow, virulently anti-American radical left-wing, there was also believed to be a CCP faction, centered about Chou En-lai, which favored ties with Washington. This latter group was characterized as fearing the Soviet Union and recognizing that the United States possessed economic assets which would be much needed to help put China back on its feet.[45] The second assumption was the core of State's Titoist policy. It was assumed that common ideology would initially put the Chinese and Soviet communists in league. However, traditional Russian imperialism would eventually sour Peking on Moscow. Chinese nationalism, it was felt, would prove a stronger force than ideological compatibility. While it was not expected that Peking would sever ties to Moscow, it was believed that the CCP would eventually deal both with the communist and non-communist blocs due to the economic and national security requirements of the Chinese state. The third assumption in State's calculus was that pandering to the CCP, caving in to its demands, or prostituting Washington's own interests out of fear of alienating Peking would backfire. The lesson that State derived from dealing with Yugoslavia's Tito was that grovelling before Moscow's potentially wayward wards would only undermine the positions of those who would defy the Kremlin. They would be accused of selling out their revolution to the hated capitalists. Moreover, it was believed that no communist, even one who was prepared to break with the Soviets, could have any respect for a foreign nation which did not act

strongly and with vigor in pursuit of its own interests.[46] All of these
ideas were evident in the way in which State handled the questions of
recognition, the violation of the Consulate in Peking, and
Washington's reaction to the Sino-Soviet Treaty.

The administration's approach to recognition became very
discernable during the period prior to and immediately following
London's own initiative. Washington had never categorically ruled
out recognition of the communist regime.[47] In testimony prepared
for Acheson's 10–12 January appearance on the Hill, Kennan, in one
of his last acts affiliated with PPS,[48] had the Staff prepare the following words for the Secretary on the subject of recognizing the CCP:

> We will not assure any benefits to ourselves just by recognition; it will
> be a question of how we handle ourselves once relations exist. But we will
> also not gain anything by withholding recognition for sentimental rea-
> sons alone, if realistic considerations indicate desirability of maintenance
> of diplomatic contact.[49]

Livingston Merchant, in a mid-January speech on the topic, pointed
out that the act of recognizing a foreign government did not imply
approval; it was merely a prerequisite for conducting the business of
diplomacy. Recognition was an act, said Merchant, "as impersonal as
laying a cable."[50] The crucial questions were those of timing and the
conditions under which recognition would be granted.

The conditions for recognizing the PRC were clearly articulated
by early 1950. Before the United States would recognize Peking it had
to be established that: (1) the communists had control of the country,
(2) the Chinese people generally recognized CCP control, and (3) the
regime demonstrated that it was prepared to honor its international
obligations and accord to foreign diplomatic personnel treatment
commensurate with their status.[51] By the close of 1949 State concluded that the first two conditions were operative. It was the third
condition which caused problems. Acheson would not recommend
granting recognition to China so long as Peking refused, as did the
Soviets in 1917, to honor international treaties and obligations
entered into by the previous regime. The Secretary of State believed
that Peking had to earn the right to be recognized by discharging its
responsibilities within the community of nations. Moreover, recognition would be withheld so long as U.S. diplomatic personnel were
harassed or incarcerated. Acheson, in a December 1949 meeting with
the Indian Ambassador, told Madame Pandit that he "considered it

an illusion to believe that a government which extended early recognition would gain gratitude or other benefits from its actions." Before considering recognition, he continued, "We should like to be better satisfied than we now are that the Chinese Communist Government would accord normal facilities to foreign diplomatic and consular officials."[52] The treatment of U.S. officials by the CCP was an issue over which Acheson was consistently intransigent. As early as June 1949 Acheson had Ambassador Stuart tell Chou En-lai that Chou's expressions of friendliness toward the United States would not suffice if relations were to be established. Chou's "protestations of pro-western sentiments," Acheson cabled Stuart, had to be "translated into deeds."[53]

CCP behavior toward U.S. diplomatic personnel reached bottom on January 6th when Clubb was informed that the communists intended to take over portions of the U.S. Consulate in Peking. Washington protested this action, to no avail, through the offices of the British Embassy in China. On January 14th, the communists made good their threat when police entered the American compound. Washington's response, making good its own threat, was to issue a notice that all U.S. officials would begin to withdraw from China, and the last consulates on the mainland (Peking, Tientsin, Shanghai, and Nanking) would be closed.[54]

From today's vantage point the CCP's violation of the Consulate and the U.S. response raises the question of whether there was any possibility at all of establishing proper (certainly not cordial) relations between Washington and Peking by the first weeks of 1950. The escalation of mutual distrust and hostility which exploded along the Sino-North Korean border later that year seemed well under way.[55] At the time, however, State did not view the affair as a terminal point in U.S.-China relations. The thinking of the day still gave reason to believe that this setback might be shortlived. In fact, Consul General Clubb was instructed by State to stay on in Peking weeks after the Consulate was closed for the purpose of seeking out Chou En-lai. Clubb believed that it might be worthwhile to attempt to engage Chou in discussions on outstanding issues between Washington and the CCP.[56] One reason why Foggy Bottom maintained confidence in its handling of Peking was because of the intelligence, rumors, and analyses it was receiving about Mao Tse-tung's long stay in Moscow.

Although the Mao-Stalin talks (December 1949–February 1950) were conducted in the utmost secrecy, reports reaching U.S. Government officials indicated that great frictions between the two communist leaders were already developing. Mao's protracted stay in Moscow, and the subsequent arrival of Chou En-lai, Nieh Jung-chen, and Li Fu-ch'un in late January fueled all sorts of speculation; including the possibility that Stalin had placed Mao under house arrest.[57] And while State treated the more outlandish rumors with the utmost circumspection, a good deal of credibility was placed in reports that Stalin was levying outrageous demands upon Mao in return for Soviet assistance. Ambassador Alan G. Kirk in Moscow was convinced, as was Clubb in Peking, that Mao's long stay was the result of the latter's hard bargaining and that Mao was "probably trying to resist sweeping Soviet demands."[58] Stories of harsh Soviet exactions were being heard in Shanghai, Peking, and even in Taipei.[59] Moscow, reportedly, was demanding half a million Chinese laborers for the Soviet Far East; "full control" of the strategic ports of Chinwangtao, Haichow, Chefoo, Weihaiwei, Tsingtao, Dairen, and Port Arthur; jurisdiction over minorities in Sinkiang, Inner Mongolia, Manchuria, and Tibet; as well as massive shipments of Chinese grains. In exchange, it was believed that Mao was asking for military supplies for the invasion of Taiwan, a large currency loan, and machinery to jump start the decimated Chinese economy.[60]

If any of this was true, argued Clubb, Mao was in danger "of returning from Moscow despoiled of certain sovereign rights and at the same time disappointed [in his] desire [for] Soviet aid for China's hungry masses and shattered economy."[61] More importantly, reports reaching Washington indicated that Soviet exactions, real or perceived, were already exacerbating tensions between the pro and anti-Soviet factions within the CCP.

Throughout January and February U.S. officials in Moscow, Shanghai, and Peking were being told by Chinese sources that in Mao's absence the pro and anti-Soviet factions within the CCP were jockeying for control of the party and a "serious cleavage" within the leadership was shaping up.[62] According to a particular source in Shanghai, seventy percent of the CCP and PLA leadership was against a subservient relationship with Moscow. Reportedly, the anti-Soviet ("China First") faction included Chu Teh, Ch'en Yi, Liu Po-ch'eng, Nieh Jung-chen, and Chou En-lai. The pro-Moscow clique was represented by Ch'en Yun, Jao Shou-shih, Li Li-san, Liu Shao-ch'i, and Lin Piao. Mao was believed to be torn and the inclinations of Yeh Chien-ying were uncertain. It was further reported that Ch'en Yi was "fed up" with Moscow's attempts to control the CCP and was prepared to act with force against Mao if he returned to China with a humiliating treaty from the Russians. Ch'en and other PLA leaders had allegedly established a secret "New China Movement" based on Chinese nationalism and a desire to be free of *all* foreign influences—to include the Soviets. On several occasions in late January and early February a Chinese claiming to be an agent of Ch'en Yi's approached U.S. Consulate officials in Shanghai for the purpose of feeling out U.S. support should the anti-Moscow faction in the CCP decide to take up arms against Peking![63]

State treated the particulars of these reports with a healthy skepticism.[64] However, a good deal of credibility was attached to the idea that the CCP was split over the issue of Soviet relations. For example, Clubb, in attempting to analyze the rationale behind the CCP's seizure of the Consulate in Peking, could not decide if the decision had the support of the entire Chinese Communist leadership (the purpose being to pressure Washington into recognition) or whether the pro-Soviet faction was attempting to humiliate the United States while Mao was in Moscow.[65] John Davies firmly believed that Peking's leaders were split. Davies, mulling over the spate of reports indicating inter-party tensions and CCP behavior toward American diplomats, counselled patience. The clock was ticking and time, he believed, was on the side of the U.S. In a memorandum sent to Rusk and Acheson in February, Davies laid out his analysis in typically confident terms.

> ...the objective facts of the situation in China are such that by spring or summer of this year, two major forces will be influencing the thinking and behavior of the individual Chinese Communist leaders, including Chen Yi. One is that Soviet imperialism will probably become more onerous in its exactions on Communist China. The second is that Communist China will feel with increasing severity its present food shortage and general economic difficulties. The pressure of these events will tend to inspire nationalistically-inclined leaders in the CCP to break with those elements in the leadership who have sold themselves out completely to the Kremlin. Whether this will mean an open split in the leadership and an attempted *coup d'etat* we cannot now prophesy. All we can say is that if there is to be a revolt against the Chinese Stalinists and if there is to be

any hope that such a revolt will be successful, it will have to come from an alliance of military men like Chen Yi with some of the more nationalistic political leaders in Peking. We should, of course, be ever on the alert for symptoms of such a break-away and should judiciously do all within our power to foster such a split.[66]

The Secretary of State acted on Davies' suggestion to exploit the situation. Acheson decided that he was going to make sure that the anti-Soviet faction in the CCP was made aware of the entire spectrum of rumors surrounding the Mao-Stalin talks; especially those detailing alleged Russian exactions. In late January and mid-February Acheson sent Ambassador David Bruce in Paris information which detailed alleged Soviet demands of Mao, and the latter's problems with Stalin. Acheson admitted that many of the stories could not be confirmed. However, he told Bruce that they could "...serve very useful propaganda purpose if skillfully released in such a manner that appearance of material cld not be traced this govt." Acheson instructed the Ambassador to have the stories "...planted as soon as possible..." Paris, it was decided, was the best place to have such information planted. Moreover, Acheson specifically named C.L. Sulzberger of the *New York Times* as the man Bruce should approach to write the stories. Sulzberger was to say that he obtained the information from "Well informed sources in Eastern Europe." To give some credibility to the sourcing Wade-Giles romanization was not to be used in the articles. Instead, Sulzberger was instructed to use the Russian transliteration of Chinese names and places. Acheson provided these in his message to Bruce. Once in print, State would have the Voice of America pick up the stories and beam them to China.[67] Livingston Merchant also believed that no opportunity to exploit Sino-Soviet tensions should be overlooked. Merchant argued that one of the great side-benefits of political, economic, and military assistance to the Bao Dai regime in Saigon was that it could very well exacerbate tensions between Moscow and Peking. In early March Merchant reported to Butterworth that one of the reasons it was important for the U.S. to assist the French in Indochina was because "...the inability of Mao Tze-tung to expand southward would increase the friction between China and Russia over Manchuria and the northern tier of Chinese provinces."[68]

Even when the Sino-Soviet Treaty was finally announced on February 14th Acheson continued to rest his China policy on the prospects of the eventual emergence of a Titoist regime in Peking. He was unconvinced that the Russians would be able to handle relations with the CCP with finesse. Just three days before the agreement was signed he cabled his views on the subject to David Bruce in Paris. The Secretary of State believed that any publicly announced treaty between Moscow and Peking would "probably breathe friendship and cooperation." Nevertheless, Acheson was sure that there would also be "secret protocols and agreements" forcing Peking to make "unpalatable" concessions to Moscow.[69] Consequently, Acheson, at least publicly, appeared unshaken when news of the Treaty was made public. In his March 15th speech before the Commonwealth Club of California the Secretary of State reiterated the analysis that the Russian-Chinese alliance was built upon a very shallow foundation.

> The Soviet Union and its most ardent supporters in China may have temporary success in persuading the people of China that these agreements refute the contention of the non-communist world that alliance with Russia holds an evil omen of imperialistic domination. These agreements promise help in the rehabilitation of China's wartorn and impoverished economy. They promise, in particular, assistance in repair and development of China's railroads and industry. The Chinese people may welcome these promises and assurances. But they will not fail, in time, to see where they fall short of China's real needs and desires. And they will wonder about the points upon which the agreements remain silent.

"It is Soviet Russia," he exclaimed in the speech, "which, despite all the tawdry pretense of the treaty terms, occupies the role of empire builder at China's expense." Acheson asked the people of China to reflect upon this reality and "...consider what it means to brush aside an established friendship for new-found and voracious friends." The people of China would soon discover that their true friend was the United States, and that America had "...fifty years of history and a world war to prove that this belief is not a mere matter of words."[70]

Acheson's confidence was bolstered by George Kennan. In a memorandum written three days after the Sino-Soviet Treaty was made public, Kennan wrote that there was no reason to feel surprised or shaken, or believe that the "...cold war...has suddenly taken some drastic turn to our disadvantage." Kennan calmly reminded Acheson that "Recent events in the Far East have been the culmination of processes which have long been apparent."

> The implications of these processes were correctly analyzed, and their results reasonably accurately predicted, long ago by our advisers in

this field...Mao's protracted stay in Moscow is good evidence that our own experts were right not only in their analysis of the weakness of the National Government but also in their conviction that the Russians would have difficulty establishing the same sort of relationship with a successful Chinese Communist movement that they have established with some of their eastern European satellites.[71]

For the moment, then, there was nothing more to be done *vis-a-vis* the mainland. The recognition carrot would remain dangling before the CCP, but it would be withheld until Peking acted civilly toward American diplomats. Opportunities to aggravate incipient tensions between Moscow and Peking would be sought. Ultimately, Truman's public announcement of U.S. military disengagement from Taiwan was intended to contrast for the CCP leadership American respect for Chinese sovereignty with Soviet territorial ambitions. Even Washington's determination to gird Southeast Asia against further communist gains was partially grounded in the belief that the CCP, frustrated in its attempt to move southward, would vent its frustrations on Soviet transgressions in the north. Time, which Washington believed was its most powerful weapon, would ultimately work to undermine the communist alliance.

While Washington played its waiting game with Peking it had to deal with Taiwan. And in the case of Taipei, Foggy Bottom—especially FE and the Office of Chinese Affairs—was not at all inclined to exercise the same patience it was adopting toward Peking, for most attitudes toward the KMT remained hardened. State was not about to let the issue of Taiwan complicate its delicate carrot and stick policy toward the CCP. Consul General McConaughy in Shanghai warned, and Acheson and his advisers agreed, that to become reinvolved deeply with Taipei at this point would only "...serve to drive the Communists further into the arms of Moscow..."[72] Consequently, State was willing to give only the most perfunctory support to the regime in Taipei.

The executive branch was bound by law to continue to provide Taiwan certain amounts of economic aid and to allow the KMT to exhaust the remaining funds of the original $125 million in the China Aid Act for the purchase of military supplies. Nevertheless, State refused to assist Taipei above and beyond what was required. In mid-January Acheson responded in the negative to Ambassador Koo's December 23rd plea for military advisers. "With reference to the request of your Government for United States military assistance," Acheson wrote Koo, "your attention is invited to the public statement made by the President on January 5, 1950..."[73] On January 26th, Acheson told Secretary of Defense Johnson that he and Rusk were opposed to a DoD suggestion that a military fact-finding mission be dispatched to Taipei to survey the Nationalists' future defense needs.[74] The State Department even placed limits on what military supplies Taipei could purchase with China Aid Act monies and Chinese government funds. For example, In early March the Nationalists applied to State for export licenses to purchase 25 Sherman tanks and 25 F-80 jet fighter aircraft. The request was disapproved. Acheson agreed with the British who feared that the probability of Taiwan's fall was too high to risk having such military equipment fall into the hands of the CCP. The threat to Hong Kong would be tremendous. Acheson informed Louis Johnson of his decision and asked the Defense Secretary to insure that no tanks from U.S. Army stocks be released to the KMT.[75]

Even Washington's diplomatic support for Nationalist China was becoming tenuous. The issue of Taipei's status in the U.N. is most telling in this regard. In January the United States was prepared to oppose the Soviet Union's resolution calling for the expulsion of the KMT from the Security Council. However, the U.S. position was not a vote of confidence for the Republic of China; it was a matter of *realpolitik*. Washington would not clear the way for Peking's membership in the U.N. since it had yet to recognize the communist regime. Moreover, the presence of Nationalist China on the Security Council was as good as another U.S. vote in that forum; a particularly good thing in as much as the Soviets and their satellites were voting as a bloc throughout the world organization. Finally, and certainly not of small consequence, it would have been almost impossible politically for the Truman administration to vote the Chinese Nationalists out of the U.N. in January 1950 given the domestic uproar over China-Taiwan policy. Nevertheless, and significantly, the U.S. was not prepared to exercise its right to veto Security Council resolutions over the question of Taiwan's continued membership. In early January Acheson sent the following instructions to the U.S. delegates at Lake Success:

> ...should any motion be presented in the Security Council to unseat the Nationalist representative or seat a representative of the Chinese Communist regime, our mission is to vote in the negative. At the same time our mission should explain that it does not regard such a negative vote as

a veto; *if the SC President rules that our vote in itself constitutes a veto, our mission is instructed to request a re-vote and abstain.*[76]

As it turned out, when the vote was taken on January 13th, the U.S.'s negative vote was accepted as not constituting a veto, and the Soviet resolution was defeated. On that day Moscow's delegate, Andrei Vishinsky, walked out of the United Nations declaring that Moscow would not recognize any U.N. action until the KMT representative was unseated.[77]

While the United States did not desire to *clear* the way for the seating of the CCP in the United Nations at that time, Washington had also decided that it would not stand in the way of granting Peking membership if a legal majority of the Security Council's members voted in favor of doing so. On January 21st, U.N. Secretary General Trygvie Lie, despondent over the issue of Chinese representation and the Soviet boycott, met with Acheson, Rusk, and Webb in Washington. Lie was given assurances that the U.S. would not exercise its veto "nor acquiesce in a veto by anyone else" if seven members of the Security Council voted to seat the PRC. Indeed, Rusk offered the opinion that it was probably only "a matter of several weeks" before Peking would have the votes it needed.[78] In effect, then, the United States was attempting to remain neutral in the U.N. battle over which China to seat. The U.S., as a regular voting member, would continue to support the seating of the Nationalist regime because doing so still supported the administration's agenda in domestic politics and foreign policy. But Washington was not willing to use its powerful veto either to keep the KMT seated or keep out the CCP.

Truman's January 5th statement, Acheson's Press Clubb speech, and luke warm support in the U.N., should have been sources of major concern for the Chinese government on Taiwan. More than likely, K.C. Wu and like-minded reformers were appropriately shaken. Nevertheless, Taipei brought relations with the United States to the brink when the Chinese Nationalist Air Force (CAF) bombed Shanghai on February 6th.

The CAF's air raid on Shanghai did tremendous damage to residential areas. The U.S. Consulate, still in the process of closing down, reported "heavy casualties" among civilians. Moreover, it was obvious to observers on the ground that the targets of the raid were the two major American-owned facilities in the city; the Standard Oil complex and the Shanghai Power Company. No American citizens were killed in the attack, but Shanghai Power lost 25% of its generating capacity. Unhappily, the aircraft and ordinance used in the raid were American-supplied.[79]

State's reaction was nothing less than outrage. With Truman's approval, Acheson directed Consul General Strong in Taipei to deliver a strongly worded note of protest to Foreign Minister George Yeh.[80] The military attaches were likewise directed to seek out the commanders of the Chinese Navy and Air Force and insure that they understood the U.S.'s position on such actions. As transmitted to Strong, Acheson's note to Yeh was as follows:

US Govt becoming increasingly concerned over CAF bombing Chi cities resulting in damage and destruction non-milit structures and injury and loss life to Chi civilian population. Amer aviation equipment was not supplied Chi Govt for use against its own defenseless people or civilian property in heavily populated areas and its employment in this manner can only result in inflaming populace against Chi Govt and in turn against US thru use Amer equipment for such purposes. Destruction caused by raids this nature gravely affects basic welfare entire Chi population in such matters as water supply, sanitation, etc. Bombing this nature cannot play any decisive part in Chi Govt military effort and must inevitably cause adverse reaction against Chi Govt on part Chi people. These raids cannot be justified in eyes Chi or Amer people as necessary part Chi Govt effort protect its position on Formosa.

The note ended by demanding that the Chinese Government inform Washington "as a matter of urgency" if Taipei intended to continue air raids of this type.[81]

Strong in Taipei delivered the note to George Yeh the next day, February 9th. Yeh's on the spot response to the *aide-memoir* irked the American Consul General. The Foreign Minister defended the raid and others like it arguing that the Shanghai Power Company was providing electricity used for military purposes by the CCP. Yeh would only guarantee that power supplied for civilian use would not be attacked again. When Strong asked if the CAF planned future attacks on American-owned oil facilities on the mainland, Yeh replied in the affirmative but added that the workers at these facilities would be warned in time to leave the area. Strong replied that this would not do. He offered Yeh his personal view that "serious difficulties would arise if such things continued."[82] As it was, the February 6th raid was not the first on Shanghai. The CAF previously attacked the city on

January 25th, and for his part, Strong was convinced that the CAF would strike again. Based upon previous talks with KMT Navy and Air Force officials Strong offered Acheson the opinion that the leaders of those two services believed that the United States "...will not retaliate in any serious way almost regardless of what they do."[83]

On the 16th of February, Taipei formally addressed in writing the Consulate's note of protest. The written response was as non-committal, vague, and alarming as Yeh's initial comments to Strong seven days earlier. The Government of China assured the United States only that "...no American property not lending itself 'to the working of the Chinese Communist war machine' would be subject to deliberate Chinese Air Force attacks."[84]

Within the Department of State, Taipei's note elicited a good deal of anger. On the day the KMT rebuttal was received Philip Sprouse (still Director of the Office of Chinese Affairs) sent to Merchant in FE a scathing denunciation of Nationalist behavior and the damage it was doing to U.S. policy toward the mainland. "It seems to me," he wrote, "that this issue should be looked at in the larger context of U.S. policy and long-range objectives. If we are to follow the policy outlined by the Secretary at his Overseas [National] Press Club speech, we must look at this in the light of the damage being done to our position in China by the use of U.S. aviation equipment to bomb the Chinese civilian population." Sprouse believed that in one fell swoop the Nationalists were able to negate "...the beneficial effect of the President's statement of January 5 regarding Formosa..."

> It should not be overlooked that the Chinese Government, in effect, exists and maintains its representation in the UN solely because of American support and that it would probably collapse overnight if that support were withdrawn. It seems incredible, therefore, that we permit the Chinese Government brazenly to do the damage to our position in China that it is doing. It is all the more incredible that we do not take stronger steps than we have already taken to make clear to that Government that, if it continues bombing attacks of this nature, we will stop all aid or at least all shipments of military supplies from this country.[85]

Dean Acheson was equally mortified by Taipei's attitude. On the evening of February 17th he telephoned Livingston Merchant, who happened to be out of town. Consequently, one of Merchant's assistants took the Secretary's message. Acheson said that the KMT response amounted to Taipei "telling us to go to hell with our protest on the Shanghai bombings." He wanted to know if this episode finally provided the U.S. the opportunity "to get out of Formosa and with-draw aid from the Nationalists." When told that the matter was "under active consideration" in FE, the Secretary said, "Fine, I just wanted to be sure that you are thinking about it."[86]

Indeed, some were thinking about the issue. It was not lost upon Sprouse and Merchant that U.S. policy toward China and Taiwan was in a state of suspended animation. Washington would not recognize Peking. At the same time, unqualified military and political support was not being given the Republic of China. Moreover, the United States was attempting to remain neutral in the U.N. controversy while both China's were pursuing policies inimical to perceived U.S. interests. Sprouse was frustrated. "We cannot drift between the two courses, as we seem to be doing at present," he complained to Merchant.[87] Merchant forwarded Sprouse's comments to Dean Rusk and added his own views. There was no reason, offered Merchant, to feel pressured at the moment to choose between the two extreme actions of quickly recognizing the PRC or extending "all-out military support to the Nationalists." Nevertheless, he told Rusk that:

> ...we should be clear in our minds in which direction we are moving in order to give a consistent emphasis in our daily actions to the policy which is fundamental. This I take it would be regaining our complete freedom of maneuver and disassociation in the Chinese mind with the Kuomintang as rapidly as events at home and abroad permit.

In the meantime, Merchant was willing to live with "some apparent confusion in our actions for some little time to come."[88] In effect, just as there was a waiting game to be played on the mainland (the belief that Sino-Soviet relations would sour on their own), Merchant saw a waiting game to played on Taiwan. It was only a matter time until there would be no Taiwan issue over which to anguish.

In State's view the situation on Taiwan looked no brighter than before. Although the economic situation was improving, KMT poli-tics continued in the usual Byzantine manner. On March 1st Chiang Kai-shek officially resumed his post as President of the Republic of China. In a telegram addressed to Li Tsung-jen (undergoing medical treatment in New York), Chiang wrote that "Our national affairs, both military and political, cannot long remain without the direct guidance of responsible chief. At this time of distress, the people have insistently reminded me of my duties towards them...I have decided resume office and continue exercise presidential functions..."[89] The

Consulate in Taipei believed that Chiang's resumption of office would not serve to unite the KMT but continue to keep it fractured. Chiang, asserted Taipei, would persist in his "divide and rule" style of leadership "with the usual fatal results."[90] Within one week of this analysis, the Consulate in Taipei reported that a purge of former Li Tsung-jen supporters was in full swing. Local sources informed the Consulate that at least 36 general officers alleged to have sympathies for Li had already been arrested. State passed on to Truman that the situation in Taiwan was now one in which "the 'crime' of supporting Li now seems to rank equally with being a Communist or advocating Formosan independence."[91]

Less than three weeks after Chiang "resumed" office the Central Intelligence Agency sent to President Truman the gloomiest forecast of Taiwan's future written to date. According to ORE 7-50, "Probable Developments in Taiwan," the island was as good as gone. The very first line in the executive summary informed the President that "No Chinese Nationalist regime on Taiwan will effect political and military adjustments sufficiently realistic to make possible a successful defense of Taiwan against a combination of internal and external threats." It was true that the economic situation was much stabilized. Nevertheless, CIA judged that the process of political disintegration on the island was so advanced that "...an invasion could be expected to precipitate a quick collapse." Much of the political instability on Taiwan was attributed to Chiang, whose "...political maneuvering...to perpetuate his personal control over the remaining National Government and Kuomintang machinery has contributed greatly to disunity." Moreover, there was no reason to believe that Chiang would be removed from power. Although reports over the past months indicated that Sun Li-jen was "planning a *coup d'etat*," Langley believed the plot was already compromised and it was unlikely that Sun was going to carry it through. CIA's assessment of K.C. Wu's recent appointment as Governor was as skeptical as State's. The appointment, "—though advertised as evidence of intended reform of the provincial administration under civilian control—is expected neither to lead to reforms nor keep down the inevitable conflict between the provincial and national governments." Wu was judged an able administrator. Nevertheless, the CIA pointed out that his freedom of action was "seriously hampered" by opposition from Ch'en Ch'eng and other conservative KMT generals. His influence would not be felt beyond the narrow field of provincial civilian affairs. As for the armed forces, the KMT had almost half a million men in uniform on the island. But they were judged ill-trained, poorly led, politically unmotivated, and highly susceptible to communist infiltration, subversion, and, ultimately, defections *en masse*. It was believed that CCP efforts to "infiltrate and disaffect" the KMT armed forces would "eventually succeed." As for the communists, CIA took Peking at its oft-expressed word that it planned to invade and "liberate" the island sometime in 1950. The PLA was judged to have adequate manpower and weapons to mount an invasion. It was estimated that the PLA's East China Field Force already possessed enough mechanically powered seacraft to land an initial invasion force of 60,000 troops "on a single lift." The supply of more traditional water craft was deemed inexhaustible. All things considered, CIA predicted that the communists would attempt an invasion of Taiwan "either just before or after the June–September typhoon season."[92]

Without United States military intervention, the communist invasion of Taiwan was expected to succeed. Without too much meddling from Washington, Sino-Soviet ties would eventually loosen. Time was the key. But U.S. domestic politics had a pace of its own. While the administration grappled with the challenges presented by Peking and Taipei, its China policy was under a most intense partisan attack.

8.3 APRIL: SIGNIFICANT PERSONNEL CHANGES AT STATE

By early 1950 the names of Whittaker Chambers, Klaus Fuchs, and Judith Coplon and the charges against them were already familiar to a public being bombarded with stories of Soviet espionage. Since the end of the Second World War the State Department was seen as *the* weak link by those who believed that subversion within the government was real and posed a grave threat to national security. The much publicized trial of former State Department official Alger Hiss merely served to keep State in the much unwanted limelight. Although Hiss was not convicted of espionage (he was named by Chambers as a Soviet agent) his perjury conviction on January 25, 1950 played into the hands of those Republicans who were prepared to turn the communists-in-government scare into a partisan weapon. Acheson was a personal friend of Hiss' and that association was used to embarrass him during his own confirmation hearings in January

1949. When asked, a year later, to comment on the case the day Hiss was convicted, Acheson caused an uproar when he was quoted as saying that "...I do not intend to turn my back on Alger Hiss."[93]

Less than three weeks later, on February 9, 1950, Senator Joseph McCarthy delivered the speech that brought the red scare to the heights of hysteria and American politics to an all-time low. His chimerical list of communists in government was aimed squarely at State. On February 20th, he spoke before the Senate to answer demands that he explain his charges. The Democrats, confident that McCarthy's charges were ridiculous, countered by immediately calling for hearings to investigate the allegations. Chaired by Millard E. Tydings (D., Maryland) the open hearings lasted until July 1950 at which time a report was issued which dismissed all of the charges as groundless. Nevertheless, in the course of the proceedings, Asian specialists in academe, in government, and those who assisted in formulating Far Eastern policy were publicly smeared; some ruined forever. Among those individuals were Owen Lattimore, Philip Jessup, and John Carter Vincent.[94]

As Tang Tsou has commented, it was almost inevitable that McCarthy's attack would be linked with the Truman administration's China policy.[95] Patrick Hurley's allegations in 1945, the *Amerasia* affair, and the defeat of the KMT insured that those officials who worked on Far Eastern policy would be among those on the list of alleged and suspected subversives. The recent battles over China-Taiwan policy when mixed with McCarthy's accusations made for a powerful and volatile weapon for Republican critics. With Far Eastern policy under attack, bipartisanship all but destroyed, and friends and respected colleagues being smeared by demagogues, Acheson, in late March and early April, made two significant personnel decisions. Walton Butterworth would be replaced as Assistant Secretary of State for Far Eastern Affairs and a prominent Republican would be brought into the department as a special advisor.

Even before McCarthy's allegations in February Walton Butterworth was more and more becoming the target of Republican attacks. Even President Truman sensed his increasing vulnerability. For example, in January 1950 it was Butterworth who brought to Truman State's position paper recommending that the U.S. close its diplomatic posts in China after the communists violated the Consulate in Peking. Truman signed the order and Butterworth began to take his leave. The President stopped him on the way out of the Oval Office, took back the paper, and wrote "I approve" (along with his initials) on the memorandum. As Butterworth recalled the incident, Truman, returning the memo, said "You better take this for your protection."[96] Moreover, in the wake of McCarthy's charges, Senators Kenneth Wherry and Styles Bridges threatened to have Butterworth served with a subpoena and begin a full-scale investigation of the Office of Far Eastern Affairs.[97] Butterworth, wrote Acheson, "served loyally and ably in highly exposed posts..." Odds were, however, that his association with China policy since the Marshall Mission would ruin him. Therefore, in order to spare him personally and save his career Acheson reassigned Butterworth at the end of March. From 1950 to 1953 he served as the Ambassador to Sweden, never to work with Asian affairs again.[98]

Into the breach stepped Dean Rusk. On March 28th he succeeded Butterworth as Assistant Secretary of State for Far Eastern Affairs. This was in fact a demotion from his previous position as Deputy Under Secretary. A grateful Acheson later recalled that Rusk was never asked to assume the post. He volunteered, as Acheson said, "for the dirtiest job in the entire Department of State when he had no call in the line of duty to do so. This was above and beyond the call of duty if anyone ever did it."[99] The appointment was a godsend to Acheson. Rusk's ability to work with Republican congressmen raised the possibility that bipartisanship in far eastern policy might still be attainable. The Republicans were pleased with the assignment.[100]

Rusk immediately began to find ways to reestablish bipartisan support for the administration's Asia policy. He engaged Republican critics in a series of conferences and used Senator H. Alexander Smith, an ally of Rusk's, as an interlocutor with his colleagues on the Far Eastern Subcommittee of the Senate Foreign Relations Committee. Regrettably, Smith reported to Rusk that the chances of reconciliation on current China-Taiwan policy were slim. The only hope of regaining any measure of support seemed to be the appointment of a prominent Republican to the State Department as a consultant; an idea which Rusk suggested to Acheson as soon he took his new post.[101] After a series of consultations in late March and early April between Rusk, Acheson, and Republican patriarch Arthur Vandenberg, it was decided that John Foster Dulles would be recommended to Truman as the candidate for a position at State.[102]

Neither Truman nor Acheson were particularly thrilled with the idea of bringing Dulles on board. As Butterworth recalls, Acheson was "initially very negative" about suggesting Dulles' appointment. For one thing, the Secretary of State was convinced that Truman would never allow Dulles into the administration given the latter's strong public criticisms of current foreign policy. Also, Acheson harbored little personal affection for the man. "Mr. Acheson might amuse himself by fencing intellectually with Mr. Dulles," said Butterworth, "but he would never waste his time in his company for pleasure." Dean Rusk was less concerned about Dulles' previous attacks on the administration. During discussions on the subject he commented that "You gentlemen just don't understand politics. Of course every two years Mr. Dulles is going to take time out to be a Republican. But in between times we're going to work with him if he's willing to work with us and get his help." Truman was convinced to allow an approach to Dulles. But he remained skeptical. The President acquiesced to the idea as long as Dulles was not allowed to work on domestic policy. Moreover, Dulles was not to be given the title of Ambassador-at-Large. The President confided to Acheson that "I don't think I have ever known a man with such a monumental ego."[103] After much haggling with Dulles over an appropriate title, the latter, on April 5th, accepted Truman's invitation to join the Department as a "top" Consultant to the Secretary of State.[104] The combination of Rusk and Dulles was soon to have a direct impact upon the direction of policy toward Taiwan.

During the Princeton Seminars Rusk claimed that he was given the job at FE for two reasons; "one was that I was willing to do it; and secondly, I had had no contact with the Far East and knew nothing about it. And that made me eminently qualified for the job in the then-existing political situation."[105] Certainly the first reason was true enough. However, Rusk's claim of detachment from far eastern policy is valid only in that he was not publicly associated with or formally charged with responsibilities in that area. The fact of the matter is that Rusk knew a great deal about the situation in the Far East and had first-hand experience during the Second World War as a member of Stilwell's staff in China. Moreover, during his tenure as Deputy Under Secretary he maintained a keen interest in policy toward Taiwan and China. The records indicate that from at least January 1949 forward Rusk attended most major meetings concerning

the Far East within State and on occasion sat in on working sessions of
the NSC. His advice was solicited and he was privy to major policy
decisions.

A complete picture of Rusk's motives for taking the position at
FE are difficult to gauge. As previously stated, Rusk's *memoire* (1990)
provided few insights into this period, and he has left no personal
papers for historians to scrutinize. Biographers have had to rely
heavily upon interviews with Rusk and those who worked with him for
insights into his pre-Secretary of State years in government.[106] There
is no reason to question the altruism of Rusk's decision to volunteer
for Butterworth's position. At the same time it appears that he seized
the opportunity to become more intimately involved in the problem
of crafting policy toward Asia for more practical reasons. As it turns
out, Rusk was uncomfortable with the Department's policy toward
Taiwan.

Rusk held no brief for Chiang Kai-shek or the Nationalist regime
per se. He recognized every fault that had brought the Kuomintang to
its ignominious defeat on the mainland as well as the disastrous policies it had pursued on Taiwan. However, the idea of allowing the
island to fall to the CCP was apparently unacceptable to him. Domestic politics was one reason. In September 1949, during a Depart-
ment-wide meeting on far eastern policy, Rusk offered to Acheson
that "U.S. opinion" would demand that Washington take some action
short of military intervention to keep Taiwan from going under.[107]
Equally important, Rusk came to believe that allowing communism to
score another victory in the Far East would undermine regional confidence in the United States and the Western powers. Rusk agreed that
there was some merit to the argument that U.S. efforts to prop-up the
regime in Taiwan would leave Washington open to charges of imperialism by the Chinese and other nations in Southeast Asia. However,
as achieving a Titoist mainland in the short-term slipped further
beyond the realm of possibility, Rusk came to the conclusion that it
was more important to show the anti-communist nations of Asia that
the U.S. had the resolve to stand fast and halt Moscow's advance into
the region. Rusk was *not* in favor of U.S. military intervention or even
increased military assistance to Taipei. But he was not convinced that
it was too late to pursue an autonomous Taiwan through the United
Nations; an idea which was raised in State, then shelved, in June 1949.
If the current regime on Taiwan was not prepared to go along with a

plan in which claims to the mainland were abandoned, then Rusk was not above pondering ways in which to shake some sense into Chiang and his recalcitrant followers. Consequently, from April 1950 until the outbreak of the Korean War, Rusk quietly explored various options by which renewed diplomatic efforts could be used to save Taiwan.

Upon assuming his new position at State, John Foster Dulles was given the responsibility of overseeing work toward concluding a peace treaty with Japan as soon as possible. This entailed reviewing the various drafts which had been prepared since 1945, negotiating the particulars with the allied powers prior to a major treaty conference, coordinating his work within the Washington bureaucracy, and rallying bipartisan support for the effort. Dulles threw himself into the work and, in the words of an admiring Rusk, Dulles was "...a one-man peripatetic conference."[108] Busy as he was with the peace treaty, Dulles was not reluctant to offer his advice on other far eastern matters. Dulles, like Rusk, was not prepared to see Taiwan go over to Peking. Also like Rusk, Dulles still seemed to think that somehow a United Nations trusteeship should be engineered to snatch the island from Mao. If nothing else, the United States, believed Dulles, had a moral obligation to the Taiwanese. "Obviously," he wrote to Vandenberg in January 1950,

> the present situation was not foreseen at Cairo or Potsdam, and it seems to me a little short of scandalous for us to adopt the theory that Formosa is part of China and that, therefore, the Formosans must be subjected to the cruel fate of being the final battleground between the Red regime and the Nationalist Army. It seems to me that the tragedy of Formosa is the Formosans...I would think that we ought to have had some respect for the six or seven million people in Formosa who, ever since Cairo, have been dealt with from a standpoint of the strategy and prestige of great powers without regard to their own welfare or desires.[109]

By the end of April Dulles was already offering Rusk his thoughts on the issue. Taiwan, he told Rusk, had made great strides within the past year. The land reform program, with its 37.5% tax ceiling, was universally welcomed by the farmers. "Today," he said, "the peasants are contented." Moreover, the infrastructure was in a good state of repair. Electricity was now widely available once again and the railroads were functioning well. Industrial production was now equal to pre-war levels. With this kind of progress, he argued, it would be foolish to allow the island to go under. As he saw it, the Nationalists were capable of performing important roles in the "world's struggle against communism." Taipei could represent for Chinese "a better way to economic improvement and national and individual freedom then through communism." Moreover, Taiwan now had "a larger and more experienced military force than all other Asian countries combined." The mere existence of this force, he offered, was an important deterrent to the expansion of the CCP into Southeast Asia. Arguing that the people on the mainland were now discouraged with CCP rule, Dulles felt the Nationalists served as an important psychological rallying point. He suggested that only "a moderate measure of aid from the United States," economic aid, was all that was needed to keep the Republic of China alive. "It seems to me," Dulles told Rusk, "that this moderate investment on the part of the United States will yield better results than any similar investment in any other region in Asia."[110]

Rusk's reaction to this particular memorandum is not known. Nevertheless, he was predisposed to be receptive to such arguments. In Dulles he had a soul mate on the issue of Taiwan. In April however, it does not appear that Rusk attempted in any way to initiate another major review of current policy toward Taiwan. But he began to pass on to Acheson intelligence products and field reports which were probably intended to start the Secretary of State thinking once again about the issue of Taiwan. In mid-April Rusk sent to the Secretary an update to CIA's March estimate; ORE 7-50, "Probable Developments in Taiwan."[111] He reminded Acheson that the intelligence services of DoD had written a formal dissent to CIA's original analysis, believing that the island could hold out longer than Langley thought. Rusk now pointed out that CIA, based on a more recent assessment of KMT capabilities, was less sure than previously about their original forecast for the longevity of the island. Central Intelligence now informed policymakers that, "The fall of Taiwan, before the end of 1950, still seems the most likely course of future developments, but the possibility of a somewhat longer survival of the Nationalist regime on the island should not be precluded."[112] In the business of intelligence, the new qualifier represented a significant change. Also in April, Rusk summarized for Acheson reports and analyses by the military attaches in Hong Kong and Taipei which claimed that the KMT military was now much improved and "are doing their most effective work since the end of World War II with morale and reliability highest in years." The service attaches pointed out that "the Nationalists are now absorbing the major attention and efforts of the Communist military forces, which if Taiwan falls may be expected to exert full pressure on Southeast Asia." The attaches in Hong Kong and Taipei were unanimous in the proposal that the KMT be given increased military assistance. Such aid, they admitted, was a "pure gamble" which could end up another "operation rathole." Nevertheless, if modest military assistance bought some time for the Nationalists, that time, they submitted, could be put to good use bolstering the defenses of Southeast Asia.[113] These reports notwithstanding, there is no indication that in April Acheson was prepared to reconsider the China-Taiwan policy which had been crafted over the past year and a half. His own thinking was revealed in a conversation with Governor Thomas Dewey who called the Secretary to clear a speech on foreign affairs he was about to present at Princeton University. Acheson took exception to a point in the talk which declared that "the only flicker of hope for China and the Far East was in Formosa." Acheson informed the Governor that "the hope in the Far East," as State saw it, "is to drive a wedge between Peking and Moscow, and to reach agreement on a Japanese Peace Treaty, or at least a Japanese settlement."[114] Apparently Taiwan, in the Secretary's grand strategy, was still of secondary importance to the greater goal of a Titoist China.

8.4 MAY: DESPERATION AFTER THE FALL OF HAINAN

On April 16th the PLA launched a major assault against the large Nationalist force on Hainan island. Within ten days the island fell and those forces of the 150,000-troop garrison which could escape retreated to Taiwan. On May 2nd Taipei announced that the island had been abandoned.[115]

The fall of Hainan jolted many on Taiwan out the false sense of security that their island fortress could not be taken. The demoralizing effect was multiplied by the Nationalists themselves, for Taipei prematurely announced victory in repulsing the communist invaders.[116] It must certainly have come as a shock to K.C. Wu. As recently as March 27th he extolled to Senator Smith the greatly improved military prowess of the Nationalist armed forces, proudly telling the Senator how communist attempts to invade Hainan had been "repeatedly beaten back" in recent weeks.[117]

Consul General Strong in Taipei reported that in fact the psychological impact of this latest defeat was "severe." It was now generally believed that the clock was ticking for Taiwan. The long-anticipated invasion could not be far off. Mainlanders of means, reported Strong, were once again making plans for yet another escape. Although the Nationalist troops defending Hainan were said to be of poor quality, the facts remained, said Strong, that the PLA successfully carried out an amphibious invasion without air and heavy naval support. Moreover, the former KMT troops which the PLA used as part of their invasion task force (Fu Tso-yi's former Peking garrison command) remained loyal to their new communist masters. Strong believed that the fate of Taiwan would be determined by what happened next in the Chusan Islands. Their capture by the PLA, he felt, would be the beginning of the end for Taiwan. Strong urged that the fall of the Chusans should be State's signal to implement plans to leave. He recommended that should the Chusans go under all private American citizens be warned to evacuate Taiwan immediately. At the same time, Strong recommended that over a three month period official U.S. Government activities (ECA, USIS, and JCRR) should begin to draw down and slowly leave Taiwan. The military attache office should be reduced and all non-essential personnel in the Consulate should be sent away. Strong commented that his analysis might be "...too pessimistic a view, but there are few grounds for optimism."[118]

Within two weeks of Strong's message the Chusan Islands were gone.[119] Taipei made the decision to evacuate rather than lose more troops to an invasion force that appeared to be preparing for an assault.[120] For once Strong and his military attaches were in agreement. They agreed that the "fate of Taiwan" was now "sealed." According to the attaches, a communist invasion of Taiwan could now take place anytime between mid-June and late July, depending upon weather, CCP capabilities, and the internal situation on Taiwan. Strong and the attaches concluded that the internal situation was the crucial variable. Interestingly, the Consul General claimed he didn't have enough intelligence on internal matters (KMT politics and the inclinations of the Taiwanese) to make an educated estimate as to how bad things were. The attaches also warned that Taiwan was now highly susceptible to air attacks. With the Chusans gone Strong now recommended that an evacuation begin. He suggested that by June 15th only a small skeleton crew in the Consulate should still be on Taiwan. He urgently requested guidance from State.[121] Two days later Washington responded. State, apparently, was not yet prepared to order a wide-scale evacuation of U.S. Government operations on the island. However, private citizens, Foggy Bottom agreed, should be told to leave Taiwan or stay at their own risk. A warning to U.S. citizens prepared in Washington was transmitted for Strong's use. At the same time, Strong was instructed not to issue the warning publicly. Incredibly, the use of registered mail was suggested, as if such news could be kept from the Chinese. If the local press asked Strong for a statement he was instructed simply to confirm that a notice was sent out to American citizens.[122]

One week later, on May 26th, the Department made some basic decisions about the evacuation of Taiwan. Washington reconfirmed its previous decision that no public announcement of a reduction of official personnel be made. It was feared that such knowledge would precipitate a general panic. Nevertheless, it was time to put an evacuation into motion. A gradual withdrawal would now commence rather than a last-minute "mass" evacuation. Assuming that the Nationalist Government would become aware of the draw down, and that Taipei would protest, Strong was instructed to tell the Foreign Ministry that the departure of diplomatic personnel from a foreign nation is fully justified (quoting international law) "in season of war or civil strife when for any reason" the safety of diplomats or their ability to perform their duties is jeopardized. Strong was informed that a liaison group was now established in Washington with which he could coordinate his evacuation plans. He was instructed to discretely seek out the British and arrange for transferring to them that which could not be shipped out or destroyed. Under no circumstances, Strong was told, should he allow administrative burdens to delay his departure at the eleventh hour. He and his staff were not to be captured. He was authorized to dispose of all U.S. property as he saw fit. Furthermore, State agreed with Strong's earlier recommendation to slowly cut down the size of the attache office and the ECA operation. At the same time, USIS personnel (two individuals) would remain until the last because of their high profile. Strong was told that the final withdrawal from Taiwan might not be accomplished until after his 15 June recommendation. He was instructed to remain flexible.[123] As the situation changed the evacuation could either be accelerated, slowed, or even reversed.

In light of Truman's January 5th statement and recent military reversals it now appeared that the Nationalist Government on Taiwan continued to exist only at the sufferance of Peking. Recent intelligence estimates that an invasion was likely within the next two months were reinforced by reports that Moscow was sending military supplies and advisers to China. In late April Dean Rusk informed Acheson that "The verified appearance of many military type planes (in addition to reports that some of them are jet types) on the Chinese mainland has raised the definite possibility of increased and highly effective Russian military assistance to the Chinese Communists..."[124] Also in late April, the CIA issued a current intelligence brief, ORE 19-50, "Reports of Current Soviet Military Activity in China." Although Langley admitted that its agents were unable to confirm first-hand most reports about specific Soviet programs, CIA judged that the large volume of field reporting about Russian military assistance should be a cause for great concern. CIA was certain that most assistance was being put into building up the PLA's air force and in conducting amphibious training in Chekiang. Soviet advisers were known to be assisting the Third Field Army "in the construction of wooden landing craft."[125]

As anticipation over the fate of Taiwan mounted, Dulles, on May 18th, sent a very strongly worded memorandum to Dean Rusk. The memo suggested nothing short of a complete reversal of current policy toward the island.

The United States faces a new and critical period in its world position.

The loss of China to Communists who, it now seems, will work in Asia as junior partners of Soviet Communism has had tremendous repercussions throughout the world. It has marked a shift in the balance of power in favor of Soviet Russia and to the disfavor of the United States.

While that *basic fact* is generally accepted, no one is yet quite sure as to the *precise extent* to which that power relationship has been shifted. Throughout the world, in Europe, the Mediterranean, the Middle East, Asia and the Pacific, governments and peoples are intently watching for the next move which will provide a measure of the extent of the power shift, so that they can orient their own policies accordingly.

The barometer most closely watched is that which seems to measure the judgment of the United States itself as to its present power and position in the world. If our conduct indicates a continuing disposition to fall back and allow doubtful areas to fall under Soviet Communist control, then many nations will feel confirmed in the impression, already drawn from the North Atlantic Treaty, that we do not expect to stand firm short of the North Atlantic area...

If our conduct seems to confirm that conclusion, then we can expect an accelerated deterioration of our influence in the Mediterranean, Near East, Asia and the Pacific. The situation in Japan may become untenable and possibly that in the Philippines. Indonesia, with its vast natural resources may be lost and the oil of the Middle East will be in jeopardy. None of these places provide good "holding" grounds once the people feel that Communism is the wave of the future and that we are retreating before it.

This series of disasters can probably be prevented if at some doubtful point we quickly take a dramatic and strong stand that shows our confidence and resolution. Probably this series of disasters cannot be prevented in any other way.

Of the doubtful areas where such a stand might be taken, Formosa has advantages superior to any other. It is not subject to the immediate influence of Soviet land power. It is close to our naval and air power. It is occupied by the remnants of the non-Communists who have traditionally been our friends and allies. Its status internationally is undetermined by any international act and we have at least some moral responsibility for the native inhabitants. It is gravely menaced by a joint Chinese-Russian expedition in formation. The eyes of the world are focused upon it.

If the United States were to announce that it would neutralize Formosa, not permitting it either to be taken by Communists or to be used as a base of military operations against the mainland, that is a decision which we could certainly maintain, short of open war by the Soviet Union. If we do not act, it will be everywhere interpreted that we are making another retreat because we do not dare risk war. If it is inferred that we do not dare take a stand that risks war unless our own citadel is directly attacked, then the disasters referred to above will almost surely happen.

...Admittedly the determination to withhold Formosa from Communists would involve complications with the Nationalist Government and with their elements on Formosa. It would involve spreading of our own military force, and possibly some actual losses. However, these aspects are of a secondary order. It is within our power to solve the political complications if we have the resolute will. Also, these same problems will embarrass us if we allow Formosa to fall. The efforts at evacuation, particularly attempts to evacuate to the Philippines large numbers of Nationalists, will pose new problems and difficulties perhaps as embarrassing as those that would be posed by an affirmative policy. It will not leave a good taste if we allow our political problems to be solved by the extermination of our war allies. That was the Russian solution of General Bor's Polish Army.

Admittedly, a strong stand on Formosa would involve a slightly increased risk of early war. But sometimes such a risk has to be taken in order to preserve peace in the world and to keep the national prestige required if we are to play our indispensable part in sustaining a free world. Action to be effective must be prompt.[126]

Dulles' argument for neutralizing Taiwan was not novel. MacArthur suggested the very same thing to President Truman in December 1949. In fact, Dulles' words were strikingly similar to those of SCAP who said that Washington should declare that "...the U.S. would treat any attempt to invade Formosa as an act of war, and similarly that it would be treated as an act of war for the Nationalist Government itself to use Formosa as a base to launch an attack against China." Senator H. Alexander Smith had also raised the issue prior to Dulles. In a letter to K.C. Wu in January 1950, Smith opined that the solution to the problem of Taiwan was to stop using the island as a base for attacking the mainland and have it "neutralized," likening its status in Asia to that of Switzerland in Europe.[127]

The origins of Dulles' suggestion to neutralize Taiwan notwithstanding, the paper had a profound impact upon Rusk. It mirrored his own instincts that sacrificing Taiwan in the pursuit of a Titoist mainland was now a losing proposition. Rusk was now ready to take action. In the last days of May he began an attempt to reverse State's hard-won "hands off" policy toward Taiwan.

On May 25th Rusk met in the Pentagon with Generals Lyman Lemnitzer (Director of the Office of Military Assistance) and James Burns (Special Assistant to the Secretary of Defense). The three men met to discuss military assistance to the Nationalists. It is clear from Burns' notes that Rusk was prepared to do all he could within State to facilitate military aid to Taiwan at this crucial moment. Burns may have been taken aback by FE's new attitude, for he felt compelled to send Rusk a copy of his understanding of what DoD and State intended to do. The bottom line was that they agreed that "every step should be taken within existing United States policy to provide assistance to the Chinese Nationalist Government on Formosa." Rusk "agreed to take the necessary action within the Department of State to determine" if Acheson's previous guidelines on military equipment permitted to be sold to the KMT out of U.S. military stockpiles could be "broadened." Rusk also agreed to do what he could to facilitate the granting of export licenses for military supplies purchased by Taipei from U.S. commercial sources. DoD agreed to "expedite" the shipment of any additional stockpiled equipment that State might now allow. Also, Defense agreed that it would insure that Taipei did not squander its purchases and that what was procured would be "items urgently required in connection with the defense of Formosa." Finally, Rusk, Burns, and Lemnitzer decided that it would be "desirable" to augment and intensify covert operations in support of the defense of Taiwan. Although they recognized that such operations held only "limited possibilities," covert operations were in fact authorized by the Mutual Dense Assistance Act of 1949, and the Section 303 funds were available to underwrite them. There was nothing to lose at this point by engaging in clandestine warfare. Rusk would seek release of 303 funds after operations were developed and approved.[128]

In spite of his inclination to shore-up the KMT's defenses, Rusk did not see U.S. military aid as anything more than a stop gap measure. The answer to Taiwan's salvation still hinged upon a solid political solution. On May 30th, during the Memorial Day Holiday, Rusk began the search for a diplomatic formula by calling a meeting at State with Jessup, Nitze, Merchant, Sprouse, and Fisher Howe (State's Deputy Special Assistant for Intelligence). He revealed to the group that he believed it was time for a reappraisal of policy toward Taiwan. Howe recorded that Rusk was:

> ...basing his thinking generally along the lines that world opinion and US opinion are generally unhappy at lack of a forthright action on our part in the Far East; that Formosa presents a plausible place to "draw the line" and is, in itself, important politically if not strategically, for what it represents in continued Communist expansion.

At the meeting Rusk informed the others that he had assembled a good deal of documentation on the issue which included past policy decisions, "changed circumstances, and alternative courses." According to Howe, Rusk was engaged in "drafting and redrafting papers with a view to presenting them to the Secretary." He intended for the participants to serve as a sounding board for his ideas.

Rusk's challenge was to find a way to preserve Taiwan from the Communists without totally alienating Peking and taking into account Acheson's great personal disdain for Chiang's regime in Taipei. To do this, Rusk suggested to the group that the three thorny issues of Taiwan's status, recognizing Peking, and Chinese representation in the United Nations somehow be linked.

The key to unknotting this tangled web rested upon doing away with the fiction that the Nationalist regime in Taipei was the government of all of China. Rusk believed that a U.N. trusteeship was the only way to both preserve Taiwan and allow some movement toward relations with Peking.

Rusk did not fool himself into believing that Chiang Kai-shek would ever go along placidly with such a scheme. Therefore, Rusk was prepared to pressure the Gimo into cooperation. Dulles was scheduled to travel to the Far East from 14 to 29 June in connection with the Japanese Peace Treaty. Rusk, recorded Howe, would propose to Acheson that Dulles approach Chiang with the following thinly-veiled ultimatum:

> (a) the fall of Formosa in the present circumstances was inevitable, (b) the US would do nothing to assist the Gimo in preventing this, (c) the only course open to the Gimo to prevent the bloodshed of his people was to request UN trusteeship.

Coming from such a cold warrior as Dulles, this proposition would likely underscore for Chiang how untenable his position had become in Washington. At the same time, Rusk would have Dulles give Chiang assurances that the U.S "would be prepared to back such a move for trusteeship and would ready the fleet to prevent any armed attack on Formosa while the move for trusteeship was pending." Although a trusteeship would virtually destroy Chiang's personal power to rule Taiwan (this would probably please Acheson), the Gimo was being offered the survival of his island province and the prospect that a new and autonomous republic could later be born. Left unsaid in the notes of the meeting was that by becoming a trustee of the U.N. the status of the Nationalist Government in that organization would probably undergo a drastic change. It is difficult to imagine that the charter of the U.N. allowed for a trustee territory to hold permanent member status or a seat on the Security Council. Thus, the current imbroglio at Lake Success over which Chinese government should be represented would disappear.

As for Peking, Acheson and Rusk were already in agreement that the United States would not exercise its veto to overrule PRC seating in the U.N. should the communists receive the appropriate support in a vote. However, Rusk, as part of his "package," was prepared to take a step, ever so slight, toward raising the possibility of establishing a dialogue with the communist regime. Rusk suggested that

Washington could make a public announcement, "...pending clarification of the situation in China," that the U.S.:

> (1) takes account of the fact that the Peking regime exercises certain de facto control in parts of China. In accordance with established international law, the United States will therefore hold that regime responsible for the discharge of international obligations wherever in China actual authority extends; (2) that it (the United States) continues to acknowledge that the Nationalist Government of China is the recognized government with which the United States maintains diplomatic and consular relations.

The two statements seem contradictory, if not self-negating. Nevertheless, it would have been difficult to hold Peking "responsible" for its obligations without establishing some form of dialogue, either directly or through a proxy such as Britain. Certainly the U.N. could not be used as Peking had yet to achieve representation. The continued recognition of Taipei would probably become a non-issue if a trusteeship could be arranged as part of Rusk's plan. Taiwan would become a ward of the world organization and even those nations that had already recognized Peking would have to support the autonomy of Taiwan. In the meantime, the onus for a real PRC-U.S. dialogue would continue to rest with Peking, awaiting such a time that its "attitude toward normal relations with others, including the treatment of foreigners" met with Washington's expectations. In effect, Rusk's thoughts in May 1950 seemed to be moving toward a formula which the CCP and KMT today still find onerous: a "One China, One Taiwan" policy.

Howe's notes of the May 30th meeting in State do not record the reactions of Jessup, Merchant or Sprouse to Rusk's ideas. It was noted, however, that there was "general agreement" that Rusk should go ahead and present to Acheson the plan for a U.N. trusteeship and the proposed approach to Chiang by Dulles. Howe noted as well that, aside from Dulles, the persons at the meeting were "the only ones who are aware of this move on Rusk's part." Rusk, according to Howe, planned to discuss these ideas with Acheson later that evening. Rusk reproduced Dulles' memo of May 18th as one of his papers for presentation to the Secretary. He added to the memo (copied verbatim) a Top Secret classification, dated it May 30th, and affixed his own name to it. By doing so one must assume that Rusk agreed completely with Dulles' reasoning. Also, it may have been that

Rusk feared Acheson would not be receptive to anything that Dulles had written on the topic.[129]

The meeting of May 30th raises questions which remain unanswered. First, the idea of a trusteeship for Taiwan backed by U.S. military force ran counter to every argument that Jessup, Case, Fosdick, Butterworth, and Sprouse had made throughout 1949 and 1950. It remains unclear as to whether Jessup and the others were prepared to reverse engines at this point. Second, there can be little doubt that the use of the Seventh Fleet to enforce a neutralized Taiwan would have undermined Acheson's and Butterworth's central theme in dealing with China: the pursuit of a Titoist mainland. The use of the fleet would be the kind "irredentist issue" which Acheson had previously argued vigorously against handing the communist Chinese. Was there now a consensus among the topmost policymakers in State that the Titoist policy was unrealistic? There is no evidence to this effect.[130] Also unknown is whether Rusk did in fact approach Acheson with the proposals he presented at the May 30th meeting. No record of a discussion between the two has been found by this researcher.[131] Moreover, if Rusk did approach Acheson the latter's reaction is also unknown.[132] All that can be stated with certainty is that Rusk, on the eve of the Korean War, seemed determined to change the course of U.S. policy toward Taiwan. But Rusk would not be able to do this quickly or single-handedly. Assuming he could convince Acheson to change horses in mid-stream (a weak assumption), State would still have to bring the issue to the National Security Council and receive Truman's approval.

8.5 JUNE: ON THE EVE OF KOREA

As May gave way to June fear of an imminent invasion heightened. In Taipei, of course, tensions were the highest. Information available to Consul General Strong indicated that Chiang Kai-shek was feeling the pressure. The Gimo, reported Strong, was "more bitter than ever" about the United States. "As is always the case when he is in a tight spot and things are going badly," said Strong, "he shouts over the telephone and at visitors, and slams objects about his office." At the same time, Sun Li-jen and Ch'en Ch'eng were still going at it with each other; this time over the recent evacuation of the Chusan Islands. Apparently, when the order to withdraw from the islands was issued the commander of the Chusan garrison (one of Ch'en Ch'eng's generals) abandoned a great deal of military equipment. Instead, commercial merchandise, which the commander and other Ch'en Ch'eng proteges had been selling to the mainland, was given priority for evacuation![133] Also in June Chiang Ching-kuo, Chief of the Ministry of Defense's General Political Department and *de facto* head of the KMT's internal security apparatus, began to increase the pressure on potential dissidents. In late May nineteen leaders of the Formosan League for Reemancipation (FLR), including the nephew of Thomas and Joshua Liao, were rounded up and arrested. In June they were formally charged with "treason involving advocacy of the overthrow of the Nationalist Government." K.C. Wu told provincial officials who appealed on their behalf that he had no power to intervene in the matter. Strong was appalled, decrying to Washington that the arrests and impending trials were a "continuation of KMT intolerant police state methods which have consistently served to alienate the population." State instructed him to ask Taipei for the particulars of the charges and evidence, but to make no comment on the affair other than the U.S. continues to hold an interest in the state of relations between mainlanders and islanders.[134]

In Washington, Senator Smith continued to lobby the administration for action to save Taiwan. His latest tactic was circulating reports which indicated that there was now on Taiwan an improved Nationalist government worth saving and appeals from concerned Taiwanese for assistance. The "Twitchell Report" is an excellent example of Smith helping the administration to keep its intelligence up to date. From April 21st until May 3rd Smith's son-in-law, H. Kenaston Twitchell, an official with the anti-communist Moral Rearmament Association, travelled throughout Taiwan and met with almost every civilian and military official of consequence (34 to be exact) from Chiang on down. At the end of his trip he prepared for Smith a lengthy report which extolled the great improvements on the island and which strongly urged the United States to take positive action to save the island. Smith subsequently sent copies to Rusk, Dulles, General Bradley, and Louis Johnson. Apparently the report caught Rusk's interest for he asked Smith for an opportunity to discuss the findings.[135] Smith also circulated a memorandum by two Chinese in Princeton, Dr. Rosy Ngeh Hsieh (Chairman of the All-Formosa Women's Association) and F.F. Liu (a former KMT military officer and Ph.D. candidate at the University). Hsieh and Liu appealed to

Smith for the help of the United States in seeing Taiwan through its current crisis by engaging in a show of force in Okinawa and in the South China Sea. They argued that a show of force would have a tremendous deterrent effect on Peking's invasion plans. But more importantly, they argued that only the development of a multiparty democracy on Taiwan could save the island. Therefore, they asked for U.S. support in putting pressure on Chiang to reform by establishing political and cultural ties with prominent Formosan leaders and organizations. The Taiwanese, they believed, were the future of Taiwan. It was they who deserved salvation, not Chiang's "inept government."[136]

As June wore on Rusk found himself caught between his own desire to pull out the stops to save Taiwan and the policies already put in place by Acheson. For example, during the senate hearings on MDAP for Fiscal Year 1951, Rusk loyally defended to an irate Senator Knowland the reasons why State would not allow Taipei to purchase jet fighter aircraft and why Indochina was a better place at the moment to take a firm stand against communist expansion in Asia.[137] At the same time, in mid-June, Rusk reversed a previous decision by State which kept the Nationalists from purchasing napalm bombs for their air force.[138] Moreover, Rusk may have been privately discussing with Senator Smith his inclination to attempt a reversal of State's thinking on Taiwan policy.[139] If Rusk was still moving forward with his plans, he was doing so quietly.

For their part the Joint Chiefs of Staff remained very unhappy with the policy toward Taiwan approved in NSC 48/2. The Navy Department especially was incensed at the constraints State had placed on the types of items Taipei could purchase from U.S. Government stockpiles and Foggy Bottom's refusal to grant export licenses for certain commercial sales. In May, Admiral Sherman (Chief of Naval Operations) tried unsuccessfully to persuade Bradley to raise with Johnson the idea of reopening the entire issue of military assistance to Taiwan in the NSC.[140] On June 19th Navy Secretary Dan A. Kimball sent to Secretary Johnson a scathing denunciation of State's non-cooperation in facilitating the purchase of even the simplest type of military equipment.[141] It appears that after the sound thrashing they took over the battle for NSC 48, neither Bradley or Johnson were prepared to take on this particular issue once again. Indeed, the two did not fight State's decision that they not visit Taiwan on their upcoming trip to the Far East. Instead, Johnson simply asked Acheson to consider allowing Chiang to visit with him and Bradley in Tokyo.[142] Johnson and Bradley were saving their bullets for the next fight: the battle over an early peace treaty with Japan.[143] In connection with this issue Johnson and Bradley left for Tokyo on the 12th of June. Dulles, representing State's interests in the matter, departed two days later. As far as a treaty with Japan was concerned, all roads led to MacArthur. And in the end it was MacArthur who attempted to reopen the issue of Taiwan. In the final days of June, with Bradley, Johnson, and Dulles in town, SCAP made his strongest statements to date.

On May 29th MacArthur transmitted to the Pentagon an urgent message stating that there was now "on-the-spot" verification that the PLA now had Soviet jet fighter aircraft. "The time has now been passed," he lectured, "when this situation can be considered by the United States from a detached or an academic standpoint." As far as MacArthur was concerned (and unless something drastic was attempted) "...the domination of Formosa by a Communist regime is an accomplished fact." He outlined in detail, as he had in the past, the consequences of Taiwan's fall to the strategic defense perimeter of the United States. Such a turn of events, he warned, would destroy the current military position of the United States in the Far East, making current war plans "no longer realistic." In the event of war between the United States and Moscow, Taiwan, if held by the communists, would be "...the equivalent of an unsinkable aircraft carrier..." Unless Formosa was "neutralized" immediately, he warned, "neither Okinawa nor the Philippines can support the offensive-defensive type of strategic operations for which these areas are best suited." He pointed out as well that his Far Eastern Command did not posses the capability to eliminate an enemy ensconced on Taiwan. "I am convinced that unless measures are taken which will prevent Communist capture of Formosa, the Joint Chiefs of Staff must modify the existing plans to provide, in the event of a general emergency, for the reinforcement of the Far East Command..."[144]

On the 22nd of June, MacArthur discussed the need to take immediate action on Taiwan with Dulles and Johnson. At the same time, he handed to both a copy of a five-page memorandum, portions of which Dulles sent back to State the same day. He reviewed, once again the disastrous impact that the island's capture would have on the American position throughout Far East. His recommendation, as a minimum, was that he be authorized to conduct a survey of the defensive needs of the KMT.

    10. At this time I am unable to recommend the exact political, economic and military measures which should be taken to prevent the fall of Formosa either into the hands of a potential hostile power or into the hands of a power who will grant military utilization of Formosa to a hostile power. It is my firm conviction that a realistic estimate of requirements can only be based upon a physical survey of the area made by experienced military, economic and political observers. I concur whole-heartedly with the recommendations made by the Joint Chiefs of Staff on 23 December 1949 to the effect that the Commander-in-Chief Far East should make an immediate survey of the need and extent of the military assistance required in Formosa in order to hold Formosa against attack. Although this recommendation was apparently not acceptable at the time to the National Security Council, I note that the Joint Chiefs reaffirmed this recommendation on 4 May 1950.

    11. Formosa has not yet fallen to Communist domination. There are conflicting reports as to the capability and will of the Chinese Nationalist Forces as now constituted and equipped to prevent either the military or . political conquest of the island of Formosa. I cannot predict what the cost may be of preventing Communist domination of that island, although I have advised the Joint Chiefs of Staff what the cost may be if such an event transpires. I am satisfied, however, that the domination of Formosa by an unfriendly power would be a disaster of the utmost importance to the United States, and I am convinced that time is of the essence. I strongly believe that the Commander-in-Chief Far East should be authorized and directed to initiate without delay a survey of the military, economic and political requirements to prevent the domination of Formosa by a Communist power and that the results of such a survey be analyzed and acted upon as a basis for United States national policy with respect to Formosa.[145]

Along with paragraph 11 of the memorandum, Dulles informed Acheson that his talks with SCAP indicated that unless MacArthur was authorized to participate in the proposed survey the exercise would be meaningless. State cabled back to Dulles that the Department acknowledged receipt of his message.[146] MacArthur's memo probably bothered Acheson to no end. At the same time, it may have heartened Rusk. This we shall never know, for seventy-two hours later an invasion did begin; the invasion of South Korea. Within seventy-two hours the entire complexion of the United States' position in Asia would change beyond anyone's wildest imagination.

Notes

1. "Unfinished Paper: Summary by George F. Kennan on points of difference between his views and those of the State Department," September, 1951, GFK/Box 24.

2. "Truman's Top Aides Divided On What to Do About China," *New York Times*, December 30th, 1949, p. 6.

3. Blum, *Drawing the Line*, p. 178. The source of this glaring security violation (NSC 48/2 was classified Top Secret) remains unknown. Blum contends (p. 178), without documentation, that "The source of this leak appears to have been the President." This is difficult to accept at face value. Gaddis Smith, also without any documentation, has written that "The leak probably came from the Defense Department." Gaddis Smith, *Dean Acheson* (New York: Cooper Square Publishers, Inc., 1972), p. 129. During the Princeton Seminars, Acheson said that he had always suspected Johnson of leaking this information, but admits that the Defense Secretary was in Florida and did not attend the NSC meeting at all. DGA/Box 75/Princeton Seminars/Reading Copy, 22–23 July 1953/Folder 2/pp. 663–665.

4. Transcript, Walter H. Judd Oral History Interview, April 13, 1970, pp. 38–48, Truman Library. Judd's recollection of the conversation is rambling and unfocused. However, the following exchange, read from his notes during his interview, gives the flavor of how the call went. "How many American soldiers do you want to put on Formosa?" asked Truman. "Not a one," answered Judd. "It would take ten divisions. I am not willing to do that," shot back the president. "Neither am I and never have been," said Judd. After having established that common ground the president excused himself and invited Judd's further comments in writing.

5. Tang Tsou, *America's Failure in China*, p. 529; Stueck, *The Road to Confrontation*, p. 141.

6. "Hoover, Taft Urge U.S. To Aid Formosa By Force If Needed," *New York Times*, January 3, 1950, pp. 1 and 10.

7. "Knowland Wants Acheson To Reveal Paper On Formosa," *New York Times*, January 4, 1950, pp. 1 and 16; "Aggressive Policy Asked," ibid., p. 16.

8. Message, Acheson to AMCONSUL Hong Kong, December 30, 1949, SDF:Reel 3; and "Red China Charges U.S.-Formosa Deal," January 4, 1950, *New York Times*, p. 16.

9. Associated Press dispatch (January 4th), *New York Times*, January 5, 1950, p. 18.

10. Blum, *Drawing the Line*, p. 179.

11. Memorandum of Conversation, Congressman John Kee, The Secretary, Mr. McFall, January 4, 1949, DGA/Box 65/MOC/ January 1950; DGA/Box 75/Princeton Seminars/Reading Copy 22–23 July 1953/Folder II/p. 651.

12. DGA/Box 75/Princeton Seminars/Reading Copy 22–23 July 1953/Folder II/p. 651.

13. STATEMENT BY THE PRESIDENT, January 5, 1950, HST/PSF/ Box 173/China, 1950–52.

14. Memorandum: Concerning Statement by the President on January 5, 1950 concerning China, January 6, 1950, GME/HST Foreign Relations, C-H/ Box 59/Formosa Policy.

15. Memorandum by Lucius D. Battle, January 5, 1950, DGA/MOC/Box 65/January 1950; Meeting with the President, January 5, 1950, DGA/MOC/ Box 65/January 1950; Elsey memorandum, January 6, 1950, GME/HST Foreign Relations, C-H/Box 59/Formosa Policy. For copies of the statement which reflected the changes asked for by Bradley, and which the president delivered, see Statement By The President, January 5, 1950, SJS/Box 18/China and Asia; GME/HST, Foreign Relations, C-H/Box 59/Formosa Policy; and "United States Policy Toward Formosa," *Statement by President Truman* [Released to the press by the White House January 5], *Department of State Bulletin,* January 16, 1950, p. 79.

16. Elsey memorandum, January 6, 1950, ibid., footnote 14.

17. Memorandum of Conversation, Acheson, McFall, Knowland, and Smith, January 5, 1950, DGA/MOC/Box 65/January 1950.

18. Blum, *Drawing the Line,* p. 181.

19. Extemporaneous Remarks by Secretary Acheson [Released to the press January 5], *Department of State Bulletin,* January 16, 1950, pp. 79–81; and HAS/Box 100.

20. Daily Summary of Opinion Developments, Department of State, January 6, 1950, GME/HST, Foreign Relations, C-H/Formosa Policy.

21. *Foreign Radio Reactions To The President's Statement On Formosa And British Recognition Of Communist China,* (6–9 January 1950), Foreign Broadcast Information Division of the Central Intelligence Agency, January 9, 1950, CMC/Box 2/China Folder #2; *Foreign Radio Reactions To The President's Statement On Formosa And British Recognition Of Communist China,* (9–12 January 1950), January 11, 1950, ibid.; *Summary Of Telegrams,* Department of State, January 11, 1949, HST/NAF/Box 22/January–April 1950.

22. Transcripts of remarks made during the debate can be found in the *Congressional Record,* XCVI, 81st Congress, 2nd Session, 1950.

23. Foster Rhea Dulles, *American Policy Toward Communist China, 1949–1969* (New York: Thomas Y. Crowell Company, Inc., 1972), p. 65.

24. Daily Summary of Opinion Developments, Department of State, January 6, 1950, GME/HST, Foreign Relations, C-H/Formosa Policy.

25. Tang Tsou, *America's Failure in China,* p. 532.

26. Daily Summary of Opinion Developments, Department of State, January 6, 1950, GME/HST, Foreign Relations, C-H/Formosa Policy.

27. Tang Tsou, *America's Failure in China,* p. 533–534; Blum, *Drawing the Line,* p. 182; Dulles, *American Policy Toward Communist China,* p. 65.

28. Blum, *Drawing the Line,* pp. 182–183; Stueck, *The Road To Confrontation,* p. 142–143; DGA/Box 75/Princeton Seminars/Reading Copy 22–23 July 1953/Folder II/pp. 672–673.

29. *Meeting with the President Item 4.*, January 5, 1950, DGA/Box
65/January 1950; DGA/Box 75/Princeton Seminars/Reading Copy 22–23 July
1953/Folder II/p. 674. The speech was published in *The Department of State
Bulletin*, January 23, 1950. However, the reprint of the speech contains neither
Acheson's opening remarks or the question and answer period following his
presentation. Those can be found in the press release of the entire affair (No.
34, January 12, 1950), copies of which are in JEW/Box 20/Dean Acheson and
GME/Box 59/HST, Foreign Relations, C-H/Formosa Policy. During his opening remarks Acheson took the opportunity to send a salvo back at Senator
Taft; an opportunity he seemed to relish.

30. Again, the best study of the defense perimeter concept and an analysis
of Acheson's remarks about it in this speech was done by John Lewis Gaddis,
"The Strategic Perspective: The Rise and Fall of the 'Defensive Perimeter'
Concept, 1947–1951," in Borg and Heinrichs, eds. *Uncertain Years*, pp. 61–119.

31. Indeed, Acheson did not consider military concerns the immediate
problem in Asia. As he said in his remarks, "...it is a mistake, I think, in considering Pacific and Far Eastern problems to become obsessed with military considerations."

32. This particular formulation was very *apropos* to U.S. policy toward
Taiwan. It was the basis of the NSC 37 series of papers, it was revalidated in
NSC 48, and was the core of the *demarche* that was delivered to Chiang in
November. If the KMT on Taiwan could reform itself, regain the confidence
of the people, then economic aid would be forthcoming. The decision not to
supply military assistance to Taipei was based not only on the reluctance of the
Joint Chiefs to expend American resources in a less than vital area. It was
based on the analysis that (1) Chiang had what military equipment he needed,
(2) the CCP did not yet have the capability to invade, and (3) the real threat was
from internal subversion made possible by the inability to reform! Had the
President, on January 5th, coupled this explanation of U.S. policy toward
Taiwan or some formulation of it with the announcement that U.S. troops
would not be used on the island, there is cause to wonder if the whole congressional row that ensued would have been possible. Stated in the above terms,
perhaps more pressure to reform would have been placed on Taipei by its
friends in the legislature as opposed to making the KMT martyrs sacrificed to
a State Department accused of being soft on communism. It is to be recalled
that a public announcement, never made, was originally intended to accompa-
ny the November *demarche*. It was much harsher in its criticism of Taipei.
However, it held out the possibility of continued economic aid and was less
susceptible to being interpreted as a final "write off" of the island than the
statement Truman issued on January 5th.

33. Walter Lippman, "Acheson Takes Long View Of the Revolution in
Asia," *Washington Post*, January 15, 1950. Parenthesis added. Italics in original
article.

34. Arthur Krock, "Position On Formosa Leaves G.O.P. 'On Limb,'" *New
York Times*, January 15, 1950. Krock also wrote that Acheson should have

explained the rationale behind the policy to the Congress before announcing it publicly and implied that the Secretary set up his Republican critics to be embarrassed.

35. In draft notes of a speech he delivered in January 1950, Livingston Merchant listed the "Missing Component" concept as George Kennan's formulation. See "Recognition," (draft notes of a speech) dated January 12, 1959, LTM/Box 17. Acheson has described his Press Club speech as extemporaneous, meaning that he had an outline rather than a full text of remarks. However, in preparing for it he had various experts in the Department write drafts from which he could draw ideas. One of those drafts (virtually ignored by Acheson in his own remarks) was prepared by Kennan and can be found in his papers. See GFK/Box 24/1-9-50, untitled notes. For Acheson's recollections about how he prepared the speech see DGA/Box 75/Princeton Seminars/Reading Copy 22-23 July 1953/pp. 674-679 and DGA/Box 76/Princeton Seminars/Reading Copy 1/13-14 February 1954/pp. 1177-1184.

36. *Office Memorandum*, Francis H. Russell (State Public Affairs) to Merchant, "Meeting of Advertising Council Business Leaders at the White House, Thursday, February 16," February 13, 1950, LTM/Box 17; Draft notes for speech to Institute for World Organization, "Recognition," 1/12/50, LTM/Box 17; Untitled speech notes, LTM/Box 17; Index cards of "White House Speech," LTM/Box 17; "White House Speech," February 15, 1950, LTM/Box 17; *Office Memorandum*, Ogburn (FE/Polinfo) to Merchant, February 15, 1950, LTM/Box 17; and Draft, "Factors Which Should Be Considered In The Formation Of Our Far Eastern Policy," 2/13/50, LTM/Box 17. Apparently Merchant did quite well in his role as a public spokesman, for immediately after the Korean invasion in June 1950, he was tasked to speak on behalf of State once again to explain to various audiences why it was necessary for the United States to fight. For example, see *Questions And Answers*, "Why is the United States fighting in Korea," LTM/Box 17; and *DRAFT*, "Why in Korea?", LTM/Box 17.

37. Raymond B. Fosdick, "Asia's Challenge to Us-Ideas, Not Guns," *The New York Times Magazine*, February 12, 1950, pp. 7, 41, 42, 43, and 44.

38. Tang Tsou, *America's Failure in China*, pp. 537-538; Blum, *Drawing the Line*, pp. 184-187; Stueck, *Road to Confrontation*, p. 136 and footnote 156, p. 280; and DGA/Box 76/Princeton Seminars/Reading Copy I/13-14 February 1954/Folder I/pp. 1176-1177.

39. Memorandum of Conversation, Acheson, Rusk, and Merchant with Bradley, Collins, Norstad, and Sherman, December 29, 1949, SDF:Reel 3.

40. Lippman, "Acheson Takes Long View Of the Revolution in Asia."

41. *The Ambassador in Thailand (Stanton) to the Secretary of State*, February 17, 1950, FR:50:VI:18-19; *The Ambassador in Thailand (Stanton) to the Secretary of State*, February 18, 1950, FR:50:VI:19-20; *Oral Report By Ambassador-at-Large Philip C. Jessup Upon His Return From the Far East*, April 3, 1950, FR:50:VI:68-76.

42. *The Secretary of State to Certain Diplomatic and Consular Offices, February 24, 1950, FR:50:VI:24–25;* Record of an Interdepartmental Meeting on the Far East at the Department of State, May 11, 1950, 11:30 a.m., FR:50:VI:87–91; and Transcript, COL. R. Allen Griffin Oral History Interview, February 15, 1974, Truman Library. For a detailed account of the mission see Samuel P. Hayes, *The Beginning of American Aid to Southeast Asia: The Griffin Mission of 1950* (Lexington, Mass.: D.C. Heath & Co., 1971). Relevant aspects of Griffin's visit to each of the countries can be found in the appropriate volumes of the *FRUS* series for 1950.

43. Tang Tsou, *America's Failure in China,* pp. 517–525.

44. *Memorandum by the Acting Secretary of State to the President, "Chinese Communist Intention to Requisition U.S. Government Property in Peiping,"* January 10, 1950, FR:50:VI:270–272.

45. *Summary of Telegrams,* Department of State, June 8, 1949, HST/NAF/ Box 21/May–June 1949; *Summary of Telegrams,* Department of State, June 15, 1949, HST/NAF/Box 21/May–June 1949; DGA/Box 75/Princeton Seminars/ Reading Copy 22–23 July 1953/Folder II/p. 695.

46. NSC 18: "The Attitude of This Government Toward Events In Yugoslavia," July 6, 1948, DNSC:Reel 1; DGA/Box 75/Princeton Seminars/ Reading Copy 22–23 July 1953/Folder II/pp. 688–689.

47. See NSC 48/2, paragraph 3*f*(1), December 30, 1949, HST/MNSC/Box 206/NSC Meeting #50, "The United States should avoid recognizing the Chinese Communist regime until it is clearly in the United States interest to do so."; *National Security Council Progress Report by the Under Secretary of State on the Implementation of The Position of the United States With Respect to Asia (NSC 48/2),* February 27, 1950, HST/MNSC/Box 206/NSC Meeting #50, "...hasty recognition should be avoided..."; Memorandum of Conversation, Acheson and Senator Smith, November 30, 1949, DGA/Box 64/October– November 1949, Acheson "...could not say that we would *never* recognize the Communist government..." (Emphasis in original.)

48. Kennan relinquished the directorship of the PPS to Paul H. Nitze in late November 1949 and remained in the Department with the title of Counselor. By January 1950 he and Nitze completed the transition and Kennan embarked on extended official travel throughout Latin America. His scheduled sabbatical to Princeton University in June 1950 was delayed by the North Korean invasion. For a comparison of the two PPS directors see Steven L. Rearden, *The Evolution of American Strategic Doctrine: Paul H. Nitze and the Soviet Challenge* (Boulder, Co., Westview Press, 1984).

49. *Memorandum by the Counselor (Kennan) to the Secretary of State,* January 6, 1950, FR:50:I:127–138.

50. Draft speech by Livingston T. Merchant, "Recognition," to the Institute of World Organization, January 12, 1950, LTM/Box 17.

51. Draft speech by Merchant, "Recognition," ibid.; Memorandum of Conversation, Acheson with Mme. Vijaya Pandit (Ambassador of India), "Recognition of Chinese Communist Regime," December 6, 1949, DGA/Box

64; Memorandum of Conversation, Acheson with Sir Oliver Franks (British Ambassador), "Far East," December 8, 1949, DGA/Box 64.

52. Memorandum of Conversation, Acheson and Madame Vijaya Pandit, December 6, 1949, DGA/Box 64.

53. *Summary of Telegrams*, Department of State, June 8, 1949, HST/NAF/ Box 21/May–June 1949.

54. *Editorial Note*, FR:50:VI:278. At the time of the decision to withdraw there were 241 U.S. officials and dependents in China. Besides the four consulates mentioned, offices of official U.S. Government organizations in Hangkow, Tsingtao, and Kunming were ordered closed as well. In effect, all official U.S.G. personnel were to leave. Approximately 3,000 private U.S. citizens remained; mostly businessmen and missionaries. Memorandum from Acheson to Truman, "United States Interests in China," January 19, 1950, HST/PSF/Box 173.

55. For an excellent interpretation of the CCP policy toward the United States during this period see Michael H. Hunt, "Mao Tse-tung and the Issue of Accommodation with the United States, 1948–1950," in Borg and Heinrichs, eds., *The Uncertain Years*, pp. 185–233

56. *The Secretary of State to the Consulate General at Peiping,* March 22, 1950, FR:50:VI:321–322. The one *proviso* in Clubb's instructions was that he should make it clear to the CCP authorities he might be able to speak with that his approach did not constitute recognition by the United States. The Chinese did not permit Clubb to meet with Chou En-lai after the Consulate closed. Although he had requested an audience with Chou, he was never able to get further than being summoned to the Peking Alien Affairs Office. Clubb refused to deal with these lowly functionaries and left China in early April. *Summary of Telegrams*, Department of State, March 23, 1950, HST/NAF/Box 22/January–April 1950; *The Consul General at Peiping (Clubb) to the Secretary of State*, January 13, 1950, FR:50:VI:276–277. See also O. Edmund Clubb Oral History Interview, June 26, 1974, Truman Library.

57. *The Secretary of State to the Embassy in France,* January 25, 1950, FR:50:VI:294–297.

58. *Summary of Telegrams*, Department of State, January 4, 1950, HST/ NAF/Box 22/January–April 1950; *The Consul General at Peiping (Clubb) to the Secretary of State,* January 20, 1950, FR:50:VI:288.

59. *Summary of Telegrams*, Department of State, January 27, 1950, HST/ NAF/Box 22/January–April 1950.

60. *The Secretary of State to the Embassy in France,* January 25, 1950, FR:50:VI:294.

61. *The Consul General at Peiping (Clubb) to the Secretary of State,* January 20, 1950, FR:50:VI:288. Parentheses added.

62. *Summary Of Telegrams*, Department of State, January 4, 1950, HST/ NAF/Box 22/January–June 1950; *Summary of Telegrams*, Department of State, January 23, 1950, HST/NAF/ Box 22/January–June 1950.

63. *The Consul General at Shanghai (McConaughy) to the Secretary of State,* January 5, 1950, FR:50:VI:264–269; *The Consul General at Shanghai (McConaughy) to the Secretary of State,* January 21, 1950, ibid., pp. 288–293; *The Consul General at Shanghai (McConaughy) to the Secretary of State,* January 26, 1950, ibid., pp. 296–300; *The Consul General at Shanghai (McConaughy) to the Secretary of State,* February 1, 1950, ibid., pp. 302–304; *The Secretary of State to the Consulate General at Peiping,* January 5, 1950, ibid., pp. 269–270.

64. *Memorandum by John P. Davies of the Policy Planning Staff,* February 2, 1950, FR:50:VI:305. Upon studying the reports concerning Ch'en Yi, John Davies penned words of wisdom for China analysts past and present.

"One learns after long dealing with China affairs that the facet of Chinese character perhaps most confusing and exasperating to the logical Western mind is a tendency toward irresponsible garrulity. In attempting to analyze the Chinese situation, the Western observer must deal with a plethora of reports and rumors, some of which are surprisingly candid and accurate, others highly embroidered and many which are plausible but airy concoctions of private political enterprise."

65. *The Consul General at Peiping (Clubb) to the Secretary of State,* January 10, 1950, FR:50:VI:273–275; *The Consul General at Peiping (Clubb) to the Secretary of State,* January 20, 1950, ibid., pp. 286–288.

66. *Memorandum by John P. Davies of the Policy Planning Staff,* February 2, 1950, FR:50:VI:305–306.

67. *The Secretary of State to the Embassy in France,* January 25, 1950, FR:50:VI:294–296; *The Secretary of State to the Embassy in France,* February 11, 1950, ibid., pp. 308–311. Acheson instructed Bruce to restrict knowledge of the operation to a small group of senior FSO's in the Embassy.

68. *Memorandum by the Acting Assistant Secretary of State for Far Eastern Affairs (Merchant) to the Secretary of State,* March 7, 1950, FR:50:VI:749–750; and especially *Memorandum by the Deputy Assistant Secretary of State for Far Eastern Affairs (Merchant) to the Assistant Secretary (Butterworth),* "Subject: French Indochina," March 7, 1950, ibid., pp. 750–751. It may be of passing interest to note that in the 1960's and 70's, the shoulder patch of the U.S. Army Military Assistance Command, Vietnam (MACV) depicted a bayonet piercing upward through a castle gate. The symbology was that of piercing the Great Wall of China from the soft underbelly—Vietnam.

69. *The Secretary of State to the Embassy in France,* February 11, 1950, FR:50:VI:308–311.

70. *Address by the Secretary of State (Acheson) before the Commonwealth Club of California, San Francsico, March 15, 1950,* in *Documents on American Foreign Relations,* VOL. XII, January 1 – December 31, 1950, Raymond Bennet and Robert K. Turner, eds. (Princeton, N.J.: Princeton University Press, 1951), pp. 519–521.

71. *Draft Memorandum by the Counselor (Kennan) to the Secretary of State,* February 17, 1950, FR:50:I:160–167.

72. *Summary of Telegrams*, Department of State, January 9, 1950, HST/NAF/Box 22/January–April 1950.

73. *The Secretary of State to the Chinese Ambassador (Koo)*, January 13, 1950, FR:50:VI:277–278.

74. Memorandum of Telephone Conversation, Secretary Johnson and Secretary Acheson, January 26, 1950, DGA/Box 65/January 1950.

75. *The Secretary of State to the Secretary of Defense (Johnson)*, March 7, 1950, FR:50:VI:316–317.

76. *Summary of Telegrams*, Department of State, January 6, 1950, HST/NAF/Box 22/January–April 1950. Emphasis added. For a review of the issue of PRC and KMT seating in the U.N. during this period see FRUS, Volume II for 1950; Tang Tsou, *America's Failure in China*, pp. 523–527, and Grasso, *Truman's Two-China Policy*, pp. 142–155.

77. The Soviet boycott lasted until August 1950. The absence of the Soviets on the Security Council facilitated the passage of U.S. resolutions in the wake of the initial invasion of South Korea on June 25th.

78. Memorandum of Conversation, Acheson, Webb, Rusk, and Hickerson with Trygvie Lie (Secretary General, U.N.) and Byron Price (Assistant Secretary General), January 21, 1950, DGA/Box 65/January 1950.

79. Footnote 1, FR:50:VI:306.

80. *Summary of Telegrams*, Department of State, February 9, 1950, HST/NAF/January–April 1950.

81. *The Secretary of State to the Embassy in China*, February 8, 1950, FR:50:VI:306–307.

82. *The Charge in China (Strong) to the Secretary of State*, February 10, 1950, ibid., pp. 307–308.

83. Footnote, ibid., p. 307.

84. *Summary of Telegrams*, Department of State, February 16, 1950, HST/NAF/Box 22/January–April 1950.

85. *Memorandum by the Director of the Office of Chinese Affairs (Sprouse) to the Deputy Assistant Secretary of State for Far Eastern Affairs (Merchant)*, February 16, 1950, FR:50:VI:312–314. Parentheses added.

86. Footnote, FR:50:VI:313.

87. *Memorandum by the Director of the Office of Chinese Affairs, (Sprouse) to the Deputy Assistant Secretary of State for Far Eastern Affairs (Merchant)*, February 16, 1959, ibid., p. 313.

88. Ibid., p. 314.

89. Telegram, Taipei to Secretary of State, March 2, 1950, HST/PSF/Box 173/China/1950–52.

90. *Summary of Telegrams*, Department of State, March 3, 1950, HST/NAF/Box 22/January–April 1950.

91. *Summary of Telegrams*, Department of State, March 8, 1950, HST/NAF/Box 22/January–April 1950.

92. CIA ORE 7–50, "Probable Developments In Taiwan," 20 March 1950, Copy NO. 1 For The President Of The United States, HST/PSF/Box 257/ORE 1949, #'s 1–17.

93. Acheson, *Present at the Creation*, pp. 251, 360; and Caute, *The Great Fear*, pp. 58–62.

94. Tang Tsou, *America's Failure in China*, pp. 540, 545; Stueck, *The Road to Confrontation*, pp. 144–145; Blum, *Drawing the Line*, pp. 187–189; and Donovan, *The Presidency of Harry S. Truman, 1949–1953: Tumultuous Years*, pp. 162–165.

95. Tang Tsou, *America's Failure in China*, p. 540.

96. Butterworth Oral History, p. 57.

97. Schoenbaum, *Waging Peace & War: Dean Rusk In The Truman, Kennedy & Johnson Years*, p. 198.

98. Acheson, *Present at the Creation*, p. 431; and Butterworth Oral History, p. 62.

99. DGA/Box 76/Princeton Seminars/Folder I/14 March 1954/p. 1476.

100. Rusk had the respect and support of Republican notables such as Arthur Vandenberg and John Foster Dulles. Dulles felt that Rusk was "reliable and responsive." Vandenburg, sang Rusk's praises to fellow party members declaring that he was "one of the most hopeful additions" at State. See Cohen, *Dean Rusk*, p. 35.

101. DGA/Box 76/Princeton Seminars/Folder I/14 March 1954/pp. 1475–1476.

102. John Foster Dulles Oral History Collection (JFDOH), Interview with Dean Rusk, 1965, Seeley Mudd Library, Princeton University, p. 2; Letter, Vandenberg to Acheson, March 31, 1950, DGA/Box 65/March 1950.

103. JFDOH, Butterworth, 1965, pp. 1 and 12; JFDOH, Rusk, 1965, p. 2; Memorandum Of Conversation With The President, Acheson and Truman, April 4, 1940, DGA/Box 65/April 1950; Letter, Truman to Acheson, April 7, 1950, HST/PSF/Box 160/Dean Acheson.

104. Memorandum of Telephone Conversation, Acheson and Dulles, April 5, 1950, DGA/Box 65/April 1950. Dulles accepted the lesser title, but told Acheson that in the opinion of Senator Smith, Senator Vandenberg, and Governor Dewey, "...the Republican Party was selling out awfully cheap." Assuring Acheson that he was not personally preoccupied with his title, his three colleagues "...were all concerned about what newspaper comment it would provoke." Memorandum of Telephone Conversation, Acheson and Dulles, April 6, 1950, DGA/Box 65/April 1950.

105. DGA/Box 76/Princeton Seminars/Folder I/14 March 1950.

106. See page ix in Cohen, *Dean Rusk*, and the preface to Schoenbaum's *Waging Peace & War* for the constraints under which these two scholars worked in preparing their biographies.

107. *Report by Mr. Charles W. Yost, Special Assistant to the Ambassador at Large (Jessup)*, "Discussion of Far Eastern Affairs in Preparation for Conversa-

tions With Mr. Bevin," September 16, 1949, FR:49:VII:1207. See fn. 35, Chapter 3 for full citation Rusk's 1990 autobiography.

108. JFDOH, Rusk, p. 3. According to Rusk; "The real Japanese Peace Conference was held through Mr. Dulles' own travels to capitals. So that when we convened in San Francisco for the purpose of signing the treaty, we convened for the purpose of signing a document which had already been concluded." For more on Dulles and the Peace Treaty see Howard Schonberger, "John Foster Dulles and the China Question in the Making of the Japanese Peace Treaty," in *The Occupation of Japan: The International Context* (The Proceedings of the Fifth Symposium Sponsored by the MacArthur Memorial, Old Dominion University, 21–22 October 1982).

109. Letter, Dulles to Vandenberg, January 6, 1950, JFD/Box 48.

110. Memorandum, Dulles to Rusk, 21 April 1950, JFD/Box 48.

111. See section 8.2 this chapter.

112. *Memorandum by the Assistant Secretary of State for Far Eastern Affairs (Rusk) to the Secretary of State*, April 17, 1950, FR:50:VI:330. According to *FRUS* Acheson did read the memorandum.

113. *Memorandum by the Assistant Secretary of State for Far Easter Affairs (Rusk) to the Secretary of State*, April 26, 1950, FR:50:VI:333–334. Robert Strong, Consul General in Taipei, was alarmed at what he considered to be the growing feeling in the field that Washington should once again commit itself to the regime in Taipei. He did not concur with the report sent in by his attaches and wrote back to Rusk that all was not well with the KMT. "I am concerned," he told Rusk, "that the representatives of other agencies of the U.S. are lining up solidly behind this regime, emphasizing the minor improvements and overlooking the major failures, and are not considering the mainland and its potentialities..." Strong still believed that only "a shooting war" in Asia might justify renewed military and economic support of the Nationalist Government. Although this last point was prescient of events soon to transpire, Strong's attitude was quickly becoming out of step with Rusk's thinking.

114. Memorandum of Telephone Conversation, Acheson and Dewey, April 10, 1950, DGA/Box 65/April 1950.

115. FR:50:VI:335; and Letter, Burton Crane to H. Alexander Smith, 19 February 1950, HAS/Box 100. The number of KMT troops on Hainan is Crane's, who visited the island in February 1950.

116. "Report On Formosa," by H. Kenaston Twitchell, Jr., May 4, 1950, HAS/Box 100.

117. Letter, K.C. Wu to H. Alexander Smith, March 27th, 1950, HAS/Box 100. The fall of Hainan may have given Wu reason to think hard about Smith's earlier offer to send his family to the States. In late January Smith extended the following invitation to the Governor of Taiwan: "Realizing that under present conditions you may all be in real danger there, and believing that it may be wise for your wife and children to leave the island before a possible Communist attack comes, Mrs. Smith has asked me to suggest to you the possibility of your wife and daughters coming to America and occupying our house

in Princeton, New Jersey until other satisfactory arrangements can be made."
Letter, Smith to Wu, January 30, 1950, HAS/Box 100.

118. *The Charge in China (Strong) to the Secretary of State*, April 27, 1950,
FR:50:VI:335–339.

119. The Chusan Islands referred to is the Chou-shan Tao (Zhoushan
Qundao) chain off the coast of Chekiang (Zhejiang) province.

120. FR:50:VI:340.

121. *The Charge in China (Strong) to the Secretary of State*, May 17, 1950,
FR:50:VI:340–341.

122. *The Acting Secretary of State to the Embassy in China*, May 19, 1950,
FR:50:VI:342–343. This message was classified restricted.

123. *The Acting Secretary of State to the Embassy in China*, May 26, 1950,
FR:50:VI:344–346. Aside from putting contingency plans in order for evacuat-
ing its Consulate, State attempted to find a home port for Chiang Kai-shek and
top members of the KMT Government. Apparently, Washington was not prepared to have the Gimo come to the U.S. if the worse came to pass. State asked
President Quirino in the Philippines if Chiang could be evacuated to Manila.
Quirino told the American Ambassador that the Generalissimo would not be
welcomed in his country. Romulo, Foreign Minister, told Ambassador Cowen
that if Chiang and his entourage showed up they would be given 24 hours to
leave.

124. *Memorandum by the Assistant Secretary of State for Far Eastern Affairs
(Rusk) to the Secretary of State*, April 26, 1950, FR:50:VI:335.

125. CIA, ORE 19–50, "Reports of Current Soviet Military Activity in
China," 21 April 1950, HST/PSF/Box 257/ORE 1949, #'s 18–29.

126. Memorandum, Dulles to Rusk, May 18, 1950, JFD/Box 47. Dulles'
memo is also printed in FR:50:I:314–316. One wonders if Dulles' argument
that a "series of disasters" would befall the U.S. if resolute action was not taken
was a precursor to the "Domino Theory" that was later offered as a justification for a strong military stand in Indochina.

127. For MacArthur's recommendation the reader is referred back to
Chapter 7, Section 7.7 (p. 238). For Smith's proposal see Letter, Smith to Wu,
January 30, 1950, HAS/Box 100.

128. *Memorandum by the Special Assistant to the Secretary of Defense for
Foreign Military Affairs and Assistance (Burns) to the Assistant Secretary of State
for Far Eastern Affairs (Rusk)*, 29 May 1950, FR:50:VI:346–347. For Acheson's
previous guidance to DoD on sales of military stockpiles see *The Secretary of
State to the Secretary of Defense (Johnson)*, April 14, 1950, FR:50:VI:325–326
and *The Secretary of State to the Secretary of Defense (Johnson)*, March 7, 1950,
FR:50:VI:316–317.

129. *Memorandum by the Deputy Special Assistant for Intelligence (Howe)
to Mr. W. Park Armstrong, Special Assistant to the Secretary of State for Intelligence and Research*, May 31, 1950, FR:50:VI:347–351. Rusk's transmittal of
Dulles' memo under his own name is included as an annex to these notes of the
May 30th meeting.

130. At least one former advocate of the Titoist policy had in fact reversed himself by late May. On June 2nd, Walter P. McConaughy, recently returned from Shanghai as Consul General, briefed 22 State and Defense Department officials on his views of the situation in China. He told the group that "deviationism among the Chinese Communists on the Titoist model should be discounted. No break between Peiping and Moscow is in the offing." *Memorandum by Mr. Charles Ogburn of the Bureau of Far Eastern Affairs,* June 2, 1950, FR:50:VI:352–356. McConaughy's revised analysis would not in itself have carried enough weight to cause high ranking policymakers to reverse themselves.

131. Robert Blum's earlier research also uncovered no evidence that Rusk approached Acheson on the results of the May 30th meeting. Neither was Blum able to register any reaction by Acheson to word of a reversal of policy in the works at FE. Blum, *Drawing the Line,* p. 196. During a week-long stay at the Truman Library in 1986 I combed the Acheson and Truman papers looking, to no avail, for documents which might give a clue as to Rusk's next moves and Acheson's guidance.

132. FR:50:VI:348. A footnote on this page indicates that during Dulles' trip to the Far East in June he did not go to Taiwan. The approach to Chiang that Rusk proposed was probably never made.

133. *The Charge in China (Strong) to the Secretary of State,* June 7, 1950, FR:50:VI:359–361.

134. *The Charge in China (Strong) to the Secretary of State,* June 2, 1950, FR:50:VI:356–357; *The Secretary of State to the Embassy in China,* June 2, 1950, ibid., p. 357.

135. Draft, "Visit to Taiwan," April 21–May 3, 1950, HAS/Box 100; Letter, Twitchell to Smith, May 4, 1950, ibid.; *Report On Formosa,* ibid., Letter, Smith to Twitchell, June 3, 1950, ibid.; Letter Omar Bradley to Smith, 27 May 1950, ibid.; Letter, Rusk to Smith, May 19, 1950, ibid.

136. Letter, Rosy Ngeh Hsieh to Smith, June 12, 1950, HAS/Box 100. Memorandum attached. Liu, of course, went on to finish his degree and publish *A Military History of Modern China: 1924–1949* (Princeton, N.J.: Princeton University Press, 1956), for years a much-used reference on the subject.

137. Executive Session, Senate Committee on Foreign Relations, "Hearings to Amend the Mutual Defense Assistance Act of 1949," June 8, 1950, SRSFC/Box 9/pp. 280–291.

138. *Memorandum by the Acting Deputy Director of the Office of Chinese Affairs (Freeman) to the Assistant Secretary of State for Far Eastern Affairs (Rusk),* Request by Chinese Government to purchase napalm bombs with money refunded under $125 million grants, June 14, 1950, FR:50:VI:363–364.

139. When Smith forwarded Rusk a copy of Hsieh's and Liu's memorandum on Taiwan (see footnote 136 above), his cover letter included the following lines: "These two people had a very interesting approach to the Formosan problem, and part of their thoughts are incorporated in this memorandum *which may have some suggestions of value to us along the lines of our recent talk on*

the Formosan subject." Letter, Smith to Rusk, June 16, 1950, HAS/Box 100. Emphasis added. Also of note, Smith was especially cordial to Rusk during the latter's testimony on MDAP and on a couple of occasions helped Rusk to dig out from under Knowland's leading questions. See SRSFC/Box 9 cited in footnote 137 above.

140. Memorandum by the Chief of Naval Operations, *Military Aid To Anti-Communist Forces On Formosa* (J.C.S. 1966/28), 3 May 1950, RJCS:Reel 2.

141. Memorandum, Secretary of the Navy to the Secretary of Defense, *Military Assistance To The Republic of China* (J.C.S. 1721/56), 19 June 1950, RJCS:Reel 1.

142. Memorandum For The File Covering Lunch From 12:30–2:00 Wednesday, June 7, Given By Secretary Johnson In His Dining Room In The Pentagon Building Regarding Japan, June 7, 1950, SWS/Box 1/White House Council, 1950–53.

143. State was still pushing for an early treaty, Defense was still opposed. For a representative sample of the respective concerns and arguments of State and DoD see, Memorandum of Conversation, Japanese Peace Treaty, April 24, 1950, DGA/Box 65/April 1950; also printed in FR:50:VI:1175–1182.

144. Message, CINCFE to DA WASH DC, C 56410, For the JCS, 29 May 1950, DM/RG 6/FECOM/Formosa.

145. MEMORANDUM ON FORMOSA, 14 June 1950. Copies can be found in RJCS:Reel 2; JFD/Box 48; GME/Box 59; and FR:50:VII:161–165. A complete transcript of the memorandum is included as an appendix at the end of this book.

146. *The Acting Political Adviser in Japan (Sebald) to the Secretary of State, From Dulles,* June 22, 1950, FR:50:VI:366–367.

EPILOGUE

Korea and the Neutralization of Taiwan

President Truman's courageous announcement of June 27 in support of Korea and with the effect of neutralizing Formosa began a new chapter in this island's history. The life of Free China, which previously seemed to be in danger of immediate extinction, was given new hope at least for the duration of the Korean fighting. For this new lease on life, and for the positive stand taken by the Free World against Communist aggression in the Far East, there was almost universal gratification in Formosa.[1]

> Karl Lott Rankin,
> Charge d'Affairs,
> Taipei

Secretary of Defense Johnson and General Bradley returned to Washington from Tokyo on the 24th of June. Johnson, with MacArthur's firm support, was determined to raise the issue of Taiwan in the NSC once again. Bradley recalled that Johnson was "fired up." The JCS Chairman was also game for a good fight over Taiwan. SCAP's memorandum of 14 June, said Bradley, "...made the case for helping Formosa more eloquently than anything the JCS produced, and I was very glad to get it."[2]

As it turned out, another Formosa offensive by the Department of Defense was unnecessary. On the 24th of June (June 25th in Korea) Washington was informed that North Korean troops had crossed the 38th parallel in force. "It would appear from [the] nature of [the] attack and [the] manner in which it was launched," reported Ambassador Muccio in Seoul, that it "constitutes [an] all out offensive against [the] ROK."[3] Muccio was quite correct.

The week that followed was one in which momentous decisions were made by the President and his advisers.[4] By the end of the week Truman, with iron resolve and broad Congressional support, com-

mitted the naval, air and land forces of the United States to the
defense of the Republic of Korea. In a moment of quiet reflection
stolen on June 26th, Truman, standing over a globe in his office,
revealed his thinking to George Elsey. "Korea," he said, "is the
Greece of the Far East. If we are tough enough now, if we stand up to
them like-we did in Greece three years ago, they won't take any next
steps. But if we just stand by, they'll move into Iran and they'll take
over the whole Middle East. There's no telling what they'll do, if we
don't put up a fight now."[5]

Of no less moment was the decision to neutralize Taiwan. Among
the President's advisers, Acheson included, there does not appear to
have been the slightest doubt that the invasion of Korea required that
Taiwan be kept out of communist hands. The decision among
Truman's advisers that it be recommended to the President that
Taiwan be neutralized was probably made during a joint State-
Defense conference held at 11:30 A.M. on June 25th, and during the
State Department's internal meetings later that afternoon.[6]
Although it is still unclear exactly which department, State or
Defense, first recommended neutralization during these initial meet-
ings, it is clear that a consensus for this move had been reached prior
to the first meeting with the President. Indeed, it was Acheson, on the
night of June 25th, who recommended to Truman during the first
Blair House conference that the Seventh Fleet be ordered "to proceed to Formosa and prevent an attack on Formosa from the mainland." "At the same time", advised Acheson, "operations from
Formosa against the mainland should be prevented."[7] Truman
deferred his decision on Taiwan until the next day. However, on June
26th the President authorized the use of the fleet to neutralize the
island.[8] Orders were issued transferring operational control of the
7th Fleet from CINCPAC in Hawaii to MacArthur. SCAP was issued
his orders.

> By naval and air action you will defend Formosa against invasion or
> attack by the Chinese Communists and will insure that Formosa will not
> be used as a base of operations against the Chinese mainland by the
> Chinese Nationalists.[9]

On the 27th of June Truman made public the decisions made up
to that point. In the presence of his advisers and influential members
of Congress, the President read a seven paragraph statement on
Korea. Two key paragraphs dealt with Taiwan:

KOREA AND THE NEUTRALIZATION OF TAIWAN   333

The attack upon Korea makes it plain beyond all doubt that Communism has passed beyond the use of subversion to conquer independent nations and will now use armed invasion and war. It has defied the orders of the Security Council of the United Nations issued to preserve international peace and security. In these circumstances the occupation of Formosa by Communist forces would be a direct threat to the security of the Pacific area and the United States forces performing their lawful and necessary functions in that area.

Accordingly, I have ordered the Seventh Fleet to prevent any attack on Formosa. As a corollary of this action I am calling upon the Chinese Government on Formosa to cease all air and sea operations against the mainland. The Seventh Fleet will see that this is done. The determination of the future status of Formosa must await the restoration of security in the Pacific, a peace settlement with Japan, or consideration by the United Nations.[10]

Within seventy-two hours of the invasion of Korea, the year and a half-long debate over whether or not the United States would intervene with military force to deny Taiwan to the Chinese communists came to a screeching halt. The MacArthur-Smith-Dulles-Rusk program of neutralization was now in effect.

It must be pointed out, however, that interposing the fleet in the Taiwan Strait was not intended to signal a policy of renewed *political* support for the regime in Taipei. Taiwan was neutralized for purely military-strategic reasons. Washington could not allow the island to be occupied by enemy forces while U.S. ground troops were committed to a land war in Korea. The previous arguments of the Joint Chiefs and MacArthur that a hostile force on Taiwan could play havoc with the U.S.'s internal lines of communication in the Pacific were valid. Moreover, there were fears that the Nationalists would inadvertently expand the fighting in Korea, at that point a localized conflict, into a general war in the Far East by continuing their attacks on the mainland and bringing the CCP and possibly the Soviets into the fight. The positioning of the 7th Fleet (and its air assets) in the Strait was as much intended to leash the KMT as it was to deter an invasion by Peking.[11]

As far as Truman and Acheson were concerned, Chiang Kai-shek and his regime were still a political liability. During the Blair House sessions Acheson made it clear that the U.S. should not "tie up with the Generalissimo" or "get mixed up with the question of the Chinese administration of the Island." Truman agreed, declaring that he would not give Taipei even "a nickel" in assistance. It was decided that MacArthur's request to send a survey team to Taiwan would not be granted at that point.[12] Washington also rejected Chiang's offer of 33,000 troops for combat in Korea under U.N. command. In July, the State Department refused to upgrade the position of Taipei's newly assigned Consul General, Karl Lott Rankin, to the rank of Ambassador (MacArthur's suggestion). Rusk told a very disappointed Rankin that, "Truman's June 27 statement regarding Formosa was based upon military factors, without prejudice to the political considerations involved. It is not desired, therefore, that your initial assignment to Formosa should involve policy implications beyond those implicit in the strengthening of our representation to meet the present grave situation."[13]

Neither is it quite correct, as Blum has written, that "...administration officials who had championed the tattered Titoist policy for the previous eighteen months kicked it over in an evening, without much apparent regret..."[14] The intent of neutralization was not to alienate the CCP, although that was the inevitable result. The President, on various occasions, attempted to reassure Peking (as well Washington's allies) that the U.S.'s initiative in the Strait was a decision made for military reasons alone and that the U.S. would not dictate the island's political future. The political effect of neutralization, argued Washington, was simply that it froze the status of Taiwan as it existed prior to the Korean invasion. The future of Taiwan could only be determined by the community of nations. On July 19th Truman tried to make this point in a major public statement.

> In order that there may be no doubt in any quarter about our intentions in Formosa, I wish to state that the United States has no territorial ambitions whatever concerning that island, nor do we seek for ourselves any special position or privilege on Formosa. The present military neutralization of Formosa is without prejudice to political questions affecting that island. Our desire is that Formosa not become embroiled in hostilities disturbing the peace of the Pacific and that all questions affecting Formosa be settled by peaceful means as envisaged in the Charter of the United Nations. With peace reestablished, even the most complex political questions are susceptible of solution. In the presence of brutal and unprovoked aggression, however, some of these questions may have to be held in abeyance in the interest of the essential security of all.[15]

Right up until Peking's intervention in Korea Washington continually attempted to reassure the PRC that it had no argument with

China or intention of grabbing Taiwan for its own. For example, during a September 1st press conference Truman went so far as to declare
that the 7th Fleet would not be needed in the Strait after hostilities in
Korea ceased.[16] On 21 September, the U.S. delegation to the United
Nations made a motion that the General Assembly consider the
future status of Taiwan during its Fifth Session; a controversial move
in that it was possible that the U.N. could vote Taiwan back to the
mainland.[17] Also in September, Acheson was interviewed on televi-
sion by Charles Collingwood of CBS News. The subject was U.S.
policy in the Far East. When asked if the Chinese would intervene in
Korea, the Secretary was given a platform from which to remind
Peking that doing Moscow's bidding would come to no good. Walking
to a map of Asia he pointed out Sinkiang, Outer Mongolia, and
Manchuria. He explained that these were areas of Soviet imperialism
and that if the Chinese sent troops to Korea Peking would only
weaken its own presence in those regions.

> Now, I give the people in Peiping credit for being intelligent enough
> to see what is happening to them. Why they should want to further their
> own dismemberment and destruction by getting at cross purposes with all
> the free nations of the world who are inherently their friends and have
> always been friends of the Chinese as against this imperialism coming
> down from the Soviet Union I cannot see. And since there is nothing in it
> for them I don't see why they should yield to what is undoubtedly pressure
> from the Communist movement to get into the Korean war.[18]

In spite of Truman's and Acheson's desires to reassure the
Chinese communists, the neutralization of Taiwan resulted only in
broadening the chasm between Washington and Peking. Neutralization was an action almost impossible to defend given the fact that it
was a unilateral initiative taken by the United States, unsanctioned by
the United Nations.[19] In the final analysis, intervention in the Strait
constituted *de facto* reinvolvement in the Chinese civil war. The
diplomatic costs *vis-a-vis* China which were engendered in a decision
based on military necessities were exorbitant.

In September 1950, the United States stood accused in the
United Nations of aggression against the People's Republic of China.
In November 1950, Peking intervened on a massive scale in the
Korean War. Then, and only then, were hopes of an early CCP break
with Moscow dashed. Mao Tse-Tito was finally dead. The United
States would continue to pursue the objective of denying China to the

USSR "as an effective ally."[20] But it would now do so along the lines which Acheson advised against in November 1949; "to harass it, needle it, and if an opportunity appeared to attempt to overthrow it."[21] Only after Chinese intervention did Washington commit itself to denying Taiwan to the mainland beyond the war in Korea. On May 1, 1951 Major General William C. Chase, U.S. Army, arrived in Taipei.[22] His mission: to reestablish JUSMAAG-China. Chiang Kai-shek had lived to witness yet another miracle.

Notes

1. U.S. Consulate, Taipei to Department of State, Political Report On Formosa—June 25 - October 10, 1950, November 1, 1950, KLR/Box 8.

2. Bradley and Blair, *A General's Life*, pp. 532, 530. On June 25th, even before news of the Korean invasion had reached him, Bradley already put his staff to work assembling a packet for the Secretary of Defense to use in resurrecting the Taiwan issue. Memorandum, Bradley to Vandenberg, Collins, Sherman, and Davis, 25 June 1950, RJCS:Reel 2. "From my discussions with Secretary Johnson both before our trip and during our trip to the Far East," Bradley informed his colleagues, "I am sure he will want to take up the question of Formosa again with the President."

3. *The Ambassador in Korea (Muccio) to the Secretary of State, Seoul*, June 25, 1950 [Received June 24–9:26 p.m.], FR:50:VII:125–126. Parentheses added.

4. The meetings and decisions of that historic week have been recounted elsewhere. See FR:50:VII (*Korea*) for transcripts of the Blair House meetings and other important decision making gatherings. Good narrative accounts are plentiful. The 1980's saw a publishing boom on the Korean War. See Bruce Cumings, *The Origins of the Korean War: Liberation and the Emergence of Separate Regimes, 1945-1947* (Princeton, N.J.: Princeton University Press, 1981; Joseph C. Goulden, *Korea: The Untold Story of the War* (N.Y.: McGraw-Hill Book Co., 1982); Callum A. MacDonald, *Korea: The War Before Vietnam* (N.Y.: The Free Press, 1986); Burton I. Kaufman, *The Korean War: Challenges in Crisis, Credibility, and Command* (Philadelphia: Temple University Press, 1986); Bevin Alexander, *Korea: The First War We Lost* (N.Y.: Hippocrene Books, 1986); and Richard Whelan, *Drawing the Line: The Korean War, 1950-1953* (Boston: Little, Brown and Co., 1990) to name just a few. Glenn D. Paige, *The Korean Decision: June 24-30, 1950* (N.Y.: The Free Press, 1968) is dated but still very useful; the same for Tang Tsou, *America's Failure in China*. Stueck, *The Road to Confrontation* is very good; and *A General's Life* by Bradley and Blair has some interesting insights. Dean Acheson, *The Korean War* (N.Y.: W.W. Norton & Co., 1969) is a condensed version of the section on Korea in his *Present at the Creation* but still of value. One of the best interpretive works to emerge on the subject of U.S. decision making during the Korean

War is Rosemary Foot's *The Wrong War: American Policy and the Dimensions of the Korean Conflict, 1950–1953* (Ithica: Cornell University Press, 1985).

5. President Truman's Conversation With George M. Elsey, June 26, 1950, GME/Box 71/Korea, June 26, 1950.

6. These are the only sessions during a week of otherwise well-documented meetings for which discussion transcripts are not available either in official documents or in personal collections. An *Editorial Note* in FR:50:VII:143–144 alludes to the State-Defense joint session. Principals did not attend. Truman was still in Missouri. Acheson and Johnson were also out of town. Rusk, Jessup, Merchant, and Davies were among the notables from State. Army Secretary Pace was the senior DoD representative. Acheson arrived at noon. George Elsey has two vague memoranda of these meetings in his papers which relate that military decisions to be recommended to Truman were discussed. No references specifically mention Taiwan. GME/Box 71/Korea, June 25, 1950, No subject, memo on State-Defense meeting taken from Secretary Acheson's Briefing Book; and GME/Box 71/ Korea, June 25, 1950, Subject: Teleconference 252230Z.

7. Memorandum of Conversation, "Korean Situation," June 25, 1950, DGA/Box 65/May–June 1950. This transcript of the first Blair House conference can also be found in FR:50:VII:157–161, *Memorandum of Conversation, by the Ambassador at Large (Jessup)*, June 25, 1950.

8. *Memorandum of Conversation, by the Ambassador at Large (Jessup)*, Korean Situation, June 26, 1950, FR:50:VII:178–183; a copy is also in GME/Box 71/Korea, June 26, 1950.

9. Message, JCS to CINCFE, 29 JUN 50, GME/Box 71/Korea, June 29, 1950; Memo, Blair House Meetings, June 26, 1950, ibid.; Memo, Teleconference with MacArthur, 270217Z, June 26, 1950, ibid.

10. Statement By The President, June 27, 1950, GME/Box 71/Korea, June 27, 1950; *Memorandum of Conversation, by the Ambassador at Large (Jessup)*, Notes on Meeting in Cabinet Room at the White House, June 27, 1950, FR:50:VII:200–203 (*Statement Issued by the President* included); also found in DGA/Box 65/May–June 1950.

11. For example, in mid-July Taipei requested that it be allowed to attack a concentration of communist jet fighters then massing on the coast of Fukien. The request went through the chain of command to the President himself who instructed SCAP to warn the KMT military representative in Tokyo that "an attack by the Chinese Nationalist Government on the Mainland will be considered an unfriendly act" toward the United States. Memorandum for the Secretary of State from the President, July 18, 1950 and Message, CINCFE to JCS, 16 July 1950, HST/PSF/Box 173/China, 1950–52.

12. *Memorandum of Conversation, by the Ambassador at Large (Jessup)*, June 25, 1950, FR:50:VII:158; *Memorandum of Conversation by the Ambassador at Large (Jessup)*, June 26, 1950, ibid., p. 180.

13. Telegram, Rankin to Rusk, July 22, 1950, KLR/Box 18; Telegram, Rusk to Rankin, July 25, 1950, ibid.

14. Blum, *Drawing the Line*, p. 215.

15. *Department of State Bulletin*, July 31, 1950, p. 166.

16. "Fleet to Quit Formosa at End Of Korea War, Says Truman," *New York Times*, September 1, 1950, pp. 1, 4.

17. Letter dated 21 September 1950 from the Chairman of the United States delegation to the Secretary General, "The Question Of Formosa," September 21, 1950, JFD/Box 8.

18. *Department of State Bulletin*, September 18, 1950, p. 463.

19. The issue of U.S. intervention in Taiwan also caused considerable strains in relations with India and London. The Indians and British feared that the U.S. risked Soviet or Chinese intervention in Korea by neutralizing Taiwan. Ambassador Douglas in London was told by the Foreign Office that "...the US legal position toward Formosa is much less secure than the position toward Korea, and added that should the USSR attempt to attack the US action in neutralizing Formosa [in the United Nations], the US could not begin to count on unanimous support among democratic nations, and might even find itself in an 'embarrassing minority position.'" Department of State, *SUMMARY OF TELEGRAMS*, July 10, 1950 (India); *SUMMARY OF TELE-GRAMS*, July 13, 1950 (United Kingdom), *SUMMARY OF TELEGRAMS*, July 25, 1950 (United Kingdom and Formosa), HST/NAF/Box 22/May–July 1950. Parenthesis added.

20. NSC 48/3: United States Objectives, Policies And Courses Of Action In Asia, April 26, 1951, HST/MNSC/Box 212/NSC Meeting #90.

21. Conversation with the President, *Item 1 – China and the Far East*, November 17, 1949, DGA/Box 64/Oct–Nov 1949.

22. Karl Lott Rankin, *China Assignment* (Seattle: University of Washington Press, 1964), p. 105.

CONCLUSIONS

Often the policy which you trotted out in great confidence at the beginning winds up badly battered in the process of running gauntlets, and you find that, happily, events have overtaken it and you won't need to call on it after all.[1]

Dean Rusk
October 1950

In January 1949 the Departments of State and Defense agreed that it would be in the interests of the United States to deny Taiwan and the Pescadores to Peking. However, in the grand mosaic of Far Eastern problems facing the United States, the survival of the Nationalist regime on Taiwan was never a prime concern. It took a backseat to the larger problem of containing the Soviets in Asia. This prime interest, in turn, required that communist China not become a satellite of Moscow, that Peking not be permitted to export its revolution to Southeast Asia, and that Japan be rehabilitated. This was not merely the perspective of the State Department. Even the Joint Chiefs of Staff refused to declare Taiwan of such vital importance to national security that they would recommend military intervention to save the island short of a situation in which a general war in the Far East was already underway. Consequently, policy toward Taiwan was subjugated to policy toward mainland China. And in the case of Peking, Washington was not prepared to do anything which would retard the emergence of a Titoist regime.

The insights into the Sino-Soviet dynamic which specialists such as Kennan, Davies, and Sprouse brought to their positions were phenomenal. The argument that a Peking-Moscow split was inevitable was brilliant. Ten years later these men would be vindicated in their predictions. However, a policy toward China which called for awaiting a Titoist regime in Peking was not without major problems.

First, this was a long-term objective, not a near-term possibility. By early 1950 it should have been apparent that the Chinese communists were intent on pursuing an adversarial relationship with the United States. Their words of anger were not mere propaganda; they were backed up by acts of hostility. And in fact, State did accept that there would be no near-term split between Peking and Moscow. Yet, Acheson continued to argue that it was still in the interests of the United States to wait six or twelve years for the split to occur. However, in the interim he and his advisers offered no logical way to handle the communists except to respond in kind to Peking's hostility; a significant contradiction. The second major problem with the Titoist concept was that State's experts could not fathom that the very Chinese nationalism which they predicted would cause a break with the Soviets worked equally to the detriment of the United States. The CCP's interpretive history of U.S.-China relations was not the same as Washington's. The very idea that the United States, the world's leading capitalist power, had ever been the friend of the "old China" or could ever be the friend or guarantor of the sovereignty of the "new China" must have been a source of major hysterics to the men who had finally triumphed in a bloody eighteen-year revolution waged in the name of communism. A third problem with the Titoist concept was the belief that the party leadership was deeply divided on the issue of relations with the Soviet Union and the United States. The idea that some senior CCP leaders were in favor of less hostile relations with Washington than others may not have been altogether wrong. However, it *was* wrong to believe that this issue was so fundamental and critical to the collective leadership that a failure to reach consensus could split the party and destroy the hard-won revolution. The strong discipline of the party's inner circle and the ability of CCP leaders with diverse views to reach consensus was (and continues to be) grossly underrated. The "split leadership" analysis of certain State Department analysts and officials resulted in false hopes for a near to mid-term Titoist China.

But from the perspectives of the times, and the men who lived them, it is not difficult to see why in 1949 and early 1950 State's China experts believed that betting on Mao Tse-Tito was safer than betting that Chiang Kai-shek could work a miracle on Taiwan. Whereas the CCP was then an unknown quantity (and anything was possible), there was intimate familiarity with the Nationalist leaders and their legacies. Men such as John Davies had lived through and observed the Nationalist's revolution. They lived through the civil wars of the 1930's and the mad hunt for the communists even as Japan was encroaching ever deeper into China. They witnessed the failures of the Nationalist revolution before the Second World War and lived the frustrations of the very strained alliance of 1941–1945. Men such as Butterworth, Sprouse, and Merchant had to live the failure of the Marshall Mission and watch from all too close the fratricide of 1945–1949 and the inability of Chiang to rally his forces. On Taiwan itself the record was brutally clear. KMT rule on the island since VJ-Day had been an abomination. As long as Chiang Kai-shek led the KMT, State's China experts would not believe that any good could come of attaching the prestige of the United States to the Nationalist cause anywhere. And it is this animus toward Chiang Kai-shek and his intimates which may account for the fact that the good intentions and relative progress which was possible on Taiwan under K.C. Wu was never taken seriously by Foggy Bottom. It cannot be overlooked that a reversal of the policy which doomed Taiwan to fend for itself could not even be attempted within State until Butterworth was replaced at FE and Davies no longer had Kennan's patronage on the PPS. Perhaps the China hands would have felt differently about the relative merits of the KMT had they stayed in China past April 1950 to observe the brutality with which the CCP consolidated its control over the country.

The Joint Chiefs of Staff also must get a mixed review for their participation in the evolution of policy toward Taiwan. It is to their credit that they realized the limits of American military power, refused to become embroiled once again in the Chinese civil war, and were unwilling to risk the start of World War III over the fate of Taiwan. It is also to the credit of General Bradley that he was able to resist the pressures put upon him by Louis Johnson and MacArthur to take up the call for a reversal of Taiwan policy as long as he did. However, the JCS, like the men at State, wanted to have their cake and eat it too. They warned that Taiwan's occupation during a general war in the Far East would be devastating to the U.S. strategic position in Asia. Yet, they continually waffled when the diplomats and policy makers asked what should be done about it. It was the Joint Chiefs, not State, which recommended diplomatic and economic measures to preclude the fall of the island during the early policy reviews of 1949.

At the same time, it was the men in the Pentagon who perpetually complained that nothing was being done in a positive way to deny the island to the CCP. If State's analysts can be accused of being overly confident in their analysis of the situation in China and on Taiwan, then the JCS, it must be said, were loud to growl their displeasure but incredibly timid in offering solutions. If State's approach to helping Taiwan was "all or nothing," then DoD's was one of half-measures which no one, even the JCS, believed (rightly or wrongly) would save the island. By their own admission, military assistance would only prolong the life of the island, not preserve it.

As one looks back at the China-Taiwan issue during this period, there is a great appreciation for the complexities of the problems faced by the men who were paid to make the great decisions. In retrospect, between January 1949 and June 1950 China-Taiwan policy was in a state of flux. Washington did not have a "One China" policy or even a "Two China" policy. It can be argued that there was in existence at the time a "No China" policy; meaning that Washington was committed neither to Peking or Taipei. The United States would not offend Peking by unilateral military intervention to save Taiwan. However, Washington refused to recognize the PRC. By April 1950 all official U.S. Government personnel were out of China. The Nationalist Government on Taiwan was still recognized as the Government of China. Yet, there was no Ambassador in residence in Taipei. Moreover, full and unconditional support of the Nationalist regime on Taiwan was never given. Taipei was looked upon with contempt, and Washington offered no assurances other than the negative ones which warned that without political and economic reform not even modest economic aid would be offered. Chiang was told point blank that the U.S. would not intervene with military force to save him from a communist invasion or an internal revolt. In the United Nations, Washington attempted to remain neutral in the debate over which China should be seated. It appears that it would have taken an event such as the invasion of Korea to move U.S. China policy one way or the other. Given its druthers, Washington would probably have preferred to straddle the fence as long as possible. And given the uncertainties on the mainland and on Taiwan, this was not necessarily a bad policy, for it preserved Washington's options. Had the Korean War not occurred, the United States probably would have maintained its policy toward Taiwan; a policy which abandoned the island to Chiang Kai-shek to fend for himself. But happily, as Dean Rusk would have put it, the "hands off" policy toward Taiwan was never put to the test.

Taiwan was neutralized in June of 1950 purely out of military necessity. And even China's later intervention in the war did nothing to endear the KMT to those at State who had worked the Taiwan problem since January 1949. "Formosa we should continue to deny to the enemy," wrote Livingston Merchant in July 1951. "To do so will not be easy. We should not let Messrs. MacArthur, Knowland and Judd to hypnotize us. I think the regime is rotten and beyond reclamation."[2] But neutralization was *de facto* salvation. In the end Washington and Taipei became allies by default.

Notes

1. "The Formulation of Foreign Policy," a speech by Dean Rusk given to students at either the National or Army War College, October 3, 1950, LTM/Box 20. July 18, 1951, LTM/Box 1.

2. "Estimate of a Princeton Graduate interested in the Far East," July 18, 1951, LTM/Box 1.

APPENDIX

14 June 1950

MEMORANDUM ON FORMOSA

1. Since the fall of 1948 when the military capability of the Chinese Communist to engulf all of the mainland of China became clearly evident I have been concerned as to the future status of Formosa and I have been convinced that the strategic interests of the United States will be in serious jeopardy if Formosa is allowed to be dominated by a power hostile to the United States. In my personal conversations with distinguished civilian and military representatives of the Government of the United States who have visited this Headquarters during the past eighteen months I have reiterated the premise that Formosa should not be allowed to fall into the hands of a potential hostile power or of a regime which would grant military utilization of Formosa to a power potentially hostile to the United States. On the 29th of May last I forwarded to the Joint Chiefs of Staff my estimate of the strategic consequences which would result from the capture of Formosa by the Chinese Communists.

2. The front line of the Far East Command as well as the western strategic frontier of the United States rests today on the littoral islands extending from the Aleutians through the Philippine Archipeligo. Geographically and strategically Formosa is an integral part of this offshore position which in the event of hostilities can exercise a decisive degree of control of military operations along the periphery of Eastern Asia. In the event of a war United States striking forces based on this line would have the capability to interdict the limited means of communication available to the Communists and deny or materially reduce the ability of the USSR to exploit the natural resources of East and Southeast Asia. This essential capability on

the part of the United States is dependent to a large degree upon the retention of Formosa by a friendly or a neutral power.

3. The geographic location of Formosa is such that in the hands of a power unfriendly to the United States it constitutes an enemy salient in the very center of that portion of our position now keyed to Japan, Okinawa, and the Philippines. At the present time there is on Formosa a concentration of operational air and naval bases which is greater than any similar concentration on the Asiatic mainland between the Yellow Sea and the Strait of Malacca. Additional bases can be developed in a relatively short time by an aggressive exploitation of World War II Japanese facilities not now utilized by the Chinese Nationalist Forces. Formosa bases are 100 miles closer to Okinawa than any point on the Chinese mainland and are 150 miles closer to Clark Field and Manila than any other area which could be acquired by Communist military forces. An enemy force utilizing those installations currently available on Formosa could increase by 100 percent the air effort which could be directed against Okinawa as compared to operations based in China proper and at the same time could direct damaging air attacks with fighter type aircraft against our installations in the Philippines which are currently beyond the range of fighters based on the mainland of Asia.

4. As a result of its geographic location and base potential, utilization of Formosa by a military power hostile to the United States may either counterbalance or overshadow the strategic importance of the central and southern flank of the United States front line position. Formosa in the hands of the Communists can be compared to an unsinkable aircraft carrier and submarine tender ideally located to accomplish Soviet offensive strategy and at the same time checkmate counteroffensive operations by United States forces based on Okinawa and the Philippines. This unsinkable carrier-tender has the capacity to operate from ten to twenty air groups of types ranging from jet fighters to B-29 type bombers as well as provide forward operating facilities for the short-range coastal submarines which are predominant in the Russian Asiatic Navy. If Formosa should be acquired by the Chinese Communists and bases thereon made available to the USSR, Russia will have acquired an additional 'fleet' which will have been obtained and can be maintained at an incomparably lower cost to the Soviets than could its equivalent of ten or twenty aircraft carriers with their supporting forces.

5. Current estimates of Soviet air and submarine resources in the Far East agreed to by both Washington and Tokyo military intelligence agencies satisfy me that the Russians have the capability to extend their forces southward from their present positions and still maintain an imposing degree of military strength in both the Maritime Provinces and the Chinese seaboard. The ability of the USSR-Chinese Communist hordes to meet promptly logistic requirements either by improvisation or by the import of critical materials from Europe is being demonstrated daily by military activities extending from Tientsin to the southern border of China. The interest of the USSR in the southward displacement of termini of the Trans-Siberian Railroad has been reported by competent observers whose information indicated that rail lines are being extended through China southward from the vicinity of Lake Baikal and eastward from Russia Turkestan in the vicinity of Alma Ata. A trans-Siberian railhead in the vicinity of Shanghai would materially assist the logistic build-up of Formosa. Pending the actual outbreak of hostilities United States military forces will be unable to prevent the stockpiling of essential military supplies on Formosa if that area is acquired by the Communists.

6. Historically Formosa has been used as a springboard for military aggression directed against areas to the south. The most notable and recent example was the utilization of Formosa by the Japanese in World War II. At the outbreak of the Pacific War in 1941, Formosa played an important part as a staging area and supporting base for the various Japanese invasion convoys. The main strength of the forces which landed at Lingayen Gulf on Luzon were staged from Keelung, Takao, and the Pescadores. The supporting air forces of Japan's army and navy were based on fields situated along Southern Formosa at Takao, Koshun, and Taichu. Takao also served as a staging area for the invasion of Java in February 1942. From 1942 through 1944 Formosa was a vital link in the transportation and communications chain which stretched from Japan through Okinawa and the Philippines to Southeast Asia. In 1944–45 Formosa was the key staging point for troops and air reinforcements deployed to the Philippines in preparation for the all-important operation to hold the Philippine areas. As the United States carrier forces advanced into the Western Pacific, the air bases on Formosa assumed an increasingly greater role in the defensive scheme of the Japanese. After the invasion of Luzon in January 1945 the Japanese air forces withdrew to Formosan fields to take up

forward operational positions to be used against our advancing forces. The military utility of Formosa is sharply underlined by the fact that Japan in 1941 controlled not only the Ryukyus but the entire periphery of China.

7. In addition to its military value, Formosa has not only been self-sufficient as regards food for its own population of more than eight million but it has exported since 1910 with a favorable balance of external trade. In normal times Fomorsa has held the position of a food surplus area in a generally food-scarce locality. Its prewar export of rice and wheat exceeded imports by approximately 600,000 metric tons annually. There is no reason to believe that able political and economic advisors cannot once more establish Formosa as a prosperous economic unit. Such a factor, particularly the availability of a food surplus, may be of considerable importance in reestablishing the economies of those Oriental nations now largely dependent upon United States assistance.

8. Formosa represents a political area of no less importance to western ideology than other areas in the Orient. The Taiwanese are a homogeneous racial group who as individuals have resisted the intrusion of foreign blood. Although Formosa was promised to China as a consequence of World War II this promise was given in consonance with a political situation entirely different than that which now exists. There is every basis from a moral standpoint to offer to the Taiwanese an opportunity to develop their own political future in an atmosphere unfettered by the dictates of a Communist police state. In view of the moral implications, as well as the geographic proximity of this area to other endangered peoples on and near the periphery of China, the future status of Formosa can well be an important factor in determining the political alignment of those national groups who have or must soon make a choice between Communism and the West.

9. There can be no doubt but that the eventual fate of Formosa largely rests with the United States. Unless the United States' political-military strategic position in the Far East is to be abandoned, it is obvious that the time must come in the foreseeable future when a line must be drawn beyond which Communist expansion will be stopped. As a means of regaining a proper United States posture in the Orient it is apparent to me that the United States should initiate measures to prevent the domination of Formosa by a Communist power. I am equally certain that it would be a fundamental error with regard to

any part of the Orient to fail to take appropriate measures in those areas still open to our influence.

10. At this time I am unable to recommend the exact political, economic and military measures which should be taken to prevent the fall of Formosa either into the hands of a potential hostile power or into the hands of a power who will grant military utilization of Formosa to a hostile power. It is my firm conviction that a realistic estimate of requirements can only be based upon a physical survey of the area made by experienced military, economic and political observers. I concur whole-heartedly with the recommendations made by the Joint Chiefs of Staff on 23 December 1949 to the effect that the Commander-in-Chief Far East should make an immediate survey of the need and extent of the military assistance required in Formosa in order to hold Formosa against attack. Although this recommendation was apparently not acceptable at the time to the National Security Council, I note that the Joint Chiefs reaffirmed this recommendation on 4 May 1950.

11. Formosa has not yet fallen to Communist domination. There are conflicting reports as to the capability and will of the Chinese Nationalist Forces as now constituted and equipped to prevent either the military or political conquest of the island of Formosa. I cannot predict what the cost may be of preventing Communist domination of that island, although I have advised the Joint Chiefs of Staff what the cost may be if such an event transpires. I am satisfied, however, that the domination of Formosa by an unfriendly power would be a disaster of the utmost importance to the United States, and I am convinced that time is of the essence. I strongly believe that the Commander-in-Chief Far East should be authorized and directed to initiate without delay a survey of the military, economic and political requirements to prevent the domination of Formosa by a Communist power and that the results of such a survey be analyzed and acted upon as a basis for United States national policy with respect to Formosa.

DOUGLAS MacARTHUR

BIBLIOGRAPHY

DOCUMENT and MANUSCRIPT COLLECTIONS

Mudd Library, Princeton University
The Papers of John Foster Dulles. (JFD)
The Papers of Raymond B. Fosdick. (RBF)
The Papers of George F. Kennan. (GFK)
The Papers of Livingston T. Merchant (LTM)
The Papers of Karl Lott Rankin. (KLR)
The Papers of H. Alexander Smith. (HAS)

Harry S. Truman Library, Independence, Missouri
The Papers of Dean G. Acheson. (DGA)
The Papers of George M. Elsey. (GME)
The Papers of Sidney W. Souers. (SWS)
The Papers of Stephan J. Springarn. (SJS)
The Papers of John D. Sumner. (JDS)
The Papers of Harry S. Truman. (HST)
    Central Files. (CF)
    The Files of Clark M. Clifford. (CMC)
    The Records of the CIA/NSC. (CIA/NSC)
    Naval Aide Files, State Department Briefs. (NAF)
    Presidential Secretary Files. (PSF)
    Meetings of the National Security Council. (MNSC)
    Official Files. (OF)
    The Papers of James E. Webb. (JEW)
Dept. of State: Selected Records of the Korean War. (SRDS)
Records of the Senate Foreign Relations Committee. (SRSFC)
The Records of the Psychological Strategy Board. (PSB)

MacArthur Memorial, Norfolk, Virginia
The Papers of Douglas MacArthur. (DM)

MICROFILM COLLECTIONS

Documents of the National Security Council. Washington, D.C.: University Publications of America, Inc., 1980. (DNSC)

O.S.S./State Department Intelligence & Research Reports. Part III, China and India. Washington, D.C.: University Publications of America, Inc., 1979.(OSS/SD)

Records of the Joint Chiefs of Staff. Part II, 1946–1953, The Far East. Washington, D.C.: University Publications of America, Inc., 1979. (RJCS)

Records of the Joint Chiefs of Staff, Meetings of the Joint Chiefs of Staff. Part II, 1946–1953. Washington, D.C.: University Publications of America, Inc., 1980. (MJCS)

The Presidential Document Series, Map Room Messages of President Roosevelt, 1939–1945. Frederick, Md.:University Microfilms of America, Inc., 1981. (MRM)

U.S. State Department Central Files: Formosa, Internal Affairs 1945–1949, Record Group 59. Frederick, Md: University Publications of America, Inc., 1985. (SDF)

ORAL HISTORY COLLECTIONS

Oral History Interviews, Harry S. Truman Library, Independence, Missouri

Walton W. Butterworth
John H. Chiles
Clark M. Clifford
O. Edmund Clubb
George M. Elsey
R. Allen Griffen
Paul G. Hoffman
U. Alexis Johnson
Walter H. Judd
Robert A. Lovett
Edwin M. Martin
Livingston T. Merchant
John J. Muccio
Louis H. Renfrow
Philip D. Sprouse

The John Foster Dulles Oral History Collection, Mudd Library, Princeton University (JFDOH)
Walton W. Butterworth
Generalissimo and Madam Chiang Kai-shek
John Foster Dulles and the Far East
Walter H. Judd
George F. Kennan
Livingston T. Merchant
Walter S. Robertson
H. Alexander Smith
Dean Rusk

GOVERNMENT PUBLICATIONS

U.S. Congress:

Military Situation in the Far East: Inquiry Into the Military Situation in the Far East and the Facts surrounding the Relief of General of the Army Douglas MacArthur From His Assignments in that Area, 5 vols. Washington, D.C: Government Printing Office, 1951.

China and U.S. Far East Policy, 1945–1966. Washington, D.C.: Congressional Quarterly Service, 1967.

U.S. Department of Defense:

United States-Vietnam Relations, 1945–1967, Book 8. Washington, D.C.: Government Printing Office, 1971.

U.S. Department of State:

Department of State Bulletin (DSB)
Foreign Relations of the United States (FR)

SECONDARY WORKS

Acheson, Dean G. *Present At The Creation: My Years At The State Department.* N.Y.: W.W. Norton & Co., 1969.

_____. *The Korean War.* N.Y.: W.W. Norton & Co., 1971.

Alexander, Bevin. *Korea: The First War We Lost.* N.Y.: Hippocrene Books, 1986.

Allison, Graham T. *Essence of Decision: Explaining the Cuban Missile Crisis.* Boston: Little, Brown & Co., 1971.

Almond, Gabriel A., Bingham, G. Powell. *Comparative Politics: A Developmental Approach.* Boston: Little, Brown & Co., 1966.

Alperovitz, Gar. *Cold War Essays*. N.Y.: Doubleday & Co., 1970.

Ambrose, Stephen E. *Rise To Globalism: American Foreign Policy Since 1938*. 4th Edition. N.Y.: Viking Penguin Inc., 1985.

Bachrack, Stanley D. *The Committee of One Million: 'China Lobby' Politics, 1953-1971*. N.Y.: Columbia University Press, 1976.

Ballentine, Joseph W. *Formosa: A Problem for United States Foreign Policy*. Washington, D.C.: Brookings Institution, 1952.

Barclay, George W. *Colonial Development and Population in Taiwan*. Princeton, N.J.: Princeton University Press, 1954.

Barron, Bryton. *Inside the State Department: A Candid Appraisal of the Bureaucracy*. N.Y.: Comet Press Books, 1956.

Bate, H. Maclear. *Report From Formosa*. N.Y.: E.P. Dutton & Co., Inc., 1952.

Beal, John R. *John Foster Dulles: A Biography*. N.Y.: 1957.

Bliss, Howard and Johnson, M. Glen. *Beyond The Water's Edge: America's Foreign Policies*. N.Y.: J.B. Lippincott Co., 1975.

Blum, Robert M. *Drawing The Line: The Origins of the American Containment Policy in East Asia*. N.Y.: W.W. Norton & Co., 1982.

Boorman, Howard L. and Howard, Richard C., eds. *Biographical Dictionary of Republican China*. 5 vols. N.Y.: Columbia University Press, 1967.

Borden, William S. The Pacific Alliance: United States Foreign Economic Policy and Japanese Trade Recovery, 1947-1955. Madison, Wisconson, 1984.

Borg, Dorothy. *American Policy and the Chinese Revolution, 1925-1928*. N.Y.: Columbia Univeristy Press, 1947.

_____. *The United States and the Far Eastern Crisis of 1933-1938*. Cambridge: Harvard University Press, 1964.

_____ and Heinrichs, Waldo, eds. *Uncertain Years: Chinese-American Relations, 1947-1950*. N.Y.: Columbia University Press, 1980.

Bardley, Omar N. and Blair, Clay. *A General's Life*. N.Y.: Simon and Schuster, 1983.

Bridgham, Philip; Cohen, Arthur; and Jaffe, Leonard. "Mao's Road and Sino-Soviet Relations: A View From Washington, 1953." *The China Quarterly* 52 (Oct-Dec 1972): 678.

Brown, Seyom. *The Faces of Power: Constancy and Change in United States Foreign Policy from Truman to Johnson.* N.Y. 1968.

Bueler, Richard. *US China Policy and the Problem of Taiwan.* Boulder, Colorado: Colorado Associated University Press, 1971.

Buhite, Russell D. *Patrick J. Hurley and American Foreign Policy.* Ithica, N.Y.: Cornell Univeristy Press, 1973.

_____. "Major Interests: American Policy Toward China, Taiwan, and Korea, 1945–1950." *Pacific Historical Review* 3 (August 1978): 425–451.

_____. *Soviet-American Relations in Asia, 1945–1954.* Norman, OK.: University of Oklahoma Press, 1981.

Bullard, Anthony. "Harry S. Truman and the Separation of Powers in Foreign Affairs." Ph.D. dissertation, Columbia Univeristy, 1972.

Byers, Gertrude C. "American Journalism and China, 1945–1950." Ph.D. dissertation, Saint Louis University, 1980.

Byrnes, James F. *All In One Lifetime.* N.Y.: Harper & Brothers, 1958.

Caute, David. *The Great Fear: The Anti-Communist Purge Under Truman and Eisenhower.* N.Y.: Simon and Schuster, 1978.

Chen Lung-chu. *Formosa, China, and the United Nations: Formosa in the World Community.* N.Y.: St. Martin's Press, 1967.

Chern, Kenneth S. *Dilemma in China: America's Policy Debate, 1945.* Hamden, Conn.: Archon Books, 1980.

Ch'i Hsi-sheng. *Nationalist China at War: Military Defeats and Political Collapse, 1937–1945.* Ann Arbor: University of Michigan Press, 1982.

Chiang Kai-shek. *China's Destiny.* N.Y.: Roy Publishers, 1947.

_____. *China's Destiny.* Translated by Wang Chung-hui. N.Y.: The Macmillan Co., and China News Service, 1947.

Chien Hou-tsung. "US Policy Toward China, 1912 To Present Emphasizing Bureaucratic Level Analysis Particularly Since 1936, of Both Nationalist and Communist Movements." Ph.D. dissertation, Northern Arizona University, 1985.

Chihiro Hosoya. "The Road to San Francisco: The Shaping of American Policy on the Eve of the Japanese Peace Treaty." Japanese Journal of American Studies 1 (1981): 90–96.

Clough, Ralph N. *Island China.* Cambridge: Harvard University Press, 1978.

Clubb, O. Edmund. *Communism in China As Reported From Hankow in 1932.* N.Y.: Columbia University Press, 1968.

_____. *The Witness and I.* N.Y.: Columbia University Press, 1974.

_____. "America's China Policy." *Current History* 80 (1981): 250–281.

Cohen, Jerome A.; Friedman, Harold C.; and Whiting, Alan S. *Taiwan and American Policy: The Dilemma in US China Relations. N.Y.: Praeger, 1971.*

Cohen, Warren I. *America's Response To China: An Interpretive History of Sino-American Relations.* N.Y.: John Wiley & Sons, 1971.

_____. "US, China, and the Cold War in Asia, 1949–1970." *Centennial Review* 24 (1980): 127–147.

_____. *Dean Rusk.* Totowa, N.J.: Cooper Square Publishers, 1980.

_____, ed. *New Frontiers in American-East Asian Relations: Essays Presented to Dorothy Borg.* N.Y. Columbia University Press, 1983.

_____. "The History of American-East Asian Relations: Cutting Edge of the Historical Profession."*Diplomatic History* Vol. 9, No. 2 (Spring 1985): 101–112.

Condit, Kenneth W. *The History of the Joint Chiefs of Staff: The Joint Chiefs of Staff and National Policy,1947–1949.* Vol. 2. Wilmington, Delaware: Michael Glazier, Inc., 1979.

Coox, Alvin D. and Conroy, Hillary, eds. *China and Japan: A Search for Balance Since World War I.* Sanata Barbara, California: ABC-Clio, Inc., 1978.

Cumings, Bruce. *The Origins of the Korean War: Liberation and the Emergence of Separate Regimes, 1945–1947.* Princeton, N.J.: Princeton University Press, 1981.

Dallek, Robert. *Franklin Delano Roosevelt and American Foreign Policy, 1932–1945.* Oxford: Oxford University Press, 1979.

_____. *The American Style of Foreign Policy: Cultural Politics and Foreign Affairs.* N.Y.: Alfred A. Knopf, 1983.

Davis, Vincent. *Postwar Defense Policy and the U.S. Navy, 1943–1946.* Chapel Hill: University of North Carolina Press, 1966.

Dennett, Raymond and Turner, Robert K., eds. *Documents on American Foreign Relations.* Vol. XI, January 1–December 31, 1949 Princeton: N.J.: Princeton University Press, 1949, and Vol. XII, January 1–December 31, 1950 (1950).

Dinwiddle, Joseph. *Aid to Nationalist China*. N.Y.: Vantage Press, 1957.

Divine, Robert A. *Roosevelt and World War II*. Baltimore: The Johns Hopkins Press, 1969.

Donovan, Robert J. *Conflict and Crisis: The Presidency of Harry S. Truman, 1945–1948*. N.Y.: W.W. Norton & Co., 1977.

_____. *Tumultuous Years: The Presidency of Harry S. Truman, 1949–1953*. N.Y.: W.W. Norton & Co., 1982.

Dulles, Foster Rhea. *American Policy Toward Communist China, 1949–1969*. N.Y.: Thomas Y. Crowell Co., 1972.

Dulles, John Foster. *War or Peace*. N.Y.: 1950.

Eastman, Lloyd E. "Who Lost China?: Chiang Kai-shek Testifies." *China Quarterly* 88 (1981): 655–688.

Eismann, Bernard N. "The Emergence of 'Two Chinas' In American Foreign Policy, 1950–1959." Masters thesis, Columbia University, 1959.

Etzold, Thomas H., ed. *Aspects of Sino-American Relations Since 1784*. N.Y.: New Viewpoints, 1978.

Fairbank, John K. *Communist China and Taiwan in United States Foreign Policy*. The Brian McMahon Lectures, The University of Connecticut, November 21, 1960.

_____. *The United States & China*. 4th edition. Cambridge: Harvard University Press, 1980.

_____. *The Great Chinese Revolution, 1800–1985*. N.Y.: Harper & Row Publishers, 1986.

Feis, Herbert. *The China Tangle*. Princeton, N.J.: Princeton University Press, 1953.

_____. *Between War and Peace: The Potsdam Conference*. Princeton, N.J.: Princeton University Press, 1960.

_____. *Japan Subdued: The Atomic Bomb and the End of the War in the Pacific. Princeton, N.J.: Priceton University Press, 1961*.

Feaver, John Hansen. "The Truman Administration and China, 1945–1950: The Policy of Restrained Intervention." Ph.D. dissertation, The University of Oklahoma, 1980.

Ferrell, Robert H. *George C. Marshall*. N.Y.: Cooper Publishers, 1966.

_____, ed. *Off the Record: The Private Papers of Harry S. Truman. N.Y.: Harper & Row Publishers, Inc., 1980*.

Fitch, Geraldine. *Formosa Beachhead*. Chicago: Henry Regnery Co., 1953.

Fleming, D.F. *The Cold War And Its Origins*. 2 vols. N.Y.: Doubleday and Co., 1961.

Foltos, Lester, J. "The Bulwark of Freedom: American Security Policy for the Far East, 1945–1950." Ph.D. dissertation, University of Illinois, 1980.

Foot, Rosemary. *The Wrong War: American Policy and the Dimensions of the Korean Conflict, 1950–1953*. Ithica, N.Y.: Cornell University Press, 1985.

_____. "Anglo-American Relations in the Korean Crisis: The British Effort to Avert an Expanded War, December 1950– January 1951." Diplomatic History Vol. 10, No. 1 (Winter 1986): 43–58.

Gaddis, John Lewis. *The United States and the Origins of the Cold War, 1941–1947*. N.Y.: Columbia University Press, 1972.

_____. *Russia, The Soviet Union, and the United States: An Interpretive History*. N.Y.: John Wiley & Sons, 1978.

_____. *Strategies of Containment: A Critical Appraisal of Post-war American National Security Policy*. N.Y.: Oxford University Press, 1982.

Gardner, Lloyd C. *Architects of Illusion: Men and Ideas in American Foreign Policy, 1941–1949*. Chicago: Quadrangle Books, 1970.

Gordon, Leonard H.D. "American Planning for Taiwan, 1942–1945." *Pacific Historical Review* 37 (1968): 201–228.

_____, ed. *Taiwan: Studies in Chinese Local History*. N.Y.: Columbia University Press, 1970.

_____. "United States Opposition To The Use Of Force In The Taiwan Strait, 1954–1962," *Journal of American History* 72 (December 1985): 637–660.

Goulden, Joseph C. *Korea: The Untold Story of the War*. N.Y.: McGraw-Hill, 1982.

Graebner, Norman A., ed. *The National Security: Its Theory and Practice, 1945–1960*. N.Y.: Oxford University Press, 1986.

Grasso, June M. "Conflict and Controversey: The United States, Taiwan and the People's Republic of China, 1948–1950." Ph.D. dissertation, Tufts University, 1981.

_____. *Truman's Two-China Policy, 1948–1950*. Armonk, N.Y.: M.E. Sharpe, Inc., 1987.

Guttmann, Allen, ed. *Korea: Cold War and Limited War*. Lexington, Mass.: D.C. Heath & Co., 1972.

Han Lih-wu. *Taiwan Today*. Taipei, 1951.

Halle, Louis J. *The Cold War As History*. N.Y.: Harper Colophon Books, 1967.

Halperin, Morton H. and Kanter, Arnold, eds. *Readings in American Foreign Policy: A Bureaucratic Perpsective*. Boston: Little, Brown & Co., 1973.

Hartman, Susan M. *Truman and the 80th Congress*. Columbia, Mo.: University of Missouri Press, 1971.

Head, William P. *America's China Sojourn: American Foreign Policy and Its Effects on Sino-American Relations, 1942–1948*. Lanham, Mass.: University Press of America, Inc., 1983.

Heinrichs, Waldo. *Threshold of War: Franklin D. Roosevelt & American Entry Into World War II*. N.Y.: Oxford University Press, 1988.

Heller, Francis H. *The Korean War: A 25-Year Perspective*. Lawrence, Kansas: The Regents Press of Kansas, 1977.

Hermes, Walter G. *The United States Army in the Korean War: Truce Tent and Fighting Front*. Washington, D.C.: Office of the Chief of Military History, United States Army, 1966.

Hull, Cordell. *The Memoirs of Cordell Hull*. 2 vols. N.Y.: The Macmillan Co., 1948.

Hunt, Michael H. *The Making of a Special Relationship: The United States and China to 1914*. N.Y.: Columbia University Press, 1983.

Huntington, Samuel P. *The Soldier and the State: The Theory and Politics of Civil-Military Relations*. Cambridge: Harvard University Press, 1957.

Isaacson, Walter and Thomas, Evan. *The Wise Men: Six Friends and the World They Made*. N.Y.: Simon and Schuster, 1986.

James, D. Clayton. *The Years of MacArthur: Triumph & Disaster, 1945–1964*. Boston: Houghton Mifflin Co., 1985.

Jansen, Marius B. *Japan and China: From War to Peace, 1894–1972*. Chicago: Rand McNally, 1975.

Johnson, Chalmers. *Peasant Nationalism and Communist Power*. Stanford, Ca.: Stanford University Press, 1962.

360 FROM ABANDONMENT TO SALVATION

360 FROM ABANDONMENT TO SALVATION

360   FROM ABANDONMENT TO SALVATION

Jones, Joseph M. *The Fifteen Weeks*. N.Y.: Viking Press, 1955.

Kahn, E.J. *The China Hands: America's Foreign Service Officers and What Befell Them*. N.Y.: Viking Press, 1972.

Kaufman, Burton I. *The Korean War: Challenges in Crisis, Credibility, and Command*. Philadelphia: Temple University Press, 1986.

Kennan, George F. *Memoirs, 1925–1950*. Boston: Atlantic Monthly Press, 1967.

————. *Memoirs, 1950–1963*. Boston: Little, Brown & Co., 1972.

Kerr, George H. *Formosa Betrayed*. Boston: Houghten Mifflin Co., 1965.

————. *Formosa: Licensed Revolution and the Home Rule Movement, 1895–1945*. Honolulu: University of Hawaii Press, 1974.

Koen, Ross Y. *The China Lobby In American Politics*. N.Y.: Octagon Books, 1974.

Korb, Lawrence J. *The Joint Chiefs of Staff: The First Twenty-Five Years*. Bloomington: Indiana University Press, 1976.

Kubek, Anthony. *How The Far East Was Lost: American Foreign Policy and the Creation of Communist China, 1941–1949*. Chicago: Henry Regnery Co., 1963.

LaFeber, Walter. *America, Russia, and the Cold War, 1945–1984*. 5th edition. N.Y.: Alfred E. Knopf, 1985.

Larson, Deborah W. *Origins of Containment: A Psychological Explanation*. Princeton, N.J.: Princeton University Press, 1985.

Lasater, Martin L. *The Taiwan Issue in Sino-American Strategic Relations*. Boulder, Co.: Westview Press, 1984.

Lattimore, Owen. *The Situation in Asia*. Boston: Little, Brown & Co., 1949.

Liu, Frederick Fu. *A Military History of Modern China, 1924–1949*. Princeton, N.J.: Princeton University Press, 1956.

Macdonald, Callum A. *Korea: The War Before Vietnam*. N.Y.: The Free Press, 1986.

Mao Tse-tung. *On the U.S. White Paper*. Peking: Foreign Language Press, 1961.

Martin, Edwin W. *Divided Counsel: The Anglo-American Response to Communist Victory in China*. Lexington, Ky.: University Press of Kentucky, 1986.

Matloff, Maurice and Snell, Edwin M. *The War Department: Strategic Planning for Coalition Warfare, 1941–1942*. Washington, D.C.: Office of the Chief of Military History, U.S. Army, 1953.

May, Earnest R. *The Truman Administration and China, 1945–1949*. N.Y.: J.B. Lippincott Co., 1975.

May, Gary. *China Scapegoat: The Diplomatic Ordeal of John Carter Vincent*. Washington, D.C.: New Republic Books, 1979.

Mayers, David A. *Cracking the Monolith: US Policy Against the Sino-Soviet Alliance, 1949–1955*. Baton Rouge, La.: Louisiana State University Press, 1986.

McLean, David. "American Nationalism, the China Myth, and the Truman Doctrine: The Question of Accommodation with Peking, 1949–50." *Diplomatic History* Vol. 10, No. 1 (Winter 1986): 25–43.

Mclellan, David S. *Dean Acheson: The State Department Years*. N.Y.: Dodd, Meade & Co., 1976.

_____, and Acheson, David C., eds. *Among Friends: Personal Letters of Dean Acheson*. N.Y.: Dodd, Mead & Co., 1980.

Mee, Charles L. *The Marshall Plan: The Launching of the Pax Americana*. N.Y.: Simon and Schuster, 1984.

Morison, Elting E. *Turmoil and Tradition: A Study of the Life and Times of Henry L. Stimson*. Boston: Houghton Mifflin Co., 1960.

Myers, Ramon H. and Peattie, Mark R., eds. *The Japanese Colonial Empire, 1895–1945*. Princeton, N.J.: Princeton University Press, 1984.

Nagai, Yonosuke and Iriye, Akira, eds. *The Origins of the Cold War in Asia*. N.Y.: Columbia University Press, 1977.

Neu, Charles E. "American Diplomats and East Asia, 1922–1932." Unpublished paper, Brown University, 1984.

Neustadt, Richard E. and May, Ernest R. *Thinking in Time: The Uses of History for Decision Makers*. N.Y.: The Free Press, 1986.

Oksenberg, Michael and Oxnam, Robert B., eds. *Dragon and Eagle: United States-China Relations Past and Future*. N.Y.: Basic Books, 1973.

Paige, Glenn D. *The Korean Decision: June 24–30, 1950*. N.Y.: The Free Press, 1968.

Patti, Archimedes. *Why Vietnam?: Prelude to America's Albatross*. Berkeley, Ca.: University of California Press, 1980.

Pogue, Forrest C. *George C. Marshall: Ordeal and Hope, 1939–1942*. N.Y.: Viking Press, 1965.

_____. *George C. Marshall: Statesman, 1945–1959*. N.Y.: Viking Penguin, Inc., 1987.

Purifoy, Lewis M. *Harry Truman's China Policy: McCarthyism and the Diplomacy of Hysteria, 1947–1951*. N.Y.: New Viewpoints, 1976.

Range, Willard. *Franklin D. Roosevelt's World Order*. Athens, Ga.: University of Georgia Press, 1959.

Rankin, Karl Lott. *China Assignment*. Seattle: University of Washington Press, 1964.

Reardon-Anderson, James. *Yenan and the Great Powers: The Origins of Chinese Communist Foreign Policy, 1944–1946*. N.Y.: Columbia University Press, 1980.

Rearden, Steven L. *The Evolution of American Strategic Doctrine: Paul H. Nitze and the Soviet Challenge*. Boulder, Co.: Westview Press, 1984.

_____. *History of the Office of the Secretary of Defense*: *The Formative Years, 1947–1950*. Washington, D.C.: Historical Office of the Secretary of Defense, 1984.

Ridgway, Mathew B. *The Korean War*. Philadelphia: The Da Capo Press, 1967.

Riggs, Fred W. *Formosa Under Nationalist Rule*. N.Y.: Macmillan Co., 1952.

Romanus, Charles F. and Sunderland, Riley. *China-Burma-India: Stilwell's Mission to China*. Washington, D.C.: Office of the Chief of Military History, U.S. Army, 1953.

_____. *China-Burma-India: Stilwell's Command Problems*. Washington, D.C.: Office of the Chief of Military History, U.S. Army, 1956.

_____. *China-Burma-India: Time Runs Out in CBI*. Washington, D.C.: Office of the Chief of Military History, U.S. Army, 1959.

Rowe, David N. *China Among the Powers*. N.Y.: Harcourt, Brace & Co., 1945.

_____. "The State Department White Paper: A Suggested Response." *Issues and Studies* 17 (1981): 35–39.

Rubin, Barry. *Secrets of State: The State Department & The Struggle Over U.S. Foreign Policy*. N.Y.: Oxford University Press, 1987.

Rusk, Dean. *As I Saw It.* N.Y.: W.W. Norton Co., 1990.

Schaller, Michael. *The United States and China in the Twentieth Century.* N.Y.: Oxford University Press, 1979.

_____. *The U.S. Crusade in China, 1938–1945.* N.Y.: Columbia University Press, 1979.

_____. "Japan, China, and Sotyeast Asia: Regional Integration and Containment, 1947–1950." In *The Occupation of Japan: The International Context,* pp. 163–184. Edited by Thomas W. Burkman. Norfolk, Va.: The MacArthur Memorial Foundation, 1984.

_____. *The American Occupation of Japan: The Origins of the Cold War in Asia.* N.Y.: Oxford University Press, 1985.

_____. "Consul General O. Edmund Clubb, John P. Davies, and the 'Inevitability' of Conflict Between the United States and China, 1949–1950: A Comment and New Documentation." *Diplomatic History* Vol. 9, No. 2 (Spring 1985) 149–160.

_____. "MacArthur's Japan: The View From Washington." *Diplomatic History* Vol. 10, No. 1 (Winter 1986): 1–25.

_____. *Douglas MacArthur: The Far Eastern General.* N.Y.: Oxford University Press, 1989.

Schnabel, James P. *The United States Army in the Korean War: Policy and Direction, The First Year.* Washington, D.C.: Office of the Chief of Military History, U.S. Army, 1972.

_____, and Watson, Robert J. *The History of the Joint Chiefs of Staff: The Joint Chiefs of Staff and National Policy, The Korean War.* Vol. 3, Part 2. Wilmington, De: Michael Glazier, Inc., 1979.

Schoenbaum, Thomas J. *Waging Peace and War: Dean Rusk in the Truman, Kennedy, & Johnson Years.* N.Y.: Simon and Schuster, 1988.

Schonberger, Howard. "John Foster Dulles and the China Question in the Making of the Japanese Peace Treaty." In *The Occupation of Japan: The International Context,* pp. 229–254. Edited by Thomas W. Burkman. Norfolk, Va.: The MacArthur Memorial Foundation, 1984.

_____. "Peacemaking in Asia: The United States, Great Britain, and the Japanese Decision to Recognize Nationalist China, 1951–1952." *Diplomatic History* Vol. 10, No. 1 (Winter 1986): 59–74.

Selden, Mark. *The Yenan Way In Revolutionary China.* Cambridge: Harvard University Press, 1971.

Shieh, Milton J.T. *Taiwan and the Democratic World.* Taipei, 1951.

Smith, Gaddis. *American Diplomacy During the Second World War.* N.Y.: John Wiley & Sons, Inc., 1965.

_____. *Dean Acheson.* N.Y.: Cooper Square Publishers, Inc., 1972.

Smith, Robert R. "Luzon Versus Formosa." In *Command Decisions,* pp. 461–466. Washington, D.C.: Office of the Chief of Military History, U.S. Army, 1960.

Spanier, John W. *The Truman-MacArthur Controversy and the Korean War.* N.Y.: W.W. Norton and Co., 1965.

_____. *American Foreign Policy Since World War II.* 10th edition. N.Y.: Holt, Rinehart and Winston, 1985.

Spector, Ronald H. *Advice and Support: The Early Years of the U.S. Army in Vietnam, 1941–1960.* N.Y.: The Free Press, 1985.

Steele, A.T. *The American People and China.* N.Y.: McGraw Hill, 1966.

Stimson, Henry L. and Bundy, McGeorge. *On Active Service in Peace and War.* N.Y.: Harper & Brothers, 1947.

Stuart, Graham. *The Department of State: A History of its Organization, Procedure, and Personnel.* N.Y.: Macmillan Co., 1949.

Stueck, William Whitney. *The Road To Confrontation: American Policy Toward China and Korea, 1947–1950.* Chapel Hill: The University of North Carolina Press, 1981.

_____. *The Wedemeyer Mission: American Politics and Foreign Policy During the Cold War.* Athens, Ga.: The University of Georgia Press, 1984.

Sulzberger, C.L. *A Long Row of Candles: Memoirs and Diaries, 1934–1954.* London, 1969.

Thomson, James C. *While China Faced West: American Reformers in Nationalist China, 1928–1937.* Cambridge: Harvard University Press, 1969.

_____; Stanley, Peter W.; and Perry, John Curtis. *Sentimental Imperialists: The American Experience in East Asia.* N.Y.: Harper & Row Publishers, Inc., 1981.

Tien Hung-mao. *Government and Politics in Kuomintang China, 1927–1937.* Stanford, Ca.: Stanford University Press, 1972.

Truman, Harry S. *The Memoirs of Harry S. Truman*. 2 vols. N.Y.: Doubleday Press, 1956. Vol 2: *1949–1952: Years of Trial and Hope*.

Tsou Tang. *America's Failure in China, 1941–1950*. Chicago: University of Chicago Press, 1963.

Tuchman, Barbara. *Stilwell and the American Experience in China, 1911–1945*. N.Y.: Macmillan Co., 1970.

————. "If Mao Had Come to Washington: An Essay in Alternatives." *Foreign Affairs* (October 1972): 44–58.

Tucker, Nancy B. *Patterns in the Dust: Chinese-American Relations and the Recognition Controversy, 1949–1950*. N.Y.: Columbia University Press, 1983.

Utley, Jonathan G. *Going To War With Japan: 1937–1941*. Knoxville, Tenn.: University of Tennessee Press, 1985.

Varg, Paul A. *The Making of a Myth: The United States and China, 1897–1912*. East Lansing: Michigan State University Press, 1968.

————. *The Closing of the Door: Sino-American Relations, 1936–1946*. East Lansing: Michigan State University Press, 1973.

Vandenberg, Arthur H. *The Private Papers of Senator Vandenberg*. Boston, 1952.

Vinacke, Harold M. *The United States and the Far East: 1945–1951*. Stanford, Ca.: Stanford University Press, 1952.

Wedemeyer, Albert C. *Wedemeyer Reports!* N.Y.: Henry Holt & Co., 1958.

Westerfield, H. Bradford. *Foreign Policy and Party Politics*. New Haven, Conn.: Yale University Press, 1955.

Whelan, Richard. *Drawing the Line: The Korean War, 1950–1953*. Boston: Little, Brown & Co., 1990.

Whiting, Allen S. *China Crosses the Yalu: The Decision to Enter the Korean War*. N.Y.: Macmillan Co., 1960.

Williams, Frederick. "The Origins of the Sino-American Conflict, 1949–1952." Ph.D. dissertation, University of Illinois, 1967.

Yates, Lawrence A. "John Foster Dulles and Bipartisanship, 1944–1952." Ph.D. dissertation, University of Kansas, 1981.

Yasuhara, Yoko. "Japan, Communist Chian, and Export Controls in Asia, 1948–1952." *Diplomatic History* Vol. 10, No. 1. (Winter 1986): 75–91.

Yergin, Daniel. *Shattered Peace: The Origins of the Cold War and the National Security State*. Boston: Houghton Mifflin Co., 1978.

Young, Arhtur N. *China and the Helping Hand, 1937–1945*. Cambridge: Harvard University Press, 1963.

Xuto, Manaspas. "United States Relations with Formosa, 1850–1955." Ph.D. dissertation, Tufts University, 1961.

Notes

1. The abbreviations for the primary sources used in the footnotes of this study are placed in parentheses next to each collection.

INDEX

demarche, 193; requests American military advisors, 195

Ch'en Yi (GEN, KMT), 45, 53–56, 59–63, 67, 77 (fn 42)

Ch'en Yi (CCP), "China First" faction, 286, 287; rumors that Ch'en will lead PLA against Mao if humiliating treaty with Soviets accepted (1950), 287

Ch'en Yun (CCP), pro-Moscow faction, 287

Chennault, Claire, "Flying Tigers" (AVG), 10; 15, 35 (fn 7); "Chennault Plan" (1949), 227

Chiang Ching-kuo, 81 (fn 96), 110; increases pressure on Taiwanese dissidents (May 1950), 314

Chiang Kai-shek, 1, 4, 7; *TIME* magazine's "Man & Wife of the Year, 1938", 9; 18; race to take surrender of Japanese troops, 23–24; comments on February Incident and March Massacre (1947), 64–65; 147, 148; emerges on Taiwan, 170; declares Mao is no Tito, 170; meeting with Elpidio Quirino, 171; as viewed by British, 185; stern *demarche* by United States, 190–197, 198–199; reaction to *demarche*, 192, 194; attempt at reforms on Taiwan, 209–216; requests for United States assistance on Taiwan, 209–210; use of intermediaries to lobby United States Government, 251–252 (fn 8); formally resumes Presidency of ROC (March 1950), 295; grows bitter about U.S. Taiwan policy, 314; State Department attempts to find Chiang a third country safe haven if Taiwan falls, 328 (fn 123)

Chiang, Madame (Soong May-ling), 9, 110; mission to the United States, 126–127 (fn 2); and former Secretary of the Navy John L. Sullivan, 213–215;

and January 5, 1950 statement on Taiwan, 272–273

Chiang Wei-kuo (KMT Armored Command), 171

China Aid Act (1948), 31, 151, 290, 291

China Bloc (in Congress), 4, 31, 42 (fn 72), 126 (fn 2); military assistance funds for China in Mutual Defense Assistance Act (1949), 164–165; 199 (fn 8); attacks NSC 48, 263–274

China Defense Supplies (CDS), 11

China's Destiny, 18–19; 38 (fn 35)

"China First" faction (CCP), 286

China Lobby, 4, 34 (fn 4), 42 (fn 72), 126 (fn 2), 199 (fn 8)

Chinese Air Force (KMT), air raid on Shanghai (February 1950), 292–295

Chinese Communist Party (CCP), prospects for Titoism, 85, 95–97 (*see also* NSC 41); on FLR, 144, 160 (fn 35); denounces North Atlantic Treaty, 168; "leans to one side", 168; possibility of accomodation with United States, 168; tells PLA soldiers United States will invade Taiwan, 169; radio broadcasts to Taiwan, 170; pro-U.S. faction, 201 (fn 23); pro-Moscow faction, 201 (fn 24); *Kwang Ming Jih Pao* alleges U.S. preparing to invade Taiwan (December 1949), 243; State Department view of factions and CCP nationalism, 283–284

Chinese Nationalist Party, *see Kuomintang*

Chou Chih-jou (Chief of Staff, KMT Air Force), 171, 202 (fn 36)

Chou En-lai, 29; "Chou *Demarche*", 168, 201 (fn 22); 201 (fn 23); viewed by State as leader of pro-U.S. faction CCP, 283; Acheson's attitude toward Chou overtures, 285; Clubb attempts to talk with Chou

(January 1950), 285; joins Mao
in Moscow (1950), 286; "China
First" faction, 286
Chu Shih-ming, (GEN, KMT),
255 (fn 30)
Chu Teh (CCP), "China First"
faction, 286
Cleaves, Francis (LT, USNR), 76
(fn 36)
Cleveland, Harlan (Director, ECA
China), 127 (fn 9)
Clifford, Clark, (White House
Special Counsul) and January
5, 1950 statement on Taiwan,
268
Clubb, O. Edmund (State), 27, 38
(fn 36), 201 (fn 23); and PRC
nationalization of U.S. Consulate in Peking, 282, 285; last
U.S. official to remain in
Peking, 285; ordered to seek
out Chou En-lai (January
1950), 285, 323 (fn 56); confused by anti-U.S. CCP actions,
287
Cold War, 7; Truman Doctrine
and Marhall Plan, 30
Collingwood, Charles (CBS),
interviews Acheson on Korean
War and China policy, 335
Collins, J. Lawton (GEN, USA),
229, 230; trusted by Omar
Bradley, 231–232; and NSC 48,
246; and 50th NSC Meeting,
248
Connally, Tom (Sen, TX), 265;
defends administration Taiwan
policy, 273
Coplon, Judith (Department of
Justice), 297
Craig, L.F. (ECA, Taiwan), 127
(fn 9)
Crane, Burton (*New York Times*),
254 (fn 20)
Crawford, (ADM, USN), 127 (fn
8)
Currie, Lauchlin, 39 (fn 42)
Daridan, Jean (French Embassy,
Washington), 141
Dau, F.J., (COL, USA), 81 (fn 88)

Davies, John Paton (State), x, 20,
38 (fn 36), 88–89; reaction to
Merchant's report, 174; firmly
convinced CCP split on issue of
relations with U.S. and USSR
(1950), 287–288
Democratic People's Republic of
Korea (North Korea), ix
Dening, Maberly E. (British
Foreign Office), meets with
Butterworth, Merchant and
Freeman on Taiwan problem,
184; British views on FLR, 185;
views on Chiang Kai-shek, 185;
Foreign Office believes Taiwan
cannot be saved, 185
Department of Defense (DoD),
118–121, 198; relations with
State worsen, 243–245
Department of State, regains
influence under Marshall,
29–30; reorganization of 1949,
199 (fn 3); relations with
Defense worsen, 243; analysis
of CCP factionalism and
Chinese nationalism, 283–284,
286–288; analysis of Mao's trip
to Moscow, 285–286; begins to
block delivery of weapons to
Taiwan (January 1950), 291;
outraged by KMT air raid on
American companies in
Shanghai (February 1950),
292–295; plans to evacuate
Taiwan (April 1950), 305–396
Dewey, Thomas E. (Gov, NY),
172, 304
Dixie Mission, 20, 89
Donovan, William J. (O.S.S.), 35
(fn 12)
Dorn, Frank, 34 (fn 3)
Draper, W.H. (Department of the
Army), 117, 129 (fn 38, 40)
Dulles, John Foster, x; becomes
advisor to Department of State,
299–300, 326 (fn 104); responsibilities at State, 302; feels
moral obligation to Taiwanese,
302; sees positive reforms on
Taiwan, 302–303; attempts to
reverse Taiwan policy, 307–309;

security objectives of United
States in Asia, 248–249; 250,
251 (fn 4); broad scope of
project, 251 (fn 5); leaked to
New York Times, 264, 318 (fn 3)
NSC 48/1, 243, 250, 262 (fn 117)
NSC 48/2, 262 (fn 117); leaked to
press, 318 (fn 3)

Office of Strategic Services
(O.S.S.), 18, wartime assessment of KMT, 37 (fn 26)

Pai Ch'ung-hsi (GEN, KMT), 65
Pandit, Vijaya Lakshmi (Indian
Ambassador, U.S.), discusses
United States recognition of
PRC with Acheson, 284
Pearl Harbor, 9
Pearson, Drew (*Washington Post*),
261 (fn 112)
Peffer, Nathaniel, 233
P'eng Hsueh-pei (KMT), 67
P'eng Meng-chi (GEN, KMT),
struggle with Sun Li-jen,
170–171; fears of defection to
CCP, 176
People's Republic of China
(PRC), recognition by various
nations, 282; nationalizes
portions of United States
Consulate in Peking, 282, 285;
Treaty of Friendship, Alliance
and Mutual Assistance with
Soviets, 282–284; recognition
issue within Truman adminis-
tration, 284–285; capture of
Hainan, 304
Philadelphia Inquirer, and Janaury
5, 1950 statement on Taiwan,
272
Policy Planning Staff (PPS,
Department of State), 20; NSC
34, 43 (fn 82); 85; established
1947, 87–88; 104 (fn 15); reac-
tion to Merchant report, 174
PPS 35, 93–95
PPS 39, 95–97, 107 (fn 42)
PPS 53, 178–181, 203 (fn 46)

Quirino, Elpidio (Philippine
President), 171; tells Washington he will not give Chiang
Kai-shek safe haven if Taiwan
falls, 328 (fn 123)

Rankin, Karl Lott (State), 331;
pushes for closer ties with
Taipei, 334
Reischauer, Edwin O., 233
Renfrow, Louis H., (BG, USA),
200 (fn 11)
Republic of China (ROC), survival of Nationalist China wartime
goal of U.S., 7, 8; German
military advisers in 1930's, 13;
censorship during Second
World War, 18; made member
of Big Four at Moscow Confer-
ence, 20; post V-J Day military
assistance from U.S., 30–31;
officially moved to Taiwan, 170;
fall of Hainan (April 1950),
304; fall of Chusan Islands
(April 1950), 305
Republic of Korea (South Korea),
Korean Aid Bill, 280; *see*
Korean War
Reston, James (*New York Times*),
on NSC 48, 264
Rhee, Syngman (President,
Republic of Korea), and Janu-
ary 5, 1950 statement on
Taiwan, 272
Ringwalt, Arthur (State), 26
Roosevelt, Franklin D., 8, 15, 20;
ignores State during Second
World War, 21; personal diplo-
macy and envoys to China, 21,
39 (fn 42); loses patience with
Chiang, 37 (fn 25)
Rossinger, Lawrence, 233
Round Table Discussion (State),
233, 259 (fn 84)
Royall, Kenneth C. (Secretary of
the Army), 125
Rusk, Dean (State), 5, 87, 92–93,
107 (fn 36); and Merchant
report, 174–176; and 50th NSC
Meeting, 246; and direction of
Taiwan policy, 295; replaces